# Combating Corruption in the Middle East

This book examines the phenomenon of 'grand corruption' in Kuwait and the pattern in the wider region.

Taking an interdisciplinary approach, the work places corruption in its sociological, political, and economic context to explore the relationship between the characteristics of Kuwait as a state with an endemic corruption problem. It then focuses on laws and regulations as key problem-solving mechanisms. In doing so, it identifies, explores, and assesses the existing counter-corruption laws and regulations in Kuwait in a broad socio-political-economic context. The work goes beyond doctrinal legal research, employing empirical methodology based on semi-structured interviews with elite politicians and professional experts from criminal justice and non-governmental organisations (NGOs). These valuable and original insights are reflected upon throughout the study.

The grand corruption that permeates the tier of high-profile officials in Kuwait is replicated in many developing countries where accountability mechanisms regularly suffer from lack of enforcement. The appeal of this book is its application to numerous jurisdictions, and the Gulf Cooperation Council (GCC) countries and Middle East in particular. It will be a valuable resource for academics, researchers, and policymakers working in the areas of financial crime and corruption.

**Khaled Al-Rashidi** is an assistant professor in the Criminal Law Department at School of Law, Kuwait University.

**The Law of Financial Crime**
Series Editor: Nicholas Ryder

Available titles in this series include:

**Financial Crime and Corporate Misconduct**
A Critical Evaluation of Fraud Legislation
*Edited by Chris Monaghan and Nicola Monaghan*

**Corporate Liability for Insider Trading**
*Juliette Overland*

**Corruption in the Global Era**
Causes, Sources and Forms of Manifestation
*Lorenzo Pasculli and Nicholas Ryder*

**Counter-Terrorist Financing Law and Policy**
An analysis of Turkey
*Burke Uğur Başaranel and Umut Turksen*

**Integrity and Corruption and The Law**
Global Regulatory Challenges
*Edited by Nicholas Ryder and Lorenzo Pasculli*

**Regulating and Combating Money Laundering and Terrorist Financing**
The Law in Emerging Economies
*Nkechikwu Valerie Azinge-Egbiri*

**Combating Corruption in the Middle East**
A Socio-Legal Study of Kuwait
*Khaled S. Al-Rashidi*

For more information about this series, please visit: www.routledge.com/The-Law-of-Financial-Crime/book-series/FINCRIME

# Combating Corruption in the Middle East

## A Socio-Legal Study of Kuwait

**Khaled S. Al-Rashidi**

Routledge
Taylor & Francis Group
LONDON AND NEW YORK

First published 2021
by Routledge
2 Park Square, Milton Park, Abingdon, Oxon OX14 4RN

and by Routledge
52 Vanderbilt Avenue, New York, NY 10017

*Routledge is an imprint of the Taylor & Francis Group, an informa business*



*British Library Cataloguing-in-Publication Data*
A catalogue record for this book is available from the British Library

*Library of Congress Cataloging-in-Publication Data*

Names: Al-Rashidi, Khaled, author.
Title: Combating corruption in the Middle East: a socio-legal study of Kuwait/Khaled Al-Rashidi.
Other titles: Law of financial crime.
Description: Abingdon, Oxon; New York, NY: Routledge, 2021. |
Series: The law of financial crime | Includes bibliographical references and index.
Identifiers: LCCN 2020046166 (print) | LCCN 2020046167 (ebook) | ISBN 9780367721763 (hardback) | ISBN 9781003153740 (ebook)
Subjects: LCSH: Political corruption–Kuwait. | Political corruption–Kuwait–Prevention. | Political corruption–Law and legislation–Kuwait.
Classification: LCC JQ1848.A56 C63 2021 (print) | LCC JQ1848.A56 (ebook) | DDC 364.1/323095367–dc23
LC record available at https://lccn.loc.gov/2020046166
LC ebook record available at https://lccn.loc.gov/2020046167

ISBN: 978-0-367-72176-3 (hbk)
ISBN: 978-0-367-72179-4 (pbk)
ISBN: 978-1-003-15374-0 (ebk)

Typeset in Galliard
by KnowledgeWorks Global Ltd.

**This book is dedicated to all stakeholders in Kuwait who have genuine intent to understand and combat corruption.**

# Contents

# List of legal and regulatory instruments

## Legal and Regulatory Instruments (Kuwait)

## Legal Instruments (UK & US)



## International Legal Instruments

# List of cases

## Cases, Explanatory Decisions, and Investigations (Kuwait)

## Cases (UK)

## Cases (European Court of Human Rights (ECtHR))

# List of acronyms and abbreviations

| Acronym | Full |
|---|---|
| ACAA | Anti-Corruption Authority and Financial Disclosure Act 2/2016 |
| ACAA-SI | Statutory Instrument No. 300/2016 of the Anti-Corruption Authority and Financial Disclosure Act 2/2016 |
| ADA | Administrative Disputes Act 20/1981 |
| AML/CFT Act | Anti-Money Laundering and Countering Financing of Terrorism Act 106/2013 |
| AML/CFT-SI | Statutory Instrument No. 37/2013 of the Anti-Money Laundering and Countering Financing of Terrorism Act 106/2013 |
| CBK | Central Bank of Kuwait |
| CLA 1960 | Criminal Law Act 16/1960 |
| CLA 1970 | Criminal Law Act 31/1970 |
| CJA | Criminal Justice Act 17/1960 |
| Civil Act | Civil Law Act 67/1980 |
| CSA | Civil Service Act 15/1979 |
| CSA-SI | Statutory Instrument of the Civil Service Act 15/1979 |
| Code 2012 | Code of Conduct of Public Officials Circular No. 11/2012 |
| CIA | Conflict of Interests Act 13/2018 |
| CIA-SI | Statutory Instrument No. 296/2018 of the Conflict of Interests Act 13/2018 |
| CAPT | Central Agency for Public Tenders |
| CFA | Criminal Finances Act 2017 |
| DPAs | Deferred Prosecution Agreements |
| ECHR | European Convention on Human Rights |
| ECtHR | European Court of Human Rights |
| EITI | Extractive Industries Transparency Initiative |
| EU | European Union |
| FATF | Financial Action Task Force |

| | |
|---|---|
| **FCB** | Financial Controllers Bureau |
| **FCPA** | US Foreign Corrupt Practices Act 1977 |
| **FDI** | Foreign Direct Investment |
| **FOI** | Freedom of Information |
| **GCC** | Gulf Cooperation Council |
| **GCCA** | GCC Common Customs Act 10/2003 |
| **GDP** | Gross Domestic Product |
| **IEO** | Illicit Enrichment Offence |
| **IMF** | International Monetary Fund |
| **ICCPR** | International Covenant on Civil and Political Rights |
| **ICIJ** | International Consortium of Investigative Journalists |
| **KAPPF** | Kuwait Association for Protecting Public Funds |
| **KBA** | Kuwait Banking Association |
| **KCCI** | Kuwait Chamber of Commerce and Industry |
| **KFIU** | Kuwait Financial Intelligence Unit |
| **KLA** | Kuwait Lawyers Association |
| **KOC** | Kuwait Oil Company |
| **KPC** | Kuwait Petroleum Corporation |
| **KSFEPK** | Kuwaiti Society for the Follow-Up Evaluation of Parliament |
| **KTS** | Kuwait Transparency Society |
| **LALD Act** | Legal Advice and Legislation Department Act 12/1960 |
| **LPA** | Legal Profession Act 42/1964 |
| **MENAFATF** | Middle East and North Africa Financial Action Task Force |
| **MoJ** | Ministry of Justice |
| **MoSA** | Ministry of Social Affairs |
| **ML Offence** | Money Laundering Offence |
| **NGOs** | Non-Governmental Organisations |
| **OCGs** | Organised Criminal Groups |
| **OECD** | Organisation for Economic Co-operation and Development |
| **OPBAS** | Office for Professional Body Anti-Money Laundering Supervision |
| **PPFA** | Protection of Public Funds Act 1/1993 |
| **POCA** | Proceeds of Crime Act 2002 |
| **SAB** | State Audit Bureau |
| **SAB Act** | State Audit Bureau Act 30/1964 |
| **SAIs** | Supreme Audit Institutions |
| **SCP** | Situational Crime Prevention |
| **SPC** | Supreme Petroleum Council |
| **STRs** | Suspicious Transactions Reports |
| **Strategy 2019–2024** | Kuwait Counter-Corruption Strategy 2019–2024 |
| **SWFs** | Sovereign Wealth Funds |

| | |
|---|---|
| **TI** | Transparency International |
| **TMA** | Trial of Ministers Act 88/1995 |
| **UAE** | United Arab Emirates |
| **UK BA 2010** | UK Bribery Act 2010 |
| **UN** | United Nations |
| **UNCAC** | United Nations Convention against Corruption |
| **UNDP** | United Nations Development Programme |
| **UNODC** | United Nations Office on Drugs and Crime |
| **UNTOC** | United Nations Convention against Transnational Organized Crime |
| **UWOs** | Unexplained Wealth Orders |
| **WPP** | Whistleblower Protection Programme |

Acknowledgement

I would like to take this opportunity to thank my supervisors, professors Clive Walker and Peter Whelan, for the high quality of their supervision, their unwavering intellectual guidance, both academically and personally. I feel very grateful to have had an opportunity to be supervised by you.

I am also grateful for the Government of Kuwait for supporting me financially; for my parents who gave everything they could give; for my precious wife, Sarah, for each inspiring word she said, and for each time she told me that she is proud of me; for my friends with whom I spent the most beautiful time in Leeds while preparing this book.

I also would like to thank the staff of the University of Leeds (and, in particular, School of Law) who were supportive and encouraging: indeed, the University of Leeds was my gate to the academia.

Last but not least, I must address a word to my memories in Leeds – the place that I have been living in for 5 years. Leeds was not just a place where I completed my studies – Leeds was home and maybe more than that. I will always miss that place where each corner in there inspired me. I also miss all moments I spent in that beautiful city, whether good or bad – the coffeeshops, the library, gatherings with friends, the Liberty Building and everywhere.

Thank you all.

# Notes for the reader

1 The author has published parts of the book in a book chapter, entitled 'Proceeds of Corruption Crime: The Kuwaiti Legal Response' in Katie Benson, Colin King and Clive Walker (eds.), *Assets, Crimes and the State: Innovation in 21st Century Legal Responses* (Routledge, Abingdon, 2020). This book chapter includes a number of passages already mentioned in chapters 2, 4, and 5. A permission was sought (Request ID: 600024516 - Request Date: 23 Sep 2020). Copyright (Khaled S. Al-Rashidi © 2020) From (Proceeds of Corruption Crime: The Kuwaiti Legal Response in Assets, Crimes and the State: Innovation in 21st Century Legal Responses/) by (Khaled S. Al-Rashidi/ Katie Benson, Colin King and Clive Walker). Reproduced by permission of Taylor and Francis Group, LLC, a division of Informa plc.

2 The provisions of some relevant statutes, which are mentioned throughout the chapters of the book, have been translated from Arabic into English by the author himself. This is because no official translated versions of those statutes are available.

3 In analysing the responses of interviewees, 'he/she' and 'his/her' have been constantly used as a means to anonymise the identity of the participant. This is an ethical issue which has been observed in the book design.

4 All the websites cited throughout the book are valid. They were last accessed in December 2019.

# 1 Introduction

## 1.1 What is this book about?

This book contends that the corruption problem in Kuwait is related to 'grand corruption', which permeates the tier of high-level officials. The corruption is also systemic in nature: it is a deep-rooted problem in the state's systems rather than an aberrant practice of individuals. The intrinsic characteristics of the state of Kuwait, such as its sociocultural systems, political structure, weak public accountability, and the government-dominated oil-based economy, are the dynamics that trigger and indulge systemic and grand corruption as prevalent corruption patterns. Consequently, this analysis of the corruption problem uncovers a link between corruption and social, political, and economic factors. Corruption, then, is perceived to be a 'governance' issue which requires an analysis of corruption within broad values such as legitimacy, transparency, accountability, human rights, and effectiveness. Although these causes suggest that corruption can be addressed by several disciplines such as sociology, politics and economics, this book approaches corruption from a socio-legal perspective, which depends on laws and regulations within broader contexts as key problem-solving mechanisms. Consequently, not only effective legalistic reforms are needed, but the conditions that surround the counter-corruption process must also be taken into consideration and reformed.

Kuwait, since its independence in 1961, has responded to corruption. Policymakers have put in place various laws and regulations to address corruption. The responses have varied between regulations directed at officeholders, civil and criminal laws, and innovative measures such as the establishment of an Anti-Corruption Authority (Nazaha) and the creation of an illicit enrichment offence (IEO). The core argument of this book is that criminal law dominates existing counter-corruption measures and public discourse about combating corruption in Kuwait. Although there is a raft of criminal laws which are comprehensive enough (in content and scope) to cover many forms of corruption crimes, they suffer from poor enforcement. Moreover, despite the adequacy of current criminal measures, criminal law alone is not adequate. Kuwait still lacks innovative measures to combat grand corruption. Grand corruption requires recourse to non-criminal measures, in particular, the adoption of more innovative approaches which address the pattern of corruption. These innovative approaches include the adoption of an 'enforcement pyramid' approach to combat corruption, an improved system of whistleblowing, enhanced prosecutorial discretion, and techniques such as civil forfeiture and unexplained wealth orders (UWOs) which target illicit assets.

In order to manage the research objectives within this book, the scope must be clearly delineated from the outset. The book scope will be determined by reference to the content and approach of the book. With regard to the content, this book aims to identify the contours of the corruption problem in Kuwait. Corruption is a complex subject. There are endless potential patterns of corruption, and each pattern has its own nature, overarching effects, and underlying causes. However, it is not helpful to consider all corruption patterns here; instead, it is necessary to focus on those relevant to Kuwait. Consequently, this book is limited to public corruption and its focus is mainly on violations of public office by public officials, namely, grand corruption (or political corruption). The core argument here is that the corruption problem in Kuwait emanates from governmental officials' frequent abuses of public duties for private interests, whether financial or otherwise. Public corruption in this sense extends to include corrupt actors from the private sector as public corruption instigators. Thus, corruption purely within the private sphere (private corruption), such as fraud between businesses and embezzlement in corporations, lies outside the scope of the book. The importance of limiting this study to public corruption is also reflected in the priority given by the Kuwait Counter-Corruption Strategy 2019–2024 (Strategy 2019–2024) to reforms of the public sector.[1]

This book aims to construct a legal and regulatory framework which will counter corruption. In accordance with the complex nature of the phenomenon of corruption, this book resorts to multiple disciplines such as the law, criminology, culture, politics, and economics in order to secure a comprehensive understanding of corruption as a phenomenon. Nonetheless, despite the interdisciplinary perspectives, the main thrust of the book focuses on the legal and regulatory perspective in terms of analyses, arguments, and solutions. While corruption can be fought using strategies such as cultural, economic, and political strategies, this book primarily adopts a legal approach to counter corruption, thereby depending on the law and regulations as key counter-corruption mechanisms. Thus, the focus will be on the following mechanisms to counter corruption: criminal law, civil law, administrative law, and other regulatory responses. The dominance of criminal law measures in the Kuwaiti legal system in the context of counter-corruption[2] further justifies both the focus of the book on criminal measures and the imbalance between criminal and non-criminal measures.

1 See Nazaha (2019). Pursuant to its remit stipulated in section 5 of the Anti-Corruption Authority and Financial Disclosure Act 2/2016 (ACAA), Nazaha issued the Strategy 2019–2024 in 2019 as a national strategy against corruption. The Strategy, and its agendas, are explored, explained and analysed throughout the book in chapters 2, 3, 4, and 5.

2 See chapter 4.

This prioritisation is due to the current primacy of criminal counter-corruption measures in Kuwait and does not affect the argument of this book that responses to corruption should be multiple.[3] Furthermore, the author aims to focus on the law, regulations, and policies as 'dynamic' phenomena which can be changed, adapted, and developed. Thus, given the limit of space, this book is not concerned with the law enforcement authorities and their modus operandi in the context of counter-corruption laws and regulations; hence, the law enforcement authorities are not part of the scope of this book. However, while this book does not subject the counter-corruption institutions to thorough analysis, addressing some institutional arrangements to combat corruption is unavoidable in specific passages.[4]

To be able to achieve the overall aim of the book, six objectives are identified. The first objective is to address the phenomenon of corruption in order to understand the complexity of corruption both globally and in Kuwait (Chapter 2). Thus, the corruption phenomenon will be analysed in four contexts: the corruption concept, its patterns, its effects, and its causes. This objective will seek to address the nature of corruption in Kuwait through the following questions: what is the factual phenomenon of corruption; why is corruption a problem in Kuwait; and what triggers it? These issues are approached with the help of the existing literature on corruption. Consequently, by conceptualising a meaning of corruption, recognising the effects of corruption, identifying the prevailing corruption patterns, and dissecting the causes of corruption, the parameters of the corruption problem in Kuwait will be identified as a prelude to tackling it.

The second objective is to investigate the literature to highlight two important aspects of counter-corruption processes: what are the outcomes of countering corruption and how corruption has been fought? (Chapter 3). This is a twofold objective: to determine the values which combating corruption instils and to identify the recommended strategies which contribute to curtailing corruption. The first aim of the objective is to probe the corruption literature in order to shed light on the desired, universally identified values of counter-corruption processes, such as transparency, accountability, and human rights, thereby answering the question about the values which should be promoted in the public sphere (public office) by countering corruption. The other aim of the objective is to explore the varied counter-corruption strategies which have been proposed in the literature. Hence, the overall objective aims to identify the values and successful strategies of counter-corruption processes in abstract and then address these two issues in the context of Kuwait in order to look at the extent to which these issues have been integrated into Kuwaiti counter-corruption policies.

The third objective is to investigate Kuwait's current experience of counter-corruption from a legal perspective by considering the criminal laws about

3 See the idea of the 'enforcement pyramid' in chapter 5.

4 For example, the counter-corruption role of the following institutions was addressed: Nazaha (chapter 3.3.2); the State Audit Bureau (chapter 5.3.4); the courts (chapter 3.2.2.2).

combating corruption (Chapter 4). The investigation takes into account a preliminary issue: to set the definition of corruption, according to which the laws can be identified and analysed. Thus, it is necessary to deconstruct the criminal counter-corruption machinery in Kuwait in order to analyse its parts and assess their genuine effectiveness in the counter-corruption process, especially regarding grand public corruption. Consequently, this objective is critical: it examines how the criminal laws can help combat corruption, the adequacy and effectiveness of Kuwaiti criminal laws on corruption and how such laws can be improved. Lastly, this objective aims to suggest innovative approaches to counter corruption, based on international practices, to further strengthen the legal response.

The fourth objective is to identify and examine current Kuwaiti non-criminal measures to combat corruption. These non-criminal responses are legal measures (including the civil and administrative laws) and broader regulatory measures (Chapter 5). This examination is achieved first by finding an appropriate definition of corruption which covers non-criminal forms of corruption. It does this by building on the definition already adopted in chapters 2 and 4. Next, this objective aims to classify the non-criminal measures based on the idea of an 'enforcement pyramid' and analyse how each type of measure is being used in Kuwait in the context of counter-corruption. Consequently, the objective here is to assess the existing non-criminal responses against corruption and how they can be improved to combat corruption more effectively alongside the criminal laws.

The fifth objective is methodological (Chapter 1). Socio-legal methodology is to be used in this book to ensure a fuller understanding of the subjects of the book. A qualitative-based study, which relies on the fieldwork technique (semi-structured interviews), is adopted to answer the research questions. Thus, the book aims to address 'law in context' in which the law is conceived to be a key aspect of the corruption problem; consequently, the law must be addressed but in the light of social and political contexts.[5] This approach makes the fifth objective a cross-cutting endeavour which addresses various questions throughout the book. The purpose is to enrich the book beyond descriptive or abstract approaches and make it empirically informed by exploring what happens in practice. The methodology will be used to achieve the following research objectives related to the phenomenon of corruption in Kuwait (Chapter 2): to determine counter-corruption values and strategies (Chapter 3), to assess Kuwaiti criminal laws on corruption (Chapter 4), and to evaluate the current non-criminal counter-corruption measures (Chapter 5).

The sixth objective is to build on the analysis and evaluation conducted in chapters 2, 3, 4, and 5 in order to establish the conclusions and recommendations of the book on how to counter corruption in Kuwait (Chapter 6). This objective specifically discusses what the prior chapters have proven and how the findings could advance the other objectives of the book. Moreover, this objective raises issues which are not addressed in the book and which could be considered for future research. The findings will also be discussed in relation to the ability

5 McConville and Chui (2007, p. 1).

to implement them in Kuwait. Thus, the objective is to conclude the book from the following standpoints: the core findings regarding the corruption problem in Kuwait, whether they have been achieved, and the feasibility of implementing the solutions suggested.

## 1.2 Originality

This section addresses the claims to originality of the book. This book advances the current literature and offers a step forward by adding significantly to the literature on corruption, specifically in the context of Kuwait. In this regard, the book sheds light on existing gaps in the literature by contributing to the scholarly efforts of describing, analysing, and criticising different issues which are relevant to the problem of corruption in Kuwait. Overall, academic efforts and contributions have enriched the literature about corruption in developing countries generally[6] and the Middle East specifically.[7] Many scholars from the Middle East have investigated and addressed the problem of corruption, whether legally, economically, or sociologically, in relation to the Arab world and under the provisions of the United Nations Convention against Corruption (UNCAC).[8] In addition, there are studies which have focused on the problem of administrative corruption, its patterns and causes, and the ways in which it might be fought in specific countries such as Saudi Arabia.[9]

With regard to Kuwait, few scholars have previously studied corruption. One example is a legal study by Al-Oumi on the provisions of the IEO. The study analysed the construction of the IEO and its legal elements, taking into account UNCAC.[10] Moreover, Al-Kanderi analysed the approach of the Kuwaiti legislature to combating corruption.[11] He studied the evolution of counter-corruption laws in the Arab world and rationalised the need which necessitated the promulgation of such laws. This approach provided a detailed study which illuminated the procedural and substantive provisions of the Anti-Corruption Authority and Financial Disclosure Act 24/2012 (ACAA).[12] Al-Qarioti also explored the problem of bribery in the Kuwaiti administration and undertook field research

6 The World Bank, for example, has a role in combating corruption in many developing countries. See World Bank (1997). The problem of corruption in developing countries has also been addressed on a sectoral basis. See Spector (2005).
7 Several scholars have addressed the corruption problem from Islamic, legal, and economic perspectives in separate studies, specifically regarding the Middle East. See Naif Arab Academy for Security Sciences (2003).
8 See Abdul Munaim (2005); Khayatt (2008).
9 Al-Asheikh (2007).
10 Al-Oumi (2015).
11 Al-Kandari (2013).
12 The Anti-Corruption Authority and Financial Disclosure Act 24/2012, establishing the anti-corruption authority (Nazaha) and financial disclosures, was enacted for the first time in 2012. However, in 2015, the Kuwaiti Constitutional Court, in Case No. 24/2015, 20/12/2015, annulled the Act for constitutional reasons. In 2016, the same Act was enacted again (Act 2/2016). So, throughout the book, Nazaha and financial disclosures are mentioned as established in 2012.

using a random sample consisting of 600 people.[13] Furthermore, Al-Zafiri[14] and Al-Mulaifi[15] explained the offences which are committed against the public purse. It is also worth noting that other scholars have studied corruption in other disciplines. From economic and sociological perspectives, for instance, Hafez insightfully studied the phenomenon of corruption as a prominent culture in the Middle Eastern world and in light of the following relevant issues: politics, economics, history, and culture (such as the rent-seeking culture).[16] Moreover, a sociological study by Al-Zu'abi and Al-Naqeeb defined corruption, highlighted 'the effects of corruption in the Arab Countries and [the] culture of corruption', and examined the causes of corruption. This study particularly explained the problem of corruption in Kuwait.[17]

Despite these valuable scholarly contributions, this book has something original to contribute about corruption in Kuwait in three ways. First, there has not yet been a major, comprehensive study which covers the key aspects of public corruption in relation to Kuwait. There is a lack, if not a complete absence, of studies in the literature which address the problem of public (grand) corruption and particularly the following issues: the conceptualisation of corruption in Kuwait in light of the international literature regarding corruption; the prevalent, problematic corruption patterns in Kuwait and the need to direct attention to them; and explanations of the corruption phenomenon in terms of the cultural, political, and economic conditions of Kuwait. These issues are critical, and it is from the analysis of these that the book derives its meaningfulness and originality. Thus, this book paves the way to answering questions which have been left unanswered in the literature about public corruption in Kuwait. The importance of such issues is clear in that the first part of the process addresses them as a preliminary phase to understanding the problem of corruption, such as its conceptualisation, patterns, and causes, thereby enabling a consideration of the counter-corruption measures in Kuwait. This book is original in the sense that it combines various aspects in order to understand the public corruption problem within a broader conceptual framework.

Second, the book achieves its originality by proposing legal reforms and showing the need for them. Consequently, it evaluates counter-corruption laws and regulations in relation to international standards. This step is crucial in order to determine whether the counter-corruption laws and regulations fit the practical problem of corruption, are effective in combating corruption, or need to be radically reformed. Thus, this book is intended to build on the current literature and address the lack of studies by answering questions and explaining issues which have not yet been considered in the literature of corruption in Kuwait. In this respect, the book sheds light on the corruption literature to provide a

13 Al-Qarioti (2013).
14 Al-Zafiri (2006).
15 Al-Mulaifi (2018).
16 Hafez (2009).
17 Al-Zu'abi and Al-Naqeeb (2007).

better and clearer grasp of real, problematic corruption in Kuwait in accordance with the latest information regarding what is said about corruption. Notably, the book draws its originality from three aspects. First, it not only analyses traditional criminal responses to corruption, it also considers current non-criminal measures against corruption, including civil and regulatory measures. Second, it analyses, for the first time, the recently issued Strategy 2019–2024 and reflects upon it.[18] Third, this book proposes innovative approaches to tackle the problem of grand corruption in Kuwait (such as civil forfeiture and UWOs).[19]

The third original contribution of this book is the way in which the book explores laws by not isolating them from practice. The book achieves this by including original data produced with an empirical methodology.[20] This methodology adopts a socio-legal approach to the corruption problem by employing methodologies which are usually applied in social science research. Consequently, while legal scholarship relies on doctrinal research as a conventional methodology which predominantly focuses on legal doctrine, this book adopts a 'law in context' approach by which the law is studied in broader social and political contexts. Such originality can be illustrated by the way the book approaches the varied corruption-related issues. In addressing some of the issues in the book, the author resorts to fieldwork as a means of evaluation in relation to reality. The interviews of the research participants enable the author to present original data. Such data are tailored to answering specific parts of the research questions. Moreover, because the book addresses grand corruption as a distinct corruption pattern, this methodology is valuable for unravelling issues which doctrinal approaches are unable to uncover. Thus, this methodology secures rich data, which prevents the book from being a purely descriptive and theoretical study. Fieldwork of this nature, which is undertaken to evaluate selected issues, has not been used previously to address corruption in Kuwait. This approach represents an important aspect of the originality of the book and reflects the observation that:

> If the work is to be of high quality, significant originality, and substantial importance or influence, the scholar, in most cases, will need to break away from the more conventional approaches and methods exhibited by the earlier stages or perspectives of legal scholarship. [21]

Consequently, this book may stimulate future research on other issues, such as the various patterns of corruption (private corruption and petty corruption) or even the institutional framework of combating corruption (via law enforcement authorities), from interdisciplinary perspectives.

18 See chapters 2–5.
19 See chapters 4–5.
20 See section 1.3 below.
21 Kissam (1988, p. 246).

## 1.3 Methodology: Socio-legal research

Research into corruption requires methodologies which consider not only the legal aspect but also the social, political, and global contexts. Consequently, this book adopts a socio-legal methodology to ensure an appropriate combination of multiple methodologies. Corruption is more effectively studied with a socio-legal approach because corruption not only raises technical legal issues but is also social and political in nature. As an exercise in the form of legal scholarship, this book mainly considers laws and regulations as key mechanisms to deal with the corruption problem and depends on doctrinal legal methodology to analyse counter-corruption responses. However, since doctrinal legal research is criticised for being an 'intellectually rigid, inflexible and inward-looking approach',[22] wider non-doctrinal methodologies are also adopted in the book. Socio-legal research enriches the doctrinal legal method and seeks to look beyond what is written in statutes and academic materials and to explore the 'law in society'.[23] It studies the law in broader social and political senses in order to understand the external factors which act upon the legal systems, thereby making it possible to answer the research questions.[24] Therefore, it enables the policymakers and, generally, readers to understand the corruption problem more practically and compare the disjunction between the law which is written in books and the law in reality. In this sense, socio-legal research goes beyond doctrinal issues and is concerned with applying the established methods of other disciplines to legal research. Thus, socio-legal research helps understand the law and how a legal system operates, which is here referred to as the 'law in context' approach. In sum, socio-legal methodology is regarded here as a generic category of research, entailing multiple techniques (such as library-based research, fieldwork research, and comparative research) which collectively shed light on research issues from diverse approaches and consider how these issues appear in the real world.[25] Overall, this section concerned with the epistemological aspect of the book. It is about the book design which has been adopted to answer the question of how the author can acquire and apply the knowledge pertaining to the research questions. It explains and justifies the various methodologies chosen for the book. These choices are based on how the methodologies help to achieve the objectives of the book. Thus, the fifth objective of the book is achieved by adopting appropriate methodologies which are applied across the book's chapters and which contribute to answering the research questions.

### 1.3.1 *Library-based research*

With library-based research, the book focuses on the analysis, reading, and reviewing of primary and secondary sources. These sources are not from one

22 McConville and Chui (2007, p. 4).
23 Bradshaw (1997, p. 99).
24 McConville and Chui (2007).
25 Banakar and Travers (2005).

discipline alone: some focus on factual and legal issues and materials (legal research), while others are concerned with social, cultural, political, and economic issues (non-legal research). Altogether, these sources not only help the book to approach the corruption phenomenon from a legal perspective but also from interdisciplinary perspectives.

Doctrinal research is the traditional research method used to address a legal topic based on the premise that legal research focuses on the text of the law itself: legal doctrine. Such research is often called 'black-letter law' research which essentially depends on statutes and judicial cases to analyse and explain the law.[26] Thus, relevant court cases and statutory provisions are used to analyse the corruption phenomenon from the legal perspective. The doctrinal method helps the book explore sources about corruption and the response to it under the umbrella of the doctrine of law. Primary sources are legislation and court decisions, while secondary resources are textbooks, journal articles, and reports. The aim is to achieve the research objectives of exploring and assessing Kuwaiti counter-corruption laws, regulations, values, and strategies. The relevance of doctrinal methodology stems from the traditional purposes of legal scholarship, as explained by Kissam: doctrinal legal analysis and synthesis, the resolution of doctrinal issues, the understanding of law, and the critique of legal doctrine.[27] As a product of legal scholarship, this book is primarily concerned with law as a normative science which asserts standards to be followed in specific conditions. Thus, the book addresses corruption-related legal issues and proposes doctrinal solutions to them.

On the other hand, various non-legal documents were used to address the research questions. These are primary resources, such as official governmental documents, and secondary resources, both of which provide useful analysis and comments on the corruption problem in general and in Kuwait. These documentary sources are of three types: personal (documents written by individuals), private (documents produced by private organisations which are published for the general public), and public (documents which are produced by governments). Each type of document is not necessarily intended or produced for research purposes.[28] With regard to private documents, instruments such as the annual reports and media statements of professional organisations, materials from the Internet and newspaper articles were analysed. For public documents, materials related to corruption in Kuwait were collected from relevant instruments, such as official documents, policy papers, and administrative records. Furthermore, some of these resources were historical because this book, to some degree, addresses the corruption phenomenon from a historical perspective: the history of corruption cases, laws, and policies related to the corruption problem (locally and globally). The book also explores domestic and international pressures since the advent of corruption as a problem in Kuwait and the establishment of relevant international organisations. Because documents are critical resources for

26 McConville and Chui (2007, p. 3).
27 Kissam (1988).
28 Scott (1990).

studying specific issues from a non-legal perspective, documentary research was utilised to rectify the limits of the legal doctrinal method, which restricts the research to focus merely on legal doctrine and achieve some research objectives.

### 1.3.2 *Qualitative research: Fieldwork study*

As this study adopts the 'law-in-context' approach, it includes qualitative research as 'a way of approaching the empirical world'.[29] Such an empirical characteristic of qualitative research is evident in the priority granted to the perspectives of those being studied rather than the preconceptions of researchers.[30] By finding a convergence point in which an interaction is secured between corruption as a problem in theory and a problem in practice, qualitative research gives issues further meaning.[31] Qualitative research is seen to be 'naturalistic' and 'participatory': it is conducted in a social, natural context where research subjects play active roles.[32] Qualitative research serves some of the research objectives which aim to understand the social and cultural context surrounding the corruption phenomenon, thereby helping to counter corruption effectively. In particular, qualitative research rectifies the limitations of doctrinal legal research in two respects. First, it brings more facts about corruption from the perspectives of privileged professional experts, an advantage that legal sources may not secure. Second, it provides critiques of the current counter-corruption measures which have not been raised elsewhere. A reflection on the success of qualitative research and the actual experience of the author will be discussed in the book's conclusion.[33]

Adopting a qualitative rather than quantitative approach is justified. First, quantitative research is ruled out because it essentially relies on accurate statistical data. Because of the absence of data on corruption crimes in Kuwait,[34] a quantitative methodology will not advance the research. Qualitative research is better at revealing insights into unrecorded crimes and undetected criminals, particularly because corruption is a form of white-collar crime committed by individuals of relatively high status.[35] Second, qualitative research enables the author to study corruption in interaction with the social world and secures more interactive results and insights of the corruption phenomenon compared with quantitative methodology. Qualitative research in this sense predominantly aims 'to "appreciate" the social world from the point of view of the criminal justice professional'.[36] Such research is of practical significance because the book includes research questions which have no answers in the literature. This

29 Taylor, Bogdan and DeVault (2016, p. 7).
30 Bryman (1989).
31 Taylor, Bogdan and DeVault (2016).
32 Kirk and Miller (1986, p. 9).
33 See chapter 6.
34 Nazaha (2019).
35 Noaks and Wincup (2004).
36 Ibid., p. 13.

deficiency can be balanced by using qualitative research to gather new information which is otherwise unavailable. Third, securing a contextualised grasp of the problem for stakeholders, such as criminal justice professionals, contributes to the development of suitable policies of crime control, especially when the research is used as an evaluation instrument, or at least has policy implications.[37] Thus, qualitative raw data were gathered from interviews and followed by analysis to enrich the content of the book.

Interviews 'are used extensively by qualitative researchers examining legal phenomena, and perceptions of law and the legal profession'.[38] Interviews of experts were used as the adopted qualitative method in order to secure a detailed grasp of the corruption phenomenon and the relevant critical issues and to evaluate the current counter-corruption measures. The author interviewed professional experts face-to-face in order to understand their perspectives 'on their lives, experiences, or situations as expressed in their own words'.[39] An expert is 'a person who has privileged access to information about groups of persons or decision processes or who is responsible for the development, implementation or control of solutions, strategies and/or policies'.[40] Qualitative research helps to gather information about corruption in Kuwait. It also helps to overcome the limits of data and literature and the sensitive nature of corruption as a topic. Indeed, the limited data drove the Kuwaiti government itself to rely on interviews of experts as a technique to prepare the Kuwait Counter-Corruption Strategy 2019–2024 (Strategy 2019–2024).[41] The interviews helped to pursue several objectives of the book: to contribute to the search for effectiveness in combating corruption, to identify the obstacles and shortcomings which are encountered in implementing counter-corruption laws in practice and to discuss the potential reforms to improve the process of fighting corruption. In particular, the expert interview technique provided information which was not published and otherwise accessible. It explained what lies behind the scenes, thereby promoting the originality of the book. Interviews then helped to achieve key research objectives by empirically studying various corruption-related issues and determining a genuine vision in terms of evaluating the Kuwaiti criminal and non-criminal measures on counter-corruption.

The development of interview schedules is important for this technique. Each schedule contains a set of questions designed to help the author ensure the standardised application of interview questions while conducting the fieldwork.[42] The standardised questions involve book chapters and are in four parts. The first part consists of questions related to the phenomenon of corruption: the meaning and causes of corruption in Kuwait and the role of state characteristics in encouraging

37 Ibid., p. 16.
38 Webley (2010, p. 935).
39 Taylor, Bogdan and DeVault (2016, p. 102).
40 Meuser and Nagel (2009, pp. 17–42).
41 Nazaha (2019).
42 Sapsford and Jupp (2006).

corruption (the first objective). The second part involves questions probing into the value of transparency and accountability in Kuwait; the counter-corruption role of courts, parliament, and civil society; and the effectiveness and fairness of the existing counter-corruption measures (the second objective). The third part encompasses questions related to Kuwaiti laws on corruption, their effectiveness, and their inherent flaws (the third objective). Finally, the fourth part consists of enforcement-oriented questions. However, because the institutional counter-corruption framework was excluded from the book's scope, the answers of the participants were used to address other issues relating to the criminal and non-criminal counter-corruption measures (the third and fourth objectives). The schedules are set out in Appendix 1.

### 1.3.3 *Comparative legal research: Policy transfer*

Comparative legal research reflects the 'increasing influence of international and supra-national legal materials' and the countervailing inability to dispense with international experiences in the various jurisdictions and operations of comparative legal systems.[43] Comparative research derives its importance from the assumption that corruption, as the subject matter addressed here, is an international phenomenon; accordingly, each jurisdiction is susceptible to it. However, although this book derived many lessons from the laws of the United Kingdom and international best practices in terms of combating corruption, the book is not a full comparative study between the United Kingdom and Kuwait. Instead, for policy considerations, the study focused on Kuwait, with special reference to the UK experience in combating corruption because the United Kingdom is a developed country and has had successful achievements in the field of fighting corruption.

This book adopts policy transfer as an 'experience-oriented' approach which depends on learning from accumulated experiences in order to face present phenomena and problems.[44] Dolowitz and Marsh define policy transfer as a process 'in which knowledge about policies, administrative arrangements, institutions and ideas in one political setting (past or present) is used in the development of policies, administrative arrangements, institutions and ideas in another political setting'.[45] With the overarching effects of globalisation, the process of policymaking in a given jurisdiction has been susceptible to external influences, beyond national borders, such as those of supranational institutions.[46] Despite the divergences between the problems which each country may encounter because of historical and institutional circumstances, there is a common area to which policies may be directed.[47] Strictly speaking, corruption is a universal

43 McConville and Chui (2007, p. 7).
44 Bennett and Howlett (1992, p. 276).
45 Dolowitz and Marsh (2000, p. 5).
46 Jones and Newburn (2007).
47 Rose (1991).

problem which is supposed to exist in, and be fought by, all states. This situation creates similarities between jurisdictions which means that the policy transfer approach is of practical relevance. Through a 'policy transfer' approach, appropriate policies from the United Kingdom may be integrated into the Kuwait policymaking process.

Having adopted the policy transfer approach, this book may help Kuwaiti policymakers to draw lessons and benefits from different jurisdictions. Among others, foreign actors are one of the sources which can be used.[48] For example, relevant global organisations address the concerns of many countries, a circumstance which creates a 'collective experience' of other jurisdictions, enabling us to evaluate the effectiveness of a specific policy: 'If the lesson is positive, a policy that works is transferred, with suitable adaptations. If it is negative, observers learn what not to do from watching the mistakes of others.'[49] Thus, international experiences, particularly those of the United Kingdom, have been, to a large extent, considered in this book. In order to illustrate the methodological importance of the policy transfer approach, however, two issues should be explained: what should be transferred and why transfer it?

With regard to the first issue, the lessons which can be drawn may take various forms. These lessons can be in the form of policy-based lessons (including goals, content, instruments, and programmes) or even in the form of 'institutions, ideologies, ideas and attitudes, and negative lessons'.[50] While exploring what international organisations and nations have undertaken to combat corruption, multiple options have enabled the author to suggest what can be drawn from these counter-corruption policies. For example, the author is able to suggest value-laden lessons, represented in the goals of counter-corruption policies; practical lessons, such as the instruments used to combat corruption; or even prevention-oriented lessons, such as avoiding the negative effects of others' experiences. The process of drawing lessons is not restricted to state actors but extends to involve other non-state societal actors who are concerned with counter-corruption policies.[51] Draftsmen working in the government and parliament, and activists of NGOs in Kuwait, are pivotal agents in this learning process.

The other issue is related to the motivation behind the policy transfer approach. Ostensibly, transferring policy from one nation to another can be a voluntary decision based on a 'rational' response to an emerging issue or problem and a desire to learn from nations' experiences.[52] However, policy transfer is more complex than a simple voluntary process. In some cases, policy transfer and learning from others can be an inevitable reaction for some countries, such as Kuwait, to an external internationally based policymaking process, particularly when international organisations and international political powers engage in

48 Dolowitz and Marsh (2000).

49 Rose (1991, pp. 4–5).

50 Dolowitz and Marsh (2000, p. 12).

51 Bennett and Howlett (1992).

52 Dolowitz and Marsh (2000, p. 14).

such a process.[53] The impetus to policy change in this manner originates from the notion that the state finds itself compelled, as a member of an international organisation, to adopt the external policies and programmes provided by this organisation, which means that any policy transfer is an 'obligated transfer'.[54]

Kuwait is a member of the United Nations (UN) and has signed and ratified the UNCAC.[55] Thus, Kuwaiti policymakers are obliged to transfer the policies which have been adopted by the global community through these international instruments in order to counter corruption. Moreover, in terms of this book addressing a global, sensitive phenomenon (corruption), Kuwait is likely to be subject to external pressures which may inspire, or even compel, a domestic policymaker to adapt policies so that they are compatible with those of the global community. Thus, analysing the causes of policy transfer signifies the importance which this methodology represents for the book.

## 1.4 Outline of the book

This book consists of six chapters, each of which aims to achieve a specific research objective. In each chapter, relevant issues are addressed in order to complement other issues in the other chapters. The aim is to fulfil the overall research objectives. An outline of the chapters is presented in subsequent paragraph.

Chapter 1 (Introduction) describes the overall content of the book. It includes the following: a book statement that explains the major problem of the book; the scope of the book, which delimits the boundaries of the book in terms of content and approach; the objectives that the book aims to achieve; the originality of the book and how this addresses the phenomenon in a way which differs from the current literature (about corruption in Kuwait); and an outline that maps the entire book. This chapter also explains the socio-legal methodology adopted to explore the core issues of the book. In particular, the chapter explains the three main methodologies used throughout the chapters of the book: library-based research (involving doctrinal legal and non-legal research), qualitative-based fieldwork and comparative research (policy transfer). Each methodology is used to answer specific research questions.

Chapter 2 (The Phenomenon of Corruption) starts by exploring the literature about corruption as a phenomenon. Thus, definitions, patterns, effects, and causes will be explained in order to identify, in abstract, the nature of the corruption problem. It is inadequate to depend solely on the law to explain and analyse the intricate issues of corruption. Consequently, it is necessary to examine corruption in a wider analytical framework with the help of established disciplines such as sociology, politics, and economics. Then, based on the reality of corruption in Kuwait, the corruption literature will be reflected in the second section of the chapter to identify the distinct nature of the corruption phenomenon in

53 Bennett and Howlett (1992).

54 Dolowitz and Marsh (2000, p. 15).

55 Ratification of the UN Convention against Corruption Act 47/2006.

Kuwait (its conceptualisation, patterns, effects and causes). Thus, this chapter is dedicated to answering the first objective of the book, encapsulated in the following question: what are the contours of the corruption problem in Kuwait?

Chapter 3 (Counter-Corruption: Values and Strategies) aims to clarify how corruption can be faced and to suggest that efforts must be exerted to propose solutions which will help confront corruption. These issues are approached by addressing the findings of the literature in general, the values promoted by counter-corruption, and the proposed strategies to combat the corruption phenomenon. Next, this chapter considers the values and strategies which can help to combat corruption in Kuwait. It evaluates how universally identified values such as transparency, accountability, and human rights can be promoted through counter-corruption measures. Further, it examines counter-corruption strategies which can be adopted by the Kuwaiti policymakers in order to fight corruption, such as enhancing proactive and reactive measures and emphasising the role of the civil society in fighting corruption alongside state institutions. This chapter follows the second objective of the book in deriving universal values and addressing the strategies of counter-corruption. It then applies the relevant values and appropriate strategies to the situation in Kuwait.

Chapter 4 (Kuwaiti Criminal Counter-Corruption Measures) is divided into three parts. The first part aims to discern an appropriate definition of corruption which helps to set the parameters of the current counter-corruption laws and measures. This definition is consistent with the definition chosen in an earlier chapter (chapter 2). The second part adopts doctrinal research to identify and explain the existing counter-corruption laws in Kuwait. In this context, the laws dedicated to addressing corruption include the following offences and measures: bribery, diversion of public funds offences, misconduct in public office (including the offence of conflict of interests), the IEO, the money laundering offence (ML offence), the proceeds of crime law, and whistle-blowing measures. The third part aims to assess the Kuwaiti laws for combating corruption in terms of their adequacy and defects. In this context, the current laws will be thoroughly scrutinised, taking into account their compliance with international standards. Innovative approaches are then suggested. Thus, this chapter achieves the third objective of the book in two ways: first, it emphasises the value of a socio-legal approach in fighting corruption; second, it assesses the law on counter-corruption in Kuwait and proposes solutions which may rectify the shortcomings of the law.

Chapter 5 (Kuwaiti Non-Criminal Counter-Corruption Measures) is divided into three parts. The first builds on the previously adopted definition of corruption to identify the existing non-criminal laws, regulations, and measures against corruption. The second identifies and investigates the current non-criminal measures. These include codes of conduct, the self-regulatory approach and other non-criminal measures as suggested by the civil and administrative laws. The third part assesses the current non-criminal measures and whether they need to be reconsidered or improved. As such, this chapter follows the fourth objective of the book to assess the non-criminal laws and regulatory counter-corruption measures in Kuwait.

Chapter 6 (Conclusion) concludes the study with recommendations and results which will help the government, legislature, and non-governmental organisations (NGOs) to combat corruption. Thus, this chapter is devoted to conclusions and recommendations about the lessons and policies learned from the prior chapters of the book and to a discussion of how the chapters of the book have advanced the research on corruption. This chapter also suggests future research, including relevant topics that have not been addressed in this book.

## Bibliography


Abdul Munaim, S. (2005). *The Corruption Phenomenon: Study on the Compatibility of Arab Legislation with the Provisions of the United Nations Convention Against Corruption.* Cairo: UNDP.

Al-Asheikh, K. (2007). *Administrative Corruption and Its Patterns, Causes and Counter Measures (the Construct of an Organizational Model): An Applied Study on Its Convicted Practitioners and Anticorruption Officials in the Kingdom of Saudi Arabia.* PhD Thesis, Naif Arab Academy for Security Sciences.

Al-Kandari, F. (2013). Philosophy of Kuwaiti and Arab Legislators in Combating Corruption. *Journal of Kuwait International Law School.* 1(4), pp. 397–452.

Al-Mulaifi, O. (2018). *The Role of the Public Prosecution in the Investigation and Disposition of Public Fund Crimes.* Kuwait: Kuwait International Law School.

Al-Oumi, N. (2015). Illicit Enrichment: Comparative Analytic Study of the Decree-Law No. 24 of 2012 of the Public Authority of Anti-Corruption and the Provisions for Financial Disclosure. *Kuwait University Journal of Law.* 39(4), pp. 65–112.

Al-Qarioti, M. (2013). Bribery Problem in Kuwaiti Administration: An Exploratory Study. In: *Proceedings of the 10th Eurasia Business and Economics Society Conference, May 23–25, 2013, Istanbul, Turkey.* Istanbul: EBES Publications, pp. 52–64.

Al-Zafiri, F. (2006). *Criminal Protection of Public Funds in Kuwaiti Act No. 1/1993.* Kuwait: Kuwait University.

Al-Zu'abi, A., Al-Naqeeb, K. (2007). Tackling Corruption in the Arab World, with Special Reference to Kuwait. *Arab World Geographer.* 10(3–4), pp. 170–188.

Banakar, R., Travers, M. (eds.) (2005). *Theory and Method in Socio-Legal Research.* Oxford; Portland, OR: Hart Publishing.

Bennett, C., Howlett, M. (1992). The Lessons of Learning: Reconciling Theories of Policy Learning and Policy Change. *Policy Sciences.* 25(3), pp. 275–294.

Bradshaw, A. (1997). Sense and Sensibility: Debates and Developments in Socio-Legal Research Methods. In: Thomas, P. (ed). *Socio-Legal Studies.* Aldershot: Dartmouth Publishing, pp. 99–122.

Bryman, A. (1989). *Research Methods and Organization Studies.* Abingdon: Routledge.

Dolowitz, D., Marsh, D. (2000). Learning from Abroad: The Role of Policy Transfer in Contemporary Policy-Making. *Governance.* 13(1), pp. 5–23.

Hafez, Z. (2009). The Culture of Rent, Factionalism, and Corruption: A Political Economy of Rent in the Arab World. *Contemporary Arab Affairs.* 2(3), pp. 458–480.

Jones, T., Newburn, T. (2007). *Policy Transfer and Criminal Justice: Exploring US Influence over British Crime Control Policy.* Maidenhead: Open University Press.

Khayatt, A. (2008). The Arab Anti-Corruption Organization. *Contemporary Arab Affairs.* 1(3), pp. 471–477.

Kirk, J., Miller, M. (1986). *Reliability and Validity in Qualitative Research.* London: SAGE.

Kissam, P. (1988). The Evaluation of Legal Scholarship. *Washington Law Review.* 63(2), pp. 221–255.

McConville, M., Chui, W. H. (2007). Introduction and Overview. In: McConville, M., Chui, W. H. (eds). *Research Methods for Law.* Edinburgh: Edinburgh University Press, pp. 1–15.

Meuser, M., Nagel, U. (2009). The Expert Interview and Changes in Knowledge Production. In: Bogner, A., Littig, B., Menz, W. (eds). *Interviewing Experts.* London: Palgrave Macmillan, pp. 17–42.

Naif Arab Academy for Security Sciences. (2003). *Arab Conference Against Corruption.* Riyadh: Naif Arab Academy for Security Sciences.

Nazaha. (2019). *Kuwait Integrity and Anti-Corruption Strategy 2019–2024.* Nazaha.

Noaks, L., Wincup, E. (2004). *Criminological Research: Understanding Qualitative Methods.* London: SAGE.

Rose, R. (1991). What Is Lesson-Drawing? *Journal of Public Policy.* 11(1), pp. 3–30.

Sapsford, R. J., Jupp, V. (2006). *Data Collection and Analysis.* London: SAGE.

Scott, J. (1990). *A Matter of Record: Documentary Sources in Social Research.* Cambridge: Polity.

Spector, B. (2005). *Fighting Corruption in Developing Countries: Strategies and Analysis.* Bloomfield, CT: Kumarian Press.

Taylor, S., Bogdan, R., DeVault, M. (2016). *Introduction to Qualitative Research Methods: A Guidebook and Resource.* Hoboken, NJ: John Wiley & Sons.

Webley, L. (2010). Qualitative Approaches to Empirical Legal Research. In: Cane, P., Kritzer, H. (eds). *The Oxford Handbook of Empirical Legal Research.* Oxford: Oxford University Press, pp. 926–950.

World Bank. (1997). *Helping Countries Combat Corruption: The Role of the World Bank.* Washington: World Bank.

# 2 The phenomenon of corruption

## 2.1 Introduction

Corruption is a universal phenomenon. As a problem of both the developed and developing worlds, corruption raises transnational concerns. Despite international efforts which recognise corruption as a serious problem, corruption endures. The complex and multifaceted nature of corruption is an integral part of the problem. First, there is no universal meaning of corruption because it is protean in nature. Second, even if it is defined, corruption has multiple patterns and varieties which are hard to confine. Third, corruption has various effects on different domains, such as economy and crime. Fourth, corruption has manifold causes, which vary depending on the surrounding conditions and the corruption patterns in question. All these features cause corruption to pose challenges to the development of a sound understanding of the corruption problem. In order to secure an appropriate grasp of it, corruption should be addressed in all respects.

This chapter proceeds as follows. Section 2.2 addresses corruption as a problem in general and how the literature approaches it. In particular, it closely examines the conceptual problem of corruption, the multiple patterns of corruption, the special nature of corruption's effects, and the causes of corruption as proposed within scholarly literature. Section 2.3 addresses each of the aforementioned issues in relation to Kuwait. The analysis of some of these issues will be enriched by information and data gathered through interviews with experts. This approach is taken by demarcating the scope of the book, limiting it to certain types of corruption (corruption within the public sector) while excluding other forms of corruption (private corruption). Consequently, this chapter aims to achieve two objectives of the book (the first and the fifth). For the first objective of the book, this chapter seeks to understand the corruption problem in a global context and build on the literature in order to delimit the parameters of the phenomenon of corruption in Kuwait so as to assimilate it. For the fifth (methodological) objective, this chapter uses socio-legal methodology to ensure a fuller understanding of the subjects of the book.

## 2.2 What is corruption? Literature review

In recent decades, corruption has rightly elicited considerable attention from scholars, governments, and policymakers to the extent that quests for counter-corruption measures exist in almost every corner of the world.[1] According to the Foreword of the United Nations Convention against Corruption (UNCAC) 2003, corruption 'is an insidious plague that has a wide range of corrosive effects on societies'. It corrodes states' legitimacy and leads to corrosive outcomes, erodes democratic practices, diminishes the rule of law, threatens the quality of life, and infringes upon human rights, and taken together amounts to a significant opportunity for organised crime and terrorism. With the eruption of corruption as a salient phenomenon in the 1990s,[2] various conventions have since prioritised corruption as a foremost political issue. Selective efforts will be considered here.[3]

On the global level, the United Nations Convention against Transnational Organized Crime (UNTOC) was adopted in 2000. It recognised that corruption and transnational organised crime are linked; thus, to fight corruption one must be able to fight organised crime.[4] Ziouvas analysed the importance of UNTOC and its applicability to corruption from a 'procedural point of view', 'substantive criminal law point of view', and 'criminological point of view'.[5] However, UNCAC is the leading international document against corruption and is considered a watershed moment in the history of curbing corruption.[6] In 2003, UNCAC was signed as 'the first truly global anti-corruption treaty'.[7]

The World Bank has also made momentous strides. It was not until 1996 that the Bank's President, James Wolfensohn, announced that 'the cancer of corruption' was a matter which could not be henceforth avoided.[8] As one of its strategies, the World Bank aims to help states and non-state actors adopt policies and schemes which reinforce public integrity and form transparent, accountable, and qualified institutions which confront corruption.[9]

The Organization for Economic Co-operation and Development (OECD) adopted on 1997 the Convention on Combating Bribery of Foreign Public Officials in International Business Transactions (OECD Anti-Bribery Convention). The

1 Heywood (2015).
2 Collier (2002).
3 The Conventions are listed at <https://www.oecd.org/cleangovbiz/internationalconventions.htm>.
4 See the General Assembly resolution 55/25 of 15 November 2000 on the UNTOC. Kuwait ratified UNTOC in 2006, pursuant to the Ratification of the UN Convention against Transnational Organized Crime Act 5/2006.
5 See Ziouvas (2018, pp. 591–596).
6 Kofi Annan contends that UNCAC's provisions are 'the first of their kind'. See the Foreword of UNCAC.
7 See Wouters, Ryngaert and Cloots (2013, p. 216).
8 World Bank (1997, p. 2).
9 Ibid.

Convention came into force on 15 February 1999 in order to establish effective standards which call for the criminalisation of the bribery of foreign public officials in the context of international business.[10]

Some international non-governmental organisations (NGOs) have also engaged in combating corruption. Transparency International (TI) is an organisation which was established in 1993, with national chapters in many countries.[11] TI has established the Corruption Perceptions Index (CPI), which was launched in 1995 to score the level of public sector corruption in countries as a means to urge the countries to react against corruption.[12] TI has also established the Bribe Payers Index (BPI), which was launched in 1999 to measure the likelihood of businesses from developed countries to be engaging in bribery practices abroad.[13] Furthermore, TI has established the Global Corruption Barometer to survey 'the experiences of everyday people confronting corruption around the world'.[14]

At the regional level, the League of Arab States issued the Arab Anti-Corruption Convention, which was signed on 21 December 2010 in Cairo and came into force on 29 March 2013.[15] In its preamble, the Convention stresses different critical issues. It emphasises the gravity of corruption and the negative impact of corruption on moral, political, and economic life. It also calls for a role to be played by the private sector and civil society organisations in countering corruption and highlights the importance of international cooperation in this regard.

In recognition of international efforts in this area, in 2016, an international anti-corruption summit was held in London. At the summit, the Global Declaration against Corruption was announced to emphasise three axes: corruption must be exposed, the corrupt should be punished and victims supported, and corruption should be eradicated. The summit focused on a number of relevant issues, inter alia, corporate secrecy, the beneficial ownership and control of companies, and money laundering.[16] Unsurprisingly, the focus on these issues is warranted because the global financial system, tax havens, and corporate secrecy can play a major role in encouraging corruption.[17] For example, in the United Kingdom, the Sanctions and Anti-Money Laundering Act 2018 was enacted and included provisions relating to 'Reports on progress towards register of beneficial owners of overseas entities'.[18]

Overall, international efforts can be summed up by the fact that persistent corruption scandals worldwide convey a vital message that corrupt behaviours cannot be tamed by international conventions or new local regulations alone;

10 Permeable of the OECD Anti-Bribery Convention.
11 See <https://www.transparency.org>.
12 Transparency International (2019).
13 See <https://www.transparency.org/research/bpi/overview>.
14 See <https://www.transparency.org/research/gcb>.
15 See<https://star.worldbank.org/star/sites/star/files/Arab-Convention-Against-Corruption.pdf>.
16 See Grimwood (2016).
17 See, for example, Christensen (2011); Schjelderup (2016).
18 Sections 50–51. See also Home Office (2019).

rather, corruption should be managed within a more sophisticated framework.[19] The attempt to find such a framework should first start by understanding what corruption is.

### 2.2.1 *Corruption: An ill-defined concept*

As a concept, corruption is ill defined and contested among analysts.[20] The complexity of the corruption concept entails a multifaceted concept which involves more than the abuse of public office or direct exchanges between individuals engaging in a corrupt practice. For example, Heidenheimer and Johnston identified three models of corruption: a public office-oriented definition, which centred on the norms and duties which govern incumbents,[21] a market-oriented definition, revolving around the notion of a corrupt individual who considers his or her office as a business tool to maximise profits,[22] and a public interest-oriented definition, which regards the abuse of public interests by a corrupt individual when he or she prioritises his or her interests over public ones.[23]

Today, societies reflect divergence in conceiving the concept of corruption: thus, the Western idea of corruption cannot be generalised and applied in other countries.[24] What is conceived as a corrupt practice in one place may be considered a praiseworthy cultural practice in another. Klitgaard stressed that corruption is a concept of a normative nature. It is hard to define because it entails a myriad of forms, which depend considerably upon domestic cultures and laws. While the accumulation of assets and private investments is a healthy practice in capitalist countries, these constitute corrupt behaviour in communist states.[25] There are even those who find it 'impossible to develop one generalizable and uncontested definition' of corruption.[26]

Even if a specific concept of corruption is adopted, operationalising the corruption concept 'is likely to differ dramatically across empirical analyses'.[27] For example, a specific definition of political corruption is likely to depend upon the political system (democratic or non-democratic) in which it was defined.[28] Corruption, because of its contestability, lends itself to be variably defined, conceptualised, and perceived. The World Bank has emphasised that the term 'corruption' should be unbundled in order to identify its specific activities and patterns.[29] A narrow definition sheds little light on the entire concept of

19 Arvis and Berenbeim (2003).
20 See Heidenheimer and Johnston (2007).
21 See Nye (1967).
22 See Leff (1964).
23 See Friedrich (1966).
24 Collier (2002).
25 Klitgaard (1988).
26 Heywood (1997, p. 422).
27 Bussell (2015, p. 24).
28 Heywood (1997).
29 World Bank (1997).

corruption and prevents us from recognising the different types of corruption.[30] Thus, 'corruption' is better conceptualised rather than defined. Rather than formulating a one-size-fits-all definition, this approach suggests a within-country or within-region analytical conceptualisation of the corruption phenomenon in order to accommodate the variation of the corruption concept.

For research purposes, an initial working concept of corruption is necessary so that this book can build on it in order to understand the multifaceted nature of corruption. Inclusivity should be considered in this concept as much as possible. Conceiving corruption as more than simply illegal transactions provides a fuller view of corruption, which enables us to discover further its manifestations and diagnose its causes.[31] In this context, the World Bank, for example, coined the corruption concept in its simplest form as 'the abuse of public office for private gain'.[32] This concept is justifiably chosen, for it serves the main thrust of the book in focusing on public corruption and excluding private corruption. This is evident in the first part of the definition, 'abuse of public office'. Moreover, the World Bank's concept is useful because it has the potential to cover various forms of corruption patterns.

### 2.2.2 *Patterns of corruption*

Patterns of corruption imply the potential of diverse forms. The literature is rich in various typologies of corruption which aim 'to identify acts which fall within the range of conduct described as "corrupt"' from diverse perspectives.[33] The corruption patterns which are referred to in this section are by no means comprehensive.[34] However, specific corruption patterns will be selectively mentioned here because they are helpful in advancing the objectives of this book (namely, understanding the phenomenon of corruption in Kuwait).

#### 2.2.2.1 *Typologies of corruption*

One typology of corruption depends upon the level of the public official who is embroiled in a corrupt practice and classifies corruption into two patterns: grand and petty corruption.[35] Grand corruption is the pattern which is related to the practices of officials who occupy either the highest levels in national government or in major governmental projects, or both. The senior officials' awards of concessions and major governmental contracts to large businesses, in exchange for bribes, are typical examples of grand corruption.[36] Also, grand

30 Bussell (2015).
31 Mills (2012).
32 Collier (2002, p. 1).
33 UNODC (2003, p. 23).
34 For other patterns, see, for example, Amundsen (1999); Thompson (2000).
35 Pradhan et al. (2000).
36 Rose-Ackerman (1999).

corruption could be described as political corruption because it involves politicians when they exploit their power.[37] In contrast, petty corruption refers to corruption which 'can involve the exchange of very small amounts of money, the granting of minor favours by those seeking preferential treatment or the employment of friends and relatives in minor positions'.[38] Petty corruption typically encompasses a small payment to a low-ranking official, such as when a corporation offers a bribe to official inspectors to overlook intentionally the irregularities which that corporation usually commits.[39] Petty corruption in this sense involves bureaucratic corruption.[40] Whilst grand corruption revolves around the core functions of a government, petty corruption is embodied 'within the context of established governance and social frameworks'.[41] This typology is supposedly advantageous for many reasons. Its ambit is wide so as to accommodate, as much as possible, other forms of corruption. Furthermore, it does not limit the concept of corruption to the public sector; instead, it includes under its umbrella the corruption which exists within the interface between the state and the private sector.

Another typology of corruption classifies corruption into state capture and administrative corruption. State capture indicates a corruption pattern which occurs when individuals, groups, and firms from the private sector, the so-called captors, act so as to influence the institutional processes of a state, such as the enactment of laws, regulations and routines, and regular administrative resolutions, and to manipulate governmental public policies to their own substantial interests by benefiting public officials with private gains through illegal and non-transparent means.[42] A typical instance is that of bribes paid to the largest possible number of MPs so that they vote on a particular piece of legislation in the interests of other. Bribes could even be offered to influence judges so that they manipulate judicial decisions.[43] In this sense, state capture takes the form of grand corruption.[44] In contrast, administrative corruption refers to a pattern of petty corruption in which non-transparent and illegal means are used to provide officials with personal gains in order to distort the enforcement of certain laws or regulations for the advantage of certain individuals and firms. Furthermore, this pattern of corruption encompasses cases wherein officeholders abuse their authority for their private interests, for example, when officials mismanage public funds by embezzling them for their own and their relatives' interests.[45]

37 Bussell (2015).
38 UNODC (2003, p. 28).
39 Arvis and Berenbeim (2003).
40 Stapenhurst, Jacobs and Pelizzo (2014).
41 UNODC (2003, p. 29).
42 Pradhan et al. (2000).
43 Hellman and Kaufmann (2001).
44 Tanzi (1998).
45 Pradhan et al. (2000).

#### 2.2.2.2 *State characteristics and corruption*

When classifying corruption, the characteristics of the state play a vital role in shaping distinctive corruption patterns. When comparing states, corruption may be either systemic or random.[46] Systemic corruption occurs when corruption is incorporated in the body of the state. It is a widespread form of corruption which pervades 'the major institutions and processes of the state' as a way of life.[47] One manifestation of systemic corruption is when there is friction between formal and informal rules; for example, bribery is illegal but may simultaneously be tolerated as routine.[48] Thus, corruption is organised in a manner which compromises the formal institutions which are responsible for guaranteeing the conformity of government practices to law.[49] Such a corruption pattern is very serious and persistently poses stiff resistance to any attempt to reform the situation because the private sector's corrupt firms and their 'allies' in the public sector, which benefit from the ingrained corruption, reject the reformative laws which establish the principles of transparency, competitiveness and openness.[50]

This corruption pattern exists in neo-patrimonial states, which are a type of state which fosters a modern form of traditional patrimonialism where there are only nominal boundaries between the public and private sectors, with a concomitant lack of awareness of these boundaries.[51] This configured concept of the patrimonial state is used to describe new nations where bureaucratic characteristics (rationality and impersonality) were injected during colonisation. Although the superstructures of a bureaucratic state were erected in these nations and still have a presence, the foundations of the patrimonial state (personalised authorities, clientelism, and patronage) still exist and pervade a wide range of state institutions.[52] The pre-modern characteristics of such nations show variance from the Western-based conceptions of politics.[53] The culture of neo-patrimonial states does not accommodate a distinctive conception of politics from other spheres of religion and social order.[54] The political construct is one of 'artificiality'[55] and is not a distinct institution where politicians should not deviate from the purpose of serving the public good. The corruption problem lies beyond the 'face values' of a formal political system or regime.[56] These formal systems are subjugated to 'veiled sources of power and influence', such as sociocultural norms, which

46 Tanzi (1998).
47 Johnston (1998, p. 89).
48 World Bank (1997).
49 Thomas and Meagher (2004).
50 Rose-Ackerman (1999, p. 17).
51 Médard (2007).
52 Pitcher, Moran and Johnston (2009).
53 Khalaf (2000).
54 Philp (2015).
55 Bacik (2008, p. 115).
56 Scott (1972, p. 2).

penetrate the state systems, engendering a dual nature, formal and informal, within state institutions.[57]

Next, random corruption takes the form of isolated individual cases, particularly when corruption is limited to the scattered practices of rogue and opportunistic officials.[58] Corruption, then, is an aberrant force in a state's systems in the sense that 'the formal institutions are sufficiently free of corruption to be able to play their constraining roles'.[59] This corruption pattern usually exists in bureaucratic states, which are the opposite of patrimonial states. A state is bureaucratic when there is a clear separation between the public and private spheres and when an official derives his/her authority from 'impersonal interests' rather than personal rights.[60] In this environment, the authority of the state's rulers is based on bureaucratic features, such as the introduction of modern 'statehood' institutions,[61] in which corruption cases are episodic and emerge as a deviant phenomenon.

State characteristics may also give rise to an extreme pattern of corruption, such as in the situation when the state itself becomes a criminal and degenerates into a 'kleptocratic state'.[62] Kleptocracy refers to a regime which is controlled by a layer of senior officials in the government 'whose primary goal is personal enrichment and who possess the power to further this aim while holding public office'.[63] In more technical language, kleptocracy is a kind of 'state crime' through which corruption becomes an organisational aim of the whole state agency.[64] Unlike an institutionalised state, in a kleptocracy, formal state institutions such as the law, which usually serve as constraints on the ultimate authority of political kleptocrats and hold them accountable, are almost absent.[65]

Rose-Ackerman stressed that the influence of kleptocrats on the policymaking mechanism in a state includes the deliberate manipulation of vital sectors in the state, such as the taxation system, regulations, price fixing, and subsidies. An example is when kleptocrats enact a regulation which levies high rates of tax to encourage individuals and corporations to engage in bribery practices.[66] This situation is not about the efficiency of regulations; it is about the desire of kleptocrats to increase their power by transferring public resources to their own accounts. In such a context, kleptocrats could be a ruling family or senior officials.[67] In some cases, the state coerces the owners of businesses to pay fees as 'protection money'

57 Brinkerhoff and Goldsmith (2002, p. 1).
58 UNODC (2004).
59 Thomas and Meagher (2004, p. 12).
60 See Weber (1978, pp. 1028–1029).
61 Bacik (2008, pp. 105–107).
62 Bloom (2014, p. 641).
63 Rose-Ackerman (1999, p. 114)
64 Green and Ward (2004, p. 16).
65 Acemoglu, Verdier and Robinson (2004).
66 Rose-Ackerman (1999).
67 Acemoglu, Verdier and Robinson (2004).

in return for 'various services'.[68] These peculiar characteristics of kleptocratic states are critical for promoting distinctive corruption patterns. Thus, corruption is embedded in a kleptocratic state's systems (systemic corruption), and the corruption of the high-level political stratum (grand corruption) becomes a factual, serious corruption pattern which is endemic in the state.

### 2.2.3 *The effects of corruption*

The prima facie effect of corruption is inevitably prejudicial. However, this is not always the case. Corruption has been argued to promote economic development, particularly for developing countries. According to Leff, corruption, especially bureaucratic corruption which is premised on 'the practice of buying favors from the bureaucrats responsible for formulating and administering the government's economic policies', acts as 'grease' which helps an economy to develop. [69] Huntington argues that corruption stimulates economic growth when productive enterprises engage in bribery to avoid the excessive bureaucratic procedures which exist in developing countries and cause inefficiency.[70] Countries such as Thailand and Indonesia have achieved economic development 'in spite of, or even because of' the high rates of corruption.[71] Because corruption may have multiple effects, two domains will be studied here: the economic effects and the relationship between corruption and crimes.

#### 2.2.3.1 *Economic effects of corruption*

It seems somewhat odd to defend corruption as a desirable phenomenon which may achieve efficiency. If Leff's view stems from good faith based on a pragmatic justification to overcome bureaucratic issues, investors will exploit this view and relentlessly attempt to avoid any burden imposed by the state, whether this avoidance is warranted or not.[72] To overcome inefficient bureaucracy, the recourse to violations of regulations is tolerated merely because the regulations neglect to consider entrepreneurs, even if the regulations exist to protect consumers and promote social-oriented productive activities. Thus, perceived economic efficiency could become a counter-productive argument. It is argued, then, that corruption is 'almost universally condemned', as Leff himself confessed.[73] The detriments of corruption overweigh its benefits as well.[74]

In a broader sense, corruption is not just a problem of the developing world. Corruption exists even in the most developed country which enjoys a good

68 Wood (2004, p. 561).
69 Leff (1964, p. 8).
70 Huntington (2006).
71 Tanzi (1998, p. 578).
72 Rose-Ackerman (1999).
73 Leff (1964, p. 8).
74 FATF (2011).

ranking in the CPI. What may differ is that developed countries are more able than developing countries to combat corruption and withstand its subversive consequences.[75] Furthermore, corruption in developed countries appears to be less rampant and thus of less concern. Unlike developing countries, when democratic institutions are well established, interest groups and businesses prefer legal channels of influence, such as lobbying and political campaigns, to corrupt practices (bribes) in order to achieve their interests.[76] This may explain the US criminalisation of bribing foreign officials[77] because the same businesses, which obey the law in developed countries, are less inhibited about violating the rules of the developing countries.[78]

Developing countries are more vulnerable to public corruption because of their characteristics, such as having less established administrations, patronage-dominated social relationships, and lack of organisational strength.[79] The World Bank emphasises corruption as 'public enemy number one' in developing countries.[80] Vulnerability comes from the fact that the public sector in developing countries plays the major role in the state, and the victims of corruption, whether citizens or foreign corporations, have no alternatives to which they can turn. Any perceived corruption inflicted on the public sector extensively impacts on people.[81] This point is reinforced when private firms stress that corruption increases the costs of establishing businesses.[82] In the field of foreign direct investment (FDI), petty corruption potentially weakens the likelihood of investing because it increases the costs of investments for investors by acting as a levied tax.[83] Corruption thus represents a serious obstacle which hampers progress towards a healthier climate for investment.[84]

One further deleterious consequence for developing countries is that corruption, particularly grand corruption and state capture, distorts the composition of government expenditure. Grand corruption is responsible for the diversion of humanitarian international aid, which should supposedly be spent on people's needs, in order to enrich a few cliques. While a government's public expenditure should be wisely spent on vital sectors, such as education, health, and economic development, the government actually expends money on sectors which are more vulnerable to corruption.[85] Tanzi and Davoodi insightfully argued that corruption increases the share of capital spending in a state's gross domestic

75 UNODC (2003).
76 Rose-Ackerman (1999).
77 See US Foreign Corrupt Practices Act (FCPA) 1977.
78 Huntington (2006, pp. 66–67).
79 World Bank (1997).
80 Heywood (2015, p. 1).
81 Klitgaard (1988).
82 Arvis and Berenbeim (2003).
83 Mauro (1995).
84 Gray, Hellman and Ryterman (2004).
85 Mauro (1998).

product (GDP) while reducing its productivity.[86] Thus, corruption contributes to the fiscal deficit of a state, which prevents the government from creating an efficient fiscal policy.[87]

Corruption also has a dynamic relation with the economic structure of a state. Notably in countries rich in natural resources, the negative impact of the economic structure on corruption is more apparent by illustrating 'the mechanism by which [the oil curse] casts its spells'.[88] Corruption is a prevailing phenomenon in oil-funded governments whose economies extensively depend upon such a specific natural resource. Despite most oil-producing countries generating much wealth, there is tangible failure in the context of their wealth and economic growth.[89] The corrupt exploitation of oil is responsible for spillovers into the status quo of a state's power economy. This explanation probably provides an answer to the question about the apparent inconsistency between oil production prosperity and slow economic growth, particularly in other industries.[90] The significant wealth created by oil distracts the interests of powerful individuals from investing in highly productive projects and instead incentivises them to take the road of rent seeking, which results in high costs for the economic growth of a state.[91] In sum, corruption, when it exists, has negative consequences for the economy of a state; hence, the notion that corruption promotes economic growth should be left aside.

#### 2.2.3.2 *The corruption–crime nexus*

A further important effect of corruption is its close relation to crime. Corruption makes a wide-ranging contribution to organised crime.[92] For the purposes of this book, organised crime can be understood as a criminal enterprise which is run by a set of criminals who threaten the integrity of the state and which provokes complex, special investigation because of the threats it poses.[93] Corruption is an opportunity which can be seized to ensure the survival of organised crime. Articles 8–9 of UNTOC assume a close relation between the phenomenon of organised crime and corruption and require the criminalisation of corruption and the enactment of effective measures to combat it. In 2019, the UN Security Council emphasised the 'potential linkages' between terrorism, organised crime, and corruption.[94] Levi contended that organised crimes are likely to prosper amid the proliferation of corruption between politicians, criminal

86 Tanzi and Davoodi (1997).
87 Tanzi (1998).
88 Sala-i-Martin and Subramanian (2013, p. 574).
89 Hafez (2009).
90 Ross (2012).
91 Tanzi (1998).
92 Campbell (2016).
93 Levi (2011).
94 See Article 3 of the Resolution 2482 (2019), adopted at its 8582nd meeting on 19 July 2019.

justice officials, and the 'suppliers of illegal commodities'.[95] This convergence between organised crime and corruption is unsurprising. The rise of organised crime in the 1990s[96] was paralleled by the growing salience of corruption in the same decade.[97]

Corruption is associated with organised crime, and more generally, crime. Organised crime is notably a source of corruption threat.[98] This interaction is an outcome of a serious criminal phenomenon, the so-called 'tactical crime displacement', which means that to secure the survival of a criminal enterprise, criminals usually tend to develop their skills and change their tactical approaches to circumvent the countervailing improvements in the criminal justice system.[99] A 'crime–corruption nexus' is established through which the intricate link between organised crime and corruption can be recognised. In many cases, corruption is but an integral part of a wider criminal enterprise.[100] In order to make use of the proceeds of corruption, corruption is essential but insufficient; thus, corruption crime may evolve into a money-laundering enterprise to disguise its illegal source and complete the criminal enterprise. The Financial Action Task Force (FATF) contends that the link between corruption and money laundering derives from the fact that ill-gotten assets and money cannot be used unless they are integrated into the legal financial market.[101] As Makarenko and Mesquita argued in the context of the 'crime–terror nexus', organised criminal groups (OCGs) and corrupt individuals may merge with each other to constitute a 'hybrid' entity which concurrently pursues the fulfilment of a multitude of purposes.[102] While terrorists can ally with the OCGs to fund their activities, corrupt individuals can also ally with OCGs to promote their purposes.

Corruption is an undesirable phenomenon. Whatever the arguments of economists who say that corruption may help an economy grow, corruption is regarded as a problem which has negative fallout, especially regarding a state's economic and political institutions. In addition, the corruption–crime nexus is a mechanism in which corruption is found to promote other criminal activities. With all these effects of corruption, particularly of grand corruption, some scholars even argue in favour of considering grand corruption as a crime against humanity which should be subjected to the jurisdiction of the International Criminal Court.[103] Thus, it may be said that one significant determinant for an economy to flourish and organised crime to be curtailed is to identify and eradicate the causes of corruption.

95 Levi (2011, p. 522).
96 Ibid.
97 Heywood (1997).
98 van Duyne (1997).
99 Rowe et al. (2013, p. 1).
100 Campbell (2016).
101 FATF (2011).
102 Makarenko and Mesquita (2014, p. 262).
103 Bloom (2014).

### 2.2.4 *Causes of corruption*

Studying the causes of corruption is so complex that it often 'opens up a number of intricate problems', not least how one can understand the concept of 'corruption', the 'causality' in social sciences, and the 'the basis of human behaviour'.[104] However, corruption in every area of the world can be an outcome of divergent reasons.[105] The causes of corruption may be a spectrum of direct and indirect factors, including individuals, institutions, and societies.[106] In this sense, analyses of corruption's causes can be broadly classified into two approaches: structural, which focuses on systemic causes related to the structure of a 'political regime, history, culture, values, norms, and loyalties', and individualist, which focuses on the incentives which encourage individuals to engage in corruption.[107]

#### 2.2.4.1 *Structural approach*

Structural analyses are preoccupied with identifying the systemic causes of corruption with the 'nature of state development'.[108] While some scholars analyse corruption in the patrimonial states,[109] others analysts attribute corruption's causes to the legal system of the relevant state.[110] Some political scientists have emphasised that when clientelism (patronage relationships) characterises a political system's organisation, it becomes the factor which is implicated in corruption.[111] Another analysis provides an explanation which perceives religious traditions as relevant to the phenomenon of corruption, whether people come from hierarchical, egalitarian, or individualistic religions.[112] Teorell suggests that corruption can be modelled 'as an institution in itself', whereby corruption may operate through the formal (such as legal contracts) and informal institutions (such as social norms) within a society.[113] Rothstein and Teorell surveyed the literature's empirical findings and found that corruption may be explained through institutional causality such as types of democracy and public administration, the size of government, and social norms such as generalised trust and religion.[114] In an empirical study, Treisman also found that corruption may be caused by different determinants; for example, exposure to democracy for decades, long-lived cultural and institutional traditions, colonial heritage, legal

104 Rothstein and Teorell (2014, p. 79).
105 Klitgaard (1988).
106 Tanzi (1998).
107 Thomas and Meagher (2004, p. 4).
108 Heywood (1997, p. 427).
109 Scott (1972).
110 La Porta et al. (1999).
111 Thomas and Meagher (2004).
112 La Porta et al. (1999).
113 See Teorell (2007, p. 8).
114 See Rothstein and Teorell (2014).

culture, and economic development.[115] Furthermore, Passas suggested that the corruption problem is systemic and not individual in nature, arguing that the structural roots of corruption reside in the 'criminogenic asymmetries', referring to 'structural disjunctions, mismatches, and inequalities in the spheres of politics, culture, the economy, and the law'.[116]

Some scholars explain corruption in a state on the basis that such a state is designed to be corrupt. In this regard, the state is characterised by a weak institutionalised structure which is unable to constrain and hold corrupt people accountable, such as in a criminal state or kleptocracy.[117] Extrapolating from a state's characteristics, this type of analysis of corruption's causes is premised on institutional theory.[118] These analyses are helpful in explaining the causes of a corruption pattern which permeates the institutions of the state: systemic corruption. However, despite the depth of structural analyses and their contribution to understanding the underlying causes of corruption, they have been criticised. Structural literature conveys a 'daunting' account of corruption's causes, in the sense that the literature provides hypotheses which are hardly operationalised and tested in practice, thereby making such hypotheses lose their 'policy relevance'.[119]

Over time, institutional transformations in the field of economics and political structures in societies have emerged to impose radical patterns on the organisation of states. Privatisation and deregulation have transferred decision-making processes from centralised government authorities to other bodies (quasi-governmental bodies).[120] This approach has had an impact on producing plentiful opportunities to follow private interest-centred decisions. For example, there has been a radical move among many prevalent discussions on corruption's causes from focusing on macro-level structural interpretations to micro-level analyses which focus on opportunities and incentives which lie beyond corrupt behaviour.[121] Consequently, faced with criticism directed at structural analyses and historical transformations, the individualist approach provides a contrasting vision of why corruption occurs.

#### 2.2.4.2 *Individualist approach*

The individualist approach provides alternative exegeses which are occupied with the circumstances and factors which encourage individuals to engage in corruption.[122] The individualist approach is informed by the agency model (the

115 See Treisman (2000).
116 Passas (1998, pp. 41–54).
117 Acemoglu, Verdier and Robinson (2004).
118 Stapenhurst, Jacobs and Pelizzo (2014).
119 Thomas and Meagher (2004, p. 12).
120 Heywood (1997).
121 Ibid.
122 Thomas and Meagher (2004).

principal–agent relationship) which suggests that corruption is, first, a result of a conflict between principals (who are assumed to favour the public interest) and agents (who favour engaging in corruption as long as the benefits outweigh the costs), and second, information asymmetry between the two (as agents have more information than principals).[123] The policy implications of the principal–agent model hold that, to reduce corruption, 'the principal should aim at negatively affecting the agent's motivations to engage in corrupt behavior' by reducing opportunities to engage in corruption.[124] Thus, the individualist approach places into the spotlight an 'individual, who has rational preferences and expectations, and who makes choices so as to maximize his own utility'.[125] In bureaucratic states, in which corruption is not an inherent part of, and aberrant to, the systems (random corruption), this analytical perspective may be helpful.

Klitgaard's explanation is one example of this individualist approach. He focused on incentives beyond corruption and argued that corruption occurs in accordance with the following formula: 'corruption = monopoly + discretion – accountability'.[126] According to the logic of this explanation, a framework is provided to explain corruption as an outcome of the highly monopolistic authority of an official, accompanied with unbridled discretion and a dearth of accountability. Similarly, Jain suggested that corruption requires three requirements to take place: discretion, economic rents (incentives), and low probability of detection and/or punishment.[127] These counter-corruption reforms, and especially those that are built on the logic of the principal–agent model, are criticised for their failure in places where corruption is rampant.[128] Because this approach is purely economic in nature, it does not analyse the role of informal institutions in corruption, such as regarding cultural norms.[129]

However, the model 'can be expanded when conditions that influence the cost-benefit calculations are taken into account'.[130] For some scholars, the individualist approach borrows the new institutional economics (NIE) approach to address the phenomenon of corruption.[131] The NIE provides an economic perspective which links corruption with both formal and informal institutions, such as regarding norms, trust, reciprocity, and legal culture, and analyses the consequential constraints which affect the interactions of human actors in their 'institutional environment' and hence their potential to engage in corruption. Thus, the NIE postulates practical interpretations of corrupt transactions in everyday life.[132] Put simply, NIE scholars consider an approach which studies 'individual

123 See Rose-Ackerman (1978).
124 Persson, Rothstein and Teorell (2013, pp. 452–453).
125 Thomas and Meagher (2004, p. 4).
126 Klitgaard (1988, p. 75).
127 Jain (2001).
128 See Persson, Rothstein and Teorell (2013).
129 Goudie and Stasavage (1998).
130 de Graaf (2007, p. 47).
131 Thomas and Meagher (2004).
132 Lambsdorff, Taube and Schramm (2005, pp. 3–4).

optimization' (when an individual is involved in rational decision making to make specific choices so that he or she can maximise his or her benefits).[133] In this regard, Collier used an 'institutional choice framework' to combine the individualist and structural approaches whereby corruption is perceived as a result of rational choice cost–benefit analysis and other structural factors.[134] In political corruption, for example, the opportunity structures of a political system may explain why politicians become involved in corruption, notably with respect to institutional arrangements pertinent to transparency and accountability.[135]

## 2.3 Kuwait and corruption

The prior section provided a review of the general literature on corruption. In this section, key issues of corruption will be considered in relation to Kuwait. In order to achieve the first objective of the book, namely, to understand the phenomenon of corruption in Kuwait, four issues will be addressed: the conceptualisation, patterns, effects, and causes of corruption. When approaching some of these issues, experts and professionals have been interviewed in order to gather data and information which shed light on the extent to which the analysis in this chapter is realistic.

### 2.3.1 *Conceptualising corruption in Kuwait*

It has been shown that there is no general consensus about the corruption concept. In Kuwait, some of the interviewees had divergent perceptions of the meaning of corruption.[136] For example, Official-5 defined corruption in a broad sense as a 'violation of formal rules and regulations to inflict damage to the public funds', while NGO-3 defined it in a narrow sense as 'financial crimes and violations that have been created in the Protection of Public Fund Act 1993, in addition to other laws, such as the State Audit Bureau Act 1964'. However, contestability, which is an intrinsic characteristic of the corruption concept, is expected to be less acute when corruption is addressed as a phenomenon in a specific context. Thus, when corruption is studied in the context of Kuwait, there should be a specific conceptual base upon which research objectives can be achieved (and to avoid any potential confusion or disagreement in the meaning of corruption within one jurisdiction). Emphasising the significant role of the law and regulations in combating corrupt behaviours also highlights the need to adopt a legalistic conception of corruption.

Reflecting reality, the concept of corruption in Kuwait may be predicated upon the public roles of public officials.[137] Consequently, the World Bank's

133 Thomas and Meagher (2004, p. 12).
134 Collier (2002, p. 13).
135 Heywood (1997).
136 MP-2; MP-3; Official-2; Official-5; NGO-2; NGO-3.
137 Gardiner (2007).

conception of corruption as 'the abuse of public office for private gain' is helpful for the purpose of this book. Official-5 argued that defining corruption with regard to public office provides policymakers with a 'comprehensive' concept that 'extend[s] to cover more than the criminal forms of corruption; it addresses forms that are not addressed in the criminal laws'. In a detailed description, the political scientist Joseph Nye demonstrated how public office can be abused: 'Corruption is behavior which deviates from the formal duties of a public role because of private-regarding (personal, close family, private clique) pecuniary or status gains'.[138] This conception of corruption implies that it typically involves a violation of formal duties. Instead of following their formal duties to meet the requirements of public roles, officeholders seek private gain.

Here, the existence of 'formal rules about official conduct', set by the legal system, prevents any potential obfuscation or variations in the meaning of corruption.[139] The meaning of corruption, proposed in this study, is a *legal-positivist* construct (norms made by the legislature) which finds support in the Kuwaiti laws which regulate public office, whether with non-criminal or criminal provisions.[140] One expert thinks that the legalistic way of defining corruption prevents any confusion with definitions of other types of corruption, such as moral corruption.[141] For example, in the civil service, officials should act disinterestedly when holding public offices in order to meet the public interest.[142] Also, the law often places a set of prohibited acts within a criminal framework.[143] The concentration upon this concept of corruption, which depends in essence upon an official's deviation from the formal standards of public office, has four merits for this book as follows.

First, it has the advantage of clarity. The criterion of deviation enables corrupt practices to be easily recognised and avoids any difficulties and contingencies. In this regard, Nye stressed that the considerations of public interest are not regarded in the corruption concept.[144] For example, one may justify a violation of public duties under the pretext of the public interest, which is a loose criterion.[145]

Second, the concept adopted helps focus on the most problematic corruption pattern in Kuwait. The focus here on public corruption is warranted. Singling out this specific meaning of corruption is derived from the reality of the size of the public sector's workforce in Kuwait. The public sector is expanding year after year, and its capacity accordingly increases to absorb the required labour force.[146]

138 Nye (1967, p. 419).
139 Gardiner (2007, pp. 26–27).
140 See chapters 4 and 5.
141 NGO-2.
142 Civil Service Act (CSA) 15/1979, ss.11, 24, and 25. In general, see chapter 5.3.2.1.
143 See chapter 4.3.
144 Nye (1967).
145 Campbell (2016).
146 Eltony (2007).

Employees who work in governmental sectors constituted the majority of the overall workforce in 2018.[147] The more the public sector dominates the economy, the greater the opportunities for corruption by officials. Consequently, offences which constitute business corruption are not included here.

Third, linking corruption to the formal duties of public office sheds light on some of the deficiencies in the definition of corruption. Restricting the meaning of corruption to some criminal laws deflates the real concept of corruption, especially when the meaning focuses on financial forms of corruption as they appear in the criminal corruption laws.[148] NGO-3 contended that corruption may take the form of violations of an administrative nature which do not necessarily result in financial losses: 'our laws focus on the financial corruption, and even if the law prohibits some administration-oriented corruption, the sanctions are weak'.[149] However, defining corruption as 'the abuse of public office for private gain' can include financial and administrative forms of corruption, a concern raised by NGO-3.

Fourth, under this concept of corruption, there can be various patterns of corruption. Grand corruption and state capture can be included under this concept, for example, when a high-ranking official, responsible for policymaking, is bribed to issue a resolution or enact a regulation in a manner which benefits a certain individual. Petty or administrative corruption by low-level bureaucrats also certainly falls under this concept of corruption. A low-ranking employee may deviate from the duties of his/her office if he/she solicits a bribe to issue a driving licence. The two examples are explicit deviations from the formal duties of public officials. Moreover, such deviations may take place routinely under institutional conditions (systemic corruption) or in individual and irregular cases (random corruption).

### 2.3.2 *Corruption patterns*

What are the prevalent corruption patterns in Kuwait? Does corruption start from the top (grand corruption and state capture) or the bottom (petty and administrative corruption)? Does it permeate the state's systems (systemic corruption)? Or are corruption cases just irregular, individual cases (random corruption)? The lack of a systematic, official database which provides reliable empirical data of corruption cases is a real obstacle which hinders the precise determination of the patterns of corruption in Kuwait. When Nazaha was preparing the Kuwait Counter-Corruption Strategy 2019–2024 (Strategy 2019–2024), the 'limited data that is nationally generated' and the newness of Kuwait's experience in combating corruption were identified as two key obstacles.[150] Although the Central

147 See Central Statistical Bureau (2018).
148 NGO-3.
149 Ibid. See chapter 5.3.4.
150 Nazaha (2019, p. 12).

Statistical Bureau is the sole source of government information and data,[151] the Bureau does not provide corruption-related information. In the absence of channels which secure reliable data, it may be a blanket statement to assert that corruption in Kuwait is either grand or petty, either systemic or random. Some have argued that defective record-keeping and poor databases are inherent attributes of governments with systemic corruption.[152]

Faced with this challenge, therefore, Tanzi believes that the Internet and newspapers,[153] or even anecdotes,[154] are alternative means of measuring corruption and help provide information about the prevalence of corruption in a certain country. Because such instruments largely reflect the public discourse on corruption, they imply that the meaning of corruption may be socially constructed. However, public discourse must be treated with caution. The reliance on public discourse presupposes that people are well informed about government activities (specifically corruption) and, more crucially, assumes a considerable amount of press freedom. Freedom of speech, of the press, and of publication are all protected by the Kuwaiti Constitution within the limits of the law.[155] Nevertheless, reality reveals that the press is free only to some extent. Freedom House classified the status of press freedom in Kuwait as 'partly free'. The media and press activities in Kuwait are subject to restrictions by the state authorities.[156] Thus, measuring corruption by using the press, or even alternative sources such as the numbers of complaints submitted and public perception, is a process fraught with challenges: 'attempts to measure corruption by counting press reports of corruption confound the incidence of corruption with the freedom of the press, the professionalism of the press, the availability of information on corrupt activities, and popular concern about corrupt acts'.[157]

With the challenges of the lack of data and only a partly free press, some would argue that evidence about corruption patterns might be inconclusive. However, such challenges should not negate the aim of this book. Scott argued that in conditions which accompany the problem of corruption, such as the lack of reliable data and openness, one should accordingly 'infer what lies below the surface from an analysis of the exposed tip of the iceberg and the general characteristics of the political system'.[158] In exploring the complex ways through which corruption takes different forms, this book draws upon two indicators to assist with the demarcation of the corruption patterns. The first indicator is the structural causes of corruption which are pertinent to the general characteristics of major institutions in Kuwait, such as the cultural, political, and economic

151 Statistics and Census Act 27/1963, s.1.
152 Thomas and Meagher (2004).
153 Tanzi (1998).
154 Klitgaard (1988).
155 Kuwaiti Constitution, arts.36–37.
156 Freedom House (2019).
157 Thomas and Meagher (2004, p. 23).
158 Scott (1972, p. ix).

institutions. The second indicator is the grand corruption scandals that Kuwait witnessed from 1978 to 2002, as compiled Al-Zu'abi and A-Naqeeb.[159] This indicator also includes objective data, such as published corruption cases.[160] With particular emphasis on the first indicator, the claim of this book is that a multi-dimensional analysis of the structural characteristics of the state of Kuwait is helpful in determining the most serious corruption pattern. As analysed below (section 2.3.4), the socio-political-economic organisation of Kuwait fosters an environment which is appropriate for 'grand' corruption to grow. Building on this analysis, there is a logical ground for inductive analysis, that is, to infer a general perception from particular instances.

The approach of Kuwaiti policymakers does not deviate far from this conclusion. In 2019, Nazaha issued the Strategy 2019–2024. The Strategy studied the corruption problem in Kuwait by collecting data from state institutions and conducting interviews with professional experts. Among other 'pillars', the Strategy concentrated on the public sector as the 'First Pillar', given the fundamental role which the public sector plays. This role is understood in a broad sense to involve legislative, executive, and judicial powers. The Strategy found the public sector to be conducive to corruption for multiple reasons: most importantly, the high number of daily transactions undertaken within governmental bodies, the huge value of these transactions, and the monopolistic position of the state in the process of public policymaking and procurement (and other activities).[161] The Strategy itself emphasises that, with a large public sector such as that in Kuwait, corruption may proliferate. This is especially so when taking into account the socio-political organisation of Kuwaiti society, where the interrelationships between individuals and the state are characterised by kinship, tribalism, and sectarianism.[162]

### 2.3.3 *Effects of corruption: The corruption–governance nexus*

Kuwait's CPI depicts the country's fluctuating but ever dismal scorecard (always below 50), exposing the country to 'massive and pervasive' corruption in the words of TI. The CPI scores reflect the omnipresent perception of corruption in Kuwait and illustrate a significant contrast in such perceptions between Kuwait and its counterparts in the Gulf Cooperation Council (GCC). Particularly evident is the decline in 2017, which placed Kuwait in the worst rank in the CPI,

159 See Al-Zu'abi and Al-Naqeeb (2007).

160 Examples of 'grand' corruption cases include: *Grupo Torras SA v Al-Sabah (No.5)* [1999] CLC 1469, Case No. 336/2012, 21/7/2013 (Supreme Court – Criminal Division), Case No. 1499/2008, 27/6/2019 (First Instance Court – Criminal Division 10), Case No. 1942/2015, 6/5/2018 (First Instance Court – Criminal Division 2) Case No. 1200/2016, 27/03/2017 (Supreme Court – Criminal Division 2), Case No. 137/1996, 23/12/1996 (Supreme Court – Criminal Division 1), and Case No. 6/2018 (Court of Ministers, no judgement has been rendered yet).

161 Nazaha (2019, p. 16).,

162 Ibid., p. 17

*Table 2.1* The CPI of Kuwait, Qatar, the UAE, and the United Kingdom (UK)

| *Country/year* | *2012* | *2013* | *2014* | *2015* | *2016* | *2017* | *2018* |
|---|---|---|---|---|---|---|---|
| Kuwait | 44 | 43 | 44 | 49 | 41 | 39 | 41 |
| Qatar | 68 | 68 | 69 | 71 | 61 | 63 | 62 |
| UAE | 68 | 69 | 70 | 70 | 66 | 71 | 70 |
| UK | 74 | 76 | 78 | 81 | 81 | 82 | 80 |

in relation to the GCC and particularly Qatar and the United Arab Emirates (UAE), and on a par with countries which have serious corruption problems (Table 2.1).[163]

As explained in section 2.2.3, corruption has adverse effects on multiple domains. In the following sections, the focus will be on 'the corruption–governance nexus' to illustrate some of the corruption effects on governance in Kuwait. Governance can be broadly understood as a concept which refers to:

> the traditions and institutions by which authority in a country is exercised. This includes (a) the process by which governments are selected, monitored and replaced; (b) the capacity of the government to effectively formulate and implement sound policies; and (c) the respect of citizens and the state for the institutions that govern economic and social interactions among them.[164]

Given that the corruption–governance nexus is further studied in the next chapter,[165] the analysis in this section is restricted to a more general issue: how corruption negatively affects the way in which state institutions are administered. The economic and managerial effects of corruption in Kuwait are studied here because of the nature of the Kuwaiti economy. Because the economy is centralised and dominated by the government,[166] corruption's effects become stark and concrete in the economic reality of Kuwait. Thus, the concentration on studying the effects of corruption on governance is justified. Although the corruption–crime nexus is also of practical relevance in Kuwait, particularly in the context of money laundering,[167] the link of corruption to governance and dysfunctional government (the corruption–governance nexus) is more critical in Kuwait than the link to organised crime (the corruption–crime nexus). According to the Strategy 2019–2024, corruption has been identified as 'one of the challenges' which Kuwait faces and which needs to be addressed in order to maximise the chances of success in achieving what Kuwaiti people want.[168] When focusing on

163 The scores work as follows: 0 is highly corrupt, and 100 is very clean. See Transparency International (2019).
164 Kaufmann, Kraay and Mastruzzi (2011, p. 222).
165 See chapter 3.2.
166 See section 2.3.4.3.
167 FATF (2011).
168 Nazaha (2019, p. 8).

corruption, the Strategy is directed at 'effective governance' and a 'prosperous economy', which are necessary to achieve 'Kuwait Vision 2035'.[169] Studying corruption in a large public sector requires attention to be paid to the consequences of corruption regarding government performance, such as, to use World Bank language, 'the quality of policy formulation and implementation, and the credibility of the government's commitment to such policies'.[170]

Corruption is highly relevant to oil-rich, developing countries because, as analysed above, grand corruption is responsible for the paradox between oil-funded rich countries and their poor economic growth, and distorts governmental public expenditure and the efficiency of public spending. The available options of fiscal policies have been limited, considering the hegemony of the public sector on the economic structure of Kuwait (which relies on oil).[171] Accordingly, there is little latitude for the Kuwaiti government to control the nature of revenues. Damage inflicted on the governmental treasury, especially highly serious damage inflicted by grand corruption, directly affects the public treasury, which inevitably affects the quality of public expenditure. The discussion here focuses on grand corruption and state capture and excludes other low-level corruption patterns, such as petty corruption. The discussion reflects the way in which Kuwait suffers most seriously. For instance, grand corruption has effects on the efficiency of public investments. The government-led economic development plans in Kuwait, which pledged to establish strategic economic policies such as diversifying the economy and developing economic growth, have been perceived as mere rhetorical prioritisation. Indeed, none of these policies has been taken seriously and some of them were considered as 'not realistic to be achieved' by the government itself.[172] Corruption increases government's capital spending on public investments and also reduces its productivity.[173] This hypothesis becomes evident if tested at the level of the GCC. In 2018, although the overall population (in relation to GDP per capita) and the ratio of government expenditure of Kuwait are higher than Qatar, the total GDP of the latter is more than that of Kuwait (Table 2.2). In the same year, Qatar ranked 62 in the CPI, while Kuwait ranked 41.[174,175]

There may be other factors than corruption which contribute to this contrast, such as the quality and nature of the products, and the policy regarding the rate of production. However, corruption can be considered as a factor responsible for increasing government spending (especially discretionary spending) when high-level officials participate in the decision-making process to direct investments towards a particular field and determine the size of investments in a manner

169 Ibid., p. 12. See also <http://www.newkuwait.gov.kw/home.aspx>.
170 See Kaufmann, Kraay and Mastruzzi (2011, p. 223).
171 Eltony (2007).
172 Ibid., p. 82.
173 Tanzi and Davoodi (1997).
174 Transparency International (2019).
175 See World Bank (2018).

*Table 2.2* Comparison of the economic growth of Kuwait and Qatar in 2018

| *Country* | *Population* | *Government final consumption expenditure (% of GDP)* | *GDP* |
|---|---|---|---|
| Kuwait | 4.137 million | 22.6% | 140.6 billion |
| Qatar | 2.781 million | 15.8% | 191.3 billion |

which allows them to achieve personal gains from such decisions.[176] Corruption associated with public expenditure illustrates that corruption is linked with senior officials who are responsible for government spending, which, potentially, renders grand corruption and state capture prevalent corruption patterns in Kuwait.

Another manifestation of the effects of corruption is the bad administration of economic policies. Since 1953, Kuwait has adopted economic diversification policies in order to address oil uncertainties and find alternatives by investing through sovereign wealth funds (SWFs). The Kuwaiti Investment Authority (KIA) is the sole governmental authority responsible for the management of two SWFs: the General Reserve Fund, whose assets from state revenues and investments are determined annually by the government, and the Future Generations Fund, which consists of a minimum of 10% annual transfers from state revenues and General Reserve Fund investments.[177] Compared with the achievements of the Abu Dhabi Investment Authority (ADIA), established in 1976 and whose funds are also derived from oil revenues,[178] the management of the SWFs by the KIA has not met the aspirations of economic diversification. The assets estimation of the Sovereign Wealth Funds Institute (SWFI) of both the ADIA and the KIA is telling (see Table 2.3).[179]

Despite the common economic generalisations between Kuwait and the UAE (regarding the dependence upon oil at least)[180] and the seniority of the KIA, the difference in these estimations implies managerial problems on the part of the KIA. The Kuwait Investment Office (KIO) in London (supervised by the KIA) was once linked to financial irregularities and accusations of fraud, such as the Grupo Torras scandal regarding Kuwaiti investments in Spain from 1984 to 1992.[181] Nonetheless, there may again be other factors than corruption which affect these figures, such as the rate of oil production and the policies of investment.

176 Tanzi and Davoodi (1997).

177 See <https://kia.gov.kw>.

178 ADIA manages the SWF of the Abu Dhabi Emirate in UAE. See <http://www.adia.ae/En/About/About.aspx>.

179 The SWFI provided a list of the 'Top 81 Largest Sovereign Wealth Fund Rankings by Total Assets'. See <https://www.swfinstitute.org/fund-rankings/sovereign-wealth-fund>.

180 Herb (2009b).

181 See *Grupo Torras SA v Al-Sabah (No.5)* [1999] CLC 1469.

*Table 2.3* The estimation of the SWFI of the KIA and the ADIA as in 2019

| *Country* | *Assets estimation* |
|---|---|
| Kuwait (KIA) | USD 592,000,000,000 |
| UAE (ADIA) | USD 696,660,000,000 |

Examples where corruption is linked to other problems abound. However, the key message here is that governance-related effects become more serious especially in Kuwait where, as the Strategy 2019–2024 stresses, an 'abundance of resources and stability' exists.[182] Grand corruption represents the most serious threat for a country with such characteristics. The association of grand corruption with high-ranking officials (including the royal family) who dominate state institutions shifts attention to problems related to government activities more than any other issues such as, for example, organised crime.

### 2.3.4 *Causes of corruption*

Corruption is associated with distinct factors which single out corruption from other crimes. Corruption's association with government activities, in which state–individual relations occur, explains the lack of cross-country correlation between corruption and other types of crime such as burglary.[183] Examining corruption patterns, particularly grand and systemic corruption, prompts the suggestion that corruption may be derived from the characteristics of the state. Since 'corruption *is* a government problem',[184] these characteristics could help explain why corruption abounds in a specific jurisdiction. Corruption is a matter of the policies, structures, political development, and social history of a country.[185] It is predominantly an internal problem for diverse state institutions, starting from the social and political institutions to the economic institutions. As Johnston argues, corruption 'is not something that "happens to" a country, but rather a symptom of deeper difficulties',[186] a point which sheds light on the 'governance–corruption' nexus (see chapter 3).

Before venturing into the causes of corruption, we should be aware of the complexity of a subject like the causality of corruption.[187] First, several causes of corruption may also be consequences of corruption.[188] Second, in the scientific enquiries on corruption, no cause can be seen as always leading to the consequence (corruption): this understanding of causation 'is such a strong one that

182 Nazaha (2019, p. 8).
183 Lederman, Loayza and Soares (2005).
184 Moene and Søreide (2016, p. 148).
185 World Bank (1997).
186 Johnston (1998, p. 88).
187 Rothstein and Teorell (2014).
188 Lambsdorff (2006).

it is not used in corruption theories'.[189] Thus, the following analysis is better not to be understood as providing a 'causal explanation', but rather, as providing factors that have positive correlation with corruption (factors having causal effects on corruption).[190] In the following sections, the dissection of the causes of corruption in Kuwait will proceed through three lenses: cultural and social, political, and economic. In this regard, the data gathered by the participants which were interviewed will be used to enrich or criticise the current analysis of the potential causes of corruption in Kuwait.

#### 2.3.4.1 *Socio-cultural backgrounds and corruption*

Culture is 'the social rules surrounding lifestyles, beliefs, customs, and values that influence a society's pursuit of its goals'.[191] In order to understand corruption, it is helpful to use a cultural framework. This approach stems from the significance of the interaction between culture and modernisation in order to understand corruption.[192] Modernity, defined by Giddens as 'modes of social life or organisation which emerged in Europe from about the seventeenth century onwards and which subsequently became more or less worldwide in their influence',[193] cannot be disregarded. Its effect is responsible for the problem of corruption, as in Huntington's metaphor, 'modernization breeds corruption'.[194] Thus, modernity is a springboard from which the analysis of other dynamics of corruption may proceed. Corruption is a stark ramification of the massive socio-economic changes which have swept Kuwait over the last decades. These changes have been attributed to the alteration in Kuwait's economy after the economic boom following the export of abundant amounts of oil in 1946. Since then, Kuwait has achieved many indices of modernisation, such as institutional transformations and the emergence of a prosperous urban society which has superseded the traditional, primitive one. This change necessitated the import of technological developments so that oil could be exploited in the service of the nascent Kuwaiti national polity.[195]

Having been subject to such transformations, the modernisation process in Kuwait has entailed some negative concomitant implications. In the same way that modernisation has brought many problematic issues to the Kuwaiti political system (a monarchical system) such as the power of the emerging parliament, the National Assembly,[196] it has also brought other far-reaching consequences. Before the advent of modernity in Kuwait, grand governmental institutions were

189 de Graaf, von Maravic and Wagenaar (2010, p. 15).
190 See Rothstein and Teorell (2014, p. 84).
191 Collier (2002, p. 7).
192 Huntington (2006).
193 Giddens (1990, p. 1).
194 Huntington (2006, p. 59).
195 Salih (1991).
196 Ibid.

largely absent.[197] Modern state institutions, however, started to develop during the modernisation process, which incidentally introduced new effects such as corruption.[198] Yet the process of modernisation did not occur in isolation from the traditional cultural systems of Kuwaiti society which, as this book argues, gave rise to many problems. Thus, the corruption concept in Kuwaiti life traces its lineage to modernity.

##### 2.3.4.1.1 CULTURAL BACKGROUND

As part of the Arab world, Kuwait's experience of the emergence of modernity has interplayed with its distinct cultural nature. In this region, the socio-economic structure is based on kinship and social relationships are formed within tribalism and sectarianism, which gives rise to diverse factions in a given society.[199] The problem, as suggested here, of the sociocultural system is summed up in the clash between traditional pre-modern values of Kuwaiti society and the institutional developments which took place during modernity in Europe, which somehow were transferred to Kuwait.[200] This clash is illustrated through different social practices in Kuwaiti society, whose societal organisation can be described as 'collectivist' and 'segregated'. It is 'collectivist' in that there are diverse groups, with each group having distinct religious and kinship relationships. It is 'segregated' in that, within the collectivist society, there is a sense of non-cooperation between the members of the divergent groups.[201] In this regard, some argue that 'Kuwait is an example of such a heterogeneous society that has divisions across tribal, as well as sectarian, lines'.[202]

Recognising the nature of Kuwaiti society serves as a useful departure point to understand the impact of cultural and social perspectives on how a society may condemn corruption, and hence how the opportunities for corruption proliferate.[203] The most critical explanations of the variation in corruption between nations are predicated on the local culture and social arrangement of each nation.[204] As a distinct model of community, collectivist culture may generate a distinct perception about corruption. Heidenheimer studied the diverse perceptions of societies across the world towards corruption and provided an outstanding argument: the different models of societies differ in their perceptions based on the strength of family relationships and community norms. What is relevant to Kuwait is that corrupt practices abound in collectivist societies,

197 Aruri (1970).
198 See Huntington (2006).
199 Al-Tarrah (2007).
200 Bacik (2008).
201 Greif (1994, p. 913).
202 Al-Kandari and Al-Hadben (2010, p. 268).
203 Heidenheimer and Johnston (2007).
204 See Scott (1972).

which are associated with a considerable amount of tolerance of corruption.[205] Heidenheimer's analysis resonates with Lawyer-3, who argued that the nature of social relationships in Kuwait encourages corruption. For example,

> within one tribe, however corrupt the person is, his tribe-based relatives will support him. This is for two reasons: first, because he is from the same tribe (so, he is my cousin), and second because he will always be allegiant to them (so, he will provide his services if he is a MP).[206]

Heidenheimer's analysis is also corroborated by the electoral corruption in Kuwait.[207] Vote-buying instances endemically proliferate in tribal elections (primary elections) where a vote's value reached KWD1000 (approximately US$3000).[208] Despite the corrupt nature of vote buying, its supposedly stigmatising effect is absent and has not dissuaded competitors from continuing with an election. Ironically, the vote-buying effect is limited in that the candidates are not perceived to be involved in a corrupt practice; hence, they do not deserve to be punished.[209] Candidates have proved that they do not have concerns about the resulting social perception of buying a vote from someone. Even with the widespread use of such a phenomenon, which is bribery par excellence, people continue to offer their votes for sale, and candidates win as a result of the votes they have bought as if this practice is not a form of corruption, although it should in fact be a source of stigma.[210] Corruption as a Western concept suffers from a degree of erosion in a kinship-based society. People are not amenable to perceiving this phenomenon as corruption, particularly when the issue concerns the interests of the tribe. What may emerge as critical here is that this cultural setting was an integral part of the modernisation process in Kuwait.

#### 2.3.4.1.2 TRADITIONAL AND WESTERN CULTURE

The modern institutional transformations which gave rise to statehood's institutions were not accompanied by cultural transformations in Kuwaiti society. The modernity which replaced the traditional social institutions has been unable to replace some of the inherent traditional values. Modernity is shallow in a society which is still committed to its historical traditions, resulting in a 'hybrid model' of state which mingles traditional values and modern conditions.[211] The modern expert systems are dominated by tradition-laden values where kinship, not merit, is the preferred standard. An individual from the royal family, a tribe akin

205 Heidenheimer (2007).
206 Lawyer-3.
207 See Ghabra (2014).
208 Salih (2011).
209 Ibid.
210 See <http://news.kuwaittimes.net/website/will-vote-money/>.
211 Bacik (2008, p. 105).

to the royal family, and an entourage of the royal family has priority for offices. Such individuals also have superiority over others and entitlement to appointments in vital positions in the state. In these societies, high-ranking positions in the state are held by individuals whose efficiency is lower than what should be expected.[212] The risk of corruption increases as long as the expert systems in which people have placed trust are not occupied by the most capable and efficient citizens. Furthermore, the cultural nature of Kuwaiti society does not only raise the issue of the 'risk of corruption' by allowing inefficient and incapable people to occupy key positions in the state, but also raise the threat of nepotism whereby the incentives to engage in corruption are embedded in social relationships rather than private material gain.[213]

Some of the interviewees were asked whether there are specific features in Kuwaiti society that encourage corruption. One participant contended that as a result of the nature of the social construction of Kuwaiti society, becoming a minister, or holding a sensitive position, is largely based on favouritism, nepotism, or cronyism.[214] Ignoring the value of meritocracy, the appointments of politicians and senior officials are based on social considerations, such as the family, tribe, and sect of the appointee.[215] In fact, at the level of sensitive positions in state institutions, what seems to be true is that 'the most appropriate man is not in the most appropriate position'.[216]

In a kinship-based society, these practices are not considered as corrupt in the Western sense. The reason is that when 'effective community-regarding norms are lacking, attitudes will be determined in individual cases in relation to who is doing the corrupting on whose behalf'.[217] Thus, corruption becomes rampant in societies where the interests of families, relatives, and tribes predominate.[218] The more a society is affected by tradition, the more instances there are of corrupt practices proliferating and being accepted.[219] The social order is shaped by the personal relationships between the state and people through 'patronage networks' in the absence of the institutionalisation of efficient administration principles.[220] The separating boundary between the nature of public roles and what constitutes private interests is of utmost importance when corruption is culturally studied in a collectivist society such as Kuwait.[221] This cultural underpinning of governmental practices weakens the capabilities of state institutions and explains why different Arabic monarchies have been called upon to replace members of the royal family with non-family members in key positions in many state

212 Peterson (2007).
213 LaPalombara (1994, p. 329).
214 NGO-1.
215 NGO-3; NGO-2.
216 Official-5.
217 Heidenheimer (2007, p. 154).
218 Huntington (2006).
219 Heidenheimer and Johnston (2007).
220 Heywood (1997, p. 427).
221 See Rose-Ackerman (1999).

apparatuses.[222] Thus, what modernisation has granted to Kuwait is a collection of modernised facades which mask unresolved cultural issues. Numerous manifestations of Western modernity were implanted in Kuwait but without an established infrastructure to act as a setting for the success of such a 'Westernisation' process.[223] 'When the legacy of the past no longer fits modern conditions', the result is an inconsistency in the values which govern the public sphere.[224]

According to an interviewee, one example where one's social relationships mediate his/her relation with the state is the phenomenon of *Wasta*, which in fact has become the prominent feature of Kuwaiti society.[225] In *Wasta,* because it depends upon a mediator (an officeholder, for example), the relation between the public and government has become indirect and somewhat personal.[226] Because *Wasta* means that official authority may be abused, the people tend to tolerate it as not corruption: 'the fact that I cannot directly get my rights from the state justifies engaging in corruption'.[227] This intrinsic characteristic of Kuwaiti society imposes a particular pattern of corruption: corruption becomes a systemic feature of the state's institutions.[228] NGO-1 described daily circumstances in the state apparatus:

> Yes, part of our daily routine involves *Wasta* practices and the exploitation of one's influence. Today, if you want to do any work in any governmental body, look for a job or even obtain a tender, you have to find someone you know so that he/she facilitates the process. This is not socially disapproved.

MP-3 had a different view about the features of Kuwaiti society and their role in the phenomenon of corruption, arguing that the main features discourage corruption. MP-3 added that such features, related to the ethics, Islamic religion, and close inter-social relationships of Kuwait society, should all contribute to disapproval of corruption. Apart from ethics and religion, the argument of MP-3 that 'close inter-social relationships' do not encourage corruption appears to differ from the prior analysis. MP-3's view seemed to depend upon how the interrelationship between society's members can deter engagement in corruption, but he/she omitted to mention the role of the same interrelationship in entrenching corruption. The negative role of the features of Kuwaiti society is supported by an idea raised by MP-3 that corruption in Kuwait, in part, is due to 'a crisis of the national identity'.[229] Indeed, such a crisis may be a result of tribal, family, and sectarian superiority over the state.

222 Peterson (2007).
223 Bacik (2008, p. 106).
224 Rose-Ackerman (1999, p. 5).
225 *Wasta* in Arabic means nepotism or clout. Official-5.
226 NGO-1.
227 NGO-3.
228 Biygautane (2015).
229 MP-3.

In general, the existence of a clear borderline between the state and society is a fundamental prerequisite for the existence of basic neutral institutions of the modern state which refuse preferential treatment and are based on principles of equality.[230] The public relationship between the state and its people should be impersonal because personal relationships (such as kinship) result in public roles which are contaminated with private interests.[231] In promoting the robust correlation between this kind of culture and the opportunity for corruption, Al-Tarrah argued that when kinship is a pillar around which all social relationships in a state revolve, this creates a belief that all the institutions are privately owned by a certain caste, a belief which is a result of 'a lack of distinction between private interests and public ownership'.[232] Boundaries between the Kuwaiti state and society are still blurred, despite modernity's institutional developments which have promoted the separation between the status of Kuwaitis as people and state institutions.[233] Paradoxically, modernisation has reinforced pre-modern values.[234]

#### 2.3.4.2 *Political system and causes of corruption*

Corruption involves the flawed administration of the state. State institutions, which are created to govern the relationships between people and the government, are exploited for personal gains for specific corrupt people.[235] Any administration consists of two parts: the political aspect, embodying diverse state institutions, and the social components who constitute the society as a whole in which such institutions actually operate. Moreover, the political structure in Kuwait comprises a diversity of political institutions which are governed by the Kuwaiti Constitution. According to this structure, and the likelihood of malfeasances, the Constitution adjusts the accountability channels and delegates the law, with authority, to regulate other accountability mechanisms. The problem here is manifold: the political culture, political system, and weak public accountability mechanisms in Kuwait.

##### 2.3.4.2.1 POLITICAL CULTURE

Because there is a mutual effect between the social practices of a community and its political organisation,[236] the Kuwaiti political system is extensively influenced by the culture of its society. The political culture is a communal area in which politics is conflated with culture, whereby the manner of exercising and

230 Bacik (2008).
231 See Lennerfors (2008).
232 Al-Tarrah (2007, p. 121).
233 Tétreault (2000).
234 Khalaf (2000).
235 Rose-Ackerman (1999).
236 Heywood (1997).

understanding politics is affected by a society's nature, blurring the boundaries between two systems.[237] Political culture is affected by the segregated social components of Kuwaiti society (clans, tribes, and sects). These segregated groups represent the constituent interest groups which are an integral part of the state. Such a socio-political construct is better understood under corporatism: a comparative politics approach which offers a useful perspective on various socio-political phenomena, such as the 'relations between society as represented by interest groups and the state or government, and hence on the dynamics of what are called state–society relations'.[238] Unlike other approaches, corporatism refers to a socio-political organisation with distinct characteristics. There is a strong directing state, with a number of interest groups (as corporate units) forming that organisation and incorporated into the political structure of state institutions. Furthermore, the government has the central role in identifying, recognising, and integrating these corporate units in the policy decision making of the state.[239]

The political culture in Kuwait exhibits these corporatist elements. The pivotal role played by the government in its relations with interest groups explains why societies such as Kuwait place power in the hands of a small ruling group who usually derive their right to reign from ties of kinship and 'social position'.[240] This form of social organisation is found in Kuwait where interest groups exist and are premised on the basis of kinship, tribalism, and sectarianism.[241] The political phenomenon of primary election (tribal election) is an instance which exemplifies the incorporation of interest groups in the Kuwaiti political system.[242] Given the absence of political parties, the tribe (as a corporate unit) chooses its representative in the general election through an informal primary election in order for the votes not to be split among other candidates, despite the illegality of this practice (criminal offence).[243] Voters from other social components are not allowed to participate in the voting process.

A number of interviewees criticised this political culture, describing it as a key cause of corruption. As one participant said, it is not the inherent feature of Kuwaiti society which encourage corruption, but the nature of the political system in Kuwait which creates a favourable climate for both corruption and the corrupt to grow.[244] NGO-2 contended that there is no 'corrupt' and 'clean' society; the system of the state has fostered the culture of corruption. While people grow indifferent to corruption in such a corrupting environment,

237 World Bank (1997).
238 Wiarda (2015, p. 5).
239 Adams (2018).
240 Collier (2002, p. 8).
241 Al-Tarrah (2007).
242 The Kuwait Chamber of Commerce and Industry is another example in which the conglomerate of merchants appears as a salient interest group.
243 National Assembly Election Act 35/1962, s.45(5) (amended by Act No. 9/1998).
244 MP-2.

the government supports this complacent society.[245] NGO-1 argued that since the beginning of the democratic process in Kuwait, the government has been 'institutionalising' the distribution of constituencies based on factors such as sectarianism and tribalism. In some cases, as NGO-3 claimed, the government may intervene in the election to support some of the tribal and sectarian candidates. These governmental practices, as NGO-3 contended, neutralise concerns about corruption and induce the people to go along with the situation. NGO-1 gave an example whereby one candidate had to be sectarian in order to win the election, although she/he had been known as 'one of the prominent antagonists to sectarianism in Kuwait'. Therefore, the political scene in Kuwait encourages you to be factional.[246]

This political culture induces interest groups (tribes, clans, and sects) to pursue individually their personal interests, interests which the government is keen to achieve. Politicians are immersed in securing the achievement of the interests of the groups to which they belong. As a corollary, corruption becomes a norm and an expectation of political life, and there is a slim chance for a consensus to be achieved around common social issues such as countering corruption. As democratisation widens the political participation of interest groups, this process represents a 'favourable condition' for corruption to thrive.[247] People are predisposed to be complacent about the abuse of public interests as long as their own interests are fulfilled. Furthermore, public apathy characterises some alienated groups which lack political representativeness because of their small numbers. Thus, identity-based political cleavages find their places in such a fragmented society.[248] Accordingly, it is assumed that when a political atmosphere is saturated by interest groups, orphan issues such as combating corruption will not be supported by public pressure and will be exploited by opportunistic politicians.

In this context, NGO-2 believed that the political culture which dominates the election system is part of the problem of corruption in Kuwait. For example, when such culture secures the success of MPs who are most able to offer services to constituents, or even the election of MPs based on social considerations, fighting corruption will not be one of the priorities of these MPs, or, in the words of NGO-2: 'what would you expect from those who came by this way?' Thus, the state's institutions will not be able to combat corruption as long as corruption is systemic and entrenched and stems from society itself.[249]

Conversely, when segregated groups' interests converge, the situation differs. In 2011, when the heyday of the Arab Spring coincided with blatant violations regarding public funds, some politicians were driven by popular sentiment

245 NGO-3.

246 NGO-1.

247 Thomas and Meagher (2004, p. 22).

248 Herb (2009a).

249 NGO-2. But MP-2 argued that corruption relates to the political environment as fostered by the government.

affected by the pan-Arab uprisings.[250] Youth organisations, parliamentarians (both Islamists and liberal), and other social activists gathered around common issues: 'Their slogans targeted combating corruption and removing the prime minister'.[251] At this time, corruption was raised as a prime issue and became more visible, especially with the contemporary bribery scandal which allegedly involved the Prime Minister and a number of MPs.[252] This scandal led to opposition which was strong enough to prompt the prime minister to resign, a circumstance which 'was something unique in the Gulf',[253] and to a decisive change in the 2012 election when 34 out of 50 MPs were reformists.[254] The outbreak of conflict between the state and this majority posed a serious challenge: a strong opposition with different social components, each of which converged around its social institutions.[255] Thus, the political system in a society, which is constructed of divergent interest groups, tends to fail to counter-corruption or to deal with common issues in general. But if the interests of the majority of social components unite under the name of public good, the government may be more vulnerable to popular demands, such as combating corruption.

Notwithstanding the ostensible victory of the opposition when interests converged to constitute unified pressure against corruption, the opposition eventually failed in 2012.[256] Why did such unified opposition fail? This issue shifts the analysis to the other major characteristics of the political structure in Kuwait. Such a structure will be examined in two aspects: the type of government and the political system (in terms of the relation between the government and the National Assembly).

#### 2.3.4.2.2 POLITICAL SYSTEM

According to its constitution, Kuwait adopts a democratic regime.[257] The type of government is a mixed government in which elements of autocracy and democracy coexist: the ruler is autocratic and comes from the Al-Sabah family on a hereditary basis (autocratic element), and the National Assembly is chosen on the basis of elections (the democratic element).[258] The political system in Kuwait is atypical because of its duality. Parliamentary aspects are espoused but compromised. The functions of the executive and legislature are fused. Characteristics of a presidential system are also injected to the effect that ministers may be chosen from outside the National Assembly. Thus, the executive power must have

250 Ulrichsen (2014).
251 Ghabra (2014, p. 11).
252 Sabrie and Hakala (2013).
253 Kinninmont (2012, p. 2).
254 Sabrie and Hakala (2013).
255 See Gause (1994).
256 Kinninmont (2012).
257 Kuwaiti Constitution, art.6.
258 Al-Saleh (2003).

the trust of the Amir instead of the National Assembly and the cabinet is responsible to the Amir (in addition to the National Assembly).[259] Thus, although the Kuwaiti political system resembles, in some aspects, 'constitutional monarchies' in which monarchs share power with parliaments,[260] it has its own peculiar nature which distances it from these regimes.

The structure of political institutions is an influential factor in terms of combating corruption. The level and nature of corruption is affected by whether the political system is parliamentary or presidential.[261] The opportunities for corruption in each system are derived from the incentives of politicians to be re-elected and what the political system provides in terms of broad-based policies (public goods) and narrowly focused benefits (group benefits) confined to a limited number of people.[262] In political systems where politicians seek to be re-elected by a wide cross section of voters, such as presidents in a presidential system, there is a propensity for politicians to defend public goods.[263] In a similar vein, what would be the result in an atypical parliamentary system where government formation is based on appointing ministers from outside elected MPs? In this instance, there is a high probability that each minister tends to prioritise the narrowly focused interests of those who are credited with his or her appointment.

The problem of ministerial appointments in Kuwait was raised by some of the interviewees. The selection of ministers in Kuwait has not been, to a great extent, predicated on merit-based factors, but on factors such as patronage, favouritism, or other social considerations.[264] A minister who has been selected in this way does not owe his/her position to the whole of society but to his/her patron, tribe, or sect. Thus, it is expected that this minister will not be keen to achieve social-wide interests, such as combating corruption. In this situation, ministers are not constrained by the need to be re-elected, or even the need to link their names to public good issues such as fighting corruption. Building on this analysis, the Kuwaiti political structure contributes to the proliferation of corruption. The departure point of this argument is that the National Assembly, as an elected institution, is supposed to be a checking institution which scrutinises the performance of the executive power, specifically the public spending through which corruption may occur.

However, the Kuwaiti political system faces structural and political challenges which affect the operation of democracy. With regard to structural obstacles, the mixed type of government and uniqueness of the political system have yielded a government which has supremacy in many instances. Two examples are used here to illustrate the way such a constitutional structure may accommodate opportunities for corruption. First, Kuwait is a 'constitutionalised monarchy'.

259 Ibid.
260 Herb (2009a, p. 134).
261 Stapenhurst, Jacobs and Pelizzo (2014).
262 Rose-Ackerman (2001).
263 Ibid.
264 MP-2; NGO-2; NGO-3; NGO-1.

This concept is mentioned here to reflect the real nature of the regime in Kuwait where power is shared between the ruling family and the National Assembly. The Amir appoints the prime minister, and the latter appoints the ministers. Both the Amir and the prime minister have the ultimate power to choose ministers without restrictions; the National Assembly has no constitutional authority to nominate a specific minister or bestow its trust on the recent formation of a cabinet. This situation contrasts with Western fully democratised systems which choose their prime ministers and ministers without the interference of monarchs.[265] The Kuwaiti system also weakens the opportunity to form a government which considers the public good, particularly in the absence of relevant parties and the existence of fragmented individual MPs who concentrate narrowly on the interests of their voters. When the benefits of some cliques are secured at the expense of the common good, 'state capture' is triggered as a frequent corruption pattern. A political system is corrupt when venal politicians replace the allocation of public benefits with their own illegal enrichment.[266]

Second, although the National Assembly is a unicameral parliament (a single legislative body) comprising 50 elected deputies, cabinet members (15 in total) have the right to vote about matters raised in the National Assembly because they serve *ex officio* as MPs, a circumstance which bestows on them a significant voting advantage.[267] This structure increases the number of MPs to 65. The inherent flaw of this constitutional structure leads to an imbalance between a strong government and weak legislature.[268] Such an outcome has fallout regarding the supervisory power of the National Assembly and fosters corruption. In 2011, the National Assembly submitted an interpellation for the prime minister over a corruption scandal. Yet, with the help of the *ex officio* votes of the government and pro-government MPs, the prime minister succeeded in the interpellation being dropped, which resulted in mass public outrage embodied in assertive street demonstrations.[269] The failure of such a parliamentary tool to achieve its purpose is attributed to the structural pitfalls of the political system in Kuwait: 'Where checks on government are weak, government actors are not prohibited from engaging in corrupt activities'.[270] As one interviewee stressed, the constitutional formation of the National Assembly is one of the obstacles in achieving the parliamentary role of overseeing the government: 'one third of the MPs are appointed by the government'.[271] With regard to the other two-thirds, the intervention of the government through 'slush funds' and the offering of other services greatly influence the attitudes of the MPs, especially in light of a

265 Herb (2009a).
266 Rose-Ackerman (2001).
267 Kuwaiti Constitution, art.80.
268 Ghabra (2014).
269 Ulrichsen (2014).
270 Thomas and Meagher (2004, p. 10).
271 Lawyer-3.

broader social context.[272] If there are reforms related to combating corruption, for instance, the government can easily hinder these by opposing them. Thus, holding the prime minister accountable was only possible by people-led street demonstrations in Kuwait, which culminated in the ousting of the prime minister.[273] Public protest acts as an alternative tool which rectifies the limits inherent in the Kuwaiti political system.

Political challenges can be more than just structural deficits: they may be ultra vires challenges. The history of the democratic experience in Kuwait has seen blatant constitutional violations which stultify democracy. By interfering, the government 'steals the elections' by designing a favourable electoral system to serve its interests. In 1980, the government divided Kuwait into 25 districts, a system which was believed to be biased and to hinder any political reforms. Such redistricting was to prevent ideological MPs from winning and instead increased the number of allegiant tribal MPs.[274] In 2012, the government intervened again and changed the electoral system to a new system whereby constituents are not allowed to vote for more than one candidate.[275] In explaining such governmental intervention, Lawyer-3 said that pre-2012, the people chose reformist MPs and challenged government control of MPs. Thus, the government reacted and 'changed the rules of the game by altering the mechanism of election', a change which constitutes further obstacles.[276]

Furthermore, the National Assembly has been unconstitutionally dissolved twice, in 1976 and 1986, and its constitutional authorities given to the Amir and the council of ministers, an act which converted Kuwait to an authoritarian country.[277] The government has an extensive impact on the decision-making process and can achieve what it intends to do. Potentially corrupt politicians can seize corrupting opportunities and be sheltered by such a flawed structure. When the structure which regulates the political arena is flawed and lacks the potential to restrain corrupt politicians, grand political corruption (engaged in by high-ranking incumbents) is apt to abound as a prevalent corruption pattern. Through these drawbacks, a government can evade censure not just for corruption but for any other illegal practices, including mismanagement and fiscal violations. Such a political structure poses challenges which hinder democracy. Thus, Kuwait is unable to achieve a fully fledged democracy, and it can be said that, at its best, Kuwait is a semi-democracy.[278]

272 Ibid. The interviewee explained that the services are offered by the government to an MP so that the latter offers them to his/her constituents to help secure popular support.
273 Ghabra (2014).
274 Herb (2009a).
275 Sabrie and Hakala (2013).
276 Lawyer-3.
277 Salih (1991).
278 Kinninmont (2012).

#### 2.3.4.2.3 PUBLIC ACCOUNTABILITY

If the corruption pattern in Kuwait is a grand one, this immediately questions the impact of public accountability as a safeguard to prevent corruption.[279] Public accountability mechanisms are tools which institutionalise accountability principles, including transparency, which makes engagement in corruption costly.[280] The World Bank suggests that where corruption is widespread among high-ranking officials, political accountability should be enhanced as an effective means to face down such a corruption pattern.[281] In Kuwait, corrupt officials can potentially be held accountable through diverse accountability mechanisms. Politically, ministers are responsible before MPs through a toolbox of mechanisms such as interpellation, parliamentary inquiry, and votes of no confidence.[282] MPs are in turn accountable before voters who may prefer not to re-elect them. The Trial of Ministers Act (TMA) 88/1995 was enacted to subject ministers, who commit crimes related to their offices, to special legal rules which are stricter than their counterparts in the Penal Code. Crucially, the Anti-Corruption Authority and Financial Disclosure Act 2/2016 (ACAA) is a groundbreaking accountability mechanism through which high-ranking officials (including ministers and MPs) are subjected to stringent substantive and procedural rules, such as the obligatory financial disclosure of wealth and the enactment of illicit enrichment crime (IEO). With these examples of accountability mechanisms, politicians and senior officeholders can be, at least theoretically, held accountable. But what is the practical application of public accountability in Kuwait?

In fact, when raising the public accountability of grand corruption, features such as limited transparency,[283] the inability to bring corruption cases to justice, and the unwillingness to enforce counter-corruption processes properly[284] are determining factors. Perhaps it is not possible to establish conclusive proof about the disinclination of domestic authorities to hold accountable those responsible, especially when the existence of domestic counter-corruption institutions implies, to a high degree, a positive perception of political will to face corruption.[285] Notwithstanding this, it is argued here that the heart of the problem is not the total absence of accountability mechanisms but their enforcement, or the way in which they are exercised. An expert noted that theoretically, all officials and politicians can be held accountable, but the extent to which the accountability may go is the 'exact' problem.[286]

Public accountability in the Kuwaiti political system is ineffective. Grand corruption can theoretically be made accountable, but in practice, prominent

279 Rose-Ackerman (1999). The value of accountability is further analysed in chapter 3.2.1.2.
280 Gray, Hellman and Ryterman (2004).
281 Ibid.
282 Kuwaiti Constitution, arts.99–101.
283 Heywood (1997).
284 Brinkerhoff and Goldsmith (2002).
285 Tanzi (1998).
286 MP-2.

corrupt politicians enjoy a type of 'informal' impunity. The misapplication of public accountability may be imputed, again, to the influence of 'political culture', which depends upon non-cooperating segregated components of society.[287]

An interviewee argued that there is a 'clear' relationship between the way in which ministers and senior officials are chosen and their 'weak' accountability.[288] Although Kuwaitis believe in political accountability through constitutional institutions, familial, kinship, and sectarian intolerance prevail regarding the operation of such institutions. Informal impunity prevents 'those responsible' from probable accountability. A common example is when a minister is alleged to be corrupt. In this instance, the MP who is related to the minister (whether because of a family-, tribe-, or sect-based relationship) is unlikely to raise a question about the minster's accountability, support a vote of no confidence in the minister, or refer the minister to the criminal justice institutions. As one participant argued:

> There is a belief in the political culture of Kuwait that the political accountability of ministers is based on 'social considerations.' For example, when the interpellation of a minister takes places, the affiliation to a tribe, sect, or family is one of the factors that determines the fate of the accountability.[289]

As such, what matters is not the existence of legal systems of accountability, but the 'legal culture' of how to execute the mechanisms.[290] For example, in 2017, the Minister of Information and Youth Affairs resigned after being held politically accountable after a gruelling hearing pertinent to fiscal violations.[291] Just a few days after his resignation, he was appointed as the President of Civil Aviation with the rank of minister.[292] Thus, the legal and political accountability of corrupt officials simply becomes an empty threat. One implication is that not only is grand political corruption the prevalent corruption pattern, but also defective political accountability promotes systemic corruption in Kuwait in which legal formal rules are replaced by cultural informal rules.[293] One interviewee said: 'the personal relationships between the low-rank and high-rank officeholders may prevent their accountability'.[294]

In a neo-patrimonial state, senior officials are selectively chosen through the mechanism of clientelism: 'a complex chain of personal bonds between political

287 See section 2.3.4.2.1 above.

288 MP-2.

289 NGO-1.

290 Treisman (2000, p. 402).

291 See <http://www.skynewsarabia.com/web/article/916241/قبول-استقالة-وزير-الإعلام-والشباب-الكويتي>.

292 See <https://www.alraimedia.com/Home/Details?id=bc8be081-1af1-4338-ab80-5f23282b7198>.

293 World Bank (1997).

294 NGO-2.

patrons or bosses and their individual clients or followers'.[295] This approach stems from the absence of boundaries which separate the public sector from the private sector: 'In political systems where ties of family and friendship are more salient … such outcomes will be even more common'.[296] It follows that the number of scandalous cases which have actually been brought to justice is low.[297] A large proportion of candidates who seem preoccupied with corruption issues during their electoral campaigns may not be serious. When an election beckons, candidates tend to stir the political atmosphere and expose other alleged corrupt practices whenever the electoral interest so requires.[298]

When they were asked about the reality of accountability of ministers, some interviewees put forward another perspective of the problem of accountability in Kuwait.[299] They responded that politicians, and in particular ministers, are still accountable. They added that ministers are the Achilles' heels in the political accountability of the Kuwaiti constitutional system; for example, they are responsible for the acts of their subordinates. However, it should not be understood that accountability is effective. NGO-2 believed that even if ministers are more accountable than others, they are so for political and not technical reasons: 'many ministers had been interpellated for issues like corruption: the ministers resigned but corruption still exists'.[300] This view is reinforced by another interviewee who said that 'as far as I know, there is no single interpellation that could solve the problem'.[301] Although this analysis may imply that political accountability of ministers is effective, it stills reveals that the accountability mechanism could be misused.

Alternatively, some of the interviewees argued that the problem of accountability in Kuwait is related not only to political accountability, but also to other forms of legal accountability. Apart from the political sphere, ministers, factually, are not legally accountable. NGO-3 observed that the Court of Ministers has never convicted a single minister since its establishment in 1995. NGO-1 argued that ministers seem less accountable than officials. There have been many cases in which the state sued an official for a negligent act which lost the state KWD 1000 (approximately USD 3000).[302] However, there have been a number of ministers who have participated in activities which inflict losses exceeding USD 2.2 billion, such as the case of Dow Chemical, and yet none of these ministers have been held accountable.[303] There are many factors which may lead to this conclusion.[304] According to the pessimistic view of a current MP, 'the

295 Brinkerhoff and Goldsmith (2002, pp. 2–6).
296 Rose-Ackerman (1999, p. 145).
297 Kuwait Transparency Society (2017).
298 Treisman (2000).
299 MP-2; MP-3; Lawyer-3.
300 NGO-2.
301 NGO-1.
302 NGO-3.
303 Ibid.
304 To avoid repetition, these factors are addressed in chapter 3.2.1.2.

high-level officeholders in Kuwait seem not to be accountable, except before the National Assembly, and through the ministerial responsibility of the minister concerned'.[305]

The structural failure of some other legal mechanisms of accountability has also been documented. For example, a 2017 judge-led inquiry by the Kuwaiti Ministry of Justice (MoJ) found that Nazaha needs to be legally and institutionally reformed because it lacks 'success requirements'. Nazaha is unable to achieve its goals because of many reasons, such as the absence of objectivity in its work, the intensification of the dispute between the members of the Board of Trustees, and the flawed legal and institutional structure of the authority.[306] The current existence of Nazaha creates a state of scepticism towards the political will underlying efforts to combat corruption.

Another drawback relates to the effective participation of civil society in combating corruption.[307] The mere participation of civil society (as an accountability mechanism) is not enough. Even with the existence of independent NGOs, their independence is necessary but insufficient.[308] The morale of NGOs which resist corruption and raise the accountability of corrupt individuals can be weakened when they lack sufficient protection against prospective governmental interventions.[309] This is what happened to the Kuwait Transparency Society (KTS) when it was suspended by the government in 2015 and the elected board of directors replaced by governmental appointees: TI then suspended KTS's membership from the organisation.[310] This dissolution is a step backwards in combating corruption. Who protects these NGOs from arbitrary governmental decisions? How can the existence of NGOs, which apply pressure, be a matter of contingency?

Public accountability should take the form of a comprehensive system. There should be specific mechanisms through which officials are held accountable and specific mechanisms to protect the powers and independence of institutions which combat corruption. Public accountability may be potentially effective, particularly when supported with transparency and openness. When governments are less reluctant to supply adequate information about corruption scandals and make them publicly accessible, citizens can be well informed and more able to assess and hold accountable those who have power.[311] These caveats are exactly what the World Bank warned about as indices of the failure of counter-corruption authorities.[312] Thus, the Kuwaiti political system encourages corruption, and public accountability of corrupt politicians is feeble, impotent, and

305 MP-1.
306 Kuwait Ministry of Justice (2017, pp. 13–15).
307 For further analysis, see chapter 3.3.1.
308 Rose-Ackerman (1999).
309 World Bank (1997).
310 The board of KTS was re-elected in 2016. See Kuwait Transparency Society (2017).
311 Rose-Ackerman (1999).
312 World Bank (1997).

susceptible to 'improper influence' exerted by diverse factors.[313] The 'political culture' undergirds corruption and relentlessly undermines any efforts to expose corruption through public accountability.

### 2.3.4.3 *Economic system and corruption*

Kuwait has experienced major economic changes since the discovery of oil. This economic transition was inevitably underpinned with complex consequences for the Kuwaiti economic system. The thrust of this section is that the very nature of the economic structure helps us to understand the phenomenon of corruption and to explain the prevailing patterns of corruption in Kuwait. The analysis may also resolve a paradox, as put forward by a current MP (former minister): 'while corruption is often linked to poor countries, Kuwait, which is a rich country, is witnessing an emerging problem of corruption'.[314]

#### 2.3.4.3.1 CENTRALISATION OF ECONOMY

The economic system is reliant on the oil sector as the most prominent, if not the sole, natural resource, constituting the largest share of its exports.[315] This reliance on oil problematically centralises economic power within government.[316] In Kuwait, oil revenues directly accrue to the government.[317] This centralisation came specifically after the 1970s' wave of oil supply nationalisation, which pulled the rug from under the dominant international oil corporations and made domestic governments the exclusive beneficiary of oil profits.[318] After the nationalisation of the entire oil sector, the Kuwait Petroleum Corporation (KPC) was established in 1980 to integrate the oil industry in Kuwait (the upstream and downstream sectors) by including all oil companies in Kuwait as subsidiaries under the control of one entity. This integration resulted in 'central planning of the industry',[319] with the Kuwaiti government becoming the sole owner and distributor of oil wealth.[320] This is evident in the relationship between the KPC and the government.

In 1974, the Supreme Petroleum Council (SPC) was created with the prime minister as the chairperson.[321] The SPC has major executive powers such as setting regulations and the presentation of the budget to the government and the National Assembly. The KPC only has the authority to propose recommendations

313 Rose-Ackerman (1999, p. 143).
314 MP-3.
315 Herb (2009b).
316 Treisman (2000).
317 El-Katiri, Fattouh and Segal (2012).
318 Ross (2012).
319 See <https://www.kpc.com.kw/about/kpc-at-a-glance>.
320 El-Katiri, Fattouh and Segal (2012).
321 Amiri Decree 1/2013 on the Establishment of Supreme Petroleum Council, s.1.

and report to the SPC, which has ultimate authority.[322] Today, the SPC is the apex of the oil industry and 'effectively the controller of KPC's operations'. The arrangement by which oil revenues go to the government's budget determines the extent to which the government dominates the oil sector. As a subsidiary of the KPC, the Kuwait Oil Company (KOC) receives its capital expenditure from the government and spends it on extracting oil from the fields. Then, the KOC has two ways to exploit the crude oil which is extracted. First, it may buy the crude oil from the government, 'deducting from the purchase price its operating expenses plus 10 per cent for a legal reserve'. The KOC then sells this crude oil in the international markets at current prices and the revenues return to the state, 'less 10 per cent for the Reserve Fund for Future Generations, in the process taking a 50 cents per barrel marketing fee'. The KOC may refine the crude oil and sell the resultant petroleum products. Second, other subsidiaries of the KPC can also refine crude oil and sell their products in international markets and return the revenues to the government.[323]

Such centralisation, however, becomes problematic when the configuration leads to the concentration of economic power in the government, particularly amidst 'weak and basic institutions'.[324] When the oil sector was nationalised, oil policy debates were common in the National Assembly since oil was Kuwait's major concern.[325] Yet, the then political and societal institutions were not competent enough to be fully aware of any economic changes. The democratic experience since 1962 has been too limited to confront such political and economic changes. Although the National Assembly was involved in the oil issue and attempted to discharge its oversight role,[326] this role was unconstitutionally dissolved in 1976 (a few months after nationalisation).[327] This reveals the political institution's weakness during such economic changes and its failure to challenge the dominance of government.

##### 2.3.4.3.2 KUWAIT: A RENTIER AND CORPORATIST STATE

'Rent' is defined as 'all sorts of inputs into the production process without their owners contributing any effort on their part'.[328] Kuwait, accordingly, is a rentier state whose government's revenues almost solely constitute economic external rents which are obtained from foreign actors.[329] Oil rents are converted directly from the international economy to the treasury of the government. As a rentier state, the government in Kuwait has a pivotal, managerial role: the management

322 Stevens (2008).
323 See ibid., p. 23.
324 Pradhan et al. (2000, p. 26).
325 Salih (1991).
326 Sabrie and Hakala (2013).
327 Al-Najjar (2000).
328 Hafez (2009, p. 460).
329 Ross (2001).

of rents extracted from selling oil.[330] Rather than managing oil rents to find opportunities to establish how to produce wealth, the government is concerned with the distribution of the windfall generated by the oil rents.[331] Such pattern of management is arguably corrupting. Oil generates rents, and oil rents per se represent a source of rents for certain recipients (the rentier class). The state management of oil rents means that the government should develop a way in which oil revenues are spent. In Kuwait, the government tends to channel the huge amount of oil rents to the public through various channels, inter alia, public employment (pensions), domestic investments, and subsidies.[332] While the centralised economy increases the contestable rents which 'the centralised economic power' has control rights upon,[333] the state becomes the most significant recourse for most of society's components, particularly private sector companies which depend on state-funded projects. One of the interviewees believed that there is a strong link between an oil-abundant country (such as Kuwait) and corruption.[334] He/she explains that such a link adopts the following mechanism:

> The nature of Kuwait's economy as a rentier centralises power in the hands of the few. The government is responsible for every aspect in the state, including pensions, public constructions, and other sectors. In particular, the government tends to allocate the rents of oil to the entities/persons/corporate units that achieve the interests of those few in the government. Individuals, and the whole of society, are in constant need of the state, despite the fact that it is the state that should need its people for its legitimisation; the equation is reversed.[335]

In parallel with the Kuwaiti political culture, corporatism in Kuwait is reflected in its economy, resulting in a 'corporatist economic system'.[336] In this system, the interests of a wide range of social stakeholders, particularly the economic interests of a conglomerate of merchants as a corporate unit, shape the role of the government in the national economy. In Kuwait, these economic interests are embodied in influential big business entities such as banks, construction companies and newspaper owners all of which belong to a limited number of local merchants. Having been introduced into the state system, stakeholders' interests are protected by the central government, which usually considers these interests in the governmental decision-making process.[337] Thus, the massive oil revenues and the way in which the government uses these revenues, particularly in

330 El-Katiri, Fattouh and Segal (2012).
331 Hafez (2009).
332 El-Katiri, Fattouh and Segal (2012).
333 Sala-i-Martin and Subramanian (2013, p. 574).
334 Lawyer-3.
335 Ibid.
336 Ammous (2012, pp. 5–6).
337 Ibid.

privileging some areas at the expense of others, cause many political troubles, of which corruption is a relevant issue.[338] Governments tend to spend oil revenues in the form of patronage, under which the vested interests of the state, through off-budget financing and influence-oriented spending such as when assigning monopoly rights, have far-reaching effects on promoting corrupt practices.

The concentration of the national wealth on extremely productive resources has allured powerful parties to seek benefits from this enormous affluence by engaging in both legitimate and corrupt transactions.[339] Oil revenues produce rental arrangements through the following machinery. For the government, huge amounts of oil revenues are incorporated in its treasury. The government seeks to create wide networks of distribution in which oil revenues can be channelled. For interest groups, enormous rental channels are created. These should be used to find ways for the oil revenues to reach the corporate units with the least effort. Thus, '[i]t is the fate of the politically connected special interest groups that is the foremost occupation of the government'.[340] In these circumstances, oil finds great opportunities for corruption.

Economically, corruption is perceived to be a form of rent-seeking activity, namely the pursuit of interest groups to seek preferential treatment by the government.[341] Interest groups, embodied in, for example, the stratum of owners of giant businesses, become a rentier class in such a process in order to generate 'unwarranted' wealth, relying on oil revenues. Rentiers accumulate their wealth not through their contributions to the production process but through 'the capture of the Other's efforts'.[342] With regard to domestic investments, for example, the government may issue a regulation in favour of some partners, or declare its need for a huge project, which secures the transfer of huge amounts of money from the state treasury to the accounts of the stakeholders without efforts which justify their entitlement to this money. By way of further evidence, MP-2 mentioned the negative effects of businesses' dependence on the public sector for securing profits. Business people prefer to be 'parasites of public funds' than invest money and efforts in building a strong private sector. In this environment, there are no interest groups which may exert legitimate pressure on the state to achieve their demands. Thus, with a weak private sector, businesses tend to take cheap, effortless, and illegitimate steps to extract rents from the state.[343]

Kuwait was affected by the leak of the so-called 'Panama Papers', which exposed the crucial mechanisms which enabled political leaders worldwide to conceal business dealings and engage in corruption, tax evasion, and other

338 Ross (2012).
339 Pradhan et al. (2000).
340 Ammous (2012, p. 6).
341 Corruption differs from other rent-seeking activities which may be legitimate. See Lambsdorff (2002).
342 Hafez (2009, p. 461).
343 MP-2.

illegalities involving the global industry of offshore companies.[344] In the aftermath of the Panama Papers, the International Consortium of Investigative Journalists (ICIJ) published a database of offshore leaks, which included offshore companies owned by several high-profile Kuwaiti merchants and influential public figures.[345] For example, an influential businessperson exploited the anonymity which such companies provide to participate indirectly in a USD 500 million military equipment contract with the Kuwaiti Ministry of Defence, in which allegations of bribing Kuwaiti officials were raised.[346] This is not to say that offshore companies were established exclusively to engage in corrupt deals; they can still be used for legal purposes. The argument put here, however, is that the creation of an offshore company as a cover behind which to engage in high value dealings is suspicious in such circumstances.

NGO-1 argued for the positive correlation between oil and corruption. He/she maintained that the fluctuation and volatility inherent in the oil sector makes people eagerly seek the benefits of this profitable sector. The reoccurring economic shocks in the oil sector often conjure up the perception that oil could run out and we will return to the pre-oil era where there was no welfare; thus, people do not enjoy psychological stability.[347] Especially after the Iraqi invasion of Kuwait in 1990 and the latter's liberation in 1991, people have started to realise the need to secure their living in case of any potential political issues in the future.[348] This situation, according to NGO-1, may explain the proliferation of 'grand corruption' cases after the Iraqi invasion in 1990.[349] This view was corroborated by another participant who argued that 'the instability of oil prices (and, therefore, its whole existence) negatively affects the people, and this is somewhat linked to their decision to secure their future'.[350]

What further promotes the oil–corruption nexus is the lack of transparency. Non-transparency implies secrecy around oil revenues in the sense that they are opaquely concealed and remain outside the public's observation. This secrecy may explain why oil revenues are commonly misused and seized.[351] The government's revenues from the sale of oil pass through invisible channels which lack sufficient transparency, depending as they do upon the complex processes through which oil production proceeds and the daily changes in oil's price.[352] Thus, a large share of the revenues are diverted to the pockets of the powerful. Opportunistic incumbents and influential politicians exploit the opaqueness of oil revenues and keep reaping their shares of huge oil rents. This is particularly

344 See Obermayer and Obermaier (2017).
345 See <https://offshoreleaks.icij.org/search?utf8=✓&q=&c=KWT&j=&e=&commit=Search>.
346 See *Westacre Investments Inc v Jugoimport SDPR Holding Co Ltd* [2000] QB 288.
347 NGO-1.
348 Ibid.
349 Ibid.
350 NGO-3.
351 Ross (2012).
352 Tanzi (1998).

true in a state where the economic structure is characterised by government hegemony.[353] In Kuwait, the activities and operations of the KPC in Europe have created controversial debates about the chances to 'disguise' oil profits from any possible scrutiny and checks.[354]

Cordesman analysed the overdependence of OPEC (the Organization of the Petroleum Exporting Countries) countries on oil and coined the term 'OPEC disease' whereby 'most [OPEC] countries have used their export revenues in ways that have distorted and damaged their economies, political structures and governance'.[355] Globally, the relationship between oil and corruption has been taken seriously. For example, Global Witness, an international NGO, has raised concerns about the 'resource curse' and oil-related corruption, referring to how far government corruption is chiefly attributable to the lack of fiscal transparency in the oil sector (and other extractive sectors).[356]

The importance of transparency in the extractive sector culminated in the establishment of the Extractive Industry Transparency Initiative (EITI) in 2002 'to promote the open and accountable management of oil, gas and mineral resources'.[357] The EITI requires that all extractive companies should report taxes and fees, and governments should also publish the incomes from their resources; such initiatives empower citizens to scrutinise the potential mismanagement of resources.[358] The United Kingdom, for instance, recognises the role of extractive industries in economic and social development through 'improved resource governance'. The UK EITI provides detailed accounts of the 'reconciliation of payments streams between companies operating in the UK extractive sector and the relevant Government agencies', including a number of companies which 'reported their 2017 payments to governments around the world'.[359] Unfortunately, Kuwait is not yet a member of the EITI, although, in 2014, the KTS prepared a proposition to induce policymakers to join.[360] Research shows that 'internal motivation' (such as the natural resource curse experience and corruption) and 'internal capacity' (including the quality of institutions) are factors affecting the decision to join the EITI.[361] This outcome is consistent with what emerges from the analysis of corruption causes in Kuwait.

Despite oil's alleged contribution to corruption, two interviewees did not agree with the assumption that Kuwait's dependence on oil is a key explanation of the corruption problem. MP-2 argued that the oil–corruption nexus is unclear, arguing that although the economy of Kuwait has depended upon oil

353 Ghabra (2014).
354 Stevens (2008, p. 6).
355 See Cordesman (2016, p. 17).
356 Global Witness calls for 'energy revenue transparency'. See Global Witness (2007, p. 4).
357 See <https://eiti.org/who-we-are>. The EITI is further addressed in chapter 3.2.1.1.
358 Haufler (2010).
359 See UK EITI Multi-Stakeholder Group (2019, pp. 5–11).
360 See <www.transparency.org.kw.au-ti.org/upload/Qanwon_Shafaf/pdf/4.pdf>.
361 Lujala (2018, p. 360).

many decades ago, the country has witnessed the eruption of grand corruption cases much more recently. Furthermore, MP-3 believed that corruption is a form of looting[362] which does not rely on the nature of resources, whether oil or otherwise: 'oil is just a natural resource, and there has never been a relationship between it and corruption'. MP-2 took Norway as proof of this argument: 'Norway has always been producing oil, and it has not ever witnessed the problems faced in Kuwait'. Although there is some literature illustrating how Norway has avoided the 'resource curse',[363] contrasting Kuwait with Norway is not a fair comparison. The quality of institutions is a major factor responsible for the variation in the effects of resource across countries.[364] In Norway, when oil was discovered, the country 'already had a long and stable tradition of democratic rule. It had a well-functioning state bureaucracy'.[365] Political culture has also been perceived as a 'fundamental' explanation for differences across countries.[366] However, the unique Norwegian experience regarding the resource curse is beyond the scope of this book.

#### 2.3.4.3.3 ECONOMIC DIVERSIFICATION AND CORRUPTION

Unlike an oil-dominated economic structure, economic diversification leads to a plurality in the structure between government and the private sector. Both government hegemony and the rents under governmental control are normally decreased in these conditions; hence, there is a decrease in corruption opportunities (according to the analysis above). The relevance of oil rents' effects on corruption is reflected in the following equation: the increased dependence upon oil, and then the increase in oil rents, is directly proportional to increases in the level of corruption. In a quantified study, Arzeki and Bruckner adopted International Monetary Fund (IMF) statistics for oil-producing countries to gauge the effect of the export value of oil on corruption. In testing the correlation, they depended upon a distinct unit which is a compound of two measures: the international price of oil interacted with the quality of oil exported rather than its quantity.[367] Among other findings, they found a correlation between an increase in oil exports (hence, increasing oil rents) and an increase in corruption. The dominance of the oil industry on a national economy has far-reaching effects upon the problem of corruption.

Arguably, the corruption problem in a concentrated economy is greater than in a diversified economy. The extent of a concentrated economy's impact on corruption becomes starker when a comparison is made between countries with

362 'Looting' was referred to as a key form of corruption. Corruption, of course, may take other forms.

363 See Holden (2013); Mehlum, Moene and Torvik (2006).

364 See Mehlum, Moene and Torvik (2006).

365 Holden (2013, p. 872).

366 See Phillips (2008).

367 Arezki and Brückner (2011).

common economic characteristics: Kuwait and the UAE. Despite the democratic practices envisaged in the Kuwaiti National Assembly, which often challenge the dominance of government, and the absence of such parliamentary power in the UAE,[368] in the CPI in 2018, the UAE ranked 70 while Kuwait ranked 41.[369] What could cause this significant difference in rank, despite the economic generalisation between Kuwait and UAE regarding the dominance of oil? While Kuwait has continued to rely entirely on oil, the UAE has successfully diversified its economy.[370] For example, with regard to FDI, the UAE is foremost among major recipients; however, Kuwait is not one of the latter. The report on world investments from 2013 to 2018 produced by the United Nations Conference on Trade and Development (UNCTAD) shows the poor growth of FDI inflows in Kuwait compared with those of the UAE: in 2018, Kuwait's FDI inflows reached USD 346 million, while the UAE had thriving FDI inflows of USD 10,385 million.[371]

Recognising the effects of a lack of economic diversification on the corruption problem, MP-2 contended that the existence of alternatives to oil means greater options for businesspersons to achieve profits. In other words, a thriving private sector dilutes the pressure on the public sector in terms of securing profits. But in the current economy of Kuwait, the weak private sector encourages dependence upon the public sector as a key profit-maximising means. Thus, the public sector is the main, dependable source of extracting profits and rents from the government, especially in light of the fact that the oil-based economy provides the government with an abundance of money.[372] As emphasised by MP-2, 'the rush on public money is mainly caused by the weakness of the private sector in Kuwait, which has encouraged businesses to depend on the public sector to make profitable transactions'.

In contrast, commenting on the role of economic diversification in the context of corruption, MP-1 opined that while the singularity of a source of wealth is not 'a good thing' for economic considerations, it says nothing about corruption. The misadministration of oil wealth is something which can be deterred and prevented by promoting the accountability of those who are responsible for its administration: 'when we talk about corruption, we should be serious about punishing the corrupt who are the apex of the administration rather than diversifying the sources of wealth'.[373] Thus, MP-1 raised the importance of accountability in preventing or combating corruption.

The importance of the characteristics of the economic structure in Kuwait can be illustrated through the patterns of corruption which they promote. The economy is oil-based, the revenues of oil usually lack transparency, oil revenues per

368 Herb (2009b).
369 Transparency International (2019).
370 Herb (2009b).
371 UNCTAD (2019).
372 MP-2.
373 MP-1.

se create oil rents which in turn provide substantial gains for all aspects of corrupt practice, and these oil rents are entirely dominated by the government. All these features make the management of oil an exclusive arena for a layer of decision makers who occupy high ranks within the political hierarchy of the state. Arguably, this distinctive economy encourages specific patterns of corruption. When oil is centrally managed by a government, this situation links corruption to senior officials, rendering grand corruption a prevalent pattern. Moreover, the mismanagement of oil rents, which channels the rents in a manner which prejudices the public good, encourages state capture. All these corruption patterns are expected to thrive in this economic milieu.

#### 2.3.4.3.4 LACK OF A TAXATION SYSTEM

One salient consequence of Kuwait being a rentier state is that its economic system does not depend upon internal income resources.[374] Kuwait lacks a taxation system, including taxes on consumption and individuals' income.[375] To date, tax is limited to the corporate income tax of foreign businesses.[376] The absence of a taxation-based economic system contributes to corruption. This argument may be supported by the fact that moral and political considerations, which underlie both the management of tax and oil revenues, differ depending upon the nature of the revenues. The illegal disposal of public money by the government through misappropriation or general mismanagement is more difficult and challenging in the context of revenues from taxes.[377]

Some scholarly works have explained the relationship between natural resources and government transparency, arguing that governments tend to make a concession of the taxation system (which requires more transparency) in exchange for gains from corruption (which is backed with less transparent administration).[378] While the literature regarding 'tax morality' emphasises the moral commitment behind paying taxes, maintaining tax morale entails a commitment on the part of a government to impose strict fiscal oversight to 'encourage greater transparency and accountability in taxation affairs, which can lead to broader, more equitable and [more] fair fiscal outcomes'.[379] This is an axiomatic inference: if oil revenues are a natural endowment, which is deemed to belong to people, tax revenues are authentically derived from the people's money. The release of the Panama Papers and the concomitant international uproar, most importantly in the context of tax evasion, is telling.[380] The release of the Global Declaration against Corruption in 2016, which was driven largely by the

374 Bacik (2008).
375 Eltony (2007).
376 Income Tax Act 3/1955.
377 See Sala-i-Martin and Subramanian (2013).
378 For example, see Mohtadi, Ross and Ruediger (2016).
379 Chohan (2016, pp. 3–4).
380 See Obermayer and Obermaier (2017).

publication of the Panama Papers, addressed many issues, inter alia, the commitment of governments to counter issues related to tax evasion.[381] This analysis underlines the importance of tax morality consideration, and, hence, the potential of taxation systems to restrict a government's management of revenues.

In contrast, the situation is different for oil revenues. The challenge faced with oil revenues is that 'there is no final consumer to whom [oil revenues] "naturally" accrue'.[382] Thus, governments have stronger discretionary authority in the management of oil revenues. When asked about whether the Kuwaiti oil-based economy contributes to corruption, Official-5 responded that 'there is an indirect relationship'. He/she further explained that the public fund, which is mostly made up of revenues from oil exports, is easy money that requires no hard effort (in the view of the people). Depicting the public fund in this way impacts our responses and reactions towards any potential abuse of the public fund: 'we have become complacent since it is not our money, so let them do what they want to do'.[383] The interviewee probably did not address the issue of lack of taxation, but the negative role of non-taxation can be logically inferred from his/her view. The 'real' ownership of the public fund, and how it is made up, may have implications on how people deal with corruption in terms of whether they are enthusiastic or indifferent.

Unlike taxation revenues, the management of oil revenues is subject to divergent considerations. The spending of oil revenues is prone to vested political considerations, particularly when revenues come from oil wells directly to a government's treasury.[384] Middle Eastern scholars have identified 'the rentier effect' when pondering the effects of oil resources on democracy in the region. Governments rely on oil revenues to dilute social pressures for the demands to have more representation, transparency, and accountability regarding the use of public funds.[385] In the same way, oil obviates the need for taxation systems. Governments which obtain tremendous revenues from oil exports do not endeavour to levy taxes on people. They adopt this approach in order to win people's satisfaction and relieve popular claims about accountability.[386] The wealth accumulated by oil revenues does not require persistent effort and the undertaking of risks; thus, the appeals for accountability should fade away.[387] Lawyer-3 emphasised that all these facts render the accountability of the government elusive. It is the government that is accountable to itself. For example, there have been many occasions where the Kuwaiti government has raised the issue of the accountability of some of its members; however, it has done so at a suitable time

381 Declared by the International Anti-Corruption Summit, held in London. See Grimwood (2016, p. 5).
382 El-Katiri, Fattouh and Segal (2012, p. 168).
383 Official-5.
384 El-Katiri, Fattouh and Segal (2012).
385 Ross (2001, p. 332).
386 Ibid.
387 Hafez (2009).

which it alone has chosen: 'this could be when the interests conflict between the government [as a patron], and one of its clients'.[388] While governments distract people's focus through the partial distribution of oil revenues to them, and while people prefer to keep the situation as it is rather than demand good governance of oil revenues and hence the levying of taxes, corruption finds an opportunity to permeate the upper domain of state bodies. An Arab economist insightfully summarises the problem as follows: 'With the marginalization of taxation, accountability and responsibility wither away as the distribution of [oil] rent is considered as "gifts" or unearned benefits to recipients who cannot therefore question their providers'.[389]

Nonetheless, this does not mean that the absence of taxation results in all patterns of corruption. Instead, it is grand corruption rather than bureaucratic corruption to which the lack of taxation arguably contributes. One may recognise, for example, that the phenomenon of corrupt tax inspectors who are bribed to overlook the taxable assets of a factory owner, is first associated with the existence of a taxation system.[390] An analysis of the underlying characteristics of an economic structure, as such, considerably signifies the contribution of the economic structure to the phenomenon of corruption as an element independent from the political structure.[391] This is why, perhaps, Scott referred to this point when stating that 'we must therefore make allowance for the effect of different economic systems when comparing the extent of corruption in different nations.'[392]

## 2.4 Conclusion

The corruption phenomenon is characterised by complexity when taking into account its contested concept, endless potential patterns, contrasting effects, and multiple causes. Thus, any attempt to simplify this complex phenomenon in Kuwait should begin by conceptualising corruption and focusing on a narrow legal conception which limits the meaning of corruption to the deviation from the duties of public office. Moreover, corruption should be treated as an undesirable phenomenon and a genuine problem which should be countered. By demonstrating its negative effects, corruption can be perceived to inflict serious damage on Kuwait's economic and political life. It has also been shown that corruption may promote crime through a complex network of relations between corruption and organised crime (the corruption–crime nexus). However, the reality in Kuwait illustrates that the managerial effect of corruption on the administration of state institutions (the corruption–governance nexus) is a starker issue and should be paid more attention, given the economic characteristics of Kuwait. Furthermore, understanding the prevailing corruption patterns

388 Lawyer-3.
389 Hafez (2009, p. 475).
390 Leff (1964).
391 Kinninmont (2012).
392 Scott (1972, p. 9).

in Kuwait is essential in order to overcome the multiplicity inherent in corruption patterns. Dissecting the causes of corruption in Kuwait is also critical in order to understand the problematic corruption patterns. The answer given here is that modernisation has collided with the institutional characteristics of Kuwait and generated corruption as a serious phenomenon. Corruption stems from the cultural, political, and economic conditions. In general, such institutional conditions tend to promote corruption as a problem embedded in the country's institutions (systemic corruption) and associate corruption with a specific stratum, namely individuals who are high-ranking officials and policymakers (grand corruption).

This chapter's objective to examine the phenomenon of corruption in Kuwait is important to understand the real nature of the problem. This understanding in turn is an essential step which must be taken before countering corruption and designing appropriate reforms. Thus, combating the corruption phenomenon in Kuwait requires efforts which are commensurate with the nature of grand corruption in order to tackle its institutional drivers. These efforts should regard the law as a principal (but not exclusive) counter-corruption instrument in any reform policies. Yet it would be a mistake for counter-corruption policies to focus on the mere existence of written laws. Systemic grand corruption is a corruption pattern which jeopardises the ability of law to act as a counter-corruption mechanism. Thus, alongside the law, there may be social, political, and economic reforms which are directed at the various institutions of the state. However, reforms of these types are beyond the scope of this book.[393]

Pessimistically, counter-corruption reforms which are mainly directed at high-ranking officials are hard to sustain. Reforms which deal with 'grand' corruption may be resisted or blocked by those who make the rules of the game and who decide on the laws and the allocation of wealth within Kuwaiti society. However, this difficulty does not justify indifference. Counter-corruption policies should be widely understood to include various elements: focusing on grand corruption in the public sphere, ensuring the adequacy of counter-corruption laws and their effective enforcement, and, before all, emphasising the broad counter-corruption values that foster a 'good governance' environment which is unfavourable for corruption and pre-emptively combats corruption.

## Bibliography

Acemoglu, D., Verdier, T., Robinson, J. (2004). Alfred Marshall Lecture: Kleptocracy and Divide-and-Rule: A Model of Personal Rule. *Journal of the European Economic Association*. 2(2–3), pp. 162–192.

Adams, P. (2018). Corporatism and Comparative Politics: Is There a New Century of Corporatism? In: Wiarda, H. (ed). *New Directions in Comparative Politics*. 3rd ed. Abingdon: Routledge, pp. 17–44.

393 Nevertheless, a social counter-corruption strategy is addressed in chapter 3.3.1.

Al-Kandari, Y., Al-Hadben, I. (2010). Tribalism, Sectarianism, and Democracy in Kuwaiti Culture. *Digest of Middle East Studies.* 19(2), pp. 268–285.

Al-Najjar, G. (2000). The Challenges Facing Kuwaiti Democracy. *Middle East Journal.* 54(2), pp. 242–258.

Al-Saleh, O. (2003). *The Constitutional System and Political Institutions in Kuwait.* Beirut: Dar Alkotob Press.

Al-Tarrah, A. (2007). Family in the Kinship State. In: Al-Sharekh, A. (ed). *The Gulf Family: Kinship Policies and Modernity.* London: Saqi in association with London Middle East Institute, SOAS, pp. 119–124.

Al-Zu'abi, A., Al-Naqeeb, K. (2007). Tackling Corruption in the Arab World, With Special Reference to Kuwait. *Arab World Geographer.* 10(3–4), pp. 170–188.

Ammous, S. (2012). *Arab Corporatism* (Working Paper No. 744). Giza, Egypt: Economic Research Forum.

Amundsen, I. (1999). *Political Corruption: An Introduction to the Issues* (Working Paper 1999: 7). Bergen, Norway: Chr. Michelsen Institute.

Arezki, R., Brückner, M. (2011). Oil Rents, Corruption, and State Stability: Evidence from Panel Data Regressions. *European Economic Review.* 55(7), pp. 955–963.

Aruri, N. (1970). Kuwait: A Political Study. *Muslim World.* 60(4), pp. 321–343.

Arvis, J.-F., Berenbeim, R. (2003). *Fighting Corruption in East Asia: Solutions from the Private Sector.* Washington, DC: World Bank.

Bacik, G. (2008). *Hybrid Sovereignty in the Arab Middle East: The Cases of Kuwait, Jordan, and Iraq.* Basingstoke, New York: Palgrave Macmillan.

Biygautane, M. (2015). Anti-Corruption Strategies in the Gulf Cooperation Council's States: Lessons Learned and the Path Forward. In: Zhang, Y., Lavena, C. (eds). *Government Anti-Corruption Strategies: A Cross-Cultural Perspective.* Boca Raton, FL: CRC Press, pp. 188–215.

Bloom, B. (2014). Criminalizing Kleptocracy? The ICC as a Viable Tool in the Fight Against Grand Corruption. *American University International Law Review.* 29(3), pp. 627–671.

Brinkerhoff, D., Goldsmith, A. (2002). *Clientelism, Patrimonialism and Democratic Governance: An Overview and Framework for Assessment and Programming.* Cambridge, MA: Abt Associates Inc.

Bussell, J. (2015). Typologies of Corruption: A Pragmatic Approach. In: Rose-Ackerman, S., Lagunes, P. (eds). *Greed, Corruption, and the Modern State: Essays in Political Economy.* Cheltenham, UK; Northampton, MA: Edward Elgar, pp. 21–45.

Campbell, L. (2016). 'Corruption by Organised Crime' – A Matter of Definition? *Current Legal Problems.* 69(1), pp. 115–141.

Central Statistical Bureau. (2018). Employment Statistic in Government Sector (Kuwaiti/Non-Kuwaiti) as of 30/6/2018. [Online]. Available from: https://www.csb.gov.kw/Pages/Statistics_en?ID=13&ParentCatID=1.

Chohan, U. (2016). The Panama Papers and Tax Morality. [Online]. Available from: https://ssrn.com/abstract=2759418.

Christensen, J. (2011). The Looting Continues: Tax Havens and Corruption. *Critical Perspectives on International Business.* 7(2), pp. 177–196.

Collier, M. W. (2002). Explaining Corruption: An Institutional Choice Approach. *Crime, Law and Social Change.* 38(1), pp. 1–32.

Cordesman, A. H. (2016). *The "OPEC Disease": Assessing the True Impact of Lower Oil Export Revenues.* Washington, DC: Center for Strategic and International Studies.

de Graaf, G. (2007). Causes of Corruption: Towards a Contextual Theory of Corruption. *Public Administration Quarterly.* 31(1), pp. 39–86.

de Graaf, G., von Maravic, P., Wagenaar, P. (2010). Introduction: Causes of Corruption – The Right Question or the Right Perspective? In: de Graaf, G., von Maravic, P., Wagenaar, P. (eds). *The Good Cause: Theoretical Perspectives on Corruption*. Opladen: Barbara Budrich, pp. 13–20.

El-Katiri, L., Fattouh, B., Segal, P. (2012). Anatomy of an Oil-Based Welfare State: Rent Distribution in Kuwait. In: Held, D., Ulrichsen, K. (eds). *The Transformation of the Gulf: Politics, Economics and the Global Order*. Abingdon: Routledge, pp. 165–187.

Eltony, M. N. (2007). The Economic Development Experience of Kuwait: Some Useful Lessons. *Journal of Economic and Administrative Sciences*. 23(1), pp. 77–102.

FATF. (2011). *Laundering the Proceeds of Corruption*. Paris: FATF.

Freedom House. (2019). Kuwait. [Online]. Available from: https://freedomhouse.org/report/freedom-world/2019/kuwait.

Friedrich, C. (1966). Political Pathology. *Political Quarterly*. 37(1), pp. 70–85.

Gardiner, J. (2007). Defining Corruption. In: Heidenheimer, A., Johnston, M. (eds). *Political Corruption: Concepts and Contexts*. 3rd ed. New Brunswick, NJ; London: Transaction Publishers, pp. 25–40.

Gause, F. G. (1994). *Oil Monarchies: Domestic and Security Challenges in the Arab Gulf States*. New York: Council on Foreign Relations Press.

Ghabra, S. (2014). *Kuwait: At the Crossroads of Change or Political Stagnation* (MEI Policy Paper 2014-2). Washington, DC: Middle East Institute.

Giddens, A. (1990). *The Consequences of Modernity*. Cambridge: Polity.

Global Witness. (2007). *Oil Revenue Transparency: A Strategic Component of U.S. Energy Security and Anti-Corruption Policy*. Washington, DC: Global Witness.

Goudie, A., Stasavage, D. (1998). A Framework for the Analysis of Corruption. *Crime, Law and Social Change*. 29(2–3), pp. 113–159.

Gray, C., Hellman, J., Ryterman, R. (2004). *Anticorruption in Transition 2: Corruption in Enterprise-State Interactions in Europe and Central Asia 1999–2002*. Washington, DC: World Bank.

Green, P., Ward, T. (2004). *State Crime: Governments, Violence and Corruption*. London: Pluto Press.

Greif, A. (1994). Cultural Beliefs and the Organization of Society: A Historical and Theoretical Reflection on Collectivist and Individualist Societies. *Journal of Political Economy*. 102(5), pp. 912–950.

Grimwood, G. (2016). *After the International Anti-Corruption Summit in May 2016: What Next?* (HC Briefing Paper 7580, 20 May 2016). London: House of Commons Library.

Hafez, Z. (2009). The Culture of Rent, Factionalism, and Corruption: A Political Economy of Rent in the Arab World. *Contemporary Arab Affairs*. 2(3), pp. 458–480.

Haufler, V. (2010). Disclosure as Governance: The Extractive Industries Transparency Initiative and Resource Management in the Developing World. *Global Environmental Politics*. 10(3), pp. 53–73.

Heidenheimer, A. (2007). Perspectives on the Perception of Corruption. In: Heidenheimer, A., Johnston, M. (eds). *Political Corruption: Concepts and Contexts*. 3rd ed. New Brunswick, NJ; London: Transaction Publishers, pp. 141–154.

Heidenheimer, A., Johnston, M. (eds) (2007). *Political Corruption: Concepts and Contexts*. New Brunswick, NJ; London: Transaction Publishers.

Hellman, J., Kaufmann, D. (2001). Confronting the Challenge of State Capture in Transition Economies. *Finance & Development*. 38(3), pp. 31–35.

Herb, M. (2009a). Kuwait: The Obstacle of Parliamentary Politics. In: Teitelbaum, J. (ed). *Political Liberalization in the Persian Gulf*. London: Hurst Publishers, pp. 133–155.

Herb, M. (2009b). A Nation of Bureaucrats: Political Participation and Economic Diversification in Kuwait and the United Arab Emirates. *International Journal of Middle East Studies*. 41(3), pp. 375–395.

Heywood, P. (1997). Political Corruption: Problems and Perspectives. *Political Studies*. 45(3), pp. 417–435.

Heywood, P. (2015). Introduction: Scale and Focus in the Study of Corruption. In: Heywood, P. (ed). *Routledge Handbook of Political Corruption*. Abingdon: Routledge, pp. 1–13.

Holden, S. (2013). Avoiding the Resource Curse: The Case Norway. *Energy Policy*. 63, pp. 870–876.

Home Office. (2019). Anti-corruption Newsletter: Summer 2019. [Online]. Available from: https://www.gov.uk/government/publications/anti-corruption-newsletter-summer-2019/anti-corruption-newsletter-summer-2019.

Huntington, S. (2006). *Political Order in Changing Societies*. London: Yale University Press.

Jain, A. (2001). Corruption: A Review. *Journal of Economic Surveys*. 15(1), pp. 71–121.

Johnston, M. (1998). Fighting Systemic Corruption: Social Foundations for Institutional Reform. *European Journal of Development Research*. 10(1), pp. 85–104.

Kaufmann, D., Kraay, A., Mastruzzi, M. (2011). The Worldwide Governance Indicators: Methodology and Analytical Issues. *Hague Journal on the Rule of Law*. 3(2), pp. 220–246.

Khalaf, S. (2000). Poetics and Politics of Newly Invented Traditions in the Gulf: Camel Racing in the United Arab Emirates. *Ethnology*. 39(3), pp. 243–261.

Kinninmont, J. (2012). *Kuwait's Parliament: An Experiment in Semi-Democracy*. London: Chatham House.

Klitgaard, R. (1988). *Controlling Corruption*. Oxford and Berkeley: University of California Press.

Kuwait Ministry of Justice. (2017). *Report of Fact-Finding Committee in the Anti-Corruption Authority*. Kuwait: Ministry of Justice.

Kuwait Transparency Society. (2017). A Press Release on the Results of the Kuwait's Corruption Perception Index 2016. [Online]. Available from: http://www.transparency.org.kw.au-ti.org/upload/moaasher/2016.pdf.

La Porta, R., Lopez-de-Silanes, F., Shleifer, A., Vishny, R. (1999). The Quality of Government. *Journal of Law, Economics, and Organization*. 15(1), pp. 222–279.

Lambsdorff, J. (2002). Corruption and Rent-Seeking. *Public Choice*. 113(1–2), pp. 97–125.

Lambsdorff, J. (2006). Causes and Consequences of Corruption: What Do We Know from a Cross-Section of Countries? In: Rose-Ackerman, S. (ed). *International Handbook on the Economics of Corruption*. Cheltenham, UK; Northampton, MA: Edward Elgar, pp. 3–51.

Lambsdorff, J., Taube, M., Schramm, M. (2005). Corrupt Contracting: Exploring the Analytical Capacity of New Institutional Economics and New Economic Sociology. In: Lambsdorff, J., Taube, M., Schramm, M. (eds). *The New Institutional Economics of Corruption*. Abingdon: Routledge, pp. 1–15.

LaPalombara, J. (1994). Structural and Institutional Aspects of Corruption. *Social Research*. 61(2), pp. 325–350.

Lederman, D., Loayza, N., Soares, R. (2005). Accountability and Corruption: Political Institutions Matter. *Economics and Politics*. 17(1), pp. 1–35.

Leff, N. (1964). Economic Development Through Bureaucratic Corruption. *American Behavioral Scientist* 8(3), pp. 8–14.

Lennerfors, T. (2008). *The Vicissitudes of Corruption: Degeneration, Transgression, Jouissance.* Luton: Ram Distribution.

Levi, M. (2011). Policing Fraud and Organised Crime. In: Newburn, T. (ed). *Handbook of Policing.* 2nd ed. Abingdon: Routledge, pp. 522–552.

Lujala, P. (2018). An Analysis of the Extractive Industry Transparency Initiative Implementation Process. *World Development.* 107,- pp. 358–381.

Makarenko, T., Mesquita, M. (2014). Categorising the Crime–terror Nexus in the European Union. *Global Crime.* 15(3–4), pp. 259–274.

Mauro, P. (1995). Corruption and Growth. *Quarterly Journal of Economics.* 110(3), pp. 681–712.

Mauro, P. (1998). Corruption and the Composition of Government Expenditure. *Journal of Public Economics.* 69(2), pp. 263–279.

Médard, J.-F. (2007). Corruption in the Neo-Patrimonial States of Sub-Saharan Africa. In: Heidenheimer, A., Johnston, M. (eds). *Political Corruption: Concepts and Contexts.* 3rd ed. Piscataway, NJ: Transaction Publishers, pp. 379–402.

Mehlum, H., Moene, K., Torvik, R. (2006). Institutions and the Resource Curse. *Economic Journal.* 116(508), pp. 1–20.

Mills, A. (2012). *Causes of Corruption in Public Sector Institutions and Its Impact on Development: Turning What We Know into What We Do.* New York: UN Public Administration Network (UNPAN).

Moene, K., Søreide, T. (2016). Corruption Control. *Crime, Law and Social Change.* 66(2), pp. 147–163.

Mohtadi, H., Ross, M. L., Ruediger, S. (2016). Oil, Taxation and Transparency. In: *Oil, Middle East, and the Global Economy Conference, 1–2 April 2016, Los Angeles.* Los Angeles, CA: University of Southern California.

Nazaha. (2019). *Kuwait Integrity and Anti-Corruption Strategy 2019–2024.* Nazaha.

Nye, J. S. (1967). Corruption and Political Development: A Cost-Benefit Analysis. *American Political Science Review.* 61(2), pp. 417–427.

Obermayer, B., Obermaier, F. (2017). *The Panama Papers: Breaking the Story of How the Rich & Powerful Hide Their Money.* London: Oneworld Publications.

Passas, N. (1998). A Structural Analysis of Corruption: The Role of Criminogenic Asymmetries. *Transnational Organized Crime.* 4(1), pp. 42–55.

Persson, A., Rothstein, B., Teorell, J. (2013). Why Anticorruption Reforms Fail—Systemic Corruption as a Collective Action Problem. *Governance.* 26(3), pp. 449–471.

Peterson, J. (2007). Rulers, Merchants and Shaikhs in Gulf Politics: The Function of Family Networks. In: Al-Sharekh, A. (ed). *The Gulf Family: Kinship Policies and Modernity.* London: Saqi in association with London Middle East Institute, SOAS, pp. 21–36.

Phillips, J. (2008). Collecting Rent: A Comparative Analysis of Oil and Gas Fiscal Policy Regimes in Alberta, Canada and Norway. [Online]. Available from: https://papers.ssrn.com/sol3/papers.cfm?abstract_id=1140306.

Philp, M. (2015). The Definition of Political Corruption. In: Heywood, P. (ed). *Routledge Handbook of Political Corruption.* Abingdon: Routledge, pp. 17–29.

Pitcher, A., Moran, M., Johnston, M. (2009). Rethinking Patrimonialism and Neopatrimonialism in Africa. *African Studies Review.* 52(1), pp. 125–156.

Pradhan, S., Anderson, J., Hellman, J., Jones, G., Moore, B., Muller, H., Ryterman, R., Sutch, H. (2000). *Anticorruption in Transition: A Contribution to the Policy Debate.* Washington, DC: World Bank.

Rose-Ackerman, S. (1978). *Corruption: A Study in Political Economy.* Cambridge, MA: Academic Press.

Rose-Ackerman, S. (1999). *Corruption and Government: Causes, Consequences, and Reform.* Cambridge: Cambridge University Press.

Rose-Ackerman, S. (2001). Political Corruption and Democratic Structures. In: Jain, A. (ed). *The Political Economy of Corruption.* Abingdon: Routledge, pp. 35–62.

Ross, M. (2001). Does Oil Hinder Democracy? *World Politics.* 53(3), pp. 325–361.

Ross, M. (2012). *The Oil Curse: How Petroleum Wealth Shapes the Development of Nations.* Princeton, NJ: Princeton University Press.

Rothstein, B., Teorell, J. (2014). Causes of Corruption. In: Heywood, P. (ed). *Routledge Handbook of Political Corruption.* Abingdon: Routledge, pp. 79–94.

Rowe, E., Akman, T., Smith, R. G., Tomison, A. M. (2013). *Organised Crime and Public Sector Corruption: A Crime Scripts Analysis of Tactical Displacement Risks* (Trends & Issues in Crime and Criminal Justice No. 444). Canberra: Australian Institute of Criminology.

Sabrie, S., Hakala, P. (2013). *Kuwait's Political Crisis Deepens.* Brussels: European Union.

Sala-i-Martin, X., Subramanian, A. (2013). Addressing the Natural Resource Curse: An Illustration from Nigeria. *Journal of African Economies.* 22(4), pp. 570–615.

Salih, K. (1991). Kuwait: Political Consequences of Modernization, 1750–1986. *Middle Eastern Studies.* 27(1), pp. 46–66.

Salih, K. (2011). Kuwait Primary (Tribal) Elections 1975–2008: An Evaluative Study. *British Journal of Middle Eastern Studies.* 38(2), pp. 141–167.

Schjelderup, G. (2016). Secrecy Jurisdictions. *International Tax and Public Finance.* 23(1), pp. 168–189.

Scott, J. C. (1972). *Comparative Political Corruption.* Upper Saddle River, NJ: Prentice Hall.

Stapenhurst, F., Jacobs, K., Pelizzo, R. (2014). Corruption and Legislatures. *Public Integrity.* 16(3), pp. 285–304.

Stevens, P. (2008). *Kuwait Petroleum Corporation: Searching for Strategy in a Fragmented Oil Sector* (Working Paper No. 78). Stanford, CA: Program on Energy and Sustainable Development (PESD), Stanford University.

Tanzi, V. (1998). Corruption Around the World: Causes, Consequences, Scope, and Cures. *IMF Staff Papers.* 45(4), pp. 559–594.

Tanzi, V., Davoodi, H. (1997). *Corruption, Public Investment, and Growth* (IMF Working Papers 97/139). Washington, DC: IMF.

Teorell, J. (2007). *Corruption as an Institution: Rethinking the Nature and Origins of the Grabbing Hand* (Working Paper Series 2007:5). Gothenburg, Sweden: Quality of Government Institute, University of Gothenburg.

Tétreault, M. (2000). *Stories of Democracy: Politics and Society in Contemporary Kuwait.* New York: Columbia University Press.

Thomas, M., Meagher, P. (2004). *A Corruption Primer: An Overview of Concepts in the Corruption Literature* (Paper No. 04/03). College Park, MD: Center for Institutional Reform and the Informal Sector (IRIS), University of Maryland.

Thompson, D. (2000). *Ethics in Congress: From Individual to Institutional Corruption.* Washington, DC: Brookings Institution Press.

Transparency International. (2019). Corruption Perceptions Index: Overview. [Online]. [1 December 2019]. Available from: https://www.transparency.org/research/cpi/overview.

Treisman, D. (2000). The Causes of Corruption: A Cross-National Study. *Journal of Public Economics*. 76(3), pp. 339–457.

UK EITI Multi-Stakeholder Group. (2019). *2017 UK EITI Reconciliation and State of Industry Report*. London: UK EITI.

Ulrichsen, K. (2014). Politics and Opposition in Kuwait: Continuity and Change. *Journal of Arabian Studies*. 4(2), pp. 214–230.

UNCTAD. (2019). *World Investment Report 2019: Special Economic Zones*. New York: UN.

UNODC. (2003). *United Nations Guide on Anti-Corruption Policies*. New York: UN.

UNODC. (2004). *United Nations Handbook on Practical Anti-Corruption Measures for Prosecutors and Investigators*. New York: UN.

van Duyne, P. (1997). Organized Crime, Corruption and Power. *Crime, Law and Social Change*. 26(3), pp. 201–238.

Weber, M. (1978). *Economy and Society: An Outline of Interpretive Sociology*. Berkeley, CA: University of California Press.

Wiarda, H. (2015). *Corporatism and Comparative Politics: The Other Great ISM*. Abingdon: Routledge.

Wood, G. (2004). Business and Politics in a Criminal State: The Case of Equatorial Guinea. *African Affairs*. 103(413), pp. 547–567.

World Bank. (1997). *Helping Countries Combat Corruption: The Role of the World Bank*. Washington, DC: World Bank.

World Bank. (2018). World Bank Open Data. [Online]. Available from: http://data.worldbank.org.

Wouters, J., Ryngaert, C., Cloots, A. (2013). The International Legal Framework Against Corruption: Achievements and Challenges. *Melbourne Journal of International Law*. 14(1), pp. 205–280.

Ziouvas, D. (2018). International Asset Recovery and the United Nations Convention Against Corruption. In: King, C., Walker, C., Gurulé, J. (eds). *The Palgrave Handbook of Criminal and Terrorism Financing Law*. New York: Palgrave Macmillan, pp. 591–620.

# 3 Counter-corruption: Values and strategies

## 3.1 Introduction

Moving on from investigating the various issues pertaining to the corruption phenomenon in the previous chapter, this chapter aims to achieve two related objectives of the book (the second and fifth objectives). In terms of the second objective, this chapter further investigates the literature on corruption regarding two issues. The first issue is the principles and values that underpin counter-corruption efforts, which, from the viewpoint of the book, countries should attempt to instil in legal and political contexts before/while combating corruption. The second research area examines various counter-corruption strategies, each of which proceeds from a distinct philosophy. Essentially, the second objective is to understand these two issues both in general and in relation to Kuwait, to bring to the centre of the discussion the compliance of Kuwaiti counter-corruption efforts with universal principles and strategies. In terms of the fifth methodological objective, this chapter uses socio-legal methodology to ensure a fuller understanding of some of the subjects of this chapter. A qualitative-based study, which relies on semi-structured interviews, is adopted to answer, in part, the second objective of this book.

The chapter is divided into two substantive sections. Section 3.2 investigates legitimacy (including transparency, accountability, human rights, morality of law, and legal certainty) and effectiveness (including the issues of an effective legal framework and evidence-based policymaking) as two key counter-corruption values, in general and in relation to Kuwait. Section 3.3 investigates a number of counter-corruption strategies in both contexts. These include the universally identified strategies of social reforms, law enforcement efforts, and situational crime prevention (SCP).

## 3.2 Counter-corruption values

For the purposes of this book, the values to be considered should be treated as instrumental. Each value is not an end in itself, but represents a means that is intricately linked to the achievement of counter-corruption objectives. The values have a 'counter-corruption' functionality in that they are targeted at the root

*Table 3.1* CPI and World Bank Worldwide Governance Indicators in 2018

| *Country/ indicator* | *CPI* | *Control of corruption* | *Voice and accountability* | *Government effectiveness* | *Rule of law* | *Regulatory quality* | *Political stability* |
|---|---|---|---|---|---|---|---|
| Kuwait | 41 | –0.29 | –0.59 | –0.09 | 0.21 | –0.04 | 0.11 |
| United Kingdom | 80 | 1.83 | 1.38 | 1.34 | 1.64 | 1.76 | 0.05 |

causes of corruption. Inculcating these values is an indirect approach to combating corruption, which involves core principles that should be recognised as the initial conditions for the success of counter-corruption strategies. The analysis here is conducted within the corruption–governance nexus. Governance can be understood as 'the traditions and institutions by which authority in a country is exercised', including the process through which the government manages the state, the government's capacity to formulate policies, and the citizens' respect for, and the legitimacy of, the state institutions.[1] Because 'curtailing corruption requires addressing the causes of mis-governance',[2] it is necessary to instil values that relate to the broader context in which a state is governed. When institutionalised, counter-corruption values govern the process in which the state is administrated and pave the way for making counter-corruption laws enforceable, legitimate, and abiding. The correlation between the Corruption Perceptions Index (CPI) and the World Bank Worldwide Governance Indicators may signify that corruption is just one symptom of a more profound problem, as indicated in Table 3.1.[3]

The counter-corruption values should be considered in Kuwait for three reasons. First, Kuwait is a developing country that adopts a democratic regime, and therefore, it accommodates an environment that supports these values. Secondly, Kuwait suffers from corruption, or at least fosters favourable conditions for corruption to grow. So, it is necessary to adopt measures to combat this phenomenon and its drivers. In particular, because of the oil-based economic structure of Kuwait, and its relation to corruption, values such as transparency and accountability should be observed.[4] Thirdly, Kuwait is part of the global community that induces its members to respect and fulfil human rights, which renders 'human rights' a value that Kuwait also endorses. After all, the universality of the values studied here is a sufficient reason to call on Kuwait to adhere to them (as well as the explicit statements in its constitution).

1 Kaufmann, Kraay and Mastruzzi (2011, pp. 222–223).
2 Huther and Shah (2000, p. 2).
3 The source works as follows: 'Estimate of governance measured on a scale from approximately –2.5 to 2.5. Higher values correspond to better governance'. See World Bank (2019).
4 See chapter 2.3.4.3.

### 3.2.1 *Legitimacy*

As an abstract concept, legitimacy is open to broad interpretation. As Beetham explains, it can be seen from three different perspectives. The first is the legal perspective, which focuses on legal validity, that is, power enjoys legitimacy 'where its acquisition and exercise conform to established law'. Second, the perspective of moral and political philosophy considers power legitimate when 'the rules governing it are justifiable according to rationally defensible normative principles'. Third, social scientists see legitimacy in a social context and argue that power is legitimate when those who are subject to it believe it to be so.[5] Because this book adopts a socio-legal approach to issues of corruption, this section is concerned with the moral and political philosophy perspective of legitimacy. It is important to step outside of the legal paradigm and question whether the law per se is justifiable and consistent with the prevailing normative ideas and values. Thus, the moral and philosophical conception of legitimacy may be more helpful here in providing universal values than social science, which may refer to values that are relative and variant across communities. However, an applied approach to moral philosophy will be used here. In outline only, this section applies existing concepts and values to the situation in Kuwait to analyse the legitimacy of counter-corruption laws in Kuwait.

Legitimacy performs a particular function for laws. It can provide the moral grounds that can secure the voluntary obedience of people to the laws.[6] Tyler put forward a normative perspective on why people obey the law. People will abstain from breaking laws when they regard them as legitimate, even if such laws conflict with their personal interests because they 'view the legal authority they are dealing with as having a legitimate right to dictate their behavior'.[7] This normative perspective contrasts with the instrumental approach, which explains that people's obedience depends on self-interest: a deterrence-based framework of incentives and punishments under the influence of the possession of power and resources.[8] The moral position of this book is that promoting the legitimacy of counter-corruption laws is premised on a normative perspective that is helpful in securing individuals' voluntary compliance with the law without the need to allocate an enormous amount of resources to compel people to obey the law.[9] As people are expected to voluntarily defer to the authority of state institutions, legitimacy helps the state to preserve most of their resources and efforts for the achievement of other goals.[10] Beetham argues that legitimacy, in turn, has effects on the 'degree of cooperation' and 'quality of performance' expected from people, enabling the state to perform more effectively.[11] So, the

5 Beetham (2013, pp. 4–8).
6 Ibid., p. 26.
7 Tyler (2006b, p. 25).
8 Beetham (2013).
9 Tyler (2006a).
10 Beetham (2013).
11 Ibid., p. 28.

legitimacy of a government is arguably a pre-condition for government-led counter-corruption efforts. The legitimacy of counter-corruption laws is contingent on the congruency between such laws and abstract universally identified values. Consequently, any discrepancy risks the erosion of the law's legitimacy.

People's obedience to the law can be linked strongly to procedural justice. Procedural justice is concerned with 'the fairness of the procedures through which institutions and authorities exercise authority'.[12] The normative view regarding when people decide whether the procedures are fair attaches more significance to process control than decision control, in the sense that 'people value having the chance to state their case' rather than having the ability to control the decisions.[13]

The importance of procedural justice resonated with the Kuwaiti experts interviewed, though they expressed it as 'fairness'.[14] They were asked: what is more important? Effectiveness or fairness? Two participants readily responded that fairness is more important than effectiveness.[15] They shared the view that laws should be fair, whatever the aims of laws are. Another participant argued that fairness is more significant than effectiveness.[16] MP-2 perceived that the fairness requirement is important because it can safeguard individuals and their freedom and rights against arbitrary practices by the executive authority. Judge-1 underlined the priority that should be given to the value of fairness: 'as a judge, I am not as much concerned with the result of the trial as whether the defendant has been able to enjoy his procedural safeguards'.[17] Fairness, as understood by Judge-1, is mainly process-based and relates to the substantive and procedural safeguards provided for the suspects by the criminal laws. When a prosecutor was asked about the importance of fairness, he/she actively defended it to the extent that he/she justified the arguably criticised judicial implementation of the money laundering offence (ML offence) on a fairness-based basis.[18] The view of Prosecutor-2 was consistent with the view of MP-2, that is, 'the effectiveness is needed, but on the basis of fairness'.

The value of legitimacy was also recognised by NGO-2, who stated that the value of fairness is more important than effectiveness because it is 'the essence of governing'. In order to enjoy legitimacy, NGO-2 asserted that the state should take into account the value of fairness in its dealings with people. NGO-2 pointed out that the belief in the importance of value over effectiveness can have many applications in the way his/her NGO works:

> We received many reports. After we had assessed them for two years, we decided not to proceed with them because the source of information was

12 Tyler (2006a, p. 328).
13 Tyler (2006b, pp. 115–116).
14 For example, Judge-1; MP-2; Official-4; Official-2; NGO-2.
15 Official-2; Official-4.
16 MP-2.
17 Judge-1.
18 Prosecutor-2. For the criticised implementation, see chapters 4.3.5 and 4.4.1.

> wittingly kept unknown. The reason behind our decision was that we thought that any information should be obtained within the legal framework; we did not want to encourage violating the law and other dishonest practices.[19]

In contrast, NGO-3 argued that in matters related to corruption, the value of effectiveness must be prioritised over fairness. He/she explained that 'since the unfair laws can achieve the effects that are intended, you may need sometimes to go beyond the fairness to hold the corrupt accountable'. His/her 'radical' view, though inconsistent with the argument of this chapter, can be justified or understood based on the professional history of that participant. As he/she narrated, the requirement of fairness can be easily exploited in the interest of defendant: 'I have been a lawyer and found that, in practice, the corrupt usually rant about the procedural safeguards as a repetitive rhetoric in courtrooms'.[20]

The Kuwaiti Constitution reflects the philosophy of democracy. It reflects: democratic rule, the role played by the nation in supporting human civilisation, and the pursuit of having a higher international standing.[21] It contends that the 'system of government is democratic; sovereignty is vested in the Nation as the source of all authority'.[22] What legitimises the state further is that the formal institutionalisation of the decision-making process, since 1962, resembles, in its essence, the customary rules of pre-1962 Kuwait society, regarding a partnership in decision making between the rulers and the ruled.[23] As this book is concerned with legitimacy beyond adherence to the established rules in a given country, the meaning of legitimacy should be analysed with reference to the very nature of democracy.

The Kuwaiti Constitution also emphasises the core democratic values upon which the political communities in democracies may be based. Described as 'the basic foundations of Kuwaiti society' and 'public rights and obligations', the Constitution stresses that freedom, justice, and equality are the community's essential pillars;[24] the achievement of social justice is the basis of the national economy, taxation, and public expenditure;[25] and individuals and groups should enjoy the right to address the public authorities.[26] In such an environment, procedural justice can potentially flourish. Enjoying values like justice, equality, and freedom, the Kuwaiti people may be as much concerned with the fairness of procedures as with the favourability of outcomes (based on the normative perspective). By adopting democracy, Kuwait has committed itself to subjecting the power relations and the wielding of authority in Kuwait to the globally identified values of the civilised world.

19 NGO-2.
20 NGO-3.
21 Preamble of the Kuwaiti Constitution. The English version of the Kuwaiti Constitution can be found at <https://www.constituteproject.org/constitution/Kuwait_1992.pdf?lang=en>.
22 Article 6.
23 Salih (1991).
24 Article 7.
25 Articles 20 and 24.
26 Article 45.

*Table 3.2* Democracy ranking of Kuwait

| *Index* | *Rank* |
|---|---|
| Economist Intelligence Unit's Democracy Index | In 2017, Kuwait scored 3.85 (on a scale of 0 to 10) and this puts it under the category of 'Authoritarian Regime'. |
| Global Democracy Ranking | In 2014–2015, Kuwait ranked 84 and was classified as a country with 'low' democracy. |

Yet, democracy suffers from societal and cultural compromises in Kuwait. One relevant feature is that Islam is the religion of the state of Kuwait, and its norms are a main source for its legislation.[27] There seems to be a hybrid conception of legitimacy in Kuwait where democratic norms, on the one hand, and Islamic norms, on the other, form two fundamental pillars to legitimise state practices. In general, culture and religion can be considered two determinants that 'affect the emergence and survival of democracy'.[28] In particular, the debate about the compatibility of the Islamic version of democracy (*shura*) and Western secular democracy raises some issues, regarding the source of legislation and political equality.[29] For example, democracy requires that every adult citizen has the right to participate in the democratic process, while in Kuwait, women were only enfranchised in 2006.[30] This problem becomes starker, especially in view of the fact that women's right to engage in elections is a sensitive issue in Islam.[31] With Islam being a source of legitimacy in Kuwait, democracy in the Western sense can be characterised as imperfect. This incongruence inevitably has negative implications for both democracy and the development of relevant counter-corruption values, as reflected by many democracy indices (Table 3.2).[32,33]

Moreover, the democratic experience in Kuwait faces multiple challenges that are responsible for its 'precarious democracy'.[34] The lack of a democratic culture and the imbalance of the power relationships encourage the phenomenon of corruption in Kuwait.[35] Faced with these challenges, this section suggests that values should be institutionalised within the state practices to legitimise its counter-corruption efforts and thus balance the adverse effects of the challenges mentioned. Five values will be considered in the following sections: transparency, accountability, human rights, morality of law, and legal certainty. These values will be examined in the abstract and in Kuwait to investigate the extent

27 Kuwaiti Constitution, art.2.
28 Clark, Golder and Golder (2017, p. 223).
29 Karagiannis (2017).
30 Salih (2011).
31 Karagiannis (2017).
32 See <https://infographics.economist.com/2018/DemocracyIndex/>.
33 See <http://democracyranking.org/wordpress/rank/democracy-ranking-2016/>.
34 See Al-Najjar (2000, p. 247).
35 See chapter 2.3.4.

to which Kuwait incorporates these values in its system as an integral part of its broader commitment to the principles of democracy.

### 3.2.1.1 *Transparency*

Transparency can be defined as 'legal, political, and institutional structures that make information about the internal characteristics of a government and society available to actors both inside and outside of the domestic political system'.[36] In terms of legitimacy and people's obedience to the law, the focus will be on 'transparency inwards' such that those outside the government can observe what is happening inside it.[37] Transparency can be achieved through 'full disclosure', which involves a series of procedures that include the collection of data by governmental institutions, and the auditing and dissemination of data to keep people informed about what is really happening around them.[38] Because counter-corruption incorporates transparency as a value in the public sphere, owing to its role in detecting corrupt practices, governments must be open in providing reliable information about their actions to prevent the problem of 'information asymmetry' between the rulers and the ruled.[39] Thus, transparency is a response that limits the principal–agent problem, in which the officials (agents) violate the interests of their principals (the citizens).[40] Transparency is considered here in terms of openness (or public disclosure), which refers to the degree of inclination of governments, as insiders, to share information with, and disclose their actions to, the public as outsiders. Freedom of information (FOI) laws are one of the most important applications of openness.

Transparency, through public disclosure, will encourage healthier governmental practices. The transparency of financial institutions can be employed to assess the efficiency of the government regarding the management of its expenditure. The leaks related to the Panama Papers galvanised the United Kingdom to declare, at the 2016 International Anti-Corruption Summit, that it would establish a 'public register of beneficial ownership of foreign companies owning or buying property in the UK' as a transparency measure to counter issues, such as corruption and tax evasion.[41] Furthermore, corruption is a form of harmful rent-seeking behaviour that usually occurs opaquely. But when transparency is promoted in transactions, the costs of corruption will be higher since any potential corruption will be more noticeable. This situation will affect the behaviours of venal officials and will induce influential groups to resort to safer means to achieve their purposes, such a lobbying, which takes place in the open.[42]

36 Finel and Lord (1999, p. 316).
37 For further analysis, see Piotrowski (2017, p. 158).
38 Ward (2004, p. 42).
39 Lindstedt and Naurin (2010, p. 303).
40 Bellver and Kaufmann (2005).
41 Grimwood (2016, p. 7).
42 Lambsdorff (2002).

Despite its importance as a democratic value, the Kuwaiti Constitution does not explicitly refer to transparency. Nevertheless, the adoption of democratic rule necessitates, inter alia, the accountability of the government and the parliament in terms of their acts towards the people and, as discussed above, people should have sufficient knowledge about government practices in order to hold the government accountable. The absence of articulation of the idea of transparency into words, therefore, does not mean that Kuwait is entitled to disclaim any responsibility for transparency. It is asked then: what is the particular importance of transparency for Kuwait and what are the attitudes of policymakers to transparency in Kuwait? The following are examples of arenas where transparency has achieved some progress.

Kuwait has made notable achievements in terms of budgetary transparency.[43] The State Audit Bureau Act (SAB Act) 30/1964 created the State Audit Bureau (SAB) as an independent oversight body, adjunct to the National Assembly, to achieve effective control over public finance. It publishes online, inter alia, reports about the results of the SAB's audit reports of the governmental departments and reports on the closing accounts of the financial department.[44] The oldest report dates back to 1995 when just one report was published online. But in subsequent years, there has been a noticeable sophistication in the reports. The increase in reports, perhaps, could be an indicator of the state's positive stance towards transparency.

The Public Tenders Act (PTA) 49/2016 established the Central Agency for Public Tenders (CAPT) and has achieved important developments that are favourable for transparency in public procurements. The Act requires the obligatory disclosure of public procurement-related information.[45] The CAPT publishes online the news of tenders, the details of the latest open tenders (including tender files, price, and bidding type), downloadable meeting records and minutes and other services pertinent to the decision-making process regarding public procurement.[46] Also, in Section 48 of the PTA, the process of opening the envelopes of bids must be published online on the CAPT's website.

The Anti-Corruption Authority and Financial Disclosure Act (ACAA) 2/2016 stipulates that one of the Kuwaiti Anti-Corruption Authority's (hereinafter Nazaha) objectives is to establish transparency and integrity in economic transactions and public administration to achieve the good governance of public funds.[47] In line with Article 52(5) of the UNCAC, the ACAA states that high-ranking officials and politicians must submit a financial disclosure of their property and assets (including their minors and those under their guardianship and custodianship).[48] These financial disclosures are investigated by Nazaha to

43 Al-Shehabi (2017).

44 Available at <https://www.sabq8.org/sabweb/home2.aspx>.

45 PTA, s.93(1)(2).

46 See <https://capt.gov.kw/en/>.

47 ACAA, s.4(1).

48 Ibid., ss.30 and 32.

achieve some degree of control over any potential, unjustifiable enrichment that may occur.[49]

The Conflict of Interests Act (CIA) 13/2018 was added to the regulatory regime. Although prohibiting the conflict of interests was already recognised in the Constitution,[50] through the Civil Service Act (CSA) 15/1979, and the Protection of Public Funds Act (PPFA) 1/1993, the CIA represents a leap towards promoting transparency in the public sphere. Not only does it deem conflicts of interest a corruption crime, it also imposes a statutory obligation on incumbents to declare and remove any conflict of interests.[51]

Despite these promising instances indicating that openness seems to be promoted by the state, transparency in Kuwait is in its infancy. Notably, Kuwait lacks any general FOI law. The fact that Kuwait has not legislated for a general FOI law contravenes its international commitment to the UNCAC, which was signed in 2003 and ratified in 2006.[52] According to Articles 10 and 13, 'each State Party shall … take such measures as may be necessary to enhance transparency in its public administration…' and to ensure 'that the public has effective access to information'. What makes the commitment to transparency more binding is that Nazaha is responsible for implementing the UNCAC.[53]

Although there have been attempts to bolster transparency, the development of the value of transparency can be characterised as piecemeal. But more effort is pending. The Kuwait Counter-Corruption Strategy 2019–2024 (Strategy 2019–2024) considers the transparency of the public administration of public finance as the 'First Priority' in relation to the reform of the public sector.[54] To achieve that, the Strategy 2019–2024 policy document has adopted five initiatives: ensuring FOI, regulating electoral campaign financing, enhancing the compliance with the financial disclosure system, preventing corruption in public procurement, and inducing governmental bodies to regularly publish information about their public activities.[55] With the issuance of the Strategy 2019–2024, the future of transparency in Kuwait could take a different tack based on two indicators. The first is that the FOI law has been included as one of the policymakers' initiatives. As the Strategy illustrates, serious steps have already been taken by stakeholders, and a draft of the FOI Act has been prepared and sent to the National Assembly, who will discuss and enact it. Second, Nazaha is preparing a draft of the 'Guiding Principles' to support government bodies to periodically disseminate information about their works.[56]

49 Ibid., s.31. See chapter 4.3.4.
50 Article 120.
51 CIA, ss.4-5. See chapter 4.3.3.2.
52 Ratification of the UN Convention against Corruption Act 47/2006.
53 ACAA, s.3(2).
54 See Nazaha (2019, p. 18).
55 See ibid., p. 21.
56 See ibid.

The potential for introducing a general FOI provision in Kuwaiti law has been recognised by different Kuwaiti professional experts. MP-3 opined that 'there is no doubt that FOI legislation contributes to the prevention and combating of corruption'. He/she argued that the availability of information leads to the truth, and such truth empowers the National Assembly and the press to shed light on corruption.[57] Another participant stated that FOI encourages effective citizenship: 'Of course, this type of legislation renders each citizen responsible and empowered to oversee the activities of his/her government'.[58] NGO-2 believed that FOI legislation can achieve positive effects: 'where there is light, the officials will work correctly'. FOI in Kuwait is of particular importance, especially in relation to the improper appointment of senior officials, because people will be able to oversee the appointees and whether they are entitled to take up the position of public office.[59]

However, NGO-2 stated that FOI will not solve all of the problems. He/she argued that there are some governmental activities that involve technicalities that are too complex to be comprehended by the 'common citizens', such as the expenditure of the government, and that this complexity may limit the effectiveness of popular oversight. NGO-3 also said that the effectiveness of FOI legislation largely depends on the number of exceptions contained. For example, the 'current proposed FOI legislation' exempts vital sectors, such as the military sector, and therefore, the intended purpose of the legislation cannot, in part, be achieved.[60] However, NGO-3 confirmed that FOI legislation, when implemented effectively, can have positive effects, since it empowers the people and promotes the role of accountability: 'the circulation of information among people deters the officeholders from engaging in any corrupt activity'.

The non-governmental organisations (NGOs) in Kuwait have played a role as stakeholders by inducing the policymakers to do more in regard to the counter-corruption policy.[61] In 2013, the Kuwait Transparency Society (KTS), TI chapter in Kuwait, prepared a detailed proposition about establishing transparency and openness between the government and individuals and regulating the right to information.[62] Furthermore, the Kuwaiti Society for the Follow-Up Evaluation of Parliament (KSFEPK) was established in 2017 to follow the activities of MPs within and outside the National Assembly and present their parliamentary works to citizens and NGOs.[63]

With the advancements in information technology in the twenty-first century, the endeavours should not stop at promoting the right to know. Collaborative

57 MP-3.
58 Official-4.
59 NGO-2
60 NGO-3.
61 Khodr (2014).
62 The draft is available at <www.transparency.org.kw.au-ti.org/upload/Qanwon_Shafaf/pdf/2.pdf>.
63 See <www.alraimedia.com/Home/Details?Id=97107ba6-c183-44f7-97fe-dd87a92b81b3>.

transparency, where public decision making becomes participatory between the government, NGOs and business,[64] ought to be incorporated into the culture of the state. With the right to form and join societies[65] and the pre-existence of the Kuwait Information Technology Society, which was established in 1982 to promote the use of information technology in both governmental and non-governmental sectors,[66] Kuwait should strive to be a member of the multilateral initiative of the Open Government Partnership (OGP) by endorsing the Open Government Declaration.[67] There are several reasons why Kuwait should join the OGP. First, the channels through which the public accesses policymaking process in Kuwait are 'more institutionalised' than in other countries in the region.[68] This step, then, may have a legitimising effect on the Kuwait democratic regime in general and specifically on its efforts to combat corruption. Secondly, enthusiasm for joining the OGP could encourage Kuwait to develop relevant local policies. To be eligible to join the OGP, Kuwait would need to achieve – based on governance indicators consisting of public data – 75% in four main pillars: fiscal transparency, access to information, public official assets disclosure, and citizen engagement.[69]

While transparency plays a role in tackling the political causes of corruption in Kuwait, transparency also can dilute the corrupting effects of the economic structure and the central governance of the national economy.[70] The transparency of the extractive sector should be applied in countries that are rich in natural resources (such as oil).[71] In this context, the Extractive Industries Transparency Initiative (EITI) is an important global initiative aimed at better governance of natural resources, including the promotion of transparency and the accountability of managing natural resources. The EITI has demonstrated that the lack of both transparency in managing natural resources and monitoring of the revenues often leads to corruption.[72] The Kuwait Petroleum Corporation (KPC) proclaims that it operates 'on the basis of trust, respect, fairness, transparency and honesty'.[73] Pursuant to the SAB Act, the finances of the KPC are subject to the financial oversight to the SAB. Thus, Kuwait, on the level of the Gulf Cooperation Council (GCC), enjoys '(relatively) publicly and independently audited, transparent final accounts of its budget'.[74] In 2008, a working paper on the KPC illustrated that, unlike other national oil companies, the KPC does

64 Fung, Graham and Weil (2007).
65 Kuwaiti Constitution, art.80.
66 See <http://kits.org.kw>.
67 See <https://www.opengovpartnership. org/open-government-declaration>.
68 Khodr (2014, p. 288).
69 See <https://www.opengovpartnership. org/how-join>.
70 See chapter 2.3.4.3.
71 Sala-i-Martin and Subramanian (2013).
72 Extractive Industries Transparency Initiative (2016).
73 KPC is responsible for the oil sector in Kuwait. See <https://www.kpc.com.kw/>.
74 Al-Shehabi (2017, p. 6).

produce fairly comprehensive annual reports and audited accounts, which, theoretically, make it possible to assess its financial performance; in practice, however, this claim is suspect, as 'reflected in a succession of missed targets and a recent series of serious accidents', according to the SAB's reports.[75]

The potential of the EITI is that it can exert greater pressure on Kuwait to promote transparency. This influence is absent in this instance. Arguably, its oil wealth deters Kuwait from seeking assistance from the international financial institutions, such as the International Monetary Fund (IMF), which could make its funding and assistance contingent on a more transparent government.[76] In its efforts to harness the instrumental role of transparency in countering corruption, the KTS has prepared a proposition for the policymakers to join the initiative and has urged the KPC to provide an annual report about its activities that are pertinent to the initiative.[77] More importantly, the interest of the Strategy 2019–2024 in transparency heralds a change in policy whereby the state has begun to heed the need for transparency in any strategy to combat corruption. However, what seems odd is that the Strategy has come without any emphasis on the necessity to promote transparency in the extractive sectors, though it pays attention to issues that arguably raise no concerns in the political reality (such as campaign financing). Nevertheless, considering transparency as a priority in the Strategy is general enough – and a promising step – to elicit the attention of policymakers in the future to other important domains where transparency plays a key role in combating corruption.[78]

#### 3.2.1.2 *Accountability*

Accountability is a relational concept that refers to the answerability of 'agents and others for whom they perform tasks or who are affected by the tasks they perform'.[79] Some scholars have deconstructed the accountability concept into two dimensions: answerability and enforcement. First, answerability revolves around the notion that A being accountable to B presumes a readiness to inform about A's decisions and to explain them. Second, enforcement implies sanctioning systems and the possibility that the accountable official suffers consequences.[80] Two sub-types of accountability will be discussed: political accountability (where the forums are political actors, such as elected representatives and the electorate) and administrative/legal accountability (where the forums are administrative and legal bodies).[81]

Political accountability revolves around the propriety of politicians' and officials' conduct, not with respect to their legality, but with regard to whether

75 See Stevens (2008, p. 6).
76 Ross (2011).
77 See <www.transparency.org.kw.au-ti.org/upload/Qanwon_Shafaf/pdf/4.pdf>.
78 See Nazaha (2019, p. 21).
79 Bovens, Goodin and Schillemans (2014, p. 6).
80 Schedler (1999).
81 See Bovens, Goodin and Schillemans (2014).

such conduct is exercised in a manner that is endorsed as satisfactory by those to whom the politicians are accountable.[82] In the parliamentary system, one crucial aspect of political accountability is ministerial responsibility.[83] Administrative/legal accountability 'is based on relationships between a controlling party outside the agency and members of the organization'.[84] Both rely 'on the existence of state agencies that are legally empowered … to take actions ranging from routine oversight to criminal sanctions'.[85] Independent institutions are established to act as auxiliary forums that help political principals hold politicians and officials accountable before the civil and criminal courts.[86] In administrative accountability, accounts are rendered to administrative bodies such as ombudsmen, inspectorates, and regulatory agencies, whereas in legal accountability, accounts are given to legal bodies, such as courts.[87]

The system in Kuwait embodies political and legal aspects of the accountability mechanisms. First, the political accountability in Kuwait takes three forms: the government's accountability to the Amir, the government's accountability to the National Assembly, and the National Assembly's accountability to the electorate. The focus here is on the two latter forms because of their direct relevance to counter-corruption issues. Although the government's political accountability to the National Assembly takes several forms,[88] ministerial responsibility has been the key tool on the part of the National Assembly to tackle corruption in many instances. According to one interviewee, the politicians, and in particular the ministers, are more accountable than other governmental actors, since ministers are the Achilles' heel in terms of political accountability.[89] The accountability of the National Assembly to the electorate is another form of political accountability. In Kuwait, the parliament is elected for four years.[90] After the end of this period, people have the opportunity to sanction and reassess the performance of each MP.

Second, the administrative/legal accountability mechanisms are essential forms of accountability to combat corruption. The Strategy 2019–2024 deemed the promotion of public accountability to be the 'Fourth Priority' in relation to the reform of the public sector. The Strategy contains multiple initiatives pertaining to the legal and administrative accountability mechanisms.[91] The following is a brief discussion of these mechanisms as reflected in a network of formal channels to hold the public authorities and officeholders accountable.

82 Philp (2001).
83 See Dicey (1989).
84 Romzek and Dubnick (1987, p. 229).
85 O'Donnell (1998, p. 117).
86 Bovens (2005).
87 Bovens, Goodin and Schillemans (2014).
88 Kuwaiti Constitution, arts.98–102.
89 MP-2.
90 Kuwaiti Constitution, art.83.
91 See Nazaha (2019, p. 19).

There are detailed forms of administrative accountability in Kuwait, such as the Government Performance Follow-Up Agency, the Financial Controllers Bureau (FCB), the SAB, Nazaha, and the Kuwait Financial Intelligence Unit (KFIU). For example, the SAB exercises reactive and proactive oversight over the public finance of the public bodies and state-owned companies. These entities are accountable to the SAB in terms of justifying and explaining any comments or irregularities detected by the SAB reports and informing them regarding what they have done about them.[92] Noticeably, the Strategy 2019–2024 directs most of its public accountability-related initiatives to this financial oversight. It focuses on public finance through developing more effective practices of financial scrutiny and inspection. It also concentrates on developing general guidelines to secure effective accountability of the state-owned companies.[93] Based on the reports of the SAB and other experts, the Strategy shows that policymakers have become more attentive to the issue of public finance. This type of accountability has a crucial function in the energy sector. The management of public finances is problematic, especially in a state rich in resources like Kuwait.[94]

In terms of legal accountability, the criminal liability of officials is one mechanism under the Penal Code and the counter-corruption laws.[95] The Trial of Ministers Act (TMA) 88/1995 has also established the Court of Ministers as a special court, dedicated to trying ministers who have engaged in corruption crimes. Moreover, in relation to the illicit enrichment offence (IEO), high-ranking officeholders are accountable to Nazaha to submit financial disclosures and to justify any unexplained increase in their wealth.[96] The Strategy 2019–2024 focuses in particular on the improvement of the IEO: it aims to revise the existing provisions of the IEO and provides, on a regular basis, information about IEO cases that have already been investigated and adjudicated.[97]

The judicial review of the government and prosecutors' decisions is another form of legal accountability. The Administrative Disputes Act (ADA) 20/1981 allows for both individuals and legal persons to file a lawsuit against a governmental body to challenge its administrative decisions. The Act specifies four grounds of judicial review: *ultra vires* (lack of legal power to issue a decision), procedural impropriety, unlawfulness, and abuse of discretion.[98] The court will review the legality of the decision challenged and examine the facts and circumstances upon which it was based to identify whether it complies with the law.[99] The remedies available to the court are quashing the administrative decision and

92 SAB Act, ss.1, 2, 5, 7, 8, 9, 26, 31, and 55.
93 See Nazaha (2019, p. 19).
94 See chapter 2.3.4.3.
95 See chapter 4.3.
96 ACAA, s.32.
97 See Nazaha (2019, p. 19).
98 ADA, s.4.
99 See Case No. 282/1998, 24/5/1999 (Supreme Court – Administrative Court).

ordering the government body to pay compensation to the parties involved.[100] Judicial review is also applied to the decisions of prosecutors to terminate an investigation. According to the Criminal Justice Act (CJA) 17/1960, sections 102–104, victims and their heirs are entitled to challenge such a decision, within two months, before the criminal court.

Following this brief description of some of the existing political and administrative/legal accountability mechanisms in Kuwait, it should be asked: are they effective? The following discussion addresses the practical implementation of political and legal accountability, respectively.

The application of ministerial responsibility has not secured the intended effect in combating corruption. The expansion and fragmentation of government activities in Kuwait, such as the creation of agencies at arm's length, has started to diminish the concept of ministerial responsibility.[101] Also, on some occasions, ministers are vulnerable to the influence of their deputy ministers, because the tenure of the latter is often longer.[102] Lawyer-3 stressed that in such cases, the factual responsible for the minister becomes the deputy minister. With these developments, the ministerial responsibility doctrine in Kuwait should be recast. There may be a delegation of political accountability of ministers to the chiefs of these kinds of authorities and other senior officials, commensurate with the powers enjoyed by the latter so that they are directly accountable to the National Assembly. When asked about the reality of ministerial accountability in Kuwait, MP-2 responded that 'it is hard to give an ultimate answer. Sometimes, the minister is politically responsible for the acts of his/her officials. But the overlap of responsibilities within the state apparatuses obfuscates the accountability'.

Another shortcoming is that the National Assembly, in general, does not play its role effectively in holding the government accountable for its corrupt practices. When asked about its role, MP-2 responded that it is hard to say that the National Assembly is effectively performing its role in combating corruption. MP-2 stressed that some MPs participate in the efforts against corruption, while others do not. The MPs exercise their authority on an individual basis: 'the current situation does not create any opportunity for potential collective actions'.[103] MP-3 said that, nowadays, the National Assembly is tolerant of corruption, or is even itself a vital actor in corruption. Its role in combating corruption is absent, which contributes to the proliferation of corruption within the government: 'the corruption of the legislative authority is one of the most serious patterns of corruption and we cannot depend on the parliament in combating corruption'.[104]

MP-3 imputed the National Assembly's weak role, in part, to the mechanism of election and, therefore, the attitudes of the winning MPs: 'an MP can keep

100 ADA, ss.5–6.
101 See Kuwait Ministry of Justice (2017).
102 Lawyer-3.
103 MP-2.
104 MP-3.

his/her office as long as the government offers him/her a package of services that he/she can provide for his/her constituents with'. Thus, MPs cannot effectively challenge the government that is eager to support such MPs. The result is that the MP is captive to the desires of the constituents, and the loyalty of the MP is not to the state, but to the constituents who support him/her during the election and to the government, which secures his/her membership. [105] NGO-3 argued that the National Assembly does not perform the role that the Constitution has entrusted it with. The mechanism of election and the distribution of constituencies encourage the people to vote based on social factors, which result in 'the services MPs' who endeavour to meet the desires of constituents: 'No MP can work correctly in this climate'.[106]

NGO-2 put forward the rather radical view that the National Assembly is part of the corruption scene. The interviewee gave an example that the other GCC states, which have no parliament, have achieved progress according to all of the international indicators, including the CPI: 'at worst, they may have one corrupt authority [executive], but not two'. NGO-2 concluded the interview with an ironic question: 'How can you solve people problems if the policeman himself is corrupt?'[107] Such analysis has implications for the National Assembly's accountability to the electorate. This accountability depends on many factors, such as the existence of a system that forces politicians to confront the electorate.[108] MP-3 stated that the accountability of parliament is ineffective. Among other reasons, this is because the popular oversight is weak, and its weakness is largely driven by causes related to the inherent features of Kuwaiti society and the interrelationships within it.[109]

Official-4 explained that the vulnerability of each MP to the surrounding political climate represents the problem inherent in the National Assembly's efforts against corruption: 'when the National Assembly decides to take an action against a specific corruption scandal/case, the decision is taken on political rather than technical grounds'.[110] But the criteria of political accountability are often contestable given 'the fluid, contingent, and ambiguous character of political agendas and political norms'.[111] One participant pessimistically concluded that 'as far as I know, there is no single interpellation that could solve the problem'.[112] According to Official-4, the political accountability in Kuwait then raises two problems. First, some cases are not referred to the investigative authorities, perhaps because of the impunity of the corrupt or because of a political compromise between the MP(s) and the responsible parties. Second, some

105 Ibid.
106 NGO-3.
107 NGO-2.
108 Lederman, Loayza and Soares (2005).
109 See chapter 2.3.4.
110 Official-4. NGO-2 also raised the same point.
111 Bovens (2005, p. 187).
112 NGO-1.

corruption cases are referred to the investigative authorities without sufficient evidence just to satisfy the public.[113]

Lawyer-3 explained the reasons responsible for the weak role of National Assembly. First, the formation of the National Assembly hinders effective accountability, especially the fact that one-third of the MPs are appointed by the government.[114] Second, for the other two-thirds, the intervention of the government through the 'slush funds' and other means has a great influence on the attitudes of the MPs, especially in the light of the broader social context: 'in 2012, when the people could overcome those two obstacles, the government changed the rules of the game by altering the mechanism of election'.[115] So, it is expected that the National Assembly has 'minimal control over the government's agenda' despite its critical role in Kuwait.[116] Lawyer-3 stated that the current parliamentary efforts (including legislation and oversight efforts) to combat corruption are the only efforts that have been allowed by the government and that the recent counter-corruption efforts could not have been fulfilled without the support of the government. Therefore, Lawyer-3 had a radical view on the political accountability of the government. Lawyer-3 went on to say that although the ministers are readily held accountable in practice, such accountability is sterile: 'The PM should be the first accountable politician in Kuwait because he is the factual administrator of the state'.

Lawyer-3's view is largely consistent with the argument of this book: due to factors mainly related to both the structure of the political institutions and the political economy of Kuwait, the government, and the ruling family in particular, enjoy a considerable degree of autonomy from any influence, especially internal influence (such as the citizens).[117] This situation corresponds to the public policy literature, which suggests that policies may be adopted when the decision-makers 'become convinced that their state is relatively deprived, or that some need exists to which other states in their "league" have already responded'.[118] Rather than being answerable to the people, the Kuwaiti government seems to have a fear of falling behind other GCC states, which could cause damage to Kuwait's international reputation and standing. This conclusion does not undermine the entire value of the government's accountability to the National Assembly and people, but this analysis precisely conveys the view that the government is not accountable to the people as much as to the global community, and that the decisions in Kuwait are prone to, and shaped by, external influences. For example, although corruption is not a new phenomenon in Kuwait, the Kuwaiti government met Lambsdorff (the creator of the CPI) in 2018 and stated that counter-corruption was a serious issue that should be prioritised in

113 Official-4.
114 Lawyer-3. On this point, see chapter 2.3.4.2.2.
115 Ibid.
116 Khodr (2014, p. 288).
117 See Ehteshami (2003). See also chapter 2.3.4.
118 See Walker (1969, p. 897).

*Table 3.3* CPI of selected GCC countries in 2016–2018

| *Country/year* | *2016* | *2017* | *2018* |
|---|---|---|---|
| Kuwait | 41 | 39 | 41 |
| Saudi Arabia | 46 | 49 | 49 |
| Qatar | 61 | 63 | 62 |
| UAE | 66 | 71 | 70 |

its agenda.[119] Such steps were taken directly when the PM expressed his dissatisfaction with Kuwait's rank in the CPI; Kuwait's counterparts in the GCC have made progress in the index (see Table 3.3).[120] But with the advent of the Strategy 2019–2024, Kuwait policymakers claim that this is a new era where no-one is immune from accountability – a claim that is yet to be proved.

Regarding legal accountability, the interviewees acknowledged that, when it comes to combating corruption, the courts should come to the fore, as they have the exclusive jurisdiction to impose sanctions on the corrupt.[121] But some participants made some comments on the relationship of courts with the overall counter-corruption process. MP-3 noted that the courts' role in combating corruption is strongly linked to the pre-trial proceedings. That said, the existing criminal proceedings used in dealing with corruption crimes resemble those used in other ordinary crimes: 'This has to change. The procedures, including the conviction, should be swifter'.[122] Among the adverse effects of this overburdened process, MP-3 believed, is that the delay in convicting the defendant has negative implications for the deterrent effect of that corruption crime. NGO-3 referred to a very important point, which is that the role of the courts cannot be addressed in isolation from the broad legal framework provided for them: 'the judges may be restricted since they deal with rigid texts [the available statutes]'. NGO-3 also argued that the courts largely rely on the rigour of the investigations and the evidence that is adduced before them. In fact, this point is strongly related to one of the values advocated in this chapter – the value of effectiveness and the need for an effective legal framework.[123] Lawyer-3 was also aware of the fact that the courts will have an effective role in combating corruption as long as they enjoy the necessary autonomy from the executive. The participant questioned the independence of the judiciary on legal grounds, stating that 'the current formation of the Supreme Judicial Council is infiltrated by governmental elements through the existence of the Deputy Minister of Justice.'[124]

119 See <https://www.kuna.net.kw/ArticleDetails.aspx?src=ilaw&id=2706647&Language=en>.

120 See <https://www.alraimedia.com/Home/Details?id=303fa340-8b4f-4790-960a-69dd0a1fe88f>.

121 Judge-1; Prosecutor-2; MP-3; Lawyer-3; NGO-3.

122 MP-3.

123 See section 3.2.2.1 below.

124 Lawyer-3.

NGO-2 argued that the ministers are not in fact accountable in 'technical terms'. Except for in political contexts, the ministers are not factually accountable to bodies that raise their accountability from legal perspectives. Despite the involvement of some politicians in a number of corruption incidents, one interviewee pointed out that the TMA has not secured the conviction of a single minister since its enactment in 1995.[125] NGO-1 attributed the lack of legal accountability of ministers to two factors. First, if ministers had to be tried in a special court, that would require more prolonged and complex procedures than the ordinary course of criminal proceedings. Second, the nature of the Court of Ministers – by virtue of its competence – may render it vulnerable to the influence of the surrounding political climate. Therefore, the patron-client networks characterising the political system in Kuwait have an influence.

It can be argued that the first factor has less impact than the second. The TMA has not brought in provisions that are more complex than those required in ordinary criminal proceedings. Except for the requirement for unanimous decisions on some issues,[126] the TMA only requires a different formation of the investigative authority and the trying court.[127] The interviewee probably meant that the parliamentary immunity that each minister enjoys may hinder the accountability of that minister.[128] However, this view does not explain the lack of accountability even in cases that were referred to the Court of Ministers after the minister had left office. Furthermore, that there is a special court by no means undermines the value of accountability. According to its Explanatory Memorandum, the TMA is a direct response to what the Kuwaiti Constitution requires in Article 132, and commensurate with the functions of the ministers who are at the apex of the civil service. In 2018, the ex-Minister of Health was referred to the Court of Ministers.[129] It is the first case that has been taken seriously. Unlike the previous cases, where the investigations were discontinued,[130] this is the first case where the investigation continued and was referred to the Court, before which the Minister of Health stood and was represented as a defendant. Commenting on this case, NGO-3 said: 'from an optimistic perspective, the case of the ex-Minister of Health may herald a change in the attitudes towards accountability; from a pessimistic perspective, the minister could have been a scapegoat in an unknown political calculation'.

In general, the problem of accountability does not relate to the absence of laws and mechanisms, but to their effective enforcement.[131] The emphasis of

125 NGO-3.

126 Such as search warrant and interim provisional orders. See TMA, s.4.

127 Ibid., ss.3, 4, 6, 8, and 10. The TMA replaces the public prosecution with an Investigation Committee consisting of judges and establishes a special court with specific formation.

128 Ibid., s.4.

129 Case No. 6/2018 (Court of Ministers).

130 See Investigation No. 1/2001, 30/10/2007 (Stand Investigation Committee of Court of Ministers); Investigation No. 4/2018, 15/10/2018 (Stand Investigation Committee of Court of Ministers).

131 The same conclusion of 'poor enforcement' is mentioned below in section 3.2.2.

the Strategy 2019–2024 on promoting the value of accountability is an implicit recognition by policymakers that much effort is needed to hold officeholders accountable in practice.[132] One interviewee emphasised that all officials and politicians can theoretically be held accountable, 'but the extent to which the accountability may go is the heart of problem'.[133] The Bertelsmann Foundation Transformation Index illustrated that although officials and politicians may potentially face legal and political sanctions for abuse of office, 'The accountability of officeholders remains limited' in Kuwait, as reflected in recent notorious cases involving high-ranking figures.[134] NGO-2 argued that there is a poor enforcement of accountability in Kuwait, and that everyone is aware that this is a result of the corruption permeating the state institutions. One of the ramifications of such corruption for accountability is that the personal relationships of the officeholders with the upper echelon can successfully prevent their accountability.[135] The cross-analysis of the views of the participants interviewed reveals a pattern, regarding the 'poor enforcement of accountability in Kuwait': high-profile officeholders have some kind of immunity to accountability. When asked about whether accountability is effective, MP-2 stated that low-level officials are more accountable than high-level officials. But, in practice, senior officeholders are more susceptible to accountability to the National Assembly through their minister.[136] NGO-3 added that the reality is that low-level officials can be more accountable than high-level officials:

> There have been many cases in which the state sued the officials for their negligent act that caused the state negligible losses (KWD 1000). Contrariwise, the many high-level ministers and officials, who participated in activities that inflicted gross losses to Kuwait which exceeded USD 2.2bn [700 Kuwaiti million], such as the case of Dow Chemical, have never been held accountable.[137]

NGO-3 explained the mechanism through which low-level officeholders can be more accountable than senior officeholders. He/she said that while the low-level officials can be easily controlled, the high-level officials cannot. When a high-profile official engages in a corrupt practice, there are often other networks of actors who might benefit from this corruption. The higher the position of the officeholder, the more complex the corruption becomes; this means more money and more beneficiaries, and hence, more complexity. In relation to procedural justice, the uneven accountability between officeholders adversely impacts the public perception of the fairness of the counter-corruption

132 See Nazaha (2019, p. 19).
133 MP-2.
134 Bertelsmann Foundation Transformation Index (2018, p. 12).
135 NGO-2.
136 MP-1.
137 NGO-3.

processes.[138] MP-3 said that the perception of their fairness is affected when the state differentiates between people in relation to the enforcement: 'you prosecute the low-level official and turn a blind eye to those who stole millions'.

#### 3.2.1.3 *Human rights*

Corruption has negative effects on human rights. Consequently, the human rights perspective claims that combating corruption not only achieves economic and political outcomes, but also promotes human rights.[139] Some scholarly trends link corruption to human rights and even contend that grand corruption can degenerate into a crime against humanity.[140] The commitment of the state to combatting corruption and its commitment to promoting human rights should be 'rooted in the same principles'.[141] This section argues that counter-corruption policies may involve statutory provisions that aim directly to protect human rights from the perspectives of both the victims and the perpetrators.

From the perspective of victims, the intersection between counter-corruption policies and human rights may materialise in the common focus on the rights of citizens directly affected by corruption and integrates them into counter-corruption policies. For example, the UNCAC, Article 35, emphasises that each state party should adopt various measures that enable each victim who has suffered loses and damages resulting from an act of corruption to initiate legal proceedings against the parties that caused the harm in order to obtain compensation. In contrast, concerns about suspects' rights may arise as counter-corruption processes can overrule their individual rights.[142] The right to a fair trial is an example. This right is established in Article 14 of the International Covenant on Civil and Political Rights (ICCPR), which states that 'all persons shall be equal before the courts and tribunals.' The considerations in the successful investigation of corruption cases raise some tensions between effective prosecution and adherence to the rights of suspects.[143] Some international instruments, which allow strict rules to ensure the effective control of corruption, might downplay the principle of the presumption of innocence. As in the IEO, to overcome the difficulties of proving the source of unjustified wealth, the burden of proof is shifted onto the suspect, which, as claimed, undermines the innocence principle.[144] Furthermore, the trend towards assets disclosure can affect the right to privacy[145] enshrined in Article 17(1) of the ICCPR that 'No one shall be subject to arbitrary or unlawful interference with his privacy'.

138 MP-3.
139 Buckley (2002).
140 See Bloom (2014).
141 Transparency International (2008, p. 2).
142 Buckley (2002).
143 Gathii (2009).
144 Gruenberg (2009). See also chapter 4.3.4.
145 See OECD (2011). See also chapter 4.3.4.

A human rights approach to corruption is of relevance to Kuwait. First, pursuant to Act No. 12/1996, Kuwait ratified the ICCPR in 1996. According to Article 70 of the Kuwaiti Constitution, the ICCPR is now incorporated into the corpus of legislation in Kuwait. Kuwait, then, is subject to the obligation to secure an environment where human rights are respected, protected, and fulfilled.[146] Second, the concept of 'human rights' is consistent with the Kuwaiti Constitution, which pledges explicitly to protect numerous rights: human rights are 'basic components of the Kuwaiti Constitution of 1962, an entire part of which is devoted to fundamental rights and freedoms in a manner consistent with the provisions of the relevant international declarations and treaties'.[147] To name but a few, the Constitution stipulates that no person will be arrested, imprisoned, or searched, save in accordance with the law;[148] there will be no crime and punishment without law, and punishment 'shall not be inflicted on the basis of ex post facto laws';[149] and the accused is presumed innocent until proved guilty in a fair trial.[150] Thus, the human rights approach extends beyond just criminalising corruption to recognising its impact on people's rights.[151] When the ICCPR was ratified, Kuwait made an interpretative declaration in Article 2(1) and 3 and made a reservation in Article 25 (b), though this reservation was partially withdrawn.[152] It is noteworthy that no reservation was made upon Kuwait's accession regarding the relevant rights addressed here.

Counter-corruption efforts should protect human rights from the perspective of victims, including, among other means, by empowering victims by conferring them with a legal standing against corruption. However, Kuwaiti law does not define 'the victims of corruption' and depends on the general provisions on the compensation of crime victims enshrined in its national legislation. In criminal prosecutions, the CJA, sections 111–115 and 117, has created a general legal mechanism for those who have been harmed (called 'plaintiffs') to initiate civil actions to claim damages from the defendant(s), during the investigation or trial. But any civil action may face some legal hurdles. This issue will be further analysed in chapter 5.3.3.

The human rights approach to fighting corruption should also consider the alleged perpetrators' perspective and their interests. Regarding the right to a fair trial, the accused is protected under the umbrella of the Kuwaiti Constitution. Statutorily, the CJA provides the accused with procedural standards that ensure a fair trial. Section 12 of the CJA prohibits self-discrimination and criminalises the torture or coercion of the accused to obtain a specific statement from

146 See Pearson (2013).
147 Human Rights Committee (2014, p. 3).
148 Article 31.
149 Article 32.
150 Article 34.
151 Pearson (2013).
152 Human Rights Committee (2014). For the partial withdrawal of reservation to Article 25(b), see <https://treaties.un.org/Pages/ViewDetails.aspx?src=TREATY&mtdsg_no=IV-4&chapter=4&clang=_en#29>.

him/her. Moreover, the CJA, section 120, guarantees prompt access to justice and the provision of legal aid in felonies, where the accused must be represented by a lawyer, and the court is obliged to appoint a lawyer if he/she cannot afford the costs of proceedings. In general, some of relevant suspect's rights will be further analysed later.[153]

The human rights approach to combating corruption resonates with Kuwaiti professional experts. One interviewee considered it necessary to have fully trained and qualified police officers who must be familiar with the rights of suspects while collecting evidence in crimes like bribery.[154] Judge-1 emphasised the 'illegitimacy' of the activities of the law enforcement authorities, which are not based on the grounds derived from the substantive and procedural safeguards established in the Constitution and the criminal justice laws. Another social activist differentiated between what the law says and what practice may reveal on a case-by-case basis: 'the counter-corruption laws, at least on paper, do not include potential infringements upon liberties'.[155] Expressing his/her own opinion on the fairness of the counter-corruption laws, Lawyer-1 did not raise any concerns regarding the rights of suspects. The participant went on to say: 'as a lawyer, I link the fairness with safeguards provided for the suspects; therefore, the [corruption] offences are fair'.[156]

The rights of the accused can be threatened in corruption cases in Kuwait. Since 2012, it has been crime for an officeholder not to be able to justify an increase in his/her wealth, derogating the right to the presumption of innocence.[157] From the perspective of human rights, the creation of the IEO has been criticised. One of the participants interviewed raised concern about the incompatibility of the reverse onus of proof and the constitutional safeguards of suspects.[158] Moreover, the asset declarations provisions in the ACAA might infringe upon the right to privacy by compelling senior officials to submit financial disclosures about their assets. Further discussion on the justification of the reverse onus of proof and the claim that asset declarations violate the right to privacy are provided in the next chapter.[159]

#### 3.2.1.4 *Morality of the law*

Underestimating the morality negatively affects the effectiveness of criminal law by undermining its moral authority and, hence, its deterrent effect.[160] Rationalising the resort to criminal law to prohibit a specific conduct should be

153 See chapter 4.3.4 (reverse burden of proof and privacy issues), chapter 5.4.2.1 (addressing some procedural safeguards), and chapter 5.4.2.2 (the right against self-incrimination).
154 Judge-1.
155 NGO-3.
156 Lawyer-1.
157 ACAA, s.48.
158 Official-5.
159 See chapter 4.3.4.
160 Green (1997).

based on a 'robust normative framework' to avoid the undesirable consequences of having morally neutral crimes.[161] Green[162] conceptualised the moral content of criminal law and divided it into three elements. First, culpability focuses on the perpetrator's state of mind (*mens rea*) while committing a crime and the extent to which he/she is blameworthy.[163] Second, the social harmfulness element focuses on the conduct itself by referring to the harms or risks that the conduct caused to others.[164] Third, moral wrongfulness also focuses on the act, but in terms of violating the pre-existing moral norms and standards of society.[165] Thus, the norms-based framework will focus on the content of conduct by illustrating the morality of corruption crimes.

The moral content of typical crimes, such as homicide, may not be controversial, for killing is usually seen as morally wrongful. However, the moral content of corruption crimes can be uncertain – a dilemma that Green called the 'moral ambiguity' of white collar crimes.[166] Several factors contribute to this dilemma, such as the nature of the conduct itself, the social norms and customs, and the legitimacy of the environment in which an act is committed.[167] Whilst many cases of bribery and extortion are examples of morally wrongful conduct, there are instances where these two examples are morally ambiguous.[168] A 'bribe' can sometimes be better categorised as just a gift or expression of gratitude, and extortion can be just a political behaviour embodied in pressure against a minister within legitimate parliamentary work. Notwithstanding this problem of moral ambiguity, it is possible to build on the literature of corruption (especially grand corruption) to establish its morality.

Regarding culpability, the blameworthiness of officials is always present in corruption crimes and is facilitated by the absence of variation in criminal liability (intent, recklessness, and negligence); the act is either corrupt or non-corrupt.[169] Equally, the harmfulness of corruption has been discussed, and affirmed, by many commentators.[170] Moreover, the opprobrious nature of corruption can be predicated on normative, political views. Corruption is seen as a deviation from the formal duties because of private interests and gains.[171] Assuming that the formal duties were conferred by a legitimate authority and in favour of the public, their violation betrays the public. Understood as such, corruption accommodates at least a minimum amount of each element of moral content. Corruption

161 Whelan (2013, p. 538).
162 Green (1997).
163 Ibid., p. 1547.
164 Ibid., p. 1549.
165 Ibid., p. 1511.
166 Green (2004, p. 502).
167 Ibid., pp. 508–518.
168 See Uslaner (2008).
169 See Underkuffler (2013).
170 See chapter 2.2.3.
171 Nye (1967).

crimes are then qualified as *mala in se,* which can be associated with typical moral reprehensibility of the criminal law.[172]

In Kuwait, establishing the morality of corruption is challenging. The difficulty is not as much concerned with the concept of corruption itself as with what is ascribed to it by ordinary people and politicians.[173] The literature points to 'cultural relativism', which asserts that many practices that are considered corruption in the West are socially acceptable in other places in the world.[174] Among the three elements of the moral content of criminal law (culpability, social harmfulness, and moral wrongfulness), what can be specifically problematic is the moral wrongfulness of corruption: can all forms of corruption offences be considered *mala in se* in Kuwait? At least some forms of corruption appear to be morally ambiguous. The clash between the traditional pre-modern values of Kuwaiti society and the modern values of institutions affects how the society sees many forms of corruption. A segment of the strongly held present social practices and prevalent norms in Kuwait is not consistent with the corruption concept in the technical, Western sense, leading the public to be complacent about these practices.[175] Corruption, then, is affected by the problem of the 'sticky norms' of a specific society 'when there is a gap between what the law regards as morally wrongful and what a significant segment of society views as such'.[176] Rothstein and Torsello, however, attribute this variation not to the moral understanding of corruption, but to how societies value and understand the difference between public and private goods.[177] The gap between what is deemed morally wrongful by the law and what is regarded as such by the society fosters the social tolerance of corruption, putting the legitimacy of counter-corruption efforts at stake.

The analysis of the questionnaires completed by 465 people from Kuwaiti society showed a 'low level of public awareness in society of the negative consequences of bribery on society' and that the 'Kuwaiti society tolerates bribery'.[178] It should not be understood from this that corruption is not condemned in Kuwait. Corruption is condemned in Islam.[179] Corruption is formally censured by several statutes that prohibit corrupt practices. It is also condemned by the civil society, as represented by its NGOs.[180] But the very nature of Kuwaiti society poses challenges to diminishing the counter-corruption efforts. The political structure of Kuwait, citizens' tolerance of corruption, and the lack of social awareness of the seriousness of corruption together impact on the morality of

172 See Green (2004).
173 See Philp (2015).
174 Scott (1972, p. 10).
175 See chapter 2.3.4.1.
176 Green (2004, p. 508).
177 See Rothstein and Torsello (2013).
178 Al-Qarioti (2013, pp. 53–63).
179 See Al-Ghazalli (2005).
180 NGO-1; NGO-2; NGO-3.

corruption. More efforts are required to raise citizens' awareness of corruption and its adverse effects on the society.

### 3.2.1.5 *Legal certainty*

The focus of legal certainty entails practical benefits by sustaining the clarity, predictability, and accessibility of the law.[181] Legal certainty, then, is a principle of importance for the criminal law, given its serious penalties. In the light of the constitutional principle that no punishment exists without law (or the principle of legality in general),[182] there is no room for criminal laws to be obscure, uncertain, or open to interpretation. Thus, the certainty of law should be bound by two requirements. First, the legal construct of a crime and its elements should be clearly stipulated in the law. Second, the legislature and courts should not create or extend the current law insofar as they criminalise conduct or an omission that was not previously punishable or impose penalties retrospectively.[183] However, the courts can, within reasonable limits, clarify and adapt the existing elements of a crime to new circumstances as long as the clarification and adaptation are in accordance with 'the original concept of the offence'.[184] The two elements are interdependent: the precision of the legislator in formulating the law prevents the deviation of judges' interpretation and public authorities' enforcement.[185] To achieve legal certainty, the accessibility of the law is a requirement that should be promoted through adequately identifiable sources.[186] The European Court of Human Rights (ECtHR) has ruled that 'the law must be adequately accessible: the citizen must be able to have an indication that is adequate in the circumstances of the legal rules applicable to a given case'.[187]

Legal certainty is one of the constitutional principles in the Kuwaiti legal system. Several constitutional provisions guarantee on paper the predictability of, and accessibility to, the legislation enacted in Kuwait. For example, treaties that affect citizens' rights should be ratified and sanctioned by an enactment of law and must then be published in the Official Gazette, and it is only after this publication that these treaties have the force of law.[188] Also, laws and regulations must be published within two weeks of their issuance, and they will come into force within one month of their publication.[189] The accessibility of the law is

181 Bingham (2011).
182 Legality is one of the principles that can be found in most constitutions. See Berger (2014).
183 International Commission of Jurists (1959).
184 *Gay News Ltd. and Lemon v United Kingdom* App No. 8710/79 (1983) 5 EHRR 123, 129.
185 Whelan (2012).
186 Bingham (2011).
187 *Sunday Times v United Kingdom* App No. 6538/74, Series A, No. 30 (1979) 2 EHRR 245, 271.
188 Kuwaiti Constitution, art.70.
189 Ibid., art.178.

achieved in Kuwait, as there are national codes that, by covering major areas of laws such as civil law and criminal law, are stable and represent the bedrock for other laws. These codes are published via a number of identifiable sources, such as the Official Gazette, which has been issued since 1954 to promulgate what is enacted in Kuwait.[190] The 'Legal Gate'[191] and the 'Legal Information Network'[192] are two sources through which legislation can be accessed. However, the extent to which these sources are updated is problematic.

In regard to the criminal law, the Kuwaiti Constitution, Article 32, determines the limits of the criminal policies and states that 'Crime and punishment will be regulated by Law' and that 'Criminal punishment shall not be inflicted on the basis of ex post facto laws'. Article 32 ensures the fulfilment of the two elements analysed above: that the criminalisation must be stipulated by the law and that the legislature should not impose sanctions retrospectively. The Constitutional Court in Kuwait emphasised legal certainty. It showed that the legislature had not violated the principle of *nullum crimen sine lege* when it examined, in one case, that the legal construct of crime, including *actus reus* and *mens rea*, was clearly stipulated so that all those subject to it know what the law is: 'the crime was not drafted in a general and loose way which would not lead to uncertainty'.[193] In 2019, the Kuwaiti Constitutional Court declared the unconstitutionality of the CIA on grounds related to the legal certainty principle: the elements of the conflict of interest crime were considered general, unclear, and ambiguous, and thus, it violates the principle of legal certainty.[194]

Legal certainty applies to the corruption laws, in particular those of a criminal nature with serious penalties. How far the counter-corruption legislation is understandable is also an issue that is relevant for legal certainty.[195] The comprehensibility of corruption laws is of particular significance, especially in Kuwait, where corruption laws are scattered throughout a number of laws (rather than being in a unified code).[196] Also, the introduction of 'indefinite legal concepts' in laws with complex technicalities to capture the various aspects of the phenomena at issue may threaten the legal certainty.[197] To face that threat, some techniques may be suggested. In the light of the absence of a thorough Explanatory Memorandum and systematic commentaries for a specific piece of legislation,[198] the dependence on decisions developed by the Supreme and Constitutional Court helps to determine the meaning of a contested concept/provision, hence

190 See <http://kuwaitalyawm.media.gov.kw>.
191 See <http://www.law.gov.kw>.
192 See <http://www.gcc-legal.org>.
193 Case No. 46-47/2015, 28/10/2015 (Constitutional Court).
194 Case No. 7/2018, 1/5/2019 (Constitutional Court). This decision is analysed in chapter 4.3.3.2.
195 See Bingham (2011).
196 See chapter 4.3.
197 Maxeiner (2007, p. 560).
198 In Kuwait, each statute is often issued with a concise and brief explanatory memorandum.

fulfilling the guidance function of legal certainty. The intelligibility of prohibited conduct is critical to 'communicate the wrongfulness of the behaviour in question to the accused' and to secure the society's respect for the criminal law (hence, its legitimacy).[199]

### 3.2.2 *Effectiveness*

What makes counter-corruption laws effective? For this book, their effectiveness depends on the extent to which such laws are able to fulfil their intended effects in reality: preventing and combating corruption. The assessment of the effectiveness of the counter-corruption framework is a composite task. It is based, first, on enumerating the state's legal responses to corruption, including its legal powers and the adequacy of the enforcement institutions. Second, it relies on an evidence-based evaluation of the laws and the performance of the enforcement institutions. These two issues are addressed in the following discussion.

#### 3.2.2.1 *Effective legal framework*

The ability of a counter-corruption policy to achieve its objectives relies largely on the extent to which such a policy is implemented by capable law enforcement authorities that are empowered with strong and relevant instruments and powers to pursue the corrupt and deter them from engaging in corruption. These objectives can be effectively achieved by enabling the various state institutions to fight corruption. Curbing corruption through producing adequate laws and their effective enforcement has been described as a 'lawyer's approach' to corruption control.[200] The scope of the discussion in this section is restricted to suggesting a specific framework within which the effectiveness of the law as a social control mechanism can be assessed. Therefore, this section does not investigate in detail whether each individual counter-corruption measure is effective in achieving the intended objectives since that is the objective of chapter 4.

In Kuwait, grand corruption is a problem that requires countervailing efforts that are commensurate with this corruption pattern. These can be embodied in sophisticated legal responses that focus on establishing, or developing, highly capable institutions empowered by a wide range of legal powers. Since 1960, Kuwait has taken repeated action against corruption. In the civil field, to name a few, the action started with the SAB Act, which created the SAB as an independent oversight body to achieve effective control over public finance.[201] The SAB Act also listed financial irregularities against the public budget and established the Disciplinary Tribunal. The CSA enacts the disciplinary offences and establishes a disciplinary system for officeholders. Moreover, the Civil Law Act (Civil Act)

199 Whelan (2012, pp. 681–682).
200 Ades and di Tella (1997, p. 497).
201 The remit of the SAB was explained in section 3.2.1.2.

67/1980 sets out the rules of the civil responsibility of both natural and legal persons, according to which liability for corrupt conduct can potentially be established. Next, the Code of Conduct of Public Officials Circular No. 11/2012 (Code 2012) sets out the standards of integrity and behaviours that should be followed by the officeholders. Recently, the Kuwaiti policymaker issued the Strategy 2019–2024, which sets out a comprehensive counter-corruption agenda.[202]

In the criminal field, this action started with the enactment of Criminal Law Act 16/1960 (CLA 1960), which created specific corruption offences, such as the bribery offences: these crimes were later revised in 1970 by the Criminal Law Act 31/1970 (CLA 1970).[203] Next, the enactment of PPFA in 1993 criminalised nine violations against public funds.[204] In 1995, the Court of Ministers was established by the TMA to try corruption crimes committed by ministers. In 2012, the ACAA created a list of corruption crimes and added, for the first time, the IEO.[205] In an important stride, the ACAA has established Nazaha as a counter-corruption body to deal with these crimes. The Anti-Money Laundering and Countering Financing of Terrorism Act (AML/CFT Act) 106/2013 established the KFIU to combat money laundering.[206] In 2018, the CIA deemed conflicts of interest to be a corruption crime.[207]

These multi-dimensional measures empower the enforcement authorities both to prevent corruption and to pursue the corrupt. How these law enforcement authorities operate is outside the scope of this book.[208] But whether the statutory powers bestowed upon them are satisfactory will be analysed in detail in subsequent chapters.[209] For the purposes of this study, a number of politicians, professional experts, and social activists were invited to express their perceptions about the effectiveness and adequacy of the existing laws.

MP-2 was satisfied with the current situation, stating that although some counter-corruption laws, such as the IEO, have been belated, the existing laws achieve most of the international requirements. However, that participant argued that the real problem revolves around the 'administration of the legislation': how Nazaha and other law enforcement authorities are being administered and how they in turn administer the laws. Despite the presence of adequate laws, the state institutions do not take any action against misconduct.[210] The participant concluded that 'the legislation is enough for the current problems, but the administration is bad, and this is the reason why we are behind'.[211] MP-3 agreed

202 See Nazaha (2019).
203 CLA 1970, ss.35–41.
204 PPFA, ss.9–19.
205 ACAA, s.48.
206 AML/CFT Act, s.16.
207 CIA, s.11.
208 See the book scope in chapter 1.2.
209 See chapters 4 and 5.
210 MP-2.
211 Ibid.

that in Kuwait there is a comprehensive system of laws against corruption. MP-3 referred to the same flaw mentioned by MP-2 that there is not a problem with the laws, but with the way in which these laws are enforced. Corruption takes place and the corrupt can go unpunished despite the existence of laws and oversight bodies: 'the problem is one that relates to the enforcement'.[212]

Official-2 raised the same issue, but from a different perspective. He/she argued that the effectiveness of the laws is strongly linked to having robust evidence in each corruption case. The evidence issue ultimately relates to how the laws are enforced in practice.[213] The interviewee believed that the poor enforcement of the laws is driven by the lack of collaboration and liaison between the law enforcement authorities in Kuwait.[214] Official-4 thought that the Kuwaiti laws are sufficient to combat corruption. He/she opined that when talking about the ACAA, at least, the Act not only aims to combat corruption, but also provides for essential pillars that are directed at the prevention of corruption, the engagement of the civil society, and the instillation of a counter-corruption culture in the society. The interviewee commented:

> With the enactment of the ACAA, and the establishment of Nazaha, the discourse of counter-corruption and the international commitments of Kuwait towards combating corruption has become predominant. The increasing awareness of the need to combat corruption has become concrete. All these facts justify the claim that the current counter-corruption *efforts* are effective.[215]

NGO-3 mentioned what he/she called a 'paradox': while Kuwait is prolific in enacting counter-corruption laws, these laws suffer from the weakness of their enforcement. He/she argued that 'the legislature seems to concentrate on the quantity of laws enacted rather than their quality'. Therefore, the rampant corruption cases in Kuwait do not reflect the inadequacy of the laws, but their ineffective enforcement.[216] NGO-2 expressed his/her view in a different manner. He/she commented that the current laws are not effective and gave an example: Nazaha has not been able to send any corrupt people to prison, and although the SAB publishes a report every year about corrupt practices, corruption continues to exist. NGO-2 said that the 'law enforcement authorities are like the police: you only supervise but cannot hold someone accountable'.[217] What that participant probably wanted to say is that the effectiveness of the laws is not linked to their adequacy, but to their effective enforcement.

212 MP-3.
213 Official-2.
214 Ibid.
215 Official-4 (emphasis added).
216 NGO-3.
217 NGO-2.

The Strategy 2019–2024 underlines the importance of effectiveness, especially the need for effective law enforcement authorities. The 'Fourth Pillar' of the Strategy is dedicated to improving the counter-corruption agencies. The Strategy focuses on developing the internal structure and the technical abilities of Nazaha and subjecting counter-corruption agencies employees to further training courses regarding their role in combating corruption. The judicial actors are part of the Strategy's agenda to improve the effectiveness of the law enforcement authorities, including training the judiciary regarding matters pertaining to counter-corruption.[218] As discussed in chapter 6, where the author reviews his fieldwork experience, more training courses are one of the most important responses to the lack of knowledge of professional experts.[219] 'Cooperation and Liaison' is one of the Strategy's priorities to consolidate the abilities of the law enforcement authorities in Kuwait. Under this priority, two critical issues have been mentioned. One is strengthening cooperation and coordination among the law enforcement authorities in the area of the investigation and prosecution of corruption cases. The second is fulfilling the obligations of Kuwait within the Implementation Review Mechanism of UNCAC 'in a participatory and effective manner'.[220]

What arguably emerges from the previous analysis is that the legal counter-corruption framework suffers more from poor enforcement than from any other defect. Since 1960, Kuwait has had in place an arsenal of laws that could effectively combat corruption, and what really matters now is improving the enforcement of those laws. The analysis of the existing counter-corruption measures (especially the criminal ones in chapter 4) will corroborate this conclusion. However, we have to be cautious about these conclusions. The adequacy of the current laws cannot be taken for granted because it has been determined based on a fallacious perception. The prominent public discourse of combating corruption among Kuwaiti experts is that corruption is only encountered criminally. That discourse is a natural result of the dominance of criminal responses against corruption, and the research participants seem to have been vulnerable to this dominant public discourse.

Paraphrasing the argument of the interviewees, the criminal measures against corruption are adequate, and the 'real' problem lies in their poor enforcement. But combating corruption is not merely an issue of criminal laws. Non-criminal measures can also have potential in preventing and combating corruption. The analysis in chapter 5, where such non-criminal measures are addressed, will open up new horizons for the potential of civil law in combating corruption in Kuwait. Thus, the argument of this book is twofold. First, one can claim that the criminal counter-corruption laws in Kuwait are adequate (though they suffer from a lack of enforcement). Second, taking into account other non-criminal responses,

218 Nazaha (2019, p. 26).
219 See chapter 6.3.
220 Nazaha (2019, p. 26).

the current counter-corruption framework in Kuwait is inadequate and lacks innovation. As will be argued, the criminal nature of Kuwaiti responses to corruption makes them inadequate and unable to deal with 'grand' corruption.[221]

### 3.2.2.2 *Evidence-based policymaking: what works?*

In order for the counter-corruption policies to be effective, ongoing assessment should be undertaken to evaluate and consider whether reforms are needed. An outcome-oriented performance evaluation is a helpful measure that is proposed here to assess the efficacy of the implemented policies. In this context, evidence-based policymaking involves:

> first, evidence of the likely effectiveness of policy options to inform decisions on what policy action to take; and, second, evidence from evaluations of policies as implemented to inform decisions on whether to continue or how to adjust and improve policies and to contribute to the evidence base to inform future consideration of policy options.[222]

Evidence-based policymaking has been associated with the increasing interest among the public sector in effectiveness and is concerned with the search for usable and relevant information that is helpful for policy development, evaluation, and improvement.[223] In the United Kingdom, for example, the 'What Works Network' was launched 'to improve the way government and other organisations create, share and use (or "generate, transmit and adopt") high quality evidence for decision-making' to promote more effective public policy in different arenas.[224] Of particular significance is the 'What Works Centre for Crime Reduction'.[225] The policymakers should adopt evidence-based practice to assess whether the implementation of counter-corruption efforts achieves their objectives and determine whether legal powers really work in practice. The UN Anti-Corruption Toolkit provides tools to undertake this evaluation and help policymakers answer questions related to what reforms are needed, what the focus should be on, and what has been gained from the actions taken.[226]

Do the Kuwaiti counter-corruption laws bring the intended effects in practice? NGO-1 commented that the effectiveness of counter-corruption measures cannot be randomly determined. He/she suggested that there is a group of measures that should first be taken in order to assess the effectiveness of the current counter-corruption laws: there should be evaluative and follow-up studies

221 See chapter 5.4.2.
222 Sanderson (2002, p. 4).
223 Head (2008).
224 See <https://www.gov.uk/guidance/what-works-network>.
225 See <http://whatworks.college.police.uk/Pages/default.aspx>.
226 UNODC (2004).

that underline the points of weakness and the strengths.[227] But evaluating the quality of the existing laws is challenging given the lack of performance evaluation. The public authorities in Kuwait do not resort to techniques like self-reflection to evaluate whether the laws bring their intended effect. Using research in policymaking faces some challenges in Kuwait, one of which is the underfunding of research.[228] An evidence-based policymaking is lacking, although the Supreme Council for Planning and Development enables the government to adopt appropriate measures to ensure effective follow-up of the policies adopted and their implementation.[229] As one interviewee put forward, there is a lack of serious steps to evaluate the laws.[230] Nevertheless, the burgeoning NGOs in Kuwait often play a crucial role in decentralising the policymaking process.[231] For example, from 2008 to 2014, the KTS developed the 'Reform Perception Index' to measure the level of transparency, accountability and respect for law, justice and equal opportunities, as well as the effectiveness and leadership in the public sector.[232]

There are, however, some means through which counter-corruption policies may be subject to evaluation. The court judgments and the investigations of public prosecutors are one of the sources for assessing the effectiveness of laws.[233] Also, the peer-review process to monitor the implementation of UNCAC is an appropriate tool to review the Kuwaiti counter-corruption laws and their compliance with the UNCAC.[234] These examples of outcome-oriented evaluations could, potentially, evaluate the effectiveness of the counter-corruption policies. Moreover, within the remit of the Nazaha are the periodic evaluation of counter-corruption laws and the legal powers related to combating the corruption process, proposing the reforms needed to comply with the international conventions ratified by Kuwait, and rectifying and improving the counter-corruption enforcement and prevention measures.[235]

In 2019, the policymakers in Kuwait started to incorporate evidence-based policymaking into their agenda. The Strategy 2019–2024 included a chapter related to the follow-up and evaluation of counter-corruption policies. The Strategy explicitly recognises that the effectiveness of the policies largely relies on whether they bring about their intended effects in practice. It realises the importance of the ongoing follow-up of the policies and observing their progress. To that end,

227 NGO-1.
228 See Khodr (2014).
229 See <https://www.scpd.gov.kw/scpdpage.aspx>.
230 NGO-1.
231 Khodr (2014).
232 See <http://www.transparency.org.kw.au-ti.org/upload/ads/prize2014/moasher2014-book.pdf>.
233 NGO-1.
234 <http://www.unodc.org/unodc/treaties/CAC/country-profile/CountryProfile.html?code=KWT>.
235 ACAA, s.5(7).

the Strategy involves gathering information annually about the implemented laws and policies from the law enforcement authorities and analysing the information with the stakeholders so that the policymakers can rectify any deficiencies.[236] To secure the implementation of the Strategy's objectives, the 'Supreme Committee' for the implementation of the Strategy 2019–2024 has been established within Nazaha.[237] Furthermore, a number of *ad hoc* sub-committees have been formed and associated to the Supreme Committee to help it perform its mission. Thus, the advent of evidence-based policymaking in the Kuwait Strategy will make a difference. The extent of this difference, however, is yet to be determined.

## 3.3 Counter-corruption strategies

There is no one-size-fits-all strategy to combat corruption. A counter-corruption strategy can be designed depending on the perspective from which corruption is regarded as a problem. While the economic perspective may depend on reducing the incentives to engage in corruption or its costs, politics suggests that corruption can be fought through reforms to enhance democratic practices, and so forth.[238] Counter-corruption policies also differ in terms of their underpinning logic. They might be 'control' policies, depending on the effective laws enforcement; 'exit' policies, relying on the creation of alternatives for public services for people by minimising the monopolistic position of the state; or 'voice' policies, focusing on the effective participation of civil society.[239] However, not all potential strategies are addressed here. This section identifies the strategies commonly devised in the abstract and used in Kuwait to counter corruption from three aspects: a social perspective (section 3.3.1), a legal perspective (section 3.3.2), and a preventive perspective (section 3.3.3). Interestingly, the three premises of counter-corruption strategies studied here are highly consistent with the underpinnings of the Strategy 2019–2024, especially with regard to its principles of 'inclusiveness' (prevention, enforcement, and awareness strategies) and 'achievability' (not distracting the efforts and focusing on what is realistically achievable).[240]

### 3.3.1 *Social empowerment*

Civil society has a critical role to play when discussing counter-corruption strategies. According to Article 13 of the UNCAC, the participation of civil society is emphasised besides the state in raising awareness of, and countering, the effects of corruption. One way of fighting corruption is to strengthen the civil society

236 Nazaha (2019, p. 28).
237 Ibid., p. 29.
238 See Rose-Ackerman (1999).
239 See Everett, Neu and Rahaman (2006, pp. 5–6).
240 Nazaha (2019, p. 16).

alongside other state institutions. This strategy can help to reduce civil society's vulnerability to political and economic influences, preventing its members from being 'the instigators or targets of corruption'.[241] It also helps to reinforce the strength, self-dependence, and autonomy of the society before the dominant political monopolies. Rather than focusing on those who combat corruption (such as law institutions), it relies on involving the victimised element (society) as a stakeholder in the plan targeted at reducing corruption.[242] In general, it depends on bottom-up reforms that aim to include the excluded, peripheral actors of the society, to expand the base of economic and political arenas, protect their activities in the state, and ensure their vigorous involvement in political life, as well as monitoring the behaviours of officials.[243]

Although social empowerment is by no means an alternative to other institutional reforms, it represents a social foundation for any potential reforms in countries where corruption is systemic, state institutions tend to perpetuate corruption, and the people are vulnerable to corruption. In general, economic and political institutional reforms are more sustainable and productive when they are backed by effective 'social processes' that enhance the political and economic contention within society.[244] Unless there is a countervailing force, the emerging powerful political leadership can easily harness the counter-corruption campaigns for perverted purposes.[245] If there is no active civil society, whose participation in the control of corruption can bring positive results, counter-corruption campaigns will be transitory and corruption then reasserts itself.[246] Thus, it is said that the social empowerment strategy has the potential to consolidate the 'reactive' measures against corruption when it makes the political influence on law enforcement authorities more difficult.[247]

Social empowerment is a mechanism of horizontal accountability, where the government's activities are not only accountable to formal institutions, but also to actors outside the governmental body.[248] When social empowerment is achieved, other institutional reforms and the conduct of officials will conform to the social values, and thereby, opportunistic politicians will be restrained. In the long run, the rule of law will be an embedded value of political life and public order.[249] Therefore, as analysed above, the values of transparency (FOI legislation) and accountability (especially political accountability through the electorate) are necessary conditions to empower the citizens. In this sense, the social empowerment strategy comprises elements that 'provide powers and incentives

241 Johnston (1998, p. 92).
242 UNODC (2003).
243 Johnston (1998).
244 See ibid., p. 87.
245 Johnston and Kpundeh (2004).
246 UNODC (2003).
247 UNODC (2004, p. 291).
248 Collier (2002).
249 Johnston (1998).

for members of the population to take appropriate action'.[250] Indeed, ensuring the basic conditions for this strategy is the threshold from which a civil society can proceed to discharge its role effectively.

The civil society in Kuwait has the potential to perform a role in social empowerment in many ways. Constitutionally, the right to form societies 'on a national basis and by peaceful means' has been stipulated and no individual shall be restrained from joining any of these societies.[251] As a result, the Associations Act 24/1962 permits citizens to form NGOs that can achieve an array of aims, including social, cultural, religious, and sport-related objectives. Also, Articles 36 and 37 of the Constitution guarantee freedom of opinion and freedom of the press and publication. Consequently, the media sector in Kuwait has been somewhat liberalised since 2006, thanks to the Press and Publication Act 3/2006 and the Audio-Visual Media Act 61/2007, which lifted some of the restrictions imposed on the newspapers and media channels.[252] Though these platforms help the society undertake its socio-political functions and exert pressure on the government, this section concentrates on the NGOs as a prominent platform.

Until 2005, there were no NGOs specialised in the counter-corruption field. In that year, the Kuwait Association for Protecting Public Funds (KAPPF) was established: to increase public awareness, to underline the importance of protecting and maintaining public funds, and to expose any misconduct to the competent authorities.[253] In 2006, more importantly, the KTS was promulgated to embody the belief in the role of civil society in the fight against corruption.[254] These NGOs probably encouraged MP-1 to argue that the civil society is performing its role in combating corruption. He/she added that 'as a person that has lived a long experience of being a MP, I can assure you that the civil society now is more effective than that society 10 years ago'. The increasing emergence of voluntary groups in the Kuwaiti society, as MP-1 argued, can be seen as a good example of the improvement in the role of the civil society. Interestingly, this interviewee stated that the NGOs have effectively been able, on several occasions, to trigger the National Assembly and the government to take action regarding corruption scandals.[255] In principle, therefore, the space for civil society to contribute to combating corruption has been constitutionally and statutorily safeguarded.

With its focus on the 'inclusiveness' principle, the Strategy 2019–2024 underlines the strategic eminence of the society-oriented reforms as the 'Third Pillar' of the Strategy. The role of NGOs has elicited the attention of policymakers. The Strategy proceeds from the fact that the society is the ultimate victim of corruption and, therefore, should be a strategic partner in combating it. Thus, the Strategy aims to 'empower' Kuwaiti society (through NGOs) to

250 UNODC (2004, p. 290).
251 Kuwaiti Constitution, art.43.
252 International Center for Not-for-Profit Law (2017).
253 The latest updates of their activities are available on their Twitter account: @KAPPF.
254 See <http://transparency.org.kw/ar/>.
255 MP-1.

build a corruption-free and integrity-based environment. The reforms focus on awareness programmes against corruption, harnessing the role of the NGOs, education, family, and media and social media platforms. Most relevantly, the Strategy aims to engage NGOs in the counter-corruption efforts through supporting their initiatives and consolidating their role in terms of popular oversight. To that end, the Strategy induces the state institutions through a specific plan to be more responsive to the issues that the NGOs raise in relation to counter-corruption.[256]

Notwithstanding the formal recognition by policymakers of the role of NGOs in combating corruption, the bottom-up social empowerment reform faces informal obstacles that lie within the social elements themselves. Ironically, the nature of the social organisation in Kuwait is part of the problem, that is, it is the first hindrance to the progress of civil society. Corruption is, as Johnston argued, 'a profoundly *social process* involving real people in concrete situations.'[257] So, what is the socio-political leverage of NGOs on the whole society? Do the Kuwaiti citizens turn to the NGOs to confront corruption?

In chapter 2, the argument was made that corruption is embedded in the cultural and social settings. The social relationships are formed within the tribalism and sectarianism, which give rise to diverse and segregated factions. The non-cooperation and lack of cohesion between the components of society affect social relationships, resulting in an imbalance in the state-society relationship. [258] In this setting, groups are vulnerable to the government.[259] NGOs do not represent an alternative political resource that citizens can resort to, and they cannot reduce the citizens' vulnerability, which eventually reinforces their dependence on the state. One governmental expert argued that the NGOs suffer from a lack of independence: 'there have been several occasions when an association has been arbitrarily dissolved because of its opinion, which did not correspond with the attitudes of the government'.[260] One social activist based his/her perception of the weak role of civil society in public matters on the intrinsic features of the society itself.[261] NGO-1 explained that the current social and political situation reveals the fact that the civil society in Kuwait has been deflated, arguing that the civil society itself is very vulnerable to the politics and is influenced by the social components. The interviewee gave an illustrative example of how the civil society is disjointed:

> The associations tend not to participate in any suggestions, initiatives and other activities that have a political dimension. The NGOs in Kuwait tend to come together on issues that are indisputable. But when it comes to the

256 Nazaha (2019, p. 17).
257 Johnston (1998, p. 88).
258 See chapter 2.3.4.1.
259 Johnston (1998).
260 Official-4.
261 NGO-1.

political issues, they do not interact. We are talking about NGOs that are negatively influenced by the surrounding political climate.[262]

Social empowerment also faces formal obstacles related to the non-supportive legal environment. The Associations Act 24/1962 represents a stumbling block that hinders the growth of social engagement in combating corruption. This Act contains governmental restrictions on the activities of NGOs and is 'founded on the notion of almost full control and discretion by the executive branch over NGOs'.[263] First, the incorporation of NGOs requires the formal approval of the Ministry of Social Affairs (MoSA).[264] Second, the Act prohibits NGOs from joining, participating in, or affiliating with any foreign entity without seeking the permission of the MoSA.[265] Finally, and more seriously, the Act grants the MoSA close supervision over NGOs, including wide discretionary power to dissolve an NGO, or replace its elected Board of Directors.[266] NGOs are not allowed to practise political activities, and if they do, their engagement triggers governmental intervention that results in their dissolution.[267] This restriction has always given rise to contention between the government and social activists. In the 1970s, some NGOs were dissolved because of their involvement in political activities.[268] In 2015, because of groundless allegations that the KTS had a political bias, the elected Board of Directors of the KTS was dissolved and replaced with a government-appointed board – this intervention was considered 'a peak in the massive harassment' and led to the suspension of the KTS as a fully accredited chapter of TI.[269] The state, then, has the ability to penetrate and control civil society through the restrictions imposed by the Associations Act 24/1962. This situation is symptomatic of broader flaws in the state's institutional structure, particularly in regard to the socio-political institutions. In general, these governmental practices are consistent with the argument that 'Arab governments are simply not used to involving a second party to share power with or allow an outsider to monitor its performance'.[270]

The theoretical analysis goes hand-in-hand with what was found empirically. The role of NGOs in relation to counter-corruption is limited.[271] NGO-2 believed that there are many restrictions on the NGOs with regard to the criticism of the government. NGO-2 gave two examples: TV stations and newspapers of both

262 Ibid.
263 International Center for Not-for-Profit Law (2017, p. 1).
264 Associations Act 24/1962, ss.1 and 30.
265 Ibid., s.30.
266 Ibid., s.27.
267 Ibid., s.6.
268 International Center for Not-for-Profit Law (2017).
269 See <https://www.transparency.org/news/pressrelease/kuwait_chapter_of_transparency_international_under_threat>.
270 Al-Kilani (2007, p. 12).
271 Official-4; NGO-2; NGO-3; NGO-1.

*Dar Al-Watan* Newspaper and *Alam Al-Youm*.[272] The interviewee stated that the government only accepts the fact that the NGOs may suggest improvements, but it does not accept criticisms of governmental practices.[273] NGO-3 said that the government imposes burdensome restrictions on the NGOs, which, in turn, deprives civil society of its role. He/she added that 'their role has been nominal rather than actual: when an association engages in a political issue, this may lead to its dissolution'.[274]

When asked whether the government takes the initiative to encourage NGOs to engage in counter-corruption matters, one participant argued that the government seems not to uphold the role of civil society, as long as it does not secure their independence.[275] Official-4 commented that 'the government tends to undermine the independence of the NGOs, such as what happened to the KTS in 2015'. Another interviewee believed that the government is keen to keep the NGOs under its control: 'it has always been intervening in the elections of those associations'.[276] Another manifestation of the lack of governmental support for NGOs was illustrated by NGO-3, who stated that that since 2005, the MoSA has stopped the financial support it used to give to the associations.

MP-1 had a different view, believing that the government encourages NGOs, albeit in a limited way. He/she asserted that 'more steps are on their way'. This different view was criticised by another participant; NGO-1 opined that the government does not believe in the role of civil society in public matters. NGO-1 argued that when the government feels that it is compelled to cooperate with NGOs to address corruption, it purports to be engaged in 'ostensible cooperation with the civil society' just to satisfy the international community. The interviewee gave an example of that 'ostensible cooperation':

> Since 2018, KTS has been dealing with the government to induce the latter to adopt a number of integrity-related programmes. However, although it has been keen to meet with the KTS, the government has not had the desire to take this step seriously; all that it wanted was to show the international communities that it was trying.[277]

In conclusion, the legislative and social environments in Kuwait have stunted social empowerment in matters related to corruption. However, social empowerment, especially through the NGOs, is possible. In regard to overcoming the

272 NGO-2 argued that the authorities withdrew the licences of these publishing companies based on alleged political reasons. See <https://cpj.org/2015/02/kuwait-shuts-down-two-outlets-after-revoking-ceos-.php> and <https://cpj.org/2015/02/kuwaiti-court-upholds-government-shutdown-of-al-wa.php>.

273 NGO-2.

274 NGO-3.

275 Official-4.

276 NGO-2.

277 NGO-1.

challenges of the social empowerment strategy in Kuwait, two points can be raised. First, empowering people to confront corruption first assumes studying their culture. Second, any potential reforms to the regulatory framework of NGOs will require intensive efforts, taking into account the dominance of the state as a prominent characteristic of the political institutions in Kuwait. It is surprising that Strategy 2019–2024 has not addressed those two critical issues; nor has it addressed the very nature of the social construction. Furthermore, it has not brought in reforms related to the statutory provisions regarding the relationship between NGOs and the state.

### 3.3.2 *Law enforcement*

Some counter-corruption strategies focus more narrowly on applying and improving legal mechanisms. These strategies place the 'substantive legal reform' at the forefront of the counter-corruption agenda.[278] Such strategies depend on criminal law as a legal framework that uses crime, punishment, and procedural law as a means to induce individuals to comply with a given public policy.[279] These strategies also depend on the enforcement element of the law, which 'concerns the capacity of a state to impose sanctions upon officials who have violated their public duties'.[280] The control of corruption, in this sense, consists of reactive mechanisms to carry out the enforcement and prosecutorial functions, such as criminal justice and criminal law.[281] This strategy has been incorporated into the UNCAC, which emphasises the effective prosecution, adjudication, and sanctions of corruption offences.[282] The discussion here focuses on three criminal law-oriented areas: the criminal laws and criminal justice, the enforcement mechanisms, and the legal powers conferred on the law enforcement authorities. To avoid overlap between the chapters, the discussion here is of a strategic nature, while the discussion in chapters 4 and 5 is related to a detailed analysis of the current laws and regulations in Kuwait.

First, the criminal law has a critical role in encountering corruption under the law enforcement strategy through the criminalisation of corruption and the determination of the penalties levied on the perpetrators. Rose-Ackerman put forward the proposition that to deter the perpetrators, the sanctioning strategies should achieve the optimal deterrence by imposing penalties commensurate with the benefits of a corrupt deal so that the penalty is positively correlated with the benefits gained from a corrupt transaction – taking into account the probability of detection.[283] Given the likelihood that corporations

278 Rose-Ackerman (1997, p. 46).
279 UNODC (2003).
280 Collier (2002, pp. 15–16).
281 Rose-Ackerman (2002).
282 Article 30.
283 Rose-Ackerman (1997). For more on the optimal deterrence, see Becker (1968).

may be involved in corruption cases, corporate criminal liability ought to be a key part of criminal law.[284]

The second aspect in the law enforcement strategy is to create anti-corruption agencies (ACAs) as a 'law enforcement mechanism'. ACAs are independent units that are erected and conferred appropriate authority to achieve counter-corruption functions.[285] This step is emphasised in Chapter III of the UNCAC where State Parties are encouraged to establish these specialised bodies with the necessary independence and resources to effectively combat corruption through law enforcement.[286] To operate effectively, international criteria for specialised ACAs have been established: ACAs should be independent of undue political influence, be specialised in relation to skilful staff and certain counter-corruption mandates, and have sufficient resources and legal powers.[287] Arguably, the ideas of Ayres and Braithwaite in *Responsive Regulation* are useful for effective ACAs. An ACA should be like 'the Benign Big Gun' model, which is an agency that speaks softly 'while carrying very big sticks'.[288] In this regard, the 'enforcement pyramid' suggests that ACAs should be empowered with enormous powers, based on a hierarchical range of sanctions.[289]

Third, the law should grant considerable legal powers to the law enforcement authorities to enable them to effectively combat corruption. Contrary to traditional criminal law techniques, shifting the burden of proof to the suspect to prove the legitimate source of the unexplained increase in his/her wealth is said to be an effective measure that achieves deterrence in corruption crimes.[290] The law should also put in place financial arrangements to deal with the proceeds and instrumentalities of corruption, including freezing orders to secure the proceeds of crime from dissipation, as well as forfeiture orders.[291] Finally, the law enforcement authorities should be permitted to make deals to uncover corruption incidences. The law could provide privileges to the parties of a corrupt deal – as embodied in leniency and reward systems. The law enforcement authorities should be able to promise to impose lower penalties, drop charges or exempt the offender from punishment to encourage the reporting of irregularities or 'coming forward with evidence' to facilitate investigations.[292]

Since 1960, Kuwaiti laws have relied on criminal laws and law enforcement strategies as a key counter-corruption strategy.[293] In chapter 4, it will be shown that the criminal responses to the challenges of corruption dominate

284 Rose-Ackerman (2002).
285 Langseth, Stapenhurst and Pope (1997).
286 Article 36.
287 OECD (2008).
288 Ayres and Braithwaite (1995, p. 40).
289 Ibid., p. 41. The 'enforcement pyramid' is addressed in chapter 5.3.1.
290 See UNODC (2003).
291 Brun et al. (2011). See also chapters 4.3.6 and 5.4.2.
292 Rose-Ackerman (2002, pp. 10–12). See also chapter 4.3.7.
293 See above section 3.2.2.

the legal system in Kuwait. When issued in 2019, the Strategy 2019–2024 re-emphasised the centrality of law enforcement strategies. One feature of the 'inclusive' Strategy is that it asserts, besides prevention and awareness, the 'punitive' nature of counter-corruption policies (the law enforcement aspect).[294] A number of initiatives throughout the Strategy underpin the law enforcement activities undertaken by the state institutions. In relation to the criminal counter-corruption laws, the Strategy aims to improve the IEO by harmonising it in accordance with the requirements of the UNCAC.[295] Moreover, the criminalisation of corruption within the private sector is part of the Strategy's agenda regarding law enforcement. The Strategy concentrates on establishing/improving the criminal liability of legal entities in corruption crimes (such as corporations) and criminalising bribery and embezzlement that entirely lie within the private sector.[296]

Regarding the specialised ACAs, Nazaha was created with full independence.[297] The ACAA has conferred on Nazaha an array of functions, ranging from prevention to enforcement-oriented functions. In terms of its law enforcement role, Nazaha receives reports related to corruption incidences, conducts an initial investigation regarding such reports, liaises with other public bodies to investigate and gather evidence about corruption cases, asks the competent bodies to initiate civil lawsuits and proceedings where necessary, refers the case dossiers to the public prosecution, and implements measures to recover the assets of corruption crimes.[298] Section 27 of the ACAA, however, has given the public prosecution exclusive authority to investigate and prosecute corruption cases. Thus, the organisational form of Nazaha is premised on the administrative model: an independent administrative authority under the supervision of the Ministry of Justice (MoJ), which forms a buffer between the reporting stage and the public prosecution.[299] Because it is not part of the judicial authorities, Nazaha does not have the legal powers of prosecutors. For example, Nazaha cannot access bank accounts in financial institutions to obtain information about those accounts, unless it obtains permission from the public prosecution.[300] Unsurprisingly, Nazaha has been included in the agenda of Strategy 2019–2024. Specifically, the Strategy aims to improve the internal structure and technical abilities of Nazaha so that it can enhance its effectiveness in undertaking its functions as stipulated by the ACAA.[301] Moreover, the Strategy is preoccupied with cooperation and coordination among the

294 Nazaha (2019, p. 16).
295 Ibid., p. 70.
296 Ibid., p. 78. Private sector bribery is mentioned in chapters 4.3.1 and 4.4.1
297 ACAA, s.3.
298 Ibid., ss.5(2), 5(6), 5(12), 5(14), and 5(15).
299 See Schott (2006).
300 ACAA, s.34.
301 Nazaha (2019, p. 93).

counter-corruption institutions as one facet of its agenda in prompting specialised institutions to be more effective.[302]

The judges, public prosecutors, and Nazaha are bestowed with legal powers that enable them to combat corruption. To name just a few, the ACAA allows for the reversing of the burden of proof to the suspect in the IEO, whereby the suspect is required to explain his/her questionable wealth[303] as a means to overcome the difficulties of prosecution in cases where the evidence is elusive.[304] Furthermore, there are two kinds of relevant legal tools that can be harnessed in corruption cases: restraint orders (such as freezing orders)[305] and the forfeiture of the proceeds of corruption.[306] Last but not least, the ACAA established the whistleblower protection programme (WPP) to encourage individuals to report crimes, and to protect them from any potential reprisals.[307] Concerning the legal powers granted to law enforcement authorities, the Strategy has directed most of its focus to the IEO and the whistleblowing system (as established by the ACAA). The IEO is to be subject to further review through keeping it as consistent as possible with the UNCAC.[308] The instrumental importance of whistleblowing in detecting corruption is also a focus of attention in the Strategy and, hence, improvements have been suggested.[309] These improvements will be addressed in chapter 4.

### 3.3.3 *Situational crime prevention (SCP)*

The situational strategy draws on the literature on crime prevention.[310] Corruption prevention here is based on SCP. Instead of thinking about the distant social causes of criminality, SCP focuses on situational features and 'seeks to reduce opportunities for specific categories of crime by increasing the associated risks and difficulties and reducing the rewards'.[311] According to SCP, crime can be prevented depending upon four tactics: 'increasing the perceived effort of crime, increasing the perceived risks, reducing the anticipated rewards, and removing excuse for crime'.[312] SCP has been subject to constant revision to include further tactics.[313] Having been recognised as 'the most important framework internationally for developing effective crime-prevention strategies', SCP

302 Ibid., p. 99.
303 However, it is not precise to say that it entails 'reverse onus of proof'. See chapter 4.3.4.
304 See Muzila et al. (2012).
305 For example, PPFA, s.24.
306 For example, ACAA, s.48. Proceeds of crime provisions are addressed in chapter 4.3.6.
307 Ibid., ss.40–43. The WPP is addressed in chapter 4.3.7.
308 Nazaha (2019, p. 70).
309 Ibid.
310 See Gorta (1998).
311 Clarke (1995, p. 91).
312 Felson and Clarke (1998, p. 24).
313 See Cornish and Clarke (2003).

can be applied to specific forms of corruption.[314] Because applications of SCP to counter-corruption policies abound, the following discussion is confined to selective examples of such applications.

From a criminological perspective, profit-oriented policies to attack criminal property in profit-driven crimes are appealing to reduce the incentives and rewards of criminality.[315] These policies may encompass innovative forfeiture techniques, such as civil forfeiture that does not require conviction to forfeit ill-gotten assets,[316] and unexplained wealth orders (UWOs), which target the proceeds of crime without a predicate crime.[317] These tools are not only reactive, in the sense that they enable law enforcement to pursue a crime after it is committed, they are also preventive in dismantling criminal enterprises and removing the proceeds of illicit activities that would be used to commit further crimes.[318] These two innovative tools will be addressed in chapter 5.4.2. The assets disclosure of officials also helps identify assets that have been acquired during the time they are in office and requires officials to prove the legitimate source of any increase in wealth.[319] According to the logic of SCP, financial disclosures have the potential to deter officeholders: they reduce the opportunity to act corruptly by increasing the risk that corruption becomes detectable.

Regarding counter-corruption efforts within the public sector, Rose-Ackerman advocates incentive-based reforms that concentrate on reducing the benefits and increasing the costs of engaging in corruption through the elimination of governmental programmes that generate opportunities for corruption.[320] The UN Anti-Corruption Toolkit emphasises a balanced system that combines elements that grant sufficient discretion to the public administration to be able to operate effectively, while, simultaneously, overseeing such discretion and holding the public administration accountable on an everyday basis.[321]

The management of public finance is a proactive stage in detecting corruption. In this context, supreme audit institutions (SAIs) are a key mechanism to examine the management of public resources. SAIs are agencies concerned with auditing government revenues and expenditure, and as such, they fulfil pre-emptive roles through acting as a watchdog over the credibility of the information reported by the state institutions.[322] SAIs may prevent

314 Graycar and Prenzler (2013, p. 71).
315 Kilchling (2001).
316 See Greenberg et al. (2009).
317 See Booz Allen Hamilton (2011).
318 Ryder (2013).
319 UNODC (2004).
320 See Rose-Ackerman (1999).
321 UNODC (2004).
322 Langseth, Stapenhurst and Pope (1997).

corruption 'through the development of financial and auditing procedures designed to reduce the incidence of corruption and increase the likelihood of its detection'.[323] The ideas of Ayres and Braithwaite about the approaches of law enforcement authorities can arguably be applied to SAIs as non-law enforcement authorities since 'governments should be responsive to the conduct of those they seek to regulate'.[324] When empowered with legal powers and enabled to use them in an escalating fashion, SAIs will be effective in persuading the supervisees to comply with the procedures of public finance. The Australian National Audit Office has adopted the 'enforcement pyramid' approach with a range of graduated responses, ranging from encouragement to comply to cancellation of the permit.[325]

Corruption prevention through manipulating the situational features in which corruption may occur provides a 'more realistic' approach to crime prevention.[326] It derives its importance from the criticism that the criminal law is 'too blunt' to be the key instrument in countering corruption because of issues related to its focus on enforcement rather than prevention, as well as the fact that it is costly, time-consuming, and fraught with evidential difficulties.[327] These issues are very important as they will bring in counter-productive consequences, for example, when a blind eye is turned to corrupt conduct just to eschew the brunt of the prosecutorial process.[328] These disadvantages can be alleviated by prevention-oriented mechanisms that either prevent the occurrence of corruption (thereby preventing the resort to criminal law) or prepare the evidence (and hence facilitate subsequent prosecutions).

Preventive arrangements have always been adopted in the Kuwait counter-corruption framework. Kuwait has founded specialised state agencies with preventive functions. The SAB, established in 1964, aims to oversee the public bodies in all matters related to public finance.[329] In terms of corruption in public procurement, each public tender whose value is KWD 100,000 or more is subject to the prior oversight of the SAB.[330] State institutions are not permitted to contract with any winning bidder, unless they obtain the permission of the SAB.[331] As such, the function of the SAB increases the risk of being detected and punished. Developing this oversight of the public finance, especially that which is conducted by the SAB, has been considered in Strategy 2019–2024. The Strategy aims to introduce improvements in the way audit reports are acted

323 Ibid., p. 515.
324 See Braithwaite (2002, p. 29).
325 See Ivec and Braithwaite (2015).
326 Clarke (1980, p. 136).
327 Langseth, Stapenhurst and Pope (1997, pp. 508–509).
328 Tanzi (1998, p. 589).
329 SAB Act, ss.2, 5, and 6.
330 Ibid., ss.13–14.
331 Ibid., s.14.

upon in the light of the best international practice.[332] The Strategy also focuses on financial oversight over state-owned companies.[333]

Kuwait has adopted several profit-oriented criminal policies to prevent corruption. Here, Nazaha performs several prevention-led corruption functions.[334] Among these, it is entrusted with implementing the assets declaration system.[335] Officials with senior positions are legally required to submit financial disclosures on different occasions.[336] These disclosures are a corruption prevention measure and serve as an oversight tool in regard to the integrity of public office and the possibility that officials can accumulate illicit wealth by abusing their position.[337] If this illicit wealth cannot be reasonably justified and a subsequent conviction is secured, the illicit wealth is liable to forfeiture.[338] Strategy 2019–2024 is rich with arrangements directed at Nazaha and its role in relation to the IEO. For example, increasing the compliance of officeholders with financial disclosures (through facilitating and securing more submissions) is one of the Strategy's preventive efforts.[339]

Given that the money laundering offence (ML offence) is strongly linked to corruption, Kuwait has criminalised any attempt to hide illegal sources of assets. To increase the likelihood that corruption is detected and to prevent the corrupt from benefiting from their crimes, preventive measures have been taken. For example, banks are not allowed to open anonymous bank accounts or accounts with fake names and they should adopt due-diligence measures and identify the purposes of accounts.[340] Most importantly, financial institutions and designated non-financial businesses and professions should report any transaction suspected to be linked to the proceeds of crime.[341] To this end, the KFIU has been established to receive and analyse suspicious transaction reports (STR) and to refer them to the public prosecution if they are suspected of being, or are linked to proceeds of crime.[342] This strategy has the potential to prevent corruption by making it less rewarding because, in the end, an offender becomes unable to benefit from his/her criminal enterprise. When a conviction in ML crime is secured, the proceeds of such a crime will be forfeited.[343] Noticeably, the potential role of the KFIU has, either wittingly or unwittingly, been overlooked by Strategy 2019–2024. The Strategy has merely concentrated on the role of the private sector in preventing corruption.

332 Nazaha (2019, p. 67).
333 Ibid., p. 68.
334 See Al-Kandari (2013).
335 ACAA, ss.30–36.
336 Ibid., s.32.
337 Al-Oumi (2015).
338 ACAA, s.48.
339 Nazaha (2019, p. 55).
340 AML/CFT Act, s.5.
341 Ibid., s.12.
342 Ibid., s.16.
343 Ibid., s.40.

With the launch of the Strategy 2019–2024, the policymakers have strongly expressed their interest in the prevention of corruption rather than the enforcement of corruption-related laws. Most of its content focuses on priorities of a preventive nature that eliminate, in the first instance, opportunities conducive to corruption. First, in relation to public office, the Strategy sets out the merit-based guidelines for appointment to public office (especially high-profile positions)[344] and reviews the codes of conduct governing public office.[345] Second, regarding public administration, the Strategy puts in place preventive arrangements regarding corruption within high-risk domains, such as public procurement,[346] aims to increase the transparency of government activities through adopting FOI legislation,[347] and aims to simplify the complexity of bureaucratic procedures within the government.[348] In general, the incorporation of risk-based systems is encouraged in each governmental sector where the risk of corruption is high.[349] With respect to the private sector, the Strategy considers the preventive role of professions and corporations and encourages them to adopt audit systems and ameliorate their governance.[350] To increase the probability of the detection of corrupt conduct, the Strategy aims to improve the whistleblowing system in both the public[351] and the private sectors.[352]

In essence, these measures aim to prevent corruption and bolster the detection of any corrupt conduct. These measures are consistent with the underpinnings of SCP in that they are directed at reducing corruption opportunities and increasing the risks of engaging in corruption so that corruption becomes a crime that does not pay. However, the analysis of the profit-oriented strategies adopted in Kuwaiti laws reveals that although Kuwaiti laws have heeded the financial arrangements of the proceeds of corruption, these arrangements lack innovative approaches to proceeds of crime, such as civil forfeiture and UWOs.[353] Although Strategy 2019–2024 might be a watershed in the history of combating corruption in Kuwait, it is disappointing that it lacks any profit-oriented tactics that involve non-criminal means. While focusing on the IEO, it has not set out a general policy regarding how to deal with the proceeds of corruption using non-criminal instruments. Kuwaiti laws still depend on the criminal law in dealing with illicit assets derived from corruption crimes – criminal conviction is the key to forfeiture. However, because of the difficulties of using traditional means of criminal law, such as punishment, to combat corruption and other

344 Nazaha (2019, pp. 58–59).
345 Ibid., pp. 61–62.
346 Ibid., p. 56.
347 Ibid., p. 71.
348 Ibid., p. 52.
349 Ibid., p. 74.
350 Ibid., pp. 75–76.
351 Ibid., p. 96.
352 Ibid., pp. 79–80.
353 See chapter 5.4.2.

crimes, the focus on financial assets has become central to the strategies that fight such crimes,[354] a point that will be subject to further analysis in the following chapters.[355]

## 3.4 Conclusion

This chapter has identified two relevant research themes: counter-corruption values and strategies. The main argument of this chapter is that corruption is symptomatic of the profound problems inherent in the state institutions in Kuwait, which has been referred to as the 'governance–corruption nexus'. Here, combating corruption is just one aspect of broader efforts to promote 'good governance' among the state institutions. Therefore, it has been argued that as well as designing a specific strategy to counter corruption, more fundamental failings need to be tackled to prepare a fertile environment for combating corruption.

Legitimacy (including other sub-values, such as transparency, accountability, human rights, morality of law, and legal certainty) and effectiveness have been found to be key values that are essential to back any potential efforts to counter corruption. Moreover, these values promote the legitimacy of any efforts to combat corruption and can secure the compliance of the public. Indeed, it has been argued that if these issues are not addressed, the counter-corruption efforts will fail. Fortunately, the basis on which institutions in Kuwait are administered is not at odds with these values. Kuwait's commitment to most of these values is an integral part of its broader commitment to democratic values. Most of these values have found explicit and implicit responses, either in the Constitution or in the laws. Yet the analysis of the mentioned values in Kuwait shows that their development is imperfect and extensive efforts are still needed in this regard. For example, the transparency value still lacks comprehensive reforms, at least regarding FOI law. It has also been shown that accountability value suffers from a flawed implementation. On the other hand, the applications of human rights are satisfactory in Kuwait, although the Kuwaiti legal system does not specify a special position for the victims of corruption and sometimes allegedly threatens the rights of suspects.

The morality of the corruption laws and their legal certainty have also been considered. It has been found that the although the morality of the criminalisation of corrupt conduct might be compromised by the underlying culture of the Kuwaiti society, there is enough room to situate corruption within a moral framework, especially in the light of the harmful nature of corruption, Islamic teachings, and the social campaigns regarding awareness of corruption. Furthermore, legal certainty has been found to be applicable to corruption laws. As shown in the Kuwaiti Constitution, laws and court

354 King and Walker (2016).
355 See chapters 4.3.6 and 5.4.2.

decisions, the Kuwaiti legal system takes into account the importance of legal certainty and its associated issues, such as clarity, accessibility, and the prohibition of retrospectivity.

The value of effectiveness in Kuwait has been found to be influenced by the counter-corruption public discourse in Kuwait, that is, the dominance of criminal law in combating corruption. Although there have been sufficient laws to criminalise the several forms of corruption since 1960, these laws suffer from a lack of enforcement – as underlined by the opinions of the experts interviewed. Also, the corruption laws are not based on evidence-based policymaking and are not subject to ongoing performance evaluation. The law enforcement authorities do not undertake independent research to evaluate whether they really work in practice. However, the adequacy and effectiveness framework should not only be observed from the perspective of criminal law. As will be discussed in chapter 5, non-criminal measures also have the potential to effectively combat corruption.

Counter-corruption strategies are also a significant theme. Given that corruption is a complex phenomenon, it cannot be combatted with a single strategy. It has been illustrated that corruption can only be fought from multi-dimensional perspectives. These strategies include empowering the society to stand against the corrupt, bolstering reactive law enforcement efforts to combat corruption after it is committed, and increasing prevention efforts to deter the corrupt from engaging in corruption or to facilitate its detection. Based on analysing the situation in Kuwait, one can see that the Kuwaiti policymaker has already integrated these various strategies into the laws to confront corruption, at least in the Strategy 2019–2024 for the future. There are designated laws to encourage civil society to participate in the public sphere, to investigate and prosecute corruption cases, and to prevent corruption from taking place. From theoretical point of view, the Strategy 2019–2024 is satisfactory in terms of content: it has addressed, inter alia, transparency and accountability as two relevant counter-corruption values, and devised overall a comprehensive counter-corruption strategy. However, assessing whether the Strategy 2019–2024 is fully effective in achieving its agendas in practice needs further time, since it has been issued only recently. Thus, the basic elements of each strategy have been identified in a strategic sense. However, a detailed analysis of those strategies, especially those that focus on laws and regulations, and their effectiveness – whether they really 'work' and serve the purposes for which they were adopted – is an issue to be addressed in the next chapters.

## Bibliography

Ades, A., di Tella, R. (1997). The New Economics of Corruption: A Survey and Some New Results. *Political Studies.* 45(3), pp. 496–515.

Al-Ghazalli, M. (2005). *Political Corruption in Arab and Islamic Societies.* Giza Governorate: Nahdet Misr Publishing House.

Al-Kandari, F. (2013). Philosophy of Kuwaiti and Arab Legislators in Combating Corruption. *Journal of Kuwait International Law School.* 1(4), pp. 397–452.

Al-Kilani, S. (2007). *Against Corruption: The Role of Arab Civil Society in Fighting Corruption*. Amman, Jordan: Arab Archives Institute.

Al-Najjar, G. (2000). The Challenges Facing Kuwaiti Democracy. *Middle East Journal*. 54(2), pp. 242–258.

Al-Oumi, N. (2015). Illicit Enrichment: Comparative Analytic Study of the Decree-Law No. 24 of 2012 of the Public Authority of Anti-Corruption and the Provisions for Financial Disclosure. *Kuwait University Journal of Law*. 39(4), pp. 65–112.

Al-Qarioti, M. (2013). Bribery Problem in Kuwaiti Administration: An Exploratory Study. In: *Proceedings of the 10th Eurasia Business and Economics Society Conference, May 23–25, 2013, Istanbul, Turkey*. Istanbul: EBES Publications, pp. 52–64.

Al-Shehabi, O. (2017). *Show Us the Money: Oil Revenues, Undisclosed Allocations and Accountability in Budgets of the GCC States*. London: LSE.

Ayres, I., Braithwaite, J. (1995). *Responsive Regulation: Transcending the Deregulation Debate*. Oxford: Oxford University Press.

Becker, G. S. (1968). Crime and Punishment: An Economic Approach. *Journal of Political Economy*. 76(2), pp. 169–217.

Beetham, D. (2013). *The Legitimation of Power*. London: Palgrave Macmillan.

Bellver, A., Kaufmann, D. (2005). *Transparenting Transparency: Initial Empirics and Policy Applications* (World Bank Policy Research Working Paper). Washington, DC: World Bank.

Berger, B. (2014). Constitutional Principles. In: Dubber, M., Hörnle, T. (eds). *The Oxford Handbook of Criminal Law*. Oxford: Oxford University Press, pp. 422–442.

Bertelsmann Foundation Transformation Index. (2018). BTI 2018 | Kuwait Country Report. [Online]. Available from: http://www.bti-project.org/fileadmin/files/BTI/Downloads/Reports/2018/pdf/BTI_2018_Kuwait.pdf.

Bingham, T. (2011). *The Rule of Law*. London: Penguin Books.

Bloom, B. (2014). Criminalizing Kleptocracy? The ICC as a Viable Tool in the Fight Against Grand Corruption. *American University International Law Review*. 29(3), pp. 627–671.

Booz Allen Hamilton. (2011). *Comparative Evaluation of Unexplained Wealth Orders: Prepared to the US Department of Justice*. Washington, DC: National Institute of Justice.

Bovens, M. (2005). Public Accountability. In: Ferlie, E., Lynn, L., Pollitt, C. (eds). *The Oxford Handbook of Public Management*. Oxford: Oxford University Press, pp. 182–208.

Bovens, M., Goodin, R., Schillemans, T. (2014). Public Accountability. In: Bovens, M., Schillemans, T., Goodin, R. (eds). *The Oxford Handbook of Public Accountability*. Oxford: Oxford University Press, pp. 1–20.

Braithwaite, J. (2002). *Restorative Justice & Responsive Regulation*. Oxford U6 - ctx_ver=Z39.88-2004&ctx_enc=info%3Aofi%2Fenc%3AUTF-8&rfr_id=info%3Asid%2Fsummon.serialssolutions.com&rft_val_fmt=info%3Aofi%2Ffmt%3Akev%3Amtx%3Abook&rft.genre=book&rft.title=Restorative+justice+%26+responsive+regulation&rft.au=Braithwaite%2C+John%2C+1951&rft.series=Studies+in+crime+and+public+policy&rft.date=2002-01-01&rft.pub=Oxford+University+Press&rft.externalDocID=b36239288&paramdict=en-US U7 - Book: Oxford University Press.

Brun, J.-P., Gray, L., Scott, C., Stephenson, K. (2011). *Asset Recovery Handbook: A Guide for Practitioners*. Washington, DC: World Bank.

Buckley, M. (2002). Anti-corruption Initiatives and Human Rights: The Potentials. In: Sano, H.-O., Alfredsson, G. (eds). *Human Rights and Good Governance: Building Bridges*. The Hague: Martinus Nijhoff Publishers, pp. 173–201.

Clark, W. R., Golder, M., Golder, S. N. (2017). *Principles of Comparative Politics.* Washington, DC: CQ Press.

Clarke, R. V. (1980). "Situational" Crime Prevention: Theory and Practice. *British Journal of Criminology.* 20(2), pp. 136–147.

Clarke, R. V. (1995). Situational Crime Prevention. *Crime and Justice.* 19, pp. 91–150.

Collier, M. W. (2002). Explaining Corruption: An Institutional Choice Approach. *Crime, Law and Social Change.* 38(1), pp. 1–32.

Cornish, D. & Clarke, R. V. (2003). Opportunities, Precipitators and Criminal Decisions: A Reply to Wortley's Critique of Situational Crime Prevention. *Crime Prevention Studies.* 16, pp. 41–96.

Dicey, A. V. (1989). Ministerial Responsibility and the Rule of Law. In: Marshall, G. (ed). *Ministerial Responsibility.* Oxford: Oxford University Press, pp. 22–24.

Ehteshami, A. (2003). Reform from Above: The Politics of Participation in the Oil Monarchies. *International Affairs.* 79(1), pp. 53–75.

Everett, J., Neu, D., Rahaman, A. S. (2006). The Global Fight Against Corruption: A Foucaultian, Virtues-Ethics Framing. *Journal of Business Ethics.* 65(1), pp. 1–12.

Extractive Industries Transparency Initiative. (2016). *What the EITI Does: Building Trust Through Transparency.* [Online]. [1 December 2019]. Available from: http://progrep.eiti.org/2016/glance/what-eiti-does.

Felson, M., Clarke, R. V. (1998). *Opportunity Makes the Thief: Practical Theory for Crime Prevention* (*Police Research Series Paper 98*). London: Home Office.

Finel, B., Lord, K. (1999). The Surprising Logic of Transparency. *International Studies Quarterly.* 43(2), pp. 315–339.

Fung, A., Graham, M., Weil, D. (2007). *Full Disclosure: The Perils and Promise of Transparency.* Cambridge: Cambridge University Press.

Gathii, J. T. (2009). Defining the Relationship Between Human Rights and Corruption. *University of Pennsylvania Journal of International Law.* 31, pp. 125–202.

Gorta, A. (1998). Minimising Corruption: Applying Lessons from the Crime Prevention Literature. *Crime, Law and Social Change.* 30(1), pp. 65–87.

Graycar, A., Prenzler, T. (2013). *Understanding and Preventing Corruption.* London: Palgrave Macmillan.

Green, S. (1997). Why It's a Crime to Tear the Tag Off a Mattress: Overcriminalization and the Moral Content of Regulatory Offenses. *Emory Law Journal.* 46(4), pp. 1533–1615.

Green, S. (2004). Moral Ambiguity in White Collar Criminal Law. *Notre Dame Journal of Law, Ethics & Public Policy.* 18(2), pp. 501–519.

Greenberg, T., Samuel, L., Grant, W., Gray, L. (2009). *Stolen Asset Recovery: A Good Practices Guide for Non-Conviction Based Asset Forfeiture.* Washington, DC: World Bank.

Grimwood, G. (2016). *After the International Anti-Corruption Summit in May 2016: What Next?* (HC Briefing Paper 7580, 20 May 2016). London: House of Commons Library.

Gruenberg, C. (2009). *Corruption and Human Rights: Integrating Human Rights into the Anti-Corruption Agenda.* Geneva: International Council on Human Rights Policy.

Head, B. (2008). Three Lenses of Evidence-Based Policy. *Australian Journal of Public Administration.* 67(1), pp. 1–11.

Human Rights Committee. (2014). *Consideration of Reports Submitted by States Parties Under Article 40 of the Covenant: Third Periodic Report of Kuwait.* New York: UN.

Huther, J., Shah, A. (2000). *Anti-Corruption Policies and Programs: A Framework for Evaluation.* Washington, DC: World Bank.

International Center for Not-for-Profit Law. (2017). *Kuwait Philanthropy Law Report.* Washington, DC: International Center for Not-for-Profit Law.

International Commission of Jurists. (1959). *The Rule of Law in a Free Society: A Report on the International Congress of Jurists, New Delhi, India, January 5–10, 1959.* Geneva: International Commission of Jurists.

Ivec, M., Braithwaite, V. (2015). *Applications of Responsive Regulatory Theory in Australia and Overseas: Update* (RegNet Working Paper No. 72). Canberra: Regulatory Institutions Network (RegNet), ANU.

Johnston, M. (1998). Fighting Systemic Corruption: Social Foundations for Institutional Reform. *European Journal of Development Research.* 10(1), pp. 85–104.

Johnston, M., Kpundeh, S. (2004). *Building a Clean Machine: Anti-Corruption Coalitions and Sustainable Reform.* Washington, DC: World Bank.

Karagiannis, E. (2017). *The New Political Islam: Human Rights, Democracy, and Justice.* Philadelphia, PA: University of Pennsylvania Press.

Kaufmann, D., Kraay, A., Mastruzzi, M. (2011). The Worldwide Governance Indicators: Methodology and Analytical Issues. *Hague Journal on the Rule of Law.* 3(2), pp. 220–246.

Khodr, H. (2014). A Preliminary Comparative Study of Policy Making in Two GCC Countries—Qatar and Kuwait: Processes, Politics, and Participants. *Politics & Policy.* 42(2), pp. 271–310.

Kilchling, M. (2001). Tracing, Seizing and Confiscating Proceeds from Corruption (and Other Illegal Conduct) Within or Outside the Criminal Justice System. *European Journal of Crime, Criminal Law and Criminal Justice.* 9(4), pp. 264–280.

King, C., Walker, C. (2016). Emerging Issues in the Regulation of Criminal and Terrorist Assets. In: King, C., Walker, C. (eds). *Dirty Assets: Emerging Issues in the Regulation of Criminal and Terrorist Assets.* Abingdon: Routledge, pp. 19–40.

Kuwait Ministry of Justice. (2017). *Report of Fact-Finding Committee in the Anti-Corruption Authority.* Kuwait: Ministry of Justice.

Lambsdorff, J. (2002). Corruption and Rent-Seeking. *Public Choice.* 113(1–2), pp. 97–125.

Langseth, P., Stapenhurst, R., Pope, J. (1997). The Role of a National Integrity System in Fighting Corruption. *Commonwealth Law Bulletin.* 23(1–2), pp. 499–528.

Lederman, D., Loayza, N., Soares, R. (2005). Accountability and Corruption: Political Institutions Matter. *Economics and Politics.* 17(1), pp. 1–35.

Lindstedt, C., Naurin, D. (2010). Transparency Is Not Enough: Making Transparency Effective in Reducing Corruption. *International Political Science Review.* 31(3), pp. 301–322.

Maxeiner, J. (2007). Legal Certainty: A European Alternative to American Legal Indeterminacy. *Tulane Journal of International and Comparative Law.* 15(2), pp. 541–607.

Muzila, L., Morales, M., Mathias, M., Berger, T. (2012). *On the Take: Criminalizing Illicit Enrichment to Fight Corruption.* Washington, DC: World Bank.

Nazaha. (2019). *Kuwait Integrity and Anti-Corruption Strategy 2019–2024.* Nazaha.

Nye, J. S. (1967). Corruption and Political Development: A Cost-Benefit Analysis. *American Political Science Review.* 61(2), pp. 417–427.

O'Donnell, G. A. (1998). Horizontal Accountability in New Democracies. *Journal of Democracy.* 9(3), pp. 112–126.

OECD. (2008). *Specialised Anti-Corruption Institutions: Review of Models.* Paris: OECD.

OECD. (2011). *Asset Declarations for Public Officials: A Tool to Prevent Corruption.* Paris: OECD.

Pearson, Z. (2013). An International Human Rights Approach to Corruption. In: Larmour, P., Wolanin, N. (eds). *Corruption and Anti-Corruption.* Canberra: ANU Press, pp. 30–61.

Philp, M. (2001). Access, Accountability and Authority: Corruption and the Democratic Process. *Crime, Law and Social Change.* 36(4), pp. 357–377.

Philp, M. (2015). The Definition of Political Corruption. In: Heywood, P. (ed). *Routledge Handbook of Political Corruption.* Abingdon: Routledge, pp. 17–29.

Piotrowski, S. (2017). The "Open Government Reform" Movement: The Case of the Open Government Partnership and US Transparency Policies. *American Review of Public Administration.* 47(2), pp. 155–171.

Romzek, B. S., Dubnick, M. J. (1987). Accountability in the Public Sector: Lessons from the Challenger Tragedy. *Public Administration Review.* 47(3), pp. 227–238.

Rose-Ackerman, S. (1997). The Political Economy of Corruption. In: Elliott, K. (ed). *Corruption and the Global Economy.* Washington, DC: Institute for International Economics, pp. 31–60.

Rose-Ackerman, S. (1999). *Corruption and Government: Causes, Consequences, and Reform.* Cambridge: Cambridge University Press.

Rose-Ackerman, S. (2002). Corruption and the Criminal Law. In: van Dijk, J., Ruggiero, V. (eds). *Forum on Crime and Society.* Vienna: UNODC, pp. 3–21.

Ross, M. (2011). *Mineral Wealth and Budget Transparency* (IBP Working Paper 2). Washington, DC: International Budget Partnership.

Rothstein, B., Torsello, D. (2013). *Is Corruption Understood Differently in Different Cultures?* (Working Paper Series 2013:5). Gothenburg, Sweden: Quality of Government Institute, University of Gothenburg.

Ryder, N. (2013). To Confiscate or Not to Confiscate? A Comparative Analysis of the Confiscation of the Proceeds of Crime Legislation in the United States of America and the United Kingdom. *Journal of Business Law.* 8, pp. 767–798.

Sala-i-Martin, X., Subramanian, A. (2013). Addressing the Natural Resource Curse: An Illustration from Nigeria. *Journal of African Economies.* 22(4), pp. 570–615.

Salih, K. (1991). Kuwait: Political Consequences of Modernization, 1750–1986. *Middle Eastern Studies.* 27(1), pp. 46–66.

Salih, K. (2011). Kuwait Primary (Tribal) Elections 1975–2008: An Evaluative Study. *British Journal of Middle Eastern Studies.* 38(2), pp. 141–167.

Sanderson, I. (2002). Evaluation, Policy Learning and Evidence-Based Policy Making. *Public Administration.* 80(1), pp. 1–22.

Schedler, A. (1999). Conceptualizing Accountability. In: Schedler, A., Diamond, L., Plattner, M. (eds). *The Self-Restraining State: Power and Accountability in New Democracies.* London; Boulder, CO: Lynne Reinner Publishers, pp. 13–28.

Schott, P. (2006). *Reference Guide to Anti-Money Laundering and Combating the Financing of Terrorism.* Washington, DC: World Bank.

Scott, J. C. (1972). *Comparative Political Corruption.* Upper Saddle River, NJ: Prentice Hall.

Stevens, P. (2008). *Kuwait Petroleum Corporation: Searching for Strategy in a Fragmented Oil Sector* (Working Paper No. 78). Stanford, CA: Program on Energy and Sustainable Development (PESD), Stanford University.

Tanzi, V. (1998). Corruption Around the World: Causes, Consequences, Scope, and Cures. *IMF Staff Papers.* 45(4), pp. 559–594.

Transparency International. (2008). *Human Rights and Corruption*. Berlin: Transparency International.

Tyler, T. R. (2006a). Psychological Perspectives on Legitimacy and Legitimation. *Annual Review of Psychology*. 57(1), pp. 375–400.

Tyler, T. R. (2006b). *Why People Obey the Law*. Princeton, NJ: Princeton University Press.

Underkuffler, L. (2013). *Captured by Evil: The Idea of Corruption in Law*. London: Yale University Press.

UNODC. (2003). *United Nations Guide on Anti-Corruption Policies*. Vienna: UN.

UNODC. (2004). *United Nations Anti-Corruption Toolkit*. Vienna: UN.

Uslaner, E. M. (2008). *Corruption, Inequality, and the Rule of Law: The Bulging Pocket Makes the Easy Life*. Cambridge: Cambridge University Press.

Walker, J. L. (1969). The Diffusion of Innovations Among the American States. *American Political Science Review*. 63(3), pp. 880–899.

Ward, G. (2004). The Role of Disclosure in Combating Corruption in Political Finance. In: Transparency International. (ed). *Global Corruption Report 2004*. London: Pluto Press, pp. 38–53.

Whelan, P. (2012). Legal Certainty and Cartel Criminalisation Within the EU Member States. *Cambridge Law Journal*. 71(3), pp. 677–702.

Whelan, P. (2013). Cartel Criminalization and the Challenge of 'Moral Wrongfulness'. *Oxford Journal of Legal Studies*. 33(3), pp. 535–561.

World Bank. (2019). Worldwide Governance Indicators. [Online]. Available from: https://info.worldbank.org/governance/wgi/

# 4 Kuwaiti criminal counter-corruption measures

## 4.1 Introduction

In the previous chapters, the book has addressed various issues relevant to the phenomenon of corruption (chapter 2) and the counter-corruption values and strategies (chapter 3). These two chapters can be linked to the current chapter. Chapter 2 helps the subsequent chapters to determine how corruption can be combatted. Chapter 3 builds on chapter 2 and studies corruption as a governance problem, suggesting necessary broader non-legal issues that should first be addressed so that the wider public are encouraged to comply with the counter-corruption laws. It also explores the literature on counter-corruption strategies. The current chapter investigates the Kuwaiti legal framework regarding how to combat corruption from the perspective of the criminal law (one law enforcement strategy that was addressed in chapter 3.3.2). It should be noted that although there is an attempt to strike a balance within the legal framework, the Kuwaiti response to corruption resides mainly in the criminal law. This justifies the direction of the book in that the criminal counter-corruption measures are dealt with first, and there is some imbalance between the criminal and non-criminal[1] responses. Therefore, this chapter derives its importance from the dominance of counter-corruption criminal measures in Kuwait.

This chapter aims to achieve two of the research objectives (the third and fifth objectives). It investigates Kuwait's current experience of counter-corruption from the perspective of criminal laws (third objective). To achieve the third objective, this chapter approaches three sub-research questions: what are the current criminal measures against corruption? how can these measures be improved? and do the current measures need innovation? Furthermore, this chapter uses socio-legal methodology to ensure a fuller understanding of the subject of this chapter (fifth objective). A qualitative-based study (semi-structured interviews) is adopted to answer the book' third objective within a practical context.

1 Discussed in chapter 5.

The chapter proceeds as follows. Section 4.2 delineates the scope of the chapter by finding a working definition of corruption through which criminal counter-corruption laws in Kuwait can be identified. Because this book relates to Kuwait, where corruption is more damaging in the public sector, the focus is on corruption crimes that are committed by public officials. Section 4.3 explores and analyses the legal framework of the criminal counter-corruption measures and their effectiveness. This section uncovers the shortcomings of the current criminal measures and is enriched by the opinions of professional experts. Section 4.4.1 builds on the analysis undertaken in section 4.3 to problematise the current criminal responses. It shows that the current criminal responses are inadequate in themselves to deal with grand corruption and suggests some reforms. In addition, faced with the shortcomings of the current criminal laws, section 4.4.2 also suggests potential innovative techniques to confront the problem of grand corruption, such as prosecutorial agreements, bounty hunting, and public mobilisation strategies.

## 4.2 What is corruption in Kuwaiti law? Setting the scope of chapter

In demarcating the scope of the chapter, this section adopts a working definition of corruption that helps the subsequent sections to delimit the Kuwaiti criminal responses to corruption.[2] In addition, this section re-states the special interest of the book in the grand corruption as prevalent pattern in Kuwait and links the analysis of counter-corruption measures with this pattern. This section does not recap that problem; rather, it identifies a link between the Kuwaiti legal responses and the problem of grand corruption. The focus on grand corruption in this book leads, among other things, to the discussion of select corruption offences, which tend to be associated with this corruption pattern. The analysis and critique of the counter-corruption measures will take a distinct tack in the context of grand corruption, given the difficulties that characterise such corruption. Grand corruption is different from petty corruption in that it often involves abuses of public office by senior officials. The sensitive decisions taken by those officials may have financial consequences, which necessitate the focus on specific offences that relate to the decision-making process or/and involve large sums of money. Also, the analysis of these offences is predicated on a presumption that they are assumed to be committed by high-level officials, which might impact the way in which they are analysed. The difficulties linked to offences committed by senior officials differ in their complexity from those committed by low-level officials.[3] Proving misconduct in a complex investment decision is more difficult than proving corruption in everyday activities undertaken by lower-level service

2 As well as the non-criminal responses in chapter 5.3.
3 Nicholls et al. (2017).

*Table 4.1* Laws and offences considered as corruption in Kuwaiti law

| *Act* | *Offences* |
|---|---|
| Anti-Corruption Authority and Financial Disclosure Act (ACAA) 2/2016 and its Statutory Instrument No. 300/2016 (ACAA-SI) | Illicit enrichment offence (IEO) and obstruction of Anti-Corruption Authority (Nazaha) |
| Anti-Money Laundering and Countering Financing of Terrorism Act (AML/CFT Act) 106/2013 and its Statutory Instrument No. 37/2013 (AML/CFT-SI) | Money laundering offence (ML offence) and terrorist act and terrorism financing offences |
| Competition Protection Act 10/2007 | Antitrust offences |
| Conflict of Interest Act (CIA) 13/2018 and its Statutory Instrument No. 296/2018 (CIA-SI) | Conflict of interest offence |
| Criminal Law Act 16/1960 (CLA 1960) | Forgery, counterfeiting and obstruction of justice offences |
| Criminal Law Act 31/1970 (CLA 1970) | Bribery and trade in influence |
| Disclosure of Commissions in Public Procurement Act 25/1996 | Non-declaration or false declaration of a commission |
| GCC Common Customs Act (GCCA) 10/2003 | Smuggling offence |
| Income Tax Act 3/1955 | Tax evasion offences |
| Protection of Public Funds Act (PPFA) 1/1993 | Offences against public funds and office |

providers. Moreover, large-scale corruption cases justify focusing on measures related to the proceeds of crime.[4] These measures can be made effective by attacking the financial incentives inherent in grand corruption cases.

There is no specific definition of 'corruption' in Kuwaiti law. Instead, Kuwait has followed the United Nations Convention against Corruption (UNCAC) in avoiding defining corruption by simply listing specific types of acts as corruption.[5] Section 22 of the Anti-Corruption Authority and Financial Disclosure Act (ACAA) 2/2016 lists the crimes that can be identified as corruption (see Table 4.1 above).

However, the crimes listed are not statutorily considered corruption crimes unless they are committed by specific individuals.[6] Corruption crime, in this sense, is subject to the special provisions provided by the ACAA. Table 4.2 illustrates the categories of officeholders stipulated by the ACAA. These categories raise the point that all of the officeholders mentioned in the table hold a sensitive position, owing to their official duties. One conclusion can be inferred, which is that the ACAA is largely driven by the problem of grand corruption in Kuwait.

As for a working definition beyond Kuwait, the focus is often upon the nature of the act. This conception is made possible by predicating corruption on the public roles of officials.[7] The World Bank's conception of corruption as 'the

4 UNODC (2003).

5 UNODC (2004b).

6 ACAA, s.2.

7 See Gardiner (2007).

*Table 4.2* Categories of officials subject to the ACAA

| *Officials* |
|---|
| Prime minister, ministers, and officials performing an executive function with the rank of Minister; |
| President and members of National Assembly |
| President and members of Municipal Council |
| Judges, prosecutors, lawyers of the Department of Legislation and Legal Advice, members of the Criminal Investigation Department, lawyers of the Municipality, arbitrators, members of the Experts Department, official receivers, liquidators, debt collectors, officials of the Land Registry, and notaries |
| Chairperson and members of the councils and authorities that perform executive functions and that are established by an Act, an Amiri decree or a Cabinet decision |
| Chairman, Deputy Chairman, Board of Trustees, Secretary General, Directors, and technical staff of Nazaha |
| Chairman, Deputy Chairman, Directors, and technical staff of the SAB |
| Officials of the Financial Controllers Bureau (FCB) |
| Senior officials, including:<br>• Deputy ministers<br>• Board of Directors, Directors, and Secretary Generals of the public authorities and agencies and other governmental bodies<br>• Ex officio senior officials in any governmental body<br>• Directors of departments in any governmental body |
| The two previous paragraphs include officials, diplomats, and military personnel who occupy such positions – permanently or temporarily |
| State representatives in the Board of Directors of companies that the state directly contributes to with 25% of its capital |
| Board of Directors of the cooperative societies and sports governing bodies |

abuse of public office for private gain' is helpful for this purpose. In general, this conception helps the chapter to focus on corruption within the public sector and to exclude private sector corruption. In particular, this definition helps the book consider a broader conception of corruption that encompasses both a wide range of criminal offences that come under the umbrella of the abuse of public office and non-criminal forms of corruption, such as disciplinary offences.[8]

Kuwaiti criminal counter-corruption laws contain many statutory provisions. However, to remain consistent with the World Bank's definition discussed above, not all criminal counter-corruption laws are addressed here; rather, specific offences are selected and analysed. Among the several offences deemed corruption in the ACAA, the definition helps to identify core corruption offences that can be perceived as violations against the public office. Also, only intentional offences are chosen. Offences based on criminal negligence are excluded, as corruption cannot be unintentional for the purpose of this chapter. Furthermore, the analysis includes the IEO and ML offence because

8 See chapter 5.3.4.

such offences are key enablers of, and associated with, corruption as a predicate crime.[9] Others acts, such as counterfeiting, smuggling, and antitrust crimes, are excluded because they may not be committed in the course of an officeholder's occupation. Reflecting Hart's view of legal rules, while corruption has 'a central core of undisputed meaning', some other corruption crimes may be perceived as a group of acts that constitute the 'penumbra' of corruption's core meaning.[10] These crimes may be dealt with as economic crimes and be subject to other laws and enforced by other law enforcement authorities in Kuwait (such as the Competition Protection Agency and Kuwait Customs).

## 4.3 Current criminal counter-corruption measures

This section explores the criminal counter-corruption framework in Kuwait. For the purposes of this section, this framework is classified into three parts. The first explains specific corruption offences, based on the criteria identified above: bribery, diversion of public funds, abuse of functions, the IEO, and the ML offence. The second addresses the financial arrangements that deal with the proceeds of corruption. The third part addresses the provisions regarding whistleblowing, especially those related to corruption crimes. Furthermore, this section analyses the effectiveness and fairness of this criminal framework in practice. The analysis is enriched by different sources, including doctrinal analysis of legal texts, comparative law, empirical data collected during the fieldwork, and interviews conducted with experts in Kuwait to illustrate the legislative history of each crime.[11]

### 4.3.1 *Bribery*

In Kuwait, prior to 1960, crimes were subject to the provisions of *Fiqh* (the theory of Islamic law based on Quran and *Sunnah*).[12] However, in 1960, just before its independence in 1961, the Kuwaiti legislation criminalised bribery offences in sections 114–119 of the CLA 16/1960 (CLA 1960). The bribery offence is one the earliest responses to corruption in Kuwait. When it was first criminalised in 1960, there was no distinct legislative history of bribery. In 1970, bribery offences were re-enacted under the chapter of 'offences against the duties of public office' in the CLA 31/1970 (CLA 1970). The 1970 amendments aimed to counter the proliferation of bribery at that time and the threats it posed to the state apparatus: 'the Kuwaiti legislature re-enacted new provisions of bribery crime with more severity'.[13] As the Explanatory Memorandum

9 UNODC (2003).

10 Hart (2012, p. 12).

11 In general, there are limited data about the legislative history of laws, especially from the government and National Assembly.

12 Explanatory Memorandum of the CLA 1960, para.2.

13 Homad (1977, p. 13).

of the CLA 1970 illustrates, the rationale beyond criminalising bribery was to protect the integrity of public office and to maintain trust in it. Bribery of national officials is specified in Article 15 of the UNCAC, which requires the criminalisation of '(a) The promise, offering or giving, to a public official, directly or indirectly, of an undue advantage,' and '(b) The solicitation or acceptance by a public official, directly or indirectly, of an undue advantage'. This section only analyses passive and active bribery of officeholders[14] and the subsequent reward offence.[15] Some of the issues arising here will be compared with the UK Bribery Act (UK BA) 2010.

There are various prerequisites for those bribery offences to have occurred. The bribed offender should be an official. The official should also be competent: he/she should have legal or factual authority to do what the bribe requires. However, bribery occurs when an official claims authority to do, or refrain from, what the bribe requires, or when the official mistakenly reckons that he/she has the legal authority.[16] The criminal law has extended the officeholder definition beyond the concept of public officials within the meaning of the administrative laws. Section 43 of the CLA 1970 stipulates that the following categories of individuals are deemed officials:

1 officials, clients, and workers of both the governmental bodies and the bodies that are supervised and overseen by the government;
2 members of parliament and other local councils (elected and appointed);
3 arbitrators, members of the Experts Department, official receivers, liquidators, and debt collectors;
4 boards of directors, directors, officials, and clients of companies and enterprises in which the state has any capital contribution; and
5 every individual that is charged with a public service.

As noted above, two bribery offences are discussed here.[17] First, active and passive bribery offences involve situations where an official asks for, or accepts for himself/herself or for others, a promise or an undue advantage in exchange for performing or refraining from one of his/her official duties.[18] The *actus reus* comprises the activity of either solicitation or acceptance, and undue advantage, including financial perks and other moral benefits.[19] The *mens rea* requires general intent.[20] Intent is defined in section 41 of the CLA 1960 as when the defendant wilfully commits the proscribed act to achieve the prohibited results.[21] The

14 CLA 1970, s.35.
15 Ibid., s.36; CLA 1960, s.118.
16 See Al-Kandari and Ghannam (2006).
17 See Appendix 2 for the full text of the offences in Arabic.
18 CLA 1970, s.35.
19 Ibid., s.38.
20 Al-Kandari and Ghannam (2006).
21 See also Hosni (2012).

official should intend to take the undue advantage offered to commit the crime. It is then immaterial whether the officeholder intends to perform or refrain from their official duties.[22] The official must also know that he/she is being bribed to perform, refrain from, or violate, a duty.[23] The official is liable to a sentence of up to 10 years' imprisonment and a fine equal to twice the value of what was given or promised.[24]

Second, the subsequent reward offence involves two forms. The first includes any official, who, without prior agreement, accepts an undue advantage as a reward from someone for whom the official has already performed, or refrained from, an act in violation of one of his/her official duties. The official is liable to a sentence of up to 5 years' imprisonment and a fine of not less than 50 Kuwaiti dinars.[25] The second form refers to the case where the performance or refraining by the official did not violate his/her official duties. For this offence, the official is liable to a sentence of up to 3 years' imprisonment and a fine equal to the bribe or the advantage.[26] The subsequent reward offence requires that the official should have already done what the briber wants and that there should be no prior agreement between the offenders.[27] Notably, the *actus reus* here is limited to the acceptance of the bribe/reward.[28] It is not crime if an official asked for a reward after he/he had performed or refrained from one of his/her duties. The latter offence is still valid, despite the controversy over whether the CLA 1970 repealed the bribery-related provisions of the CLA 1960. The courts have emphasised that section 118 of the CLA 1960 does not contradict the new provisions of the CLA 1970, and each Act criminalises a different form of bribery.[29]

Official-2 emphasised that 'the current law on bribery aims to criminalise a wide range of potential abuses of the public office'. The CLA 1970 sends a message to officials that bribery is unacceptable to the extent that it criminalises 'just thinking about engaging in bribery and even if the official does not have the official capacity to do what he or she promises'.[30] The ability to apply bribery to many potential cases has led some professionals to think that bribery, as a legal text, is effective.[31] It is not surprising then that NGO-3 stated that, 'based on the relatively high rate of referrals by the public prosecutors and convictions by the courts, bribery is more effective than other corruption crimes'. Judge-1 also concluded that, 'since its criminalisation, there have been numerous bribery cases that have ended with convictions'.

22 CLA 1970, s.35.
23 Case No. 770/2009, 26/10/2010 (Supreme Court – Criminal Division) 16.
24 CLA 1970, s.35.
25 Ibid., s.36.
26 CLA 1960, s.118.
27 Al-Kandari and Ghannam (2006).
28 CLA 1960, s.118; CLA 1970, s.36.
29 Case No. 19/1990, 19/3/1990 (Supreme Court – Criminal Division) 6.
30 Official-2.
31 Lawyer-2; Judge-1.

Despite this endorsement by the interviewees, the bribery offence has been beset with many practical problems and criticised by Kuwaiti professionals. Across the interviews, 'the problem of difficulty with proving bribery' could be inferred as an emerging pattern.[32] Some participants concluded that bribery, in the current situation, is not effective and is unable to bring the intended effect – that is, ensuring the integrity of officials. Lawyer-1 stated that, 'from a practical perspective, the law on bribery in Kuwaiti law is of little value in combating bribery offences.' Because of the requirements of the law, bribery is difficult to prove.[33] Lawyer-1 stated that the 'bribery offence is difficult to prove in many cases as the Act requires that the benefit or the undue advantage should be proven to be in the possession of the offender.' Official-4 added that the requirement that the offenders should be caught *in flagrante delicto* (caught red-handed) proves to be almost impossible, and 'this is why there are many cases that have ended with acquittal'. Official-4 believed that the strict requirements of the bribery offence, which caused the perceived difficulty in proving it, lead to contradictions in implementing it: 'while some low-level officials are easily caught for being bribed, other high-ranking officials escape justice although they have abused the public office'. The interviewees proposed solutions to overcome this difficulty. The legislature may encourage whistleblowers and grant them some privileges, such as criminal impunity.[34] Judge-1 also suggested that the agents working in the law enforcement authorities should be well trained as one important factor that could enhance the effectiveness of the bribery offence.

The views of Lawyer-1 and Official-4 are arguably insufficient as explanations of the law. What they said (that the benefit should be proven to be in the possession of the offender, or they should be caught red-handed) are not requirements of the bribery offences in Kuwaiti law. The Kuwaiti criminal courts have emphasised on many occasions that the bribery offence may be proved by all means or types of evidence. In one bribery case, the court applied the general rule on criminal evidence established by the Kuwaiti Supreme Court, asserting that what matters in criminal trials is that the judge is persuaded by the evidence adduced; that the judge can infer the guilt or innocence of the defendant(s) from any admissible evidence or the facts of the case; and that the judge can decide whether what occurred – the offence as depicted by the prosecutor – is true or not.[35] Consequently, the bribery offence does not have to be proved in a particular way. The tactics that police officers often use to catch bribed offenders *in flagrante delicto* should not be conflated with what the elements of the bribery offence in the statutes are: that is just evidence to be used to strengthen the case.

32 Lawyer-1; Lawyer-2; Official-2; Official-4; Judge-1.

33 For example, Lawyer-1; Judge-1.

34 Judge-1.

35 See, for example, Case No. 328/2011, 13/2/2012 (Supreme Court – Criminal Division).

Official-2 mentioned a new aspect of proof-based difficulties, stating that criminal activities have become too complex to be proven: 'the undue advantage may take the form of buying real estate abroad, and this complexity affects the ability to prove bribery, and hence, its effectiveness'. Bribery is a conventional offence, in the sense that the law requires material physical or moral benefits to be accrued to the official. This conception of bribery hinders it from keeping up with the complex forms that bribery may take nowadays. Lawyer-2 summarised the problem: 'Bringing in evidence on bribery is difficult; it is not easy to find an official who is being bribed. In practice, bribes are not being paid through bank transfers but in cash. An important example of this problem is the "multi-million deposit scandal"'. Therefore, the bribery law should be improved to keep pace with the non-traditional approaches used in committing bribery, such as an exchange of benefits that does not take the form of explicit bribery: 'when an officeholder exploits his/her discretion with the intention of simultaneously achieving benefits for himself/herself and for others'.[36] Lawyer-1 argued that 'the criminalisation of conflicts of interest in the Conflict of Interests Act rectifies some drawbacks that bribery is plagued with'. The conflict of interest offence can be described as a 'modernised form of bribery' as the legislature has criminalised other forms of unnamed benefits and advantages, such as the assumption that the possession by an official of a share in a business that deals with that official's employer is a form of undue advantage.[37]

Official-4 referred to another problem related to the *mens rea* required in bribery offences. This practice reveals another trick that is used by lawyers, which jeopardises the effectiveness of the bribery offence. Under the current law, it is difficult to prove that what is paid is in return for what the official did (especially when he/she discharged his/her duty properly). Some lawyers state, as a defence, that what has been paid is, in fact, just a debt that the official owed to the person.[38] Lawyer-1, Lawyer-2, and Official-4 stated that the current law must be revised and amended in order for the bribery offence to be effective. Lawyer-1 suggested that the law should not require that all of the elements of bribery be proven by the prosecutor. In particular, Official-4 suggested the law should be revised in relation to the *mens rea*. The requirement of proving the offender's knowledge that the bribe was paid because of what the official performed in order for bribery to occur is strict and obstructs the application of bribery in many cases. However, this problem of *mens rea* arises because of the legal construction of the bribery offence in section 35 of the CLA 1970 which covers cases where the bribed official discharges his/her responsibilities properly. In the latter case, it may be difficult to establish a link between the bribe paid and what the official did. In contrast, the *mens rea* is not expected to raise problems under the provisions of the UK BA 2010 where a bribe is 'essentially an inducement or reward to a person with public

36 Lawyer-1.
37 Ibid.
38 Official-4.

or private responsibilities to discharge those responsibilities improperly'.[39] It is easier for the prosecutors to establish a link between the bribe paid and the improper performance of the officeholder.

Two interviewees emphasised the potential of financial disclosures, as stipulated in the ACAA, in combating bribery.[40] They should be extended to include the junior officials because the existing financial disclosures are limited to specific types of high-ranking officials.[41] Lawyer-2 stated that, to facilitate the prevention of bribery, the exclusion of non-Kuwaiti officials from submitting financial disclosures may lead to the displacement of bribery to other non-Kuwaiti actors. In practice, non-citizens occupy sensitive positions. One perceived risk is that bribes may be given to a non-Kuwaiti official who acts as a secretary of a high-level official (as in the reality of the public administration in Kuwait). Abusing the trust given to him/her, the secretary may engage in bribery in return for violating their public duties.[42]

The awareness of the public has also been recognised as one measure to ensure that the bribery offence is effective. In 2013, a researcher studied bribery in Kuwait based on a sample of 600 persons. Among the results, he found that people tolerate bribery although they realise its illegality.[43] He recommended that the government should develop strategies to raise people's awareness. As stressed by one interviewee, 'to ensure the effectiveness of the bribery offence, the civil society's awareness of bribery and corruption should be raised'.[44] NGO-3 said, 'we are aware of the need to help people raise their awareness', and that is why the non-governmental organisations (NGOs) and '… [our association] launched the campaign of "Report" to encourage people to report any bribery to increase the exposure of the corrupt'. This interest of the NGOs perhaps reflects the importance of whistleblowing and the potential role of informers in uncovering inherently secretive corruption acts.[45]

Regarding the fairness of the bribery offence, the majority of the participants who discussed bribery did not mention any specific concerns about its fairness.[46] As for its legitimate purpose, Lawyer-1 stated that bribery is a fair offence given that it aims to protect the integrity of the public office. With regard to respect for constitutional rights – safeguards provided for the suspect – NGO-3 contended that 'bribery is fair and does not involve any potential infringements upon the civil liberties of people'. Judge-1 concluded that:

> With respect to the constitutional rights of the suspect, bribery is a fair offence that is surrounded by several substantive and procedural safeguards

39 Sullivan (2011, p. 88).
40 Official-4; Lawyer-2. Financial disclosures are addressed in section 4.3.4.
41 Lawyer-2.
42 Ibid.
43 Al-Qarioti (2013).
44 NGO-3.
45 Analysed in sections 4.3.7 and 4.4.2.1.
46 Lawyer-1; Lawyer-2; Official-2; Judge-1; NGO-3.

> that are established in the constitution and in the criminal justice laws … if the procedures are violated, evidence gained based on those procedures then loses its legal value/validity.

The bribery offence was perceived on other occasions to be 'incomplete', 'not ideal', or even 'unfair'.[47] Official-2 stated that 'we cannot say that bribery is unfair; rather, the fairness of bribery is "incomplete"'. This participant based his/her argument on the fact that bribery of employees in the private sector is not criminalised and 'this does not correspond to the power of the private sector in Kuwait, which comprises individuals who have financial affluence, and a constant need to deal with the government'. As Official-2 emphasised, the existing bribery law does not correspond to the potential role of the private sector in Kuwait, where the public sector prevails: 'the dependent, affluent private sector always needs a decision from an official so that it can penetrate the public sector'. The potential role of the private sector in the bribery offence becomes a more serious issue, 'particularly in a rentier state like Kuwait'.[48] Another participant shared this view on bribery and went on to say that the non-criminalisation of private sector bribery '… does not make bribery unfair' and that 'there is a difference between being fair and ideal; the way in which bribery is criminalised in Kuwait is fair, but not ideal'.[49] The existing bribery law also provides more leniency for private sector actors.[50] Because of this lenient treatment, the current law could be perceived as unfair. In Kuwait, both the briber (who can be from the private sector) and the bribed (always an official) are subject to the same punishment – 10 years' imprisonment.[51] However, the CJA 1970 differentiates between them on different occasions. First, if what the briber asked for is legal, whereas the bribed official is still liable for 10 years' imprisonment, the briber will be subject to just 5 years' imprisonment.[52] Second, if the officeholder did not accept the bribe, the briber is liable for 5 years' imprisonment, or 3 years' imprisonment if what they asked for is legal.[53]

Though private sector bribery is beyond the scope of the book, two points related to the criminalisation of private sector bribery might be mentioned. First, the public-private distinction in Kuwait is justified based on the purpose of the existing bribery law, that is, protecting the integrity of public office.[54] As Green argued, while private bribery should be criminalised, public sector bribery should be dealt with distinctly because of its 'moral and political character'.[55] Second, criminalising bribery that occurs wholly within the private sector

47 Official-2; Lawyer-1; Official-5.
48 Official-2.
49 Lawyer-1.
50 Official-2.
51 CLA 1970, s.39, para.1.
52 Ibid., s.39, para.2.
53 Ibid., s.41, paras.1–2.
54 Explanatory Memorandum of the CLA 1970.
55 Green (2013, p. 65).

necessitates a transformation in how the Kuwaiti policymakers perceive bribery. For example, Alldridge stressed that the changes in the bribery law in the United Kingdom are based on the assumption that the UK BA 2010 'gave up the idea that the essence of bribery is that it is an offence of disloyalty and embraced the idea that bribery undermines the proper operation of markets'.[56] Therefore, it may be argued that it is too early to call for the criminalisation of private sector bribery in Kuwait. Under the present circumstances, where corruption pervades the public sector in Kuwait, the focus should be on the bribery offences that involve the abuse of public office, including public sector corruption that involves actors from the private sector.[57]

The construction of the bribery offence was a reason why some professionals perceived it as unfair. Official-5 criticised it for not including any legal excuses. According to the CLA 1970, it is considered bribery when an official receives an advantage from external parties in regard to performing legal activities that lie within his/her official capacity, and 'this may lead, in some situations, to an unfair application of bribery'.[58] Official-5 mentioned the *Zakat House* case. In this case, the *Zakat House* – a public body responsible for charitable fundraising – received funds from a philanthropist. Part of those funds went to the officials who were responsible for the distribution of the funds to the eligible poor.[59] In the aftermath, the public prosecution charged a number of officials with bribery when they received payments. The charge was inconsistent with *Sharia* law, according to which those officials were entitled to that payment as 'workers on *Zakat*' (those who collect alms).[60] Again, this problem is linked to the construction of bribery offence in Kuwait (in particular, section 35) that extends to cases where the officials discharged their responsibilities properly. Compared with the UK BA 2010, this issue is not expected to arise because 'One important limiting factor is that the giving or taking of the advantage must be linked to the improper performance of a relevant function or activity'.[61]

### 4.3.2 *Diversion of public funds*

This section is concerned with offences involving the diversion of public funds by officeholders from their public purpose to someone's personal interests. In particular, this category includes embezzlement and misappropriation as two core offences that have been addressed in the PPFA.[62] Before 1993, crimes against the public purse had been stipulated in sections 44–52 of the CLA 1970. However, the PPFA aimed to fill the loopholes in the CLA 1970 and was a response

56 See Alldridge (2012, p. 1181).
57 On this point, see self-regulation in private sector in chapter 5.3.2.2.
58 Official-5.
59 Ibid.
60 Ibid. See Quran, *Surat Al-Tawbah* (Repentance), Verse 9:60.
61 Sullivan (2011, p. 89).
62 See Appendix 2 for extracts of the full text of the PPFA.

to the statutory deficiencies exposed by some notorious pre-1993 Kuwaiti internal and external investments that involved several corruption scandals.[63] In those scandals, the public funds were blatantly abused and the stolen money was sent abroad to jurisdictions that supported the bank's secrecy and where the money was untraceable.[64] The criminalisation of those two core offences is consistent with Article 17 of the UNCAC, which suggests that each state should consider criminalising 'the embezzlement, misappropriation or other diversion by a public official'.

Two preliminary points should be explained. First, both the embezzlement and misappropriation offences require that the offender should be an office-holder within the meaning of section 43 of the CLA 1970.[65] The second is that 'public funds' have a peculiar meaning within Kuwaiti law. The PPFA adopts a broad definition of public funds in order to extend the protection. Public funds comprise a wide array of property, including property in Kuwait and abroad that is owned or administered by one of these entities (hereinafter public bodies): the state and its institutions, and companies in which the entities mentioned above have no less than a 25 per cent stake, whether held directly or indirectly.[66] One manifestation of the expansive definition of public funds is that the PPFA considers the funds owned by companies as public funds, even if they are not appropriated for the public domain.[67]

### 4.3.2.1 *Embezzlement*

In Kuwaiti law, embezzlement occurs when an official embezzles money, documents or other property entrusted by virtue of his/her official capacity or position.[68] Thus, there is a distinct prerequisite for the embezzlement offence: the embezzled property should be in the possession of the official by virtue of his/her position. Such a requirement distinguishes the embezzlement offence from other offences. In the embezzlement offence, however, the element of public funds is not a requirement that should be realised in all cases. Having been placed in the custody of the official, it does not matter whether the embezzled property was public funds or private property.[69]

The *actus reus* involves any act whereby the offender transfers his/her precarious possession of property to full possession so that he/she assumes the full rights of an owner.[70] For the *mens rea*, the official must intend to perform the act and know that he/she embezzled what was placed in his/her custody

63 Explanatory Memorandum of the PPFA, paras.1–2.
64 See the Explanatory Memorandum of the PPFA.
65 PPFA, s.3.
66 Ibid., s.2.
67 Al-Melhem (1995).
68 PPFA, s.9.
69 Al-Mulaifi (2018).
70 Case No. 34/2002, 13/5/2003 (Supreme Court – Criminal Division).

because of his/her position (general intent) to assume the full rights of an owner with the intention of permanently depriving the owner of his/her property (specific intent).[71] Embezzlement is punished with at least 5 years' imprisonment. Sentencing is aggravated and is no less than 7 years if it is indivisibly linked to another felony offence.[72] The judgment shall include the dismissal of the offending officeholder, an order to return what was embezzled, and a fine equal to twice what was embezzled.[73]

#### 4.3.2.2 *Misappropriation and facilitation thereof*

Misappropriation takes place when an official misappropriates or facilitates others to misappropriate money, documents or other property that is owned, or controlled, by the public bodies.[74] The misappropriated funds may be public funds or private funds that are under the control of the public bodies.[75] In Kuwaiti laws, the misappropriation offence is different from embezzlement in terms of the nature of the link between the official and the funds: in the misappropriation offence, the misappropriated property is not necessarily in the possession of the offending official by virtue of his/her position.[76] The official may misappropriate what has been entrusted to other officials or individuals.

The *actus reus* comprises an act whereby property is transferred from the possession of the owner to the possession of the offender/others so that the latter assumes the full rights of an owner.[77] Regarding the *mens rea*, the officeholder must intend to perform the act, knowing that he/she is an official and has misappropriated property (general intent) to assume the full rights of an owner with the intention of permanently depriving the owner of his/her property (specific intent).[78] Misappropriation is punished with at least 5 years' imprisonment. Sentencing can be aggravated and is no less than 7 years if it is linked to another felony offence.[79] The judgment shall include the dismissal of the offending officeholder, an order to return what was misappropriated, and a fine equal to twice what was misappropriated.[80]

The views of the experts interviewed on the effectiveness of the diversion of public funds offences were divergent. Some interviewees perceived the embezzlement and misappropriation offences as effective. Official-4 and Official-5 believed

71 Ibid.
72 PPFA, s.9.
73 Ibid., s.16.
74 Ibid., s.10.
75 Ibid., ss.2 and 10. See Case No. 308/2011, 5/3/2012 (Supreme Court – Criminal Division 2) 6.
76 Al-Zafiri (2006).
77 Case No. 184/2004, 28/6/2005 (Supreme Court – Criminal Division). See also Hosni (2005).
78 Case No. 59/1998, 8/2/1999 (Supreme Court – Criminal Division).
79 PPFA, s.10.
80 Ibid., s.16.

that the PPFA brings in comprehensive provisions that cover all cases where money is embezzled or misappropriated. Lawyer-1 stated that such offences are effective, especially when they are backed by other accountability mechanisms: 'their effectiveness is largely dependent on the supervisory role of the State Audit Bureau (SAB), which keeps the law enforcement authorities informed'. In 2018, while preparing an audit report on the work of the Kuwait Ports Authority, an SAB team suspected that several corrupt transactions had taken place within the authority that had deliberately been kept hidden. The team reported such suspicious transactions, and this report led to the conviction of seven offenders for misappropriating public funds.[81] The SAB's report was used by the court as key evidence for the conviction.

The effectiveness of the embezzlement and misappropriation offences is further evidenced by the fact that the number of these offences investigated increased from 900 in 2017 to 1400 in 2018.[82] This increase is perceived to be 'an indication of their effectiveness in covering an array of forms of abuses of public funds'.[83] This is a sweeping statement, however. These numbers may not be a reliable measure of their effectiveness. Before asserting their effectiveness based on the number of offences investigated, the limitations of statistics regarding crime and criminal justice should be considered. Among other things, we must be cautious about underreported offences and the outcomes of the investigations, especially the number of convictions secured in comparison with the number of cases detected.[84]

Lawyer-1 also stated that the effectiveness of such offences is enhanced by the provision that they are not subject to the statute of limitation. Judge-1 agreed with the view that these offences are effective: 'we, as judges, are provided with a wide range of deterrent punishments.' The PPFA also encourages the offender to return the money embezzled and misappropriated; the mitigating factors will not apply unless the offender returns the money.[85] The Act also provides the judge with discretion, if the harm is not serious, to make the offence a misdemeanour and limit additional penalties. In practice, this judicial discretion has effectively encouraged many offenders to return the money.[86] Prosecutor-2 accepted that view that 'the offences are effective and well-defined' and that 'the penalties are proportional to the offences'. In reality, there are many convictions, which is perceived as a good indication of their effectiveness.[87] Prosecutor-2 added that where there is sufficient evidence, it is difficult for the offender to escape liability.

81 Case No. 1942/2015, 6/5/2018 (First Instance Court – Criminal Division) 25.

82 How many cases were discontinued or prosecuted is nowhere discussed.

83 Lawyer-1 stressed that this number represents all cases against public purse and not only the embezzlement and misappropriation offences.

84 See Eurostat (2017).

85 Judge-1.

86 Ibid.

87 Prosecutor-2.

The embezzlement and misappropriation offences, nevertheless, are not sophisticated enough to deal with complex situations. They are built to address primitive cases where public money is stolen in a simple manner. Yet, they are financial crimes that are more complex than they seem, which has practical implications. Lawyer-2 stated that direct theft from the public budget is the form that dominates the mentality of the public prosecutors, while in fact these offences are often committed in a more complex manner, such as offences that are linked to investment processes.[88] Lawyer-2 concluded that 'the offences do not fit the recent embezzlements that have occurred in Kuwait'. He/she explained that, in reality, they take complex forms that sometimes require specialised prosecutors who can deal with their complexity. Perhaps this conclusion explains what was noted by NGO-3, which is that referrals by the prosecutors often tend to be based on 'weak evidence'.

The PPFA, including the embezzlement and misappropriation offences, lack the necessary pre-trial measures to ensure their effectiveness.[89] As noted by some professionals, there is a need for legal powers enabling prosecutors to negotiate with the suspects in certain situations.[90] Lawyer-1 suggested that the discontinuance of criminal proceedings should be permitted if the suspect takes the initiative to return the money during the investigation, based on 'negotiation and agreement', especially if there is no serious harm. When it is clear to the suspect that returning what he/she has embezzled will not exempt him/her from being prosecuted, it is then logical that the suspect will be discouraged from cooperating or returning the assets.[91] In reality, the law enforcement authorities are expected to fail to recover the embezzled and misappropriated funds even after the enforcement of a punishment.[92]

The effectiveness of the offences in question may also depend on other factors, such as enforcement selectivity. As stated by Prosecutor-2, 'when enacted in 1993, the aim of the PPFA was to confront the then blatant abuses of public money that involved massive amounts of stolen money'. But in practice, the prosecutors are being overwhelmed with trivial cases that do not involve serious abuses of public funds.[93] To be able to deal with the more serious crimes, which is the key purpose of the PPFA, there should be clear financial criteria upon which cases are selected and prosecuted.[94]

Although there is a potential role to be played by the public or officials in reporting crimes, the PFFA does not uphold this role. In any case, where a prosecutor decides to discontinue an investigation, section 104 bis of the CLA 1960 provides victims with the right to appeal against such a decision. However,

88 Lawyer-2.
89 See below section 4.4.2.2.
90 Prosecutor-1; Lawyer-1.
91 Lawyer-1.
92 Ibid.
93 Prosecutor-2.
94 Ibid.

Lawyer-1 cited some cases where individuals who reported an offence were not allowed to appeal against the discontinuance decision as they did not have a 'direct interest'. Lawyer-1 explained that this is a judicial attitude regarding who can be considered a victim in public funds offences and stated that 'the current law preserves this right only for the victim state institutions.' Lawyer-1 pointed out a significant issue that the legislature heeded in 2014. An amendment was introduced to the Trial of Ministers Act (TMA) 88/1995 to allow an individual who reports a crime committed by a minister to appeal against the decision to discontinue the investigation within two months.[95] Thus, and only in the context of crimes committed by ministers, the TMA settled the issue by granting such individuals the power to appeal as victims.

The embezzlement and misappropriation offences were perceived to be fair by most of the participants interviewed.[96] One interviewee stressed that, 'as a lawyer, I link the fairness with the safeguards provided for the suspects … such offences do not bring in any provision that violates the suspect's rights'.[97] In terms of the severity of the punishments, Lawyer-1 added that the excessive punishments set out for those offences are proportional given the legitimate objective of the PPFA, that is, protecting public funds. Other professionals also emphasised the fairness of these offences, based on the fact that they do not violate the safeguards provided for the suspect. Generally, the law is fair when considering the safeguards provided in the constitution, which are consistent with the principles of justice.[98]

By contrast, some professionals viewed the embezzlement and misappropriation offences as unfair. This perception was due to the unclear objectives of the PFFA: does it protect public funds or the integrity of public office? Official-5 stated that although the PPFA should protect public funds, the embezzlement and misappropriation offences only apply to public officials. The theft of public funds by non-officials is still a criminal offence, yet the same act can be seen as a felony or a misdemeanour based on the character of the perpetrator. The PPFA unjustifiably differentiates between offenders, which affects the fairness of the offences. This differentiation, however, is not intended. The PPFA is perceived to protect, in the first place, public funds. The title of the PFFA (the protection of public funds) is a misnomer. It would be better if the PFFA were called 'the integrity of public office', as it aims to maintain the trust of the public in office-holders and to protect the integrity of the public administration.[99] In responding to this critique, one interviewee justified the distinction between officials and non-officials, as they are not equal: 'the officials are entrusted with specific roles and duties that require special treatment'.[100]

95 TMA, s.6 bis (amended by Act No. 29/2014).

96 For this offence, the interviewees were Official-4; Official-5; Lawyer-1; Lawyer-2; Judge-1; Prosecutor-2.

97 Lawyer-1.

98 Judge-1; Prosecutor-2.

99 Al-Mulaifi (2018, p. 31).

100 Prosecutor-2.

In regard to the PFFA's offences (including embezzlement and misappropriation), unless the offender returns the money embezzled or misappropriated, section 20 of the PPFA prevents the judge from applying the mitigating circumstances that lessen the seriousness of the guilt, such as the circumstances of the offender and the crime's triviality.[101] This provision is problematic, especially when seen from the perspective of the decision of the Kuwaiti Constitutional Court in Case No. 1/2018, 24/10/2018 (Constitutional Court). In that case, an application was submitted to review the unconstitutionality of section 42 of the AML/CFT Act, which includes the non-applicability of mitigating circumstances.[102] The constitutional ground of the application was that section 42 of the AML/CFT Act violated the constitutional principles pertaining to the defendant's right to a fair trial, the separation of powers, and the independence of the judiciary.[103] The Court decided that section 42 was not compatible with the principles of the Kuwaiti Constitution, since it represented a breach of the safeguards of a fair trial, an interference in the affairs of justice, and an explicit violation of the individualisation of punishment principle, which revolves around individual criminal responsibility and the idea that the punishment must be proportional to the crime, and is associated with the offender and his/her intention.[104]

Applying this decision to section 20 of the PPFA is possible. However, section 20 is distinct in two respects. First, the applicability of mitigating circumstances is conditional on the defendant's behaviour. The judge is prevented from considering the circumstances unless the defendant takes the initiative to return the illicit assets. Thus, the rationale here is to encourage the defendant to return the proceeds of the crime. Second, the second paragraph of section 20 has its own mitigating factors. It allows for the judge to consider whether the harm caused by the offence is negligible. In that case, the judge can substitute the original punishment for a sentence of not more than three years and a fine of not more than KWD 3000 or one of these punishments. The PPFA's special arrangement of mitigating factors has been subject to divergent views. As mentioned above, section 20 was seen by Judge-1 as one of the effective measures provided by the PPFA. On the contrary, Lawyer-1 was concerned that 'the restricted discretion of the trial judge negatively affects the fairness that the law should uphold'. The lack of fairness of the embezzlement and misappropriation offences also has legal ramifications for their effectiveness. One interviewee argued that:

> … there are many cases where the judge was convinced that the offender was guilty but would not engage in any further offence in the future. Because of the section 20 [of the PPFFA], which prevented the judge from applying

101 The mitigating circumstances are stipulated in section 81 of the CLA 1960.
102 This section is the counterpart of section 20 of the PPFA.
103 Case No. 1/2018, 24/10/2018 (Constitutional Court) 2–5.
104 Ibid., 5–7.

> the mitigating circumstances, the judge had to acquit the offender ... This really undermines the value of the stigmatising role of the criminal law.[105]

### 4.3.3 *Abuse of function*

This section addresses a set of offences that can be labelled 'abuse of function'.[106] The PPFA consists of five offences of this kind.[107] Some of these offences are excluded from the discussion here because they are outside the chosen definition of corruption. The analysis is restricted to two offences: misconduct in public office and the conflict of interest offence. These two offences are in line with what Article 19 of UNCAC stipulates that an abuse of function involves 'the performance of or failure to perform an act, in violation of laws, by a public official in the discharge of his or her functions, for the purpose of obtaining an undue advantage for himself or herself or for another person or entity'.

#### 4.3.3.1 *Misconduct in public office*

According to the PPFA, misconduct in public office takes two forms: the intentional harm offence and the exploitation of office offence.[108] Both of these offences require two prerequisites to occur. The first is that the offender should be an officeholder. The second is that the official should have exploited his/her official capacity: there should be a link between the formal duties of that official and the gains he/she gained.[109] The history of these offences is similar to the history of the diversion of public funds crimes, for all of them were enacted in the PPFA and under the same circumstances.[110]

The first offence (the intentional harm offence) involves any act by an official in violation of his/her duties whereby he/she wilfully inflicts harm on a public body to achieve benefits for himself/herself or for others. This offence occurs when that official is charged with maintaining the interest of that public body in a transaction, process or case, or is assigned to negotiate or contract with any party in relation to the affairs of that body.[111] The *actus reus* arises from any act that inflicts harm on a public body to obtain benefits for the official or for others.[112] The *mens rea* is proved when the official wants to inflict harm on the funds and interests entrusted to him/her to obtain benefits for himself/herself or for others.[113] If found guilty, the official is liable to either life imprisonment or at

105 Lawyer-1.
106 UNCAC, art.19.
107 PPFA, ss.1–114 and 17.
108 See Appendix 2 for the full text of the offences in Arabic.
109 Al-Zafiri (2006).
110 See section 4.3.2.
111 PPFA, s.11.
112 Case No. 662/2012, 14/7/2013 (Supreme Court – Criminal Division 2) 9.
113 Case No. 17/2007, 24/6/2008 (Supreme Court – Criminal Division) 7.

least 7 years' imprisonment.[114] The judgment must include: the dismissal of the offending officeholder, an order to return the gains obtained, and a fine equal to twice the gains.[115]

The second offence (the exploitation of office offence) refers to an official, who directly or indirectly, illegally obtains, or conspires to obtain, benefit for himself/herself or for others from contracting, procurement or works related to a public body. The official should have the duty to manage or supervise those works.[116] The *actus reus* involves all forms of exploitation of one official's job to illegally obtain, or attempt to obtain, benefits. Neither the occurrence of harm nor the obtaining of gains is required for such an offence to occur. The *mens rea* is fulfilled when the officeholder knows the elements of the offence and intends to illegally obtain benefits and gains for himself/herself or for others.[117] If convicted, the official is liable to at least 7 years' imprisonment.[118] The judgment must include: the dismissal of the offender, an order to return the gains obtained, and a fine equal to twice the gains.[119]

In evaluating the effectiveness of both offences, the professionals raised some practical issues. Lawyer-2 and Official-5 compared the difficulty of these offences with that faced with the bribery offence; that is, the practical difficulty of proving that an official has received benefits for himself/herself or for others. Added to that, one interviewee pointed out the difficulty in determining that an official intended to inflict the harm, especially with the intentional harm offence, where the infliction of harm is part of the *actus reus*.[120] Lawyer-2 contended that, in the area of investments, proving the intent to cause harm is one of the most difficult aspects in practice: 'how can we prove that an official, entrusted to decide on investment matters, had the intent to cause financial damage to the state, especially if that official has performed his/her statutory role?' In this context, the role of internal supervision within the victimised state institutions may help prove the intention of the official based on, for example, proving the relation between the offender and the other parties.[121] As they are close to the circumstances of the individual case, these institutions may provide documents that reveal information that can assist the prosecutors during the investigation.

This difficulty was also recognised by Judge-1, who emphasised that the application of these offences faces some practical difficulties. While there are cases where the intention to inflict harm is clear, Judge-1 found that the 'intentional harm offence' is challenging, especially in cases related to investments, where

114 PPFA, s.11.
115 Ibid., s.16.
116 Ibid., s.12.
117 Case No. 1138/2015, 19/5/2016 (Supreme Court – Criminal Division 3) 9.
118 PPFA, s.12.
119 Ibid., s.16.
120 Lawyer-2.
121 Official-5.

'the concepts become vague and elastic'. The problem is that those cases depend on economic assumptions that may not have taken place. Lawyer-1 raised the same point, that the harmful consequences may be 'unforeseeable' in some cases. Lawyer-1 cited an illustrative example. The inclusion of an 'arbitration clause' in a contract (to which the government was party) and its later use by the other party may incur extra costs for the government. In this case, the official who signed on behalf of the government may be said to have caused harm to his/her employer so that the other party could secure some gains. There could be a case although the resort to arbitration might be unforeseeable and contingent on the behaviours/decisions of others.

The ambiguity of some economic and investment assumptions also applies to the second offence – the exploitation of office. In one case, the Vice-Chairman of the Board of Directors of a state-owned company was charged with exploitation of office.[122] The prosecutor stated that the Vice-Chairman had illegally attempted to achieve gains for other parties by signing an investment contract with a fare less than the fare for similar contracts. Acquitting the accused, the trial judge had a different view. The intent of the offender to achieve illegal gains for others – including his/her knowledge that the contract signed would do so – was not proven. The acquittal was based on an expert report, which concluded that there were no clear mechanisms based upon which the fares could have been determined during the contracting process. Thus, economic issues may cause confusion for some cases, thereby jeopardising the effectiveness of the law. The long interval between the time at which an official undertook the criminal conduct and the time of reporting or prosecuting it further complicates the problem.[123] Lawyer-2 mentioned the Public Institution for Social Security case when one of the offenders was charged for his wrongful decision in specific investments: though prosecuted in 2008 and referred to the court in 2011, the act was committed in 1998.[124] It is not surprising, then, to find that both Lawyer-2 and Judge 2 drew the same conclusion: such complex offences 'need technical experience, an accurate understanding of the process undertaken [by the official], and specialised judges'.[125] The effectiveness of such offences can also be affected by the inexperience of the judges in such cases. Having experienced judges is critical. The lawyer who defended one of the offenders in the Public Institution for Social Security case was astonished that the judge imposed a sanction that was not stipulated in the PPFA.[126]

In the light of this uncertainty, the fairness of such offences is questionable, particularly when the PPFA restricts the authority of the judge when considering the circumstances under which an act was conducted (as mentioned

122 Case No. 1138/2015, 19/5/2016 (Supreme Court – Criminal Division 3).
123 Lawyer-2.
124 See Case No. 1200/2016, 27/03/2017 (Supreme Court – Criminal Division 2).
125 Judge 2.
126 Lawyer-2.

above in section 4.3.2.2). Judge-1 expressed concern about justice in each case where the seriousness of the guilt is not clear or certain. Moreover, although Official-5 believed that these offences are fair because of the requirement of criminal intent, Lawyer-1 raised another issue regarding fairness related to the uncertainty of the 'intentional harm offence'. An official can be prosecuted even in the case where the consequences are 'unforeseeable'. Lawyer-1 emphasised that the current drafting of this offence is very general and extends to all activities performed by officials whenever there is harm inflicted on the state, even if the official was unaware of those harms. In such cases, this offence may be perceived to be unfair since the PPFA does not match up to the seriousness of the offender's guilt.[127]

Another issue, related to 'the exploitation of office offence', was noted by Official-5, who argued that this offence is unfair in terms of the fact that it does not consider the differences in the laws between Kuwait and other jurisdictions. One of the cases that the interviewee had investigated related to an official – entrusted with contracting on behalf of the state – who received a commission from a foreign company. In some countries, it may be permissible for a company to give a commission to an official for just meeting with that company. However, the PPFA criminalises the receipt of such a commission and considers it a form of exploitation of office without any regard for foreign laws.[128]

### 4.3.3.2 *Conflict of interest*

Under the CIA 13/2018 and its Statutory Instrument No. 296/2018 (hereinafter CIA-SI), conflict of interest has become a corruption crime.[129] Before the introduction of its criminal form in 2018, conflict of interest was regulated in the Code of Conduct of Public Officials Circular No. 11/2012 (Code 2012).[130] Now, it takes two forms: a criminal offence in the CIA and a disciplinary offence in the Code 2012 and CIA-SI. One advantage of criminalising conflict of interest is that it empowers the state to deal with money gained at the expense of the integrity of the public office through its confiscation. This section focuses only on the criminal form. The Explanatory Memorandum of the CIA emphasises, though in a terse statement, that it is a direct response to Kuwait's international commitment to the UNCAC, Article 7(4), which requires having in place systems that prevent conflicts of interest.[131] However, the CIA was declared unconstitutional in Case No. 7/2018, 1/5/2019 (Constitutional Court).[132] Nevertheless, this section addresses the annulled provisions of the CIA to articulate reforms that may rectify the constitutional deficiencies of the CIA.

127 Lawyer-1.
128 Official-5.
129 See Appendix 2 for extracts of the full text of the CIA in Arabic.
130 Section 6 of the Code 2012.
131 No further legislative history of the CIA has been documented.
132 As will be discussed later in this section.

The conflict of interest offence is defined in the CIA, section 1, as any situation where the officeholder has a physical or moral interest, or can benefit from his/her official capacity, in a manner that conflicts, absolutely or relatively, with the integrity of public office, including those situations that cause illicit enrichment for an official or for others. The subjects of the CIA include those who are referred to in section 43 of the CLA 1970 and the categories of officials in section 2 of the ACAA.[133]

Section 1 of the CIA classifies two types of benefits or interests that result from a conflict of interest. The first is 'physical interest', which involves certain or likely financial gains or harms. The second is 'moral interest', which comprises non-financial interests, arising from personal, family or other relationships, which affect decision making. Section 3 of the CIA extends the 'physical' and 'moral' interests to include interests related to: kinship ties of the official up to the fourth degree (and up to the second degree in the case of affinity); any natural or legal person associated with the official in a work relationship, mediation, agency or legal representation; and any natural or legal person associated with the official within two years preceding the case in which the decision is taken or participated in.

The CIA also differentiates between 'relative' and 'absolute' conflict. Section 1 of the CIA defines 'relative' conflict as a situation that is likely to cause harm to the public interest or the office. An official is in a 'relative' conflict in the following cases:

1 an official owning any share or percentage in any activity having financial transactions with his/her employer, if he/she participates in decisions related to those transactions and no gains are achieved and no harms are inflicted;
2 an official, or his/her minor children, spouse, or those under his/her guardianship or custody, who own a share in a company or business activities associated with that official's duties, if he/she participates in decisions related to those transactions and no gains are achieved and no harms are inflicted; and
3 an official acting as an intermediary, agent, or consultant for any private company whose activities relate to his/her employer, if no gains are achieved and no harms are inflicted.[134]

An 'absolute' conflict encompasses a situation that results in direct and certain harm to the public interest or the office.[135] An official is in 'absolute' conflict in the following cases:

1 if the official is in a situation that certainly or directly inflicts harms;
2 if a physical or moral interest is achieved in terms of one of the categories mentioned in section 3 of the CIA by any act or omission of an official's duties, whether performed individually or through participation with others;

133 CIA, s.1.
134 CIA-SI, s.4.
135 CIA, s.1.

3 if a physical or moral interest is achieved for any natural or legal person associated with the official within two years preceding the case in which the decision is taken or participated in (related-party transaction); and
4 if physical or moral interest is achieved for an official through acting as an intermediary, agent, sponsor, or consultant for any private company whose activities relate to his/her employer.[136]

The key conflict of interest offence takes two forms (both are related to absolute conflict). The first involves any act or omission of an official's duties, individually or through participation with others, that achieves a physical or moral interest in terms of one of the categories mentioned in section 3 of the CIA.[137] The second involves an official owning any share or percentage of work in any activity that has financial transactions with his/her employer.[138] In all of the cases mentioned above, the official is liable to one year's imprisonment, or up to 5 years' imprisonment, and a 3000 KWD fine, or a fine of up to KWD 10,000, or one of these punishments. The judgment shall include: the dismissal of the official, the invalidity of the actions taken, and an order to return or forfeit the benefits or gains.[139]

When a conflict of interest arises, there is a duty to disclose relevant information.[140] Each official, within 10 days of the day on which the conflict of interest arises, should submit the disclosure to the competent body.[141] Within 60 days of the disclosure, the official should remove this conflict either through an interest waiver or by leaving the public office and should take all necessary measures to prevent harm and remove the conflict.[142] The body responsible should examine the disclosures and take the following actions. First, if the official is in a relative conflict that is not a crime, and he/she has removed the conflict, the body responsible shall dismiss the case. Second, if the official is one of the categories in section 2 of the ACAA (who are subject to the financial disclosure),[143] and there are reasonable grounds to assume that a conflict of interest has occurred, the body responsible should refer the case to Nazaha, which shall present the case to the examination committees established in the ACAA to examine the financial disclosures. Third, if the official is not in the categories in section 2 of the ACAA and falls within one of the criminal situations of conflict of interest, the body responsible should refer the case to the public prosecution.[144] If the official fails to remove the conflict that he/she has declared, the body

136 CIA-SI, s.3.
137 CIA, s.4(1).
138 Ibid., s.4(2).
139 Ibid., s.11.
140 Ibid., ss.1 and 5.
141 CIA-SI, ss.4 and 6.
142 Ibid., s.7.
143 As examined below in section 4.3.4.
144 CIA-SI, s.8.

responsible should refer the case to Nazaha or the public prosecution (depending on the category of the official).[145]

Upon asking the interviewees to assess the CIA's effectiveness, there were no definitive responses. Some interviewees commented that they were not able to assess its effectiveness, as this Act has only recently been enacted.[146] However, this fact did not prevent some of the interviewees from expressing their views, or even concerns, about the effectiveness of this Act. Some of them were optimistic. The CIA was perceived as providing new provisions that criminalise modern forms of bribery: 'conflict of interest is better described as bribery but in a sophisticated form'.[147] Lawyer-1 underlined a critical aspect of the effectiveness of the CIA, stating that it rectifies the ineffectiveness of the bribery offence caused by the difficulties related to proof. The CIA solves two difficulties. First, it assumes that the officeholder has benefited from the exploitation of their official position without the need to prove that they received a bribe – undue advantage. Second, the CIA considers a wide range of benefits and undue advantages that accrue to officials as a result of the violation of their official duties.[148]

By contrast, Official-4 was pessimistic: 'although the Act has just been enacted, I can assume that it will not be effective'. Its ineffectiveness was perceived to be due to its exaggerated requirements. The Act was issued to include all officials in government bodies, including their family members, up to the fourth-degree relative.[149] The CIA obliges all officials to declare the share they have in companies that deal with their employer and requires them to remove this conflict. In Kuwait, however, there are so many companies that people (including officials) have shares in that this may lead to a 'massive applicability' of the CIA to a large number of officeholders. Thus, the effectiveness of the CIA is at stake.[150] Lawyer-2 referred to a similar point, stating that this Act is important in Kuwait but, given the social construct in the country, the Act seems 'unrealistic'. The population in Kuwait is small, and professional people know each other. The intra-society relationships are mostly based on interest, and therefore, 'each public official has an interest everywhere'.[151] The Kuwaiti society is built on kinship and tribalism, where each individual depends on the other. For a society like this, the applicability of the Act to the fourth-degree relative of the officeholder is problematic.

The CIA was perceived by NGO-3 to be a fair measure in view of its aim to protect the integrity of public office. For NGO-3, the prevention of conflicts of interest is but an embodiment of an international practice and reflects

145 Ibid, s.9.
146 Official-4; Official-5; Judge-1; NGO-3.
147 Lawyer-1.
148 Ibid.
149 This extends to include parents, siblings, grandparents, uncles, and first cousins.
150 Official-4.
151 Lawyer-2.

the 'implementation of one of the requirements of the UNCAC'. However, Official-4 explained that the fairness of any law is assessed not only based on its purpose, but also on the condition that the law does not exceed the limits prescribed by the Constitution and does not deviate from its key aim. The problem pertains to sections 4(2) and 8 of the CIA. Those sections criminalise situations whereby an officeholder, or his/her spouse, minor children, or anyone under his/her guardianship has a share in any company/business that deals with his/her employer. The officeholder is prohibited from participating in governmental decisions whenever such decisions relate to such a company/business. Although this prohibition is apparently acceptable, it leads to unrealistic consequences. Many Kuwaitis have a share in several businesses or companies because of the initial public offerings (public subscription) that were made available by the government.[152] A recent example of public subscription occurred in 2019 when all Kuwaiti citizens were invited to the public subscription in the shares of Boursa (a Kuwaiti Securities Company).[153] When one of these businesses/companies deals with one officeholder's employer, the officeholder has limited options. The officeholder is obliged to choose between either leaving office, leaving their position, or divesting their private interest. One interviewee emphasised:

> the current provisions of the CIA have departed from its basic purpose: from the prevention of conflicts of interest in public office and the maintenance of public decision-making to intervention in the private property of individuals, which is safeguarded in Article 18 of the Constitution.[154]

Official-4 stated that that CIA involves provisions that are inconsistent with the constitutional and criminal law principles; some of the provisions amount to a violation of the individual criminal responsibility.[155] The CIA has expanded criminalisation and prohibits some conflict of interest cases based on family and affinity relationships. Because of activities undertaken by others (for example, a father-in-law who wants to deal with the employer of the official), that official is obliged to leave office; otherwise he/she will be liable. Official-4 suggested that the CIA should decrease the scope of the categories for which the official is responsible. Second, other provisions negatively affect the certainty of criminal law. The CIA criminalises situations where a conflict of interest is based on non-financial, moral interests arising from personal and family relationships. While the criminal law should be based on certainty, 'the moral interest is uncertain, vague and based on prospects and not facts.'[156]

152 Official-4.
153 <https://www.cma.gov.kw/en/web/cma/cma-board-releases/-/cmaboardreleases/detail/989629>.
154 Official-4.
155 See Kuwaiti Constitution, art.33
156 Official-4.

These provisions have serious implications as they are of a punitive nature. For the sake of certainty, the moral interest must be well defined and involve actual interests.[157]

The CIA's constitutionality was challenged in Case No. 7/2018, 1/5/2019 (Constitutional Court). The application was based on several constitutional grounds pertaining to the legal certainty principle, non-retrospectivity of criminal laws, property rights, and the principle of individual criminal responsibility. In May 2019, the Constitutional Court declared the CIA unconstitutional. In particular, the Court decided that Article 32 of the Constitution establishes the principle of legality regarding crime and punishment, which requires that the elements of each crime be ascertainable and unambiguously specified. The subjects of a law must be able to identify the proscribed acts/omissions so that they can avoid them. In violation of the legal certainty, the proscribed acts in section 4 of the CIA had been drafted 'in so broad and general sense that they may bear, and be open to, different interpretations' – the Act had left determining the meaning of the acts to the executive power. Moreover, the terms used in the Act, such as 'the likely financial gains or harms' and 'non-financial interest', could confuse the formation of the crime in question.[158]

Other issues raised by the Court were that the Act was 'expansive' in determining the criminal responsibility of the officeholder for extended ties of kinship and affinity, and, in particular, that the Act did not specify the extent of the harms that such ties may inflict on the public office and whether the official had the intent to inflict such harms.[159] The Act also did not take into consideration that in some cases, a conflict of interest is 'simple and does not affect the officeholder's decision regarding his/her formal duties', or it may even involve low-rank officeholders who are not among the decisionmakers. The Court also decided that the 'generality' of the CIA's provisions derogated the constitutional property rights of individuals. The mere owning of any share in any activity that involves having financial transactions with someone's employer was a form of conflict of interest that required either leaving office or divesting the private financial interests, although the Act did not specify the limits of that property and whether it negatively affected the integrity of public office. The Court stated that, 'what made things worse is that the Act did not provide other options, including stepping down from participating in the decision'.[160] In aftermath, Nazaha stated that it would study the Court's decision to eradicate the constitutional deficiencies that had marred the annulled Act in the future drafting of legislation.[161]

157 Ibid.

158 See Case No. 7/2018, 1/5/2019 (Constitutional Court) 7.

159 Ibid., 9–10.

160 Ibid., 10–11.

161 See <https://www.alraimedia.com/Home/Details?id=5df8f27f-dd46-4034-9a97-299299eeed8d>.

### 4.3.4 *Illicit enrichment offence (IEO)*

Responding to Article 20 of the UNCAC, which urges states to establish an IEO, the ACAA introduced the IEO as an innovative tool.[162] With the difficulties related to prosecuting corruption offences, the IEO strengthens the ability of the state to combat corruption and recover illicit assets.[163] This argument is consistent with the legislative history of the IEO. The ACAA was a result of a number of crises that Kuwait witnessed, which exposed the failure of the state institutions to deal with some corruption incidents.[164] These incidents, known as the 'multi-million deposits', involved unexplained increases in the wealth of a number of MPs in 2011.[165] Despite these unwarranted increases, the Attorney General discontinued the investigation as there was no evidence of the illegality of the provenance of the increases. The Attorney General called for statutory amendments to fill the loopholes through the introduction of the IEO.[166] Official-5 stated that it is possible now to expose any potential increase in the wealth of an official without the need to provide further evidence: 'this offence would have helped prosecute cases like the multi-million deposits scandal'.

The ACAA defines an IEO as an increase in the wealth or decrease in the obligations of an official, including his/her minor children and those under his/her guardianship, because of the assumption of public office, when that increase or decrease cannot be reasonably explained and justified in terms of their legal resources.[167] There are specific prerequisites for an IEO. First, the offender should be an officeholder within the meaning of the ACAA. Second, the illicit enrichment should occur during the tenure of the officeholder. Third, illicit enrichment should be detected through the financial disclosure submitted to Nazaha.[168] In terms of the *actus reus*, the ACAA does not mention any specific forms of conduct. However, from a through reading of the illicit enrichment definition, particularly 'an increase in the wealth' and 'cannot be reasonably explained and justified', one can conclude that the *actus reus* involves any act by an official resulting in an increase in his/her wealth, whereby this increase is not commensurate with his/her legitimate sources of income. In regard to the *mens rea*, an IEO is an intentional crime that requires general intent. The official must intend to achieve illicit enrichment through abuse of public office, knowing that such enrichment is due to the exploitation of public office.[169] The IEO is based on a presumption of law that a corruption

162 ACAA, ss.1, 22, and 48.
163 Muzila et al. (2012).
164 Explanatory Memorandum of the 2012 version of the ACAA, para.3.
165 Sabrie and Hakala (2013, p. 10).
166 See <http://www.alraimedia.com/Home/Details?Id=bdfdcbd0-6dca-4a80-aea3-96b85e4dc1a1>.
167 ACAA, s.1. See Appendix 2.
168 Al-Oumi (2015).
169 Ibid. See also Boles (2014a).

crime underlies the unexplained wealth; hence, the IEO requires both *actus reus* and *mens rea*.[170]

Financial disclosure is one of the significant provisions set out in the ACAA and its Statutory Instrument No. 300/2016 (ACAA-SI).[171] Pre-defined high-ranking officials must submit financial disclosures to Nazaha about their property and legal obligations (including their minor children and those under their guardianship and custody), whether inside Kuwait and abroad.[172] These disclosures are examined by specialised examination committees in Nazaha.[173] If they suspect that an IEO has taken place, the Attorney General may, upon request, order anyone to enable Nazaha to access or obtain documents related to accounts and deposits in banks or financial institutions.[174] Other individuals, who are reasonably suspected to have benefited from the IEO, may be asked to provide documents proving their wealth so that Nazaha can check whether there has been an unjustifiable increase in their wealth.[175] These measures can be contrasted with the 'disclosure orders' in the UK Proceeds of Crime Act (POCA) 2002.[176] The examination committees prepare reports about the suspects and refer them to the public prosecution.[177] If found guilty, the official is liable to up to 5 years' imprisonment and a fine equal to the value of the illicit enrichment gained. The judgment shall include: the dismissal of the official and disqualification from holding office, and an order to forfeit the illicit gains.[178]

As of 23 April 2018, Nazaha had collected 11,023 out of the 11,642 required financial disclosures, which represents 95% of the disclosures that should have been submitted (see Table 4.3). Despite these submissions, the IEO has not led to any convictions, and Nazaha has not recovered any stolen assets yet.[179] One hundred referrals were made to the public prosecution office: these were limited to the offence of failure to submit the financial disclosures. In regard to suspicious increases in wealth, Prosecutor-2 stressed that as of December 2018, not a single case had been referred to by Nazaha, and any attempt to judge the effectiveness of this device would be 'hasty'. However, in July 2019, Nazaha declared that it had referred its first illicit enrichment case to the public prosecution office.[180,181,182]

170 Wilsher (2006).
171 Sections 11–36.
172 ACAA, ss.1 and 30.
173 Ibid., s.35.
174 Ibid., s.34
175 ACAA-SI, s.54.
176 See section 357 of the POCA as amended by the Criminal Finances Act (CFA) 2017. See also <https://www.gov.uk/government/publications/circular-0062018-criminal-finances-act-disclosure-orders/circular-0062018-criminal-finances-act-disclosure-orders>.
177 ACAA, s.35.
178 Ibid., ss.48–49.
179 Prosecutor-2.
180 See <http://www.nazaha.gov.kw/AR/Lists/News/DispForm.aspx?ID=236&Source=/AR/Pages/default.aspx>.
181 Official statistics presented by Official-2.
182 However, in July 2019, Nazaha referred one case.

*Table 4.3* The number of financial disclosures up to 23 April 2018

| *Officials/type of financial disclosure/action taken* | *Total* |
|---|---|
| Number of officials who should submit disclosures | 11,642 |
| Financial disclosures that have actually been submitted | 11,023 |
| • First disclosure | 10,451 |
| • Final disclosure | 576 |
| Referrals to the public prosecution office (failure to submit financial disclosures) | 100 |
| Referrals to the public prosecution office (suspicious increases in wealth) | 0 |

The interviewees expressed various views about the effectiveness of the IEO. Official-4 stated that the application of the IEO is challenging. In Kuwait, the justification of any increase in the wealth is easy. An official can explain his/her wealth based on various explanations. Domestically, there are different activities that can be a reason for making easy money, such as the camel trade. One could claim that the source of his/her increased wealth is a recent deal in such a trade. The problem with such activities is that there are no specific clear financial criteria to evaluate claims about suspicious increases in wealth.[183] In fact, this criticism is inaccurate. In examining any suspicious increase in wealth, the examination committees in Nazaha can always check the credibility and accuracy of explanations through recourse to experts.[184] These experts help validate whether an explanation is realistic or a sham.

The IEO raises some concerns regarding the principle of presumption of innocence.[185] Globally, some commentators have addressed the claim that the IEO involves an infringement of international instruments of human rights establishing the presumption of innocence principle, such as Article 14(2) of the International Covenant on Civil and Political Rights (ICCPR).[186] In the IEO, the prosecutor is relieved from the 'full burden of proof' and from adducing 'direct' evidence of corruption.[187] The IEO is also alleged to violate two rights associated with the principle of presumption of innocence, that is, the right to silence and the right against self-incrimination.[188] However, the focus here is on the allegation that the IEO reverses the burden of proof for this allegation has given rise to controversy in Kuwait.

In the Kuwaiti context, the IEO has been seen to violate Article 34 of the Kuwaiti Constitution, regarding the right to be presumed innocent until proven

183 Official-4.
184 ACAA-SI, s.28(5).
185 For general discussion about the threats to this principle, see Ashworth (2006).
186 See, for example, Kofele-Kale (2012).
187 See Wilsher (2006, p. 29).
188 See Boles (2014a). For the right against self-discrimination in Kuwaiti law, see Al-Eifan (2016).

guilty.[189] This criticism resonates with Kuwaiti professionals. The IEO is perceived to be unfair because it relaxes this right by shifting the burden of proof onto the suspect.[190] In fact, using the expression 'reverse burden of proof' is inaccurate and 'its continuing use invariably leads to controversy'.[191] The existing legal framework of the IEO in Kuwait does not depart from the conventional rules of criminal law regarding evidence.

In Case No. 4/2017, 8/11/2017 (Constitutional Court), it was decided that the IEO does not contravene the Kuwaiti Constitution. The claim that the IEO involves reversing the onus of proof was incorrect because the IEO requires that the prosecutors should first provide evidence of each element of the crime (*actus reus* and *mens rea*). More importantly, the Court emphasised that the IEO does not establish an 'arbitrary' assumption that the defendant is guilty, and hence, it does not reverse the burden of proof and place the onus on the defendant to prove his/her innocence.[192] Indeed, 'presumptions of fact or of law operate in every criminal-law system', and what matters is that the presumptions should take into account 'the importance of what is at stake and maintain the rights of the defence'.[193] Consequently, it may be said that, at worst, the Kuwaiti Constitutional Court read down the IEO as establishing a rebuttable assumption that the defendant(s) is always permitted to rebut. This view has already been adopted by the Legislative Guide for the UNCAC, which states that:

> ... there is no presumption of guilt and [...] the burden of proof remains on the prosecution, as it has to demonstrate that the enrichment is beyond one's lawful income. It may thus be viewed as a rebuttable presumption. Once such a case is made, the defendant can then offer a reasonable or credible explanation.[194]

In Kuwait, illicit enrichment is proven through the financial disclosures submitted by the official, and the burden first rests on the prosecutor to prove that there is an unwarranted increase in wealth. The officeholder (defendant) is only required to refute this point by providing the legitimate source of the increase.[195] The use of financial disclosures (as the first part of the dual approach to combat the IEO) may dilute the concerns regarding human rights. Some commentators argue that the adoption of financial disclosures is one the measures that seek to

189 See Case No. 4/2017, 8/11/2017 (Constitutional Court).
190 Official-5.
191 Jayawickrama, Pope and Stolpe (2002, p. 29).
192 Case No. 4/2017, 8/11/2017 (Constitutional Court) 7.
193 See European Court of Human Rights (2019, p. 62). See also *Salabiaku v France* App No. 10589/83, Series A No. 141-A (1988) 13 EHRR 379, 388.
194 UNODC (2012a, p. 84).
195 The Hong Kong's Court of Appeal had a comparable justification. See Jayawickrama, Pope and Stolpe (2002).

prevent the IEO's alleged violation of human rights. They argue that, with the financial disclosures, it is the prosecutors who bear the legal burden; they must collect evidence of the unexplained wealth from the disclosures submitted and use it in the IEO cases.[196]

The analysis of the types of burdens of proof in common law systems may be relevant to the discussion here because the type of burden imposed on the defendants may determine the degree of compatibility of the IEO with the presumption of innocence principle. Two types of burden are of particular relevance: the legal burden of proof (also called the burden of persuasion) and the evidential burden of proof (also called the burden of production).[197] In criminal cases, the legal burden requires that 'the prosecution bear the burden of proving the elements of the offence charged, to the standard of beyond reasonable doubt'.[198] This burden does not shift during the trial.[199] In contrast, the evidential burden is 'the obligation to adduce sufficient evidence to raise an issue for the court to consider'.[200] Once sufficient evidence is adduced to raise an issue, the responsibility for proving or disproving that issue shifts to the prosecution; thus, this burden involves no more than raising 'a reasonable doubt as to guilt'.[201] Where this burden rests on the defendant, it is 'for his own safety' to make some answer, and in this context, the prosecutor can choose whether to give any evidence on that issue.[202] Ashworth emphasises that evidential burden is not a burden of proof, but rather, it is a burden of adducing evidence, and that it is 'a common and logical way of dealing with defences, exceptions and provisos to offences'.[203] In general, the party who bears the legal burden also bears the evidential burden: however, sometimes, one party is relieved of adducing evidence on a specific point and is only required to bring evidence of the essential elements forming the crime.[204] Drafting the IEO such that the evidential rather than the legal burden is placed on the defendant is seen to be consistent with the human rights standards.[205]

Emmerson and Ashworth argue that any shift in the presumption of innocence relies on the legislative technique adopted in drafting the statutory crime.[206] Applying this analysis to the IEO in the Kuwaiti law, the IEO may be read as follows: the prosecutors should first prove all of the elements of the offence, that is, the increase in the wealth of the officeholder and that this increase is unjustifiable in relation to his/her legitimate sources of income (legal burden).

196 See Boles (2014a); Wilsher (2006).
197 See Prakken and Sartor (2016).
198 Dennis (2010, p. 452).
199 See Kofele-Kale (2006).
200 Dennis (2010, p. 452).
201 Emmerson and Ashworth (2001, p. 256).
202 Williams (1963, p. 185).
203 Ashworth (2006, p. 269).
204 Dennis (2010).
205 Wilsher (2006).
206 Emmerson and Ashworth (2001).

After that, the burden rests on the defendant to justify by all means that that this increase has come from legitimate sources of income (evidential burden). The evidential, not the legal burden is seen to overcome some difficulties associated with proving corruption.[207] Although the evidential burden appears to be less demanding, in that it may only require the defendant to adduce evidence that the unexplained wealth does not have illicit origins, Boles argues that when comparing the legal and evidential burdens, 'the practical ramifications essentially remain the same'.[208] However, this argument does not take into account the differences in the nature of the burdens, not least that the evidential burden does not require 'the accused to assume the risk of being convicted because he fails to prove one matter relating to his innocence'.[209] As emphasised by some scholars, the evidential burden 'is not a grave departure from traditional principles' and 'is not incompatible with the presumption of innocence'.[210] Lord Steyn reasoned that 'a transfer of a legal burden amounts to a far more drastic interference with the presumption of innocence than the creation of an evidential burden on the accused'.[211]

The analysis of the developments in competition matters in the European Union (EU) is useful here, in particular the fact that the 'proof-proximity principle' has emerged in the EU courts to overcome information asymmetry and evidentiary issues.[212] This principle 'provides that the evidential burden of proof is allocated upon the party in whose hands evidence is more likely to be available'.[213] The principle of 'proof proximity' is aligned with the idea that there may be a party who discharges the legal burden of proof and another who bears the evidential burden.[214] To abridge the process of fact-finding and alleviate the conventional principle governing the evidential responsibility of the parties, the guilt of the defendant may be inferred from a number of indicia; for example, the absence of other reasonable explanations may form evidence that a crime has been committed. Thus, there is no statutory presumption of guilt here, but rather, it is all about the nature of the evidence, which can be described as circumstantial evidence.[215]

Independent of such a crime, and regardless of whether an IEO involves the reverse onus, other jurisdictions have sometimes warranted reversing the onus of proof on the accused on different utilitarian bases in regard to promoting public policy or practical considerations.[216] As Ashworth asserted, 'In no system

207 Wilsher (2006).
208 Boles (2014a, p. 860).
209 Kofele-Kale (2012, p. 14).
210 See Williams (1963, p. 158); Emmerson and Ashworth (2001, p. 256).
211 *R v Lambert* [2002] 2 AC 545, 572.
212 Volpin (2014, p. 1159).
213 Ibid., p. 1173.
214 See Kalintiri (2015).
215 See Volpin (2014).
216 See Kofele-Kale (2006).

of human or constitutional rights is the presumption of innocence regarded as absolute'.[217] In the United Kingdom, even after incorporating the European Convention on Human Rights (ECHR) into the Human Rights Act 1998, Lord Steyn was satisfied that 'there is an objective justification for some interference with the burden of proof' in cases where prosecutors face 'real difficulties' regarding proof.[218] Moreover, the House of Lords decided 'that transferring the burden of proof… would not result in an unfair trial to the defendant' and 'that the transfer of the onus satisfies the test that it has a legitimate aim in the public interest'. It must be borne in mind that the justification is also subject to the principle of proportionality; whether there is a 'pressing necessity' that justifies imposing the burden on the accused, and that 'there is a reasonable relationship of proportionality between the means employed and the aim sought to be realised'.[219] In *R v Webster*, the Court of Appeal decided that under the Prevention of Corruption Act 1916, section 2, 'the imposition upon him [the appellant] of the legal burden of disproving guilt was no longer necessary and the means of imposition was unreasonable and disproportionate', and consequently, read it down to an evidential burden of proof so that it was compatible with Article 6 of the ECHR.[220]

Adapting the criterion of 'proportionality' to the situation in Kuwait, the adoption of the IEO can be said to be a proportionate response to the legitimate aim of the suppression of corruption. Although this test or criterion is established by the European Court of Human Rights (ECtHR) in the context of the EU States, its importance stems from its leading position as 'the first international human rights tribunal to argue in favour of treating reverse burden clauses as no more than "reasonable limits" on the presumption of innocence'.[221] As conceived by the Kuwaiti Constitutional Court, the IEO is underpinned by the legitimate aim of maintaining Kuwait's public interest through combating corruption, maintaining the integrity of public office, and protecting public funds.[222] Thus, the criticism of Glanville Williams, regarding some offences in English criminal law, that 'there has never been any reason of expediency for these departures from the cherished principle [presumption of innocence]; it has been done through carelessness and lack of subtlety', does not apply to the IEO in Kuwait.[223] Finally, believing that there is no shift of the burden of proof onto the official in the IEO, Prosecutor-2 argued that the IEO is driven by a legitimate

217 Ashworth (2006, p. 257).

218 *R v Lambert* [2002] 2 AC 545, 571. In this case, the defendant was charged with 'possession of a class A controlled drug with intent to supply'.

219 Ibid., 625. See also *Salabiaku v France* App No. 10589/83, Series A No. 141-A 10589/83 (1988) 13 EHRR 379.

220 [2010] EWCA Crim 2819.

221 Kofele-Kale (2012, p. 94).

222 Case No. 4/2017, 8/11/2017 (Constitutional Court) 7. See also Muzila et al. (2012, p. 31).

223 Williams (1963, pp. 184–185).

aim that was considered within reasonable limits, as evident in the limited scope of its criminalisation:

> The ACAA does not question an officeholder for the increased wealth in his or her private life. Rather, the offence is basically concerned with examining the illicit enrichment because of the assumption of the office; in particular, it aims to examine the link between the increase in wealth and the office.[224]

Another controversial issue among Kuwaiti professionals is the compatibility of the IEO with the principle of equality. The existing IEO leads to inequality between state officials. One interviewee argued that such differentiation between public officials is justified.[225] High-ranking officials hold sensitive positions, and hence they are more vulnerable to engaging in corruption. On the contrary, low-level officials often do not have the capacity to contribute to public decision making, which makes them less disposed to corruption. In 2017, the Kuwaiti Constitutional Court ruled on an application regarding the equality of the ACAA, including the IEO. The judgment did not address the inequality that resulted from the non-criminalisation of the IEO for low-level officeholders, but the inequality in general that results from choosing specific individuals and subjecting them to the ACAA. The Court went on to state that this is one of the matters that lies within the discretion of the legislature and that there is no restriction on such discretion unless the Constitution stipulates otherwise.[226]

Financial disclosures were allegedly claimed to infringe upon individuals' constitutional right to privacy. In 2017, a group of judges submitted an application to the Kuwaiti Constitutional Court, challenging the constitutionality of financial disclosures. Among the issues they raised was that financial disclosures violate the right to privacy and represent a 'flagrant violation' of Article 30 of the Constitution, which stipulates that 'Personal liberty is guaranteed'.[227] The application based its argument on the previous explanation of Article 30 made by the Constitutional Court in 1982, where it was stated that safeguarding personal liberty necessarily implies constitutional protection of the privacy of individuals.[228] In 1986, the Constitutional Court also struck a balance between the National Assembly's supervisory role over the government's (executive's) performance and individuals' right to privacy. While it was decided that the bank's secrecy (and the confidentiality of bank clients) is not ultimate and cannot be a legitimate cause to hinder the National Assembly's oversight, the Court imposed a restriction on the National Assembly's oversight. The Court stated that the

224 Prosecutor-2.

225 Official-5.

226 See Case No. 4/2017, 8/11/2017 (Constitutional Court) 5.

227 See ibid.

228 See Explanatory Decision No. 3/1982, 8/11/1982 (Constitutional Court).

oversight is limited just to access to the financial disclosures of the bank's clients (including the names, identities, details and financial statements of their accounts); however, the oversight should not extend to the exposure of, and the interference with, the financial disclosures, which violates their right to privacy, which is constitutionally protected.[229]

Though not explicitly mentioned in the Kuwaiti Constitution or laws, the individual's right to privacy has been inferred by the Constitutional Court from a number of relevant constitutional principles, most notably the right to personal liberty.[230] In 2017, however, the Constitutional Court took another view on whether financial disclosures violate the right to privacy. The Court explained that a law will not infringe on the privacy of individuals as long as it is driven by, to use its words, 'national interest'.[231] Arguably, the terse justification of the Court cannot even be considered as an attempt to strike a balance between the right to privacy and the public interest. Perhaps the Court could have justified the infringement based on public interest, but it was rather extreme when it said that there is no violation at all. In dismissing the argument of the claimants, the Court decided that:

> The claim that the financial disclosures violate the right to privacy and infringe upon the personal liberty of individuals is refutable: the law does not violate the privacy of individuals whenever the legislature aims to achieve a 'national interest', as required by the public interest of Kuwait in combating corruption, maintaining the integrity of public office, and protecting the public funds.[232]

Official-4 argued that the ACAA does not infringe upon the right of officials to privacy. The assumption of high-ranking positions implies their consent to accountability. Added to that, the financial disclosures submitted by officials are statutorily safeguarded and treated as confidential: 'according to the ACAA, the confidentiality is surrounded by criminal safeguards, such as criminalising the divulgation of information related to the financial disclosures'.[233] Thus, unlike jurisdictions that treat financial disclosures as public records, the ACAA holds the financial disclosures in private to protect the reputation of those involved.[234] Official-3 stressed that law enforcement authorities in Kuwait are aware of privacy and confidentiality issues. He/she went on to say that, 'we do not probe into the financial details of individuals' bank accounts unless there are reasonable grounds justifying our intervention'.[235] This view denies the seriousness of the claim that the ACAA threatens the privacy of officials.[236]

229 See Explanatory Decision No. 1/1986, 14/6/1986 (Constitutional Court).
230 See Al-Assar (2015).
231 See Case No. 4/2017, 8/11/2017 (Constitutional Court) 7.
232 Ibid.
233 Official-4. See sections 29 and 45 of the ACAA.
234 See Muzila et al. (2012).
235 Official-3.
236 Official-4.

### 4.3.5 *Money laundering offence (ML Offence)*

The Kuwait AML laws have experienced two phases. The first was from 2002 to 2013 and was governed by the Anti-Money Laundering Act 35/2002 (AML Act 2002) when the ML offence was introduced for the first time to address the legal deficit regarding the tracing of proceeds of illicit activities and to counter the adverse consequences of the ML activities, including the phenomenon of 'easy money' and using ML to hide other criminal activities.[237] The second phase is from 2013 to the present and is governed by the AML/CFT Act 106/2013.[238] The 2013 Act aims to keep abreast of the developments in the AML arena, and in particular, the increasing global concern regarding the financing of terrorism.[239]

'Proceeds of crime' and 'predicate crime' are two concepts that should first be explained in order to study the ML offence. Proceeds of crime are defined as money that is derived or obtained, directly or indirectly, from committing a predicate crime. Proceeds of crime also refer to what this money yields, including profits, interests, rents, or any other gains – whether they remain as they are, or they are, fully or partially, converted into other forms of money.[240] The concept of a predicate crime was redefined and expanded in the 2013 Act.[241] It concerns both acts constituting crimes according to the Kuwaiti laws, and acts committed abroad, constituting crimes according to the laws of the country where the act was committed and to the Kuwaiti laws.[242] Therefore, a person commits the ML offence when he or she, knowing that the money is proceeds of crime, intentionally:

a converts, transfers or substitutes the proceeds of crime, with the purpose of hiding or disguising their illicit source, or helps the offender involved in the predicate crime to avoid the legal consequences of his or her activities;
b hides or disguises the original nature, source, place, disposition, movement and ownership of proceeds of crime, or the rights related to them; and
c acquires, possesses, or uses proceeds of crime.[243]

If the money is proven to be proceeds of crime, the non-conviction of the offender in the predicate crime does not hinder his/her conviction for the ML offence.[244] The offender is liable to a sentence of up to 10 years' imprisonment, and a fine of no less than the half the value of the money (the subject matter of the offence) and no more than its full value. The illicit gains and the instruments

237 Explanatory Memorandum of the AML Act 35/2002.
238 See Appendix 2 for extracts of the full text of AML/CFT Act.
239 Explanatory Memorandum of the AML/CFT Act.
240 AML/CFT Act, s.1.
241 See Jusic (2017).
242 AML/CFT Act, s.1.
243 Ibid., s.2.
244 Ibid., s.2.

used in the ML offence shall also be forfeited.[245] Among the aggravating factors that raise the sentence to up to 20 years' imprisonment and a fine of up to twice the illicit gains is when the ML offence is linked to the abuse of public office.[246]

This section assesses the effectiveness of the AML/CFT Act from two perspectives. The first perspective depends on the number of successful prosecutions and convictions that have been secured. Prosecutor-1 stressed that the AML/CFT Act is effective. He/she measured the effectiveness of the AML/CFT Act in terms of the number of successful prosecutions that have been secured and concluded that 'the AML law then is supposed to be working'. Statistically, from 2013 to 2017, the number of AML cases that were referred to the public prosecution office was 194. However, only 79 cases were prosecuted, of which 15 ended with a conviction. Convictions for the ML offence represent 8% of the cases referred.[247] Therefore, the dependence on the number of successful prosecutions is fallacious.

The second perspective is whether these prosecutions and convictions reflect the intended results that combating the ML offence aims to achieve, or, in other words, the rationale behind the AML/CFT Act.[248] Section 2 of the AML/CFT Act states that when proving the illegality of the source of money, it is not required that the offender is convicted of a predicate crime. Although this provision facilitates the implementation of the AML/CFT Act, the practice shows a misunderstanding in its implementation.[249] The ML offence is often simultaneously prosecuted with a predicate offence. Prosecutor-1 referred to the fact that the current judicial attitude jeopardises the effectiveness of this Act. The courts tend to acquit the offender if he/she is not convicted of the predicate offence, or if the courts failed to prove the offender's knowledge of the illegal source of the money. This interviewee stated that acquittals happen, although proving the offender's knowledge is not limited to specific events (as judges currently view it); knowledge can be proven through a set of facts.[250] Judge-1 stated:

> I think that the ML offence is complex and not easy to deal with. In all the cases that I have dealt with, the money laundering offences were referred to the court associated with the predicate offences. I have not dealt with a single case where the offender was charged with the ML offence alone.

The analysis of the current implementation of the AML/CFT Act underlines the importance of the second perspective. The effectiveness of the AML/CFT Act

245 Ibid., s.28.
246 Ibid., s.30.
247 Statistical Report (dated 31 January 2018) provided by the Attorney General. See Al-Oumi (2018).
248 See Sproat (2007) for relevant analysis of the rationale behind the AML regime in the United Kingdom.
249 Prosecutor-1.
250 Ibid.

should reflect the rationale behind it. As Gallant illustrates, in the ML offence, 'the financial aspect of the crime incurs criminal culpability, a liability that is not dependent on the underlying offence'.[251] Building on the way in which this Act is understood in Kuwait, it can be said that the AML/CFT Act is ineffective. Surveying some ML offence cases illustrates that the ML offence was simultaneously prosecuted with usury offences,[252] theft,[253] fraud,[254] embezzlement,[255] extortion,[256] and drug offences.[257] It was possible for the court in these cases to conclude that the offender was also guilty of the ML offence when he/she possessed, used, transferred, or disguised criminal property that resulted from those offences. Nevertheless, the rationale behind the AML/CFT Act – and the intention of the legislature as well – is not to replace the offences created in other laws. The same case has been seen in the United Kingdom where theft has also been seen as an ML offence.[258] It has been described as 'bad practice for the prosecution to add additional counts of that kind unless there is a proper public purpose in doing so'.[259]

The ML offence is also subject to similar criticism to that faced in the context of the IEO: the difficulty of proving the illegal source of the money. In reality, the launderer can easily manipulate the process of laundering by manufacturing evidence.[260] The source of the money can be justified with different explanations, which, in turn, vary from one person to another. Official-5 gave the example that portraits in London or Paris differ in value from portraits in Kuwait. This divergence can be problematic in practice.[261] Official-5 also referred to the misuse of legal structures, as posed by the consultancy activities undertaken by lawyers because their actual value is hard to determine. Prosecutor-1 added that in Kuwait, there are 'suspicious trades' that put the effectiveness of the AML/CFT Act at stake, such as the livestock and perfume trades. Some suspects can explain suspicious transactions based on explanations related to those businesses. As Alldridge described, rather than using bank accounts and moving funds internationally, the criminals use devices that are 'concrete, quotidian, easily comprehensible, and difficult to regard as a global threat'.[262] One participant said: 'although these explanations seem to be absurd, the law

251 Gallant (2004, p. 16).
252 Case No. 907/2016, 16/3/2017 (Supreme Court – Criminal Division 3).
253 Case No. 158/2014, 4/2/2016 (Supreme Court – Criminal Division 3); Case No. 133/2016, 19/2/2017 (Supreme Court – Criminal Division 1).
254 Case No. 610/2015, 19/6/2016 (Supreme Court – Criminal Division 1); Case No. 1325/2016, 22/5/2017 (Supreme Court – Criminal Division 2).
255 Case No. 369/2011, 20/5/2012 (Supreme Court – Criminal Division 1).
256 Case No. 103/2012, 30/9/2012 (Supreme Court – Criminal Division 1).
257 Case No. 671/2007, 24/6/2008 (Supreme Court – Criminal Division 1).
258 Doig (2015).
259 *R v GH* [2015] UKSC 24, 48.
260 Lawyer-1.
261 Official-5.
262 Alldridge (2016, p. 4).

does not secure effective and fair mechanisms to validate such explanations'.[263] Accordingly, both Official-5 and Prosecutor-1 argued that there should be an official system of evaluation to determine the legality of the wealth source by recourse to experts:

> I suggest that in each governmental body, there should be officials specialised in evaluating the value of goods: for example, a commission in the Public Authority for Agriculture Affairs and Fish Resources to evaluate the value of livestock, and a commission in Kuwait Customs and the Ministry of Commerce to determine the value of perfumes and so on.[264]

Arguably, the establishment of specialised bodies to evaluate the value of goods is unnecessary. In fact, the participants interviewed overlooked the legal powers granted to both the prosecutors and the Kuwaiti Financial Intelligence Unit (KFIU). Prosecutors can ask individuals with technical experience in any area to give, under oath, an opinion on any matter.[265] Moreover, KFIU is statutorily mandated to take any appropriate action within its jurisdiction.[266] The KFIU can cooperate with experts to subject the explanations of the sources of money to further validation. Thus, these legal measures, provided for the prosecutors and the KFIU, have the potential to deal with the criticism raised by the practitioners in this regard.

Lawyer-1 expected that the difficulty in proving the illicit sources of the money may lead to a 'major failure' in the AML/CFT Act. Lawyer-1 argued that the problem lies in section 2 of the Act, which requires that for an ML offence to take place, the money should be proceeds of crime. However, in the light of the evidential difficulties, 'if the law enforcement authorities fail to prove the illegal source of money, we will have an offence that is unable to do anything', especially as the individuals cannot be legally obliged to explain their wealth on different occasions, other than in regard to the AML.[267] As shown above, the current judicial attitudes in construing the ML offence are part of the problem. The tendency of Kuwait' courts to acquit the defendants when the prosecutor fails to prove the predicate crime makes the evidential problem worse. While proving the unlawfulness of wealth provenance is difficult, proving the exact predicate crime is more daunting, if not impossible.

To face this risk, Lawyer-1 suggested that the legislature should introduce amendments to the AML/CFT Act, emphasising 'the idea of logicality and reasonability' in the explanation provided by the suspect; he/she stated that, in particular, 'these must be realistic'. Thus, the failure to explain the

263 Lawyer-1.
264 Prosecutor-1.
265 CJA, s.100.
266 Section 5 of the Resolution No. 1532/2013 on the Establishment of the KFIU.
267 Lawyer-1.

source of the money – based on logical and reasonable explanations – can be taken as evidence against the offender in the prosecution of the ML offence. Two examples illustrate the problem. The first is that some offenders may claim that the source of the money was 'sorcery' activities. They may say that because the predicate crime in this case has not been criminalised, and the money cannot be proceeds of crime.[268] The second example relates to investigations into suspicious activities in the bank accounts of a group of social media influencers in Kuwait. Those individuals explained the suspicious transactions and justified their legal source (profits from business advertisements).[269] What emerges here is that the law cannot ignore the popularity and influence of social media platforms and the threats they pose by being perfect instruments through which dirty money may be disguised or channelled. The reasonableness of the explanation of the money's source may be helpful in those two examples.

Although the Kuwaiti Constitutional Court declared some provisions of the AML/CFT Act to be unconstitutional,[270] the fairness issue addressed here is restricted to the ML offence as a core offence rather than the AML/CFT Act as a whole. In this narrow context, the professionals, who were asked to comment on the fairness of the ML offence, raised no issues. For example, one interviewee assessed the fairness of the ML offence based on the interest it aims to protect. The ML offence is fair insofar as it aims to combat the incorporation of illegal money into the legitimate economy of the state: 'fighting the easy money, in turn, upholds the principle of equal opportunity between people'.[271] Prosecutor-1 based his/her assessment of the fairness of the ML offence on constitutional grounds: its criminalisation has not brought in unfair provisions, especially those affecting the constitutional rights of the suspect.

### 4.3.6 *Proceeds of crime*

This section explores the Kuwaiti legal response to proceeds of crimes and how the law enforcement authorities are empowered to deal with the dirty money acquired through corruption offences.[272] Unlike the IEO and ML offences (which can also deal with proceeds of crime), this section classifies the measures that are directed at proceeds of crime into two broad categories: pre-conviction measures (provisional measures) and post-conviction measures (confiscation or forfeiture). Since the proceeds of crime may be located outside the jurisdiction of Kuwait, this section also deals with available mechanisms for international cooperation.

268 Lawyer-1.
269 See <https://alqabas.com/614327/>.
270 See above section 4.3.2.2.
271 Official-5.
272 See Al-Rashidi (2020).

#### 4.3.6.1 *Pre-conviction measures*

Illicit assets can be hidden or moved outside a jurisdiction. When an investigation begins, it is critical that expeditious actions are taken in advance to protect assets that are liable to be confiscated from dissipation, loss, or transfer to third parties. The preservation methods include provisional measures, such as restraining orders that are directed at natural/legal persons or properties.[273] In Kuwait, if there are reasonable grounds to suspect that offences against public funds,[274] the IEO[275] or ML offence,[276] have been committed, the Attorney General can take any provisional measure to prevent the suspect from travelling (travel ban) or restrain the suspect from disposal and administration of the relevant property, whether it is in the possession of the suspect or other individuals.[277] The provisional measures also include the preventive detention of the suspect.[278] The law enforcement authorities can also submit an application for restraint orders to the Attorney General. The provisional measures will not be discharged until the financial sanctions are enforced (or the case is dismissed).[279] The state institutions are also mandated to take any type of provisional measures to prevent the disposal, dissipation or movement of assets, whether in Kuwait or abroad.[280]

The provisional measures were perceived as effective by the participants interviewed.[281] Prosecutor-1 stated that the provisional measures in Kuwaiti law are broad enough to enable the prosecutors to protect the illicit assets from dissipation. Prosecutor-2 also argued that the provisional measures are effective in preserving the recoverable assets and the prosecutors often consider taking preventive measures during an investigation: 'Examples abound, but in general it is uncommon to see cases involving huge amounts of money without provisional measures'.[282] The provisional measures are widely applied to cover everything that is suspected of being associated with corruption crimes.[283] Prosecutor-1 referred to the effective liaison between the public prosecution and the Central Bank of Kuwait (CBK). In practice, the CBK is expeditiously responsive to the provisional measures: 'the CBK in turn secretly asks the banks to freeze the accounts of the suspects.'[284]

Official-4 also believed that the provisional measures are effective, and that the prosecutors have been able, on many occasions, to preserve recoverable

273 Greenberg et al. (2009).
274 PPFA, s.24.
275 ACAA, s.36.
276 AML/CFT Act, s.22.
277 PPFA, s.24; ACAA, s.36.
278 CJA, ss.48–68 and 74(a) bis.
279 PPFA, s.27.
280 Ibid., s.24.
281 Prosecutor-1; Prosecutor-2; Lawyer-2; Official-4; Official-5.
282 Prosecutor-2.
283 Ibid.
284 Prosecutor-1.

illicit assets: 'a recent example is the case of the Public Institution for Social Security where more than 300 properties were successfully identified and frozen'. Official-4 based his/her view on the broad discretion granted to the prosecutors during the pre-trial stage. The interviewee approved of Kuwait's practice in regard to the provisional measures, whereby the jurisdiction is granted to the investigative authority (prosecutors): 'the current statutory arrangements secure swifter actions'.[285] Official-4 cited the role played by the Ministry of Justice (MoJ) as the central authority for mutual legal assistance (MLA) as a manifestation of effectiveness.

However, in practice, the provisional measures have faced some challenges. Prosecutor-1 argued that the belated crime reports render the provisional measures useless, especially when the offender has had the chance to launder the assets or move them abroad. The delay in reporting crimes is problematic even if the assets are not laundered or moved outside Kuwait. When investigating crimes that were committed a relatively long time ago, the prosecutors will hardly be able to identify or differentiate between legitimate and illegitimate assets associated with the crime reported.[286] Official-2 argued that despite the comprehensive framework of provisional measures, their issuance takes a relatively long time. Comparing the views of Official-4 and Official-2 (regarding the time that the provisional measures take to implement), it seems that Official-2 referred to the time taken for applications to be approved when submitted to the public prosecution office, while Official-4 spoke of the spontaneous actions taken by the prosecutors while investigating cases.

Lawyer-2 stressed that the prosecutors can effectively exercise their authority in applying provisional measures. Yet in practice, the application of the provisional measures tends to be dismissed without clear reasons being given.[287] Some applications have been dismissed although there was sufficient evidence of a link between the property and the crime, which threatens the effectiveness of the provisional measures, especially since there is no statutory mechanism to appeal against the dismissal decision.[288] Lawyer-2 argued that 'the prosecutors should consider the preventive nature of provisional measures'. When asked about this point, Prosecutor-1 commented that the applications that were dismissed were 'either random or unsubstantiated'. Prosecutor-2 stated that, 'the applications of the provisional measures have often been driven by animosity between individuals.' The prosecutors should be aware of the potential abuse of such application.[289]

The provisional measures were seen as fair by the interviewees. Prosecutor-1 stressed that the legal framework of provisional measures is not expected to raise

285 Official-4.
286 Prosecutor-1.
287 Lawyer-2.
288 Ibid.
289 Proseuctor-2.

fairness concerns. Their temporary nature does not result in permanently depriving the suspect of their property, and reasonable grounds are always required to take the provisional measures.[290] Official-5 believed that the provisional measures are fair as long as they are not used arbitrarily and they are applied for a reasonable period.[291] What further increases the fairness of the provisional measures is that they are always appealable.[292] They are subject to judicial oversight as a safeguard. Every suspect can appeal against the provisional measures taken by the prosecutors before the court, whose authority includes amending and annulling those measures.[293]

#### 4.3.6.2 *Post-conviction measures*

Post-conviction measures include confiscation and forfeiture, referring to 'the permanent deprivation of assets by order of a court or other competent authority'.[294] Confiscation and forfeiture are 'closely related' concepts that are often used interchangeably.[295] For the purposes of the analysis in this chapter, these two concepts must be differentiated. Forfeiture will be used to refer to 'the seizure of property by the state because of its use in the commission of crime', and confiscation will refer to 'an order made against a convicted defendant to pay the state a sum equivalent to the proceeds that s/he has gained by crime'.[296] While forfeiture is limited to assets immediately associated with a crime, confiscation includes depriving the offender of his/her proceeds and profits of crime.[297] Forfeiture and confiscation are very important responses to corruption cases. Where wealth accumulation is the essential aim of the corrupt, these are common mechanisms 'to deprive criminals of the financial benefit of their illegal activities'.[298] However, there is no recognised hard boundary between the nature of forfeiture and confiscation orders in Kuwaiti law. But for the present purposes, forfeiture and confiscation will be used within the meanings already mentioned.

Kuwaiti laws have long recognised forfeiture and confiscation. The courts are empowered in all 'intentional' criminal cases to forfeit any property that was used, or could be used, in committing an offence, and that extends to the assets derived from that criminal property.[299] In bribery offences, the court shall forfeit the money that was paid as a bribe.[300] However, the forfeiture of things used to

290 Lawyer-2.
291 Official-5.
292 Prosecutor-1.
293 PPFA, s.26.
294 Brun et al. (2011, p. 13).
295 Broadbridge (2001, p. 9).
296 Alldridge (2002, pp. 781–782).
297 Broadbridge (2001).
298 Ryder (2013, p. 3).
299 CLA 1960, s.78.
300 CLA 1970, s.42.

facilitate crimes (by association) is distinct from forfeiture/confiscation of the proceeds of crime.[301] For offences against the public purse, the PPFA, section 16, does not use the forfeiture or confiscation concepts. Rather, each judgment shall include an order to return the assets embezzled or misappropriated or the benefits gained from misconduct in public office offences. The courts construe that as a restitutionary remedy whereby the offender(s) is ordered to restore the property/benefits to the owner (the state).[302] This remedy is used as an ancillary order to compensate the lack of forfeiture provisions in offences against the public purse in the PPFA.[303] To facilitate the process of restitution, transactions that were carried out with the assets/property associated with crimes shall be rendered invalid,[304] the restitution order is immediately enforceable,[305] and offences against the public purse are not subject to the statute of limitations.[306]

For the IEO, the judgment shall include a forfeiture order in relation to ill-gotten gains.[307] The court can include in the trial any individual or legal entity that has benefited from the IEO, so that the forfeiture order can be effective against them.[308] As understood in regard to section 48 of the ACAA, the forfeiture order is limited to the illicit enrichment and does not cover the benefits associated (so this is not technically a confiscation order as defined above). The court can, in IEO and other corruption cases, exempt the offender from the punishment if they enable the authorities, during the investigation process, to identify or locate the assets.[309]

For the ML offence, section 40 of the AML/CFT Act includes more than the forfeiture of property connected with the crime. It also requires the courts to order the confiscation of the 'proceeds of crime', as defined in the AML/CFT Act. In particular, the confiscation order includes the proceeds of the crime and the funds intermingled with, derived from, or exchanged for these proceeds and income and other gains from the proceeds of the crime.[310] However, if the forfeiture and confiscation of the proceeds of the crime is not possible because they cannot be located or are no longer available, the court shall order the offender to pay an amount of money equivalent in value to the proceeds of the crime.[311]

From the previous analysis, two points can be concluded regarding the effectiveness of post-conviction measures. First, and most notably, as Official-3

301 See Gallant (2005).
302 Case No. 1942/2015, 6/5/2018 (First Instance Court – Criminal Division 2); Case No. 1499/2008, 27/6/2019 (First Instance Court – Criminal Division 10).
303 See Al-Oumi (2018).
304 PPFA, s.23. This may be based on the 'relation-back doctrine'. See Gallant (2005).
305 Ibid., s.28.
306 Ibid., s.21 bis.
307 ACAA, s.48.
308 Ibid., s.55.
309 Ibid., s.44.
310 AML/CFT Act, s.1.
311 Ibid., s.40.

stressed, the confiscation provisions in the AML/CFT are being effectively used in practice to deprive offenders of the proceeds of crime in all crimes. Thanks to the broad definition of 'proceeds of crime' in the AML/CFT Act, it is possible to confiscate the tainted profits of any crime when the offenders are simultaneously charged with a predicate crime and the ML offence.[312] Such a practice arguably rectifies the potential deficiencies in the forfeiture provisions dedicated to other corruption crimes that are limited to the deprivation of assets immediately connected with the crime. Nevertheless, in those cases, restricting the forfeiture to specific assets (immediately connected to the crime) may not be a deficiency, but rather, it may reflect the legitimate rationale underpinning the forfeiture as considered by the legislature.[313]

Second, criminal forfeiture/confiscation is allowed in cases in which the defendant died after the criminal charge was instituted. In offences against the public purse,[314] the IEO,[315] and ML offences,[316] the death of the defendant brings an end to the criminal proceedings, but it does not preclude the forfeiture/restitution of the proceeds of the crime. The state institutions can also file a compensation claim against the heirs and all those who benefited from the crime.[317] In an unprecedented case that involved public funds embezzled by an deceased official, the Kuwaiti Supreme Court explained that in order to forfeit the proceeds of the crime (when the proceedings were brought to an end), the prosecutor should include the inheritors and all those who had benefited from the crime in the case.[318] Moreover, the absconding of the defendant does not constitute an impediment to a forfeiture/confiscation order. The CJA, section 122, allows for a criminal trial to proceed *in absentia* when the court has ascertained that the suspect is a fugitive and is not expected to be arrested in a timely manner.

Thus, Kuwaiti law deals with the proceeds of crime depending on the criminal law. One relevant issue is the standard of proof that should be used to prove whether the identified assets are linked to the crime.[319] The Kuwaiti law has not clarified this issue. But the fact that the ML offence in Kuwait is dealt with by criminal proceedings suggests the standard used in criminal trials, proof beyond reasonable doubt, which further complicates the use of criminal law-based arrangements in regard to proceeds of crime. Moreover, the developments in the criminal financial arrangements regarding proceeds of crime can be characterised as piecemeal. There is a lack of a systematic strategy to deal with proceeds of crime through a defined forfeiture regime, but rather, they

312 Official-3.
313 On this issue, see Alldridge (2018).
314 PPFA, s.22.
315 ACAA, s.48.
316 AML/CFT Act, s.40.
317 PPFA, s.22.
318 See Case No. 1410/2017, 21/7/2019 (Supreme Court – Criminal Division 1).
319 Gallant (2005).

are dealt with by provisions that are scattered throughout the criminal laws. In this regard, the criminal law may fall short in dealing with proceeds of crime. There are situations where the money may be proven to be proceeds of crime, but it cannot be forfeited/confiscated because no potential offender can be identified or suspected. Because the criminal arrangements regarding proceeds of crime are *in personam* in nature, illicit assets cannot be forfeited/confiscated unless they are linked to a specific offender. Furthermore, in the worst cases, even if the offender is identified, the court may acquit him/her because there is a violation of the procedural safeguards provided for the defendant.[320] Faced with such assumptions, it is argued that adherence to the criminal law approach leads to 'illogical' consequences, embodied in the failure of the law enforcement authorities to recover assets that are proven to be illegal.[321] The Stolen Asset Recovery Initiative (StAR) asserted that criminal forfeiture is not always an effective tool for proceeds of corruption and recommended that there should be alternatives for the asset recovery process, in particular civil forfeiture and unexplained wealth orders (UWOs).[322] Since these two approaches might be undertaken before civil courts without criminal proceedings, they will be addressed later in chapter 5, where non-criminal measures against corruption are explained.

#### 4.3.6.3 *International cooperation*

In grand corruption cases, it is commonplace for the proceeds of corruption to transcend the national borders and to be re-invested or hidden abroad. Therefore, international cooperation between jurisdictions in criminal matters becomes imperative. The importance of international cooperation is evident in two relevant scenarios. The first is when a corruption crime is prosecuted in Kuwait, but forensic evidence related to that case can only be gathered from other jurisdictions. The second is when the case prosecuted involves recoverable assets belonging to Kuwait, but they are located in a foreign jurisdiction.[323] In those scenarios, the law enforcement authorities in Kuwait may cooperate with their counterparts in other jurisdictions to obtain evidence to help secure the conviction of the perpetrator, identify assets associated with the crime, and eventually recover the proceeds of the crime. This section focuses on pursuing assets derived from corruption crimes and the international cooperation in that regard. Therefore, issues pertaining to extradition are excluded from the discussion here. It should be noted that despite its relevance, the interviewees did not raise or emphasise any point or issue in terms of the international cooperation in

320 More scenarios are mentioned by Greenberg et al. (2009, p. 15).

321 See Al-Oumi (2018, p. 93).

322 Gray et al. (2014, p. 68).

323 There is another scenario where the recoverable assets, belonging to a foreign country, are located in Kuwait. However, the emphasis here is on Kuwait as a party requesting for the assistance.

criminal matters, which may be attributable to the lack of expertise in that aspect of the counter-corruption field in Kuwait.[324]

There are two ways in which states can cooperate with each other. The first is informal assistance, whereby unofficial information transmission can be utilised through police-to-police or agency-to-agency communication with no need to resort to formal channels.[325] Informal requests are regularly made when the use of coercive powers is not needed.[326] The second is a formal MLA request, which is 'an international cooperation process by which states seek and provide assistance in gathering evidence for use in the investigation and prosecution of criminal cases, and, in tracing, freezing, seizing and ultimately confiscating criminally derived wealth'.[327] The MLA request covers a wide range of assistance forms, including 'requests to gather physical evidence, identify witnesses and obtain testimony, produce documents, conduct forensic tests and similar assistance'.[328] There are four legal bases of MLA requests: international conventions, bilateral agreements, domestic legislation, and the promise of reciprocity.[329]

Kuwait has already ratified a number of international conventions providing provisions for international cooperation.[330] Most importantly, the UNCAC may provide the option to use the Convention as a framework of international cooperation through which MLA requests are made. Kuwait ratified the UNCAC in 2006, and since then, it has had the force of law.[331] The significance of the UNCAC is that it provides the option to use the Convention as a framework through which MLA requests are made (especially in the absence of another basis for MLA). Although Kuwait lacks a comprehensive legal framework in relation to international cooperation in criminal matters,[332] its monist legal system unifies the international and domestic laws. Article 70 of the Kuwaiti Constitution stipulates that: 'After ratification, sanction and publication in the Official Gazette the treaty shall have force of law'. Accordingly, the UNCAC is an integral part of the legal system in Kuwait and constitutes a direct legal action upon which the MLA can be offered. According to the UNCAC, Article 46(13), the MoJ is the central authority responsible for the MLA in criminal matters in Kuwait.[333]

Next, bilateral treaties also are a 'common' and 'effective' vehicle that has been used for international cooperation.[334] Kuwait is party to bilateral

324 See chapter 6.3.
325 UNODC (2012b).
326 Hatchard (2014).
327 UNODC (2004b, p. 120).
328 UNODC (2004a, p. 551).
329 Ziouvas (2018).
330 See Kuwait Ministry of Justice (2015, pp. 15–16).
331 Ratification of the UN Convention against Corruption Act 47/2006.
332 Nazaha (2017a, p. 57).
333 Ratification of the UN Convention against Corruption Act, s.1(c).
334 UNODC (2012b, p. 19).

and multilateral agreements regarding MLA, which form 'a broad basis for assistance in relation to criminal matters and meet all of the requirements of the UNCAC'.[335] Furthermore, in relation to AML matters, based on the existing MLA agreements, mutual agreements regarding cooperation or the principle of reciprocity, the Attorney General in Kuwait is responsible for the exchange of cooperation requests with foreign authorities in criminal matters, including those related to the ML offence or other predicate crimes.[336] The KFIU may, spontaneously, or upon request, provide any competent foreign authority with information.[337] This mechanism of international cooperation helped Kuwait to enter the Egmont Group in 2017 – a network of 155 FIUs that aims to secure mutual international cooperation in AML matters.[338]

When a corruption crime takes place, Kuwait may seek assistance from other jurisdictions to obtain evidence to strengthen the case being investigated. In a recent case, a letter rogatory (a letter of request) issued by the public prosecution in Kuwait to its counterpart in Switzerland provided details about financial transactions made by suspects charged with the misappropriation offence. Those documents constituted evidence that helped secure the conviction of the offenders.[339] More importantly, during an investigation or upon conviction, it may be found, with the help of evidence obtained from other states, that there are illicit assets associated with the crime that lie outside Kuwait. Thus, a mere conviction is not helpful in this situation. The pursuit of the illicit assets necessitates further cooperation with those states where the assets are located. The MLA requests in this case consist of forms of assistance that facilitate 'surveillance of transactions and the searching of financial records to trace assets … the use of legal powers to "freeze" suspect assets … and to confiscate them by having legal title transferred to the competent authorities'.[340] The MLA may also be helpful in the direct or indirect enforcement of foreign forfeiture or confiscation orders (the recognition and enforcement of orders).[341] Finally, the UNCAC considers asset recovery a 'fundamental principle' of the convention and requires states parties 'to afford one another the widest measure of cooperation and assistance in this regard'.[342] Once the assets are forfeited or confiscated, international cooperation is crucial to secure their repatriation.[343]

In general, in order to be more effective in combating grand corruption and its financial consequences, Kuwait should not only depend on the relevant provisions provided by the UNCAC, for they face a number of challenges.[344]

335 UNODC (2013, p. 11).
336 AML/CFT Act, s.23.
337 Ibid., s.19.
338 See <https://egmontgroup. org/en/content/kuwait-kuwaiti-financial-intelligence-unit>.
339 Case No. 1499/2008, 27/6/2019 (First Instance Court – Criminal Division 10) 14–15.
340 UNODC (2004a, p. 552).
341 Brun et al. (2011). See also Articles 54–55 of the UNCAC.
342 UNCAC, art.51.
343 Brun et al. (2011). See also Article 57 of the UNCAC.
344 See Ziouvas (2018).

It could expand the number of states with which it has MLA treaties to facilitate cooperation. In this context, Kuwait should concentrate on developing cooperative relations with the jurisdictions where dirty assets are often well hidden. These jurisdictions include states that offenders often target to hide the assets derived from corruption crimes due to a number of factors, such as the fact that they enjoy economic stability and are prominent financial centres. The recent MLA treaty with the United Kingdom is an example of an effective step towards combating corruption. In 28 January 2018, the Government of the United Kingdom of Great Britain and Northern Ireland and the Government of the State of Kuwait signed a Treaty on Mutual Legal Assistance in Criminal Matters. Article 1 of the Treaty covered a wide range of areas, including '(b) providing documents, records and items of evidence, including bank records ... d) search and seizure; e) restraining and confiscating the proceeds and instrumentalities of criminal activities ...; i) return of assets ...'.[345]

### 4.3.7 *Whistleblowing*

Modern organisations are so complex that it becomes less likely that 'outsiders' will be aware of wrongdoing inside such organisations.[346] Rose-Ackerman argues that the 'successful detection of corruption depends on insiders to report wrongdoing'.[347] Without whistleblowers informing about wrongdoing, many corrupt actions would go unreported. Whistleblowing is broadly defined as 'the disclosure or reporting of wrongdoing, including but not limited to corruption ... and acts to cover up of any of these'.[348] Supposedly, whistleblowers can refer more and early information to those who can do something with it.[349] This section addresses the Kuwaiti law regarding the act of exposing wrongdoing. The existing whistleblowing system in Kuwait is generally categorised into two parts. The first is the general duty to report crime as a core issue. The second part is the whistleblowing system set out for corruption crimes. Upon identifying the whistleblowing provisions in Kuwait, this section simultaneously approaches the evidence-related difficulties confronted in corruption offences.

In general, Kuwaiti criminal law imposes a limited obligation to report crime.[350] It is a criminal offence for anyone who was aware of a criminal project to have refrained from reporting it at a time when it could have been prevented. However, such a duty is confined to three offences: murder, arson, and theft.[351]

345 See <https://www.gov.uk/government/publications/cs-kuwait-no22018-ukkuwait-treaty-on-mutual-legal-assistance-in-criminal-matters>.
346 Miceli, Near and Dworkin (2008, p. 2).
347 Rose-Ackerman (1999, p. 53).
348 Transparency International (2018, p. 7). See also Miceli, Near and Dworkin (2008).
349 Dworkin and Near (1997).
350 This is 'a matter of the extent of the duties recognised' by the legislator. See Ashworth (1989, p. 424).
351 CLA 1960, s.143.

It is also a criminal offence if an individual, who is aware that an offence has been committed, refrains from reporting in favour of the offender(s), including concealing evidence to help an offender escape justice. The mere refraining is not criminal unless it is accompanied by an intention to help the offender(s).[352]

The duty to report corruption crimes is broader. The ACAA, section 37, has imposed a duty on individuals to report all corruption crimes. To that end, it is crime for any person to abstain from reporting any 'corruption crime' when he/she knows that such a crime has been committed.[353] The Act exempts the spouse, ascendants, and descendants of the offender from this duty.[354] The Kuwaiti law is so flexible that it even encourages offenders to self-report. In bribery offences, the briber will be immune from punishment if he/she reports it even after its commission, and the bribe paid will be returned to the briber.[355] In other corruption crimes, the offender shall also be given immunity from punishment when he/she spontaneously reports any criminal enterprise before embarking on that enterprise.[356] Even after committing the crime, the court can exempt the offender from the punishment, if the offender, before the start of the investigation, voluntarily reports a corruption crime; and if he/she enables the investigative authority to arrest the other offenders, locate the money that is the subject of the offence, or arrest the offenders of other crimes that are similar in their seriousness.[357]

Researchers generally agree that the reliance on 'purely altruistic' whistleblowing imposes an 'unrealistically high standard'.[358] Therefore, since 2012, whistleblowing in Kuwait has taken on a more sophisticated shape.[359] Several measures have been introduced to induce people to act on the civic duty to report corruption crimes. Section 37 of the ACAA aims to safeguard the 'freedom and safety' of the whistleblower, establishing a general rule that no whistleblower may be prejudiced by reason of his/her report. The whistleblower protection programme (WPP) is set out in the ACAA. The WPP is extendable to the whistleblower's immediate relatives and, if necessary, other persons close to the whistleblower.[360] The protective measures provided for the whistleblower take into account different repercussions and fall into three categories of protection: security, criminal, and administrative.

In terms of the security aspect, the whistleblower's identity and home address should be anonymised and kept confidential, and if necessary, personal protection

352 CJA, s.14; CLA 1960, s.133.
353 ACAA, ss.20 and 45.
354 Ibid., s.45.
355 CLA 1970, ss.39–42.
356 ACAA, s.44.
357 Ibid. See also CJA, s.160.
358 See Miceli, Near and Dworkin (2008, p. 37).
359 See Al-Haidar (2018).
360 ACAA, s.40.

and a new home may also be provided.[361] Criminally, the whistleblower will be immune from any criminal prosecution.[362] The divulgation of the whistleblower's identity or home is also criminalised.[363] The administrative protection involves protecting the whistleblower from any potential retaliatory measures being imposed by his/her employer. The WPP sets out two arrangements. First, it is a disciplinary offence for any officeholder to take any disciplinary action (as a reprisal) against the whistleblower because of his/her role in counter-corruption efforts. Second, the disciplinary procedure taken against the whistleblower shall be invalid.[364] Outside the workplace, whistleblowers (such as former officials) are also immune and protected from any retaliatory legal actions, such as civil lawsuits.[365]

To prevent potential abuses, whistleblowers should act in good faith when reporting a corruption act. When reporting such an act, they should have reasonable evidence that justifies the correctness of their belief that a corruption crime has been committed.[366] A claim is not considered substantive if it lacks documents, or if it just refers to the facts of the case without any plausible evidence.[367] The 'good faith' requirement does not refer to the proper motivation of the whistleblower, but rather to the information disclosed.[368] Although the 'reasonable belief' threshold prevents frivolous claims, this provision is argued to be an overdeterrent, because it may prevent employees from reporting when they have 'risky information'.[369] Nevertheless, the threshold of 'reasonable belief' is not intended to deter would-be whistleblowers, but is a safeguard against abuses of whistleblowing. The ACAA strikes a balance between encouraging individuals to report crimes and the right of individuals not to be discredited/defamed. Deliberate false disclosure is not protected and is punishable by up to 3 years' imprisonment and dismissal from office.[370]

The public disclosure of wrongdoing made to non-official platforms, such as the media, might be misused and cause detrimental consequences to third parties. Transparency International (TI) suggests that public disclosure should not be protected unless it satisfies certain requirements, such as 'in case of urgent or grave public or personal danger'.[371] In Kuwait, public disclosures are criminally protected if they meet three requirements. First, disclosures should be based on a reasonable belief that what is being disclosed has actually occurred.

361 Ibid., s.41(1).
362 Ibid., s.41(3).
363 Ibid., s.51.
364 Ibid., s.52.
365 Ibid., s.41(3).
366 Ibid., s.38.
367 ACAA-SI, s.37. Section 38 also imposes further formalities.
368 This requirement avoids many practical problems. See Transparency International (2018, p. 15).
369 Al-Haidar (2018, p. 1025).
370 ACAA, s.53.
371 Transparency International (2018, pp. 40–41).

Second, the intention behind the disclosure must be to protect the public interest. Third, the public disclosure must be as limited in scope and content as possible just to protect the public interest.[372] Therefore, it is not a defamation offence if an individual publicly discloses a truthful wrongdoing if the public interest justifies such a public disclosure, including misconduct related to an officeholder and his/her public duties.[373]

However, the collateral consequences of misreporting are controllable and less devastating as long as they remain in the hands of the official bodies. Thus, the requirement of reporting to official bodies represents a safeguard against any potential abuses. To encourage whistleblowing to official bodies (such as Nazaha or the public prosecution), the ACAA restricts the effects of WPP to those who have followed the designated channels.[374] The WPP does not include those who report externally to other third parties. Furthermore, the Kuwait Counter-Corruption Strategy 2019–2024 (Strategy 2019–2024) aims to establish a 'National Electronic Platform' through which individuals can securely report to Nazaha any wrongdoing and provide any information they may have. Nazaha will put in place specific criteria that measure the effectiveness of this platform.[375]

The ACAA acknowledges the role of the relief measures and the financial incentives in encouraging whistleblowing. A whistleblower is entitled to two types of incentives: relief remedies for injury and a reward system. The state should compensate whistleblowers for any potential moral and physical injuries and damages resulting from the act of whistleblowing.[376] Nazaha shall also bear the expenses of the whistleblower's treatment and social care.[377] The ACAA also grants whistleblowers moral and financial incentives.[378] Nazaha may grant the whistleblower financial rewards or honour rewards and acknowledgements, provided that his/her report is the only direct cause of the detection of the corruption crime. The financial reward may be a portion of the assets recovered. Because the assets of a crime may disappear, the ACAA allows Nazaha in determining the financial rewards on a case-by-case basis.[379]

The whistleblowing system in Kuwait is consistent with most of the guiding principles stipulated by the TI[380] and seems to be comprehensive: starting from depicting the obligation to report corruption as a prosocial behaviour and the incorporation of the prisoner dilemma technique in the course of the investigation (such as the criminal immunity granted in self-reporting),[381] to the WPP.

372 CLA 1960, s.215
373 Ibid., s.214
374 ACAA, s.40; ACAA-SI, ss.38 and 61.
375 Nazaha (2019, pp. 79–80).
376 ACAA, s.43.
377 ACAA-SI, s.66.
378 ACAA, s.43.
379 ACAA-SI, s.41.
380 See Transparency International (2018).
381 See Yadlin (2006).

*Table 4.4* Number of the corruption cases reported by whistleblowers to Nazaha

| *Procedure taken* | *Number* |
|---|---|
| Under investigation | 59 |
| Recommended that the investigation be discontinued | 44 |
| Investigations closed | 23 |
| Referred to the public prosecution | 19 |
| Investigation discontinued and referred to other competent bodies | 6 |
| Attached to previous investigation | 5 |
| Investigations discontinued | 1 |
| *Total:* | *157* |

The positive effects brought by the current whistleblowing system are evidenced by the relatively high number of reports filed by individual whistleblowers.[382] Between April 2016 and December 2017, Nazaha received 90 reports: 75 of them were filed by individuals.[383] Up to November 2018, the number increased to 157 reports. Some reports triggered investigations into financial disclosures submitted by officeholders to check whether there had been an unexplained increase in their wealth. Of those investigated, 19 reports were referred to the public prosecution (see Table 4.4).[384]

In the Strategy 2019–2024, the policymakers have shown their acknowledgement of the importance of whistleblowing. Nazaha has initiated initiatives to promote whistleblowing in the public sector. These initiatives basically aim to increase the number of governmental bodies that incorporate procedures to encourage their respective officials to report wrongdoings and to protect them from any potential abuse.[385] Furthermore, one of the agenda items of the Strategy 2019–2024 is to encourage and support whistleblowing from the private sector. The Strategy aims to regularly review the number of private entities that incorporate whistleblowing systems that both encourage and protect their employees when reporting corruption incidents. For that purpose, Nazaha has formed a special team that provides technical assistance for private sector entities to put in place effective whistleblowing policies.[386]

In conclusion, the experience of the whistleblowing system, especially the WPP and the reward scheme, is recent and it needs more time to be reasonably assessed. Some potential reforms and innovative approaches are suggested in section 4.4.2.1. There is one final point to be raised, however. In order for the whistleblowing system to achieve its intended effect, the law enforcement authorities and NGOs must ensure that it is known about and understood by those whom it concerns, that is, would-be whistleblowers.

382 Official-2.
383 Nazaha (2017a, pp. 63–64).
384 Official statistics presented by Official-2 during the interview on 21 November 2018.
385 Nazaha (2019, p. 96).
386 Ibid., pp. 79–80.

## 4.4 Critique of the Kuwaiti criminal response to corruption and suggested reforms

This section addresses two issues. First, it evaluates the adequacy and effectiveness of the existing Kuwaiti criminal laws in dealing with grand corruption. This overall assessment is built upon the analysis in the previous section (section 4.3). Second, the section examines how the law can be changed and improved especially regarding grand corruption. In examining the second aspect, this section explores innovative techniques and suggests how these could be incorporated into Kuwaiti laws. These innovative approaches could be harnessed to rectify and further strengthen the legal response based on international practices.

### 4.4.1 *Assessment of existing criminal counter-corruption measures*

As emerged from the previous analysis, the criminal law dominates in Kuwait as the key instrument being employed to counter corruption domestically, as evidenced by the number of corruption offences created and the provisions for the proceeds of crime. In fact, Kuwait has put in place a constellation of corruption crimes that arguably cover most, if not all, potential corruption cases. The legal analysis of the criminal laws, supported by the judgments of courts and the opinions of professional experts, allows us to contend that the criminal texts related to corruption are sufficient to deal with corruption cases in Kuwait. Kuwait has achieved notable progress in the arena of criminal counter-corruption measures[387] and the AML law.[388] However, this is not to say that the criminal law is enough to combat the phenomenon of corruption. The criminal law, per se, is, by no means, enough. The following is overall assessment of what has previously been said.

The bribery offence has been criticised for being fraught with difficulties that mar the effectiveness of the offence. In particular, two issues should be revised: the difficulty of proving bribery and the strict requirement of *mens rea*.[389] Different solutions may be suggested. For example, inducing insiders to report, backed by an effective system of whistleblowing, could increase the possibility of detecting bribery cases.[390] Some participants also thought that the creation of the IEO and the associated financial disclosures are means to besiege the bribed: if bribery is not detected when committed, it will then be detected later as an 'unjustified' increase in wealth.[391] Altogether, the whistleblowing system and financial disclosures have been effective in overcoming the difficulties

387 See UNODC (2013).
388 See MENAFATF (2015).
389 See chapter 4.3.1.
390 Judge-1.
391 Official-4; Lawyer-2.

related to proof. As stated by Nazaha, one report by a whistleblower who had a reasonable belief that a senior officeholder had engaged in a bribery offence triggered an investigation into the financial disclosure already submitted by that official. The investigation successfully enabled Nazaha to identify suspicious transactions in the suspect's bank accounts and he could not provide a reasonable justification for their legitimate provenance.[392] Thus, with ameliorations in the counter-corruption provisions, the difficulties inherent in proving bribery could be less stark.

The non-criminalisation of private sector bribery in Kuwait has been said to affect the fairness of the bribery offence.[393] However, that there is a need for a private bribery offence is debatable. The large dependence on the public sector in Kuwait casts doubt on the exigency of criminalised private bribery, at least for the time being this argument is not meant to downplay the several adverse consequences of private bribery.[394] Instead, it is a matter of prioritisation in the jurisdiction of Kuwait. Attention should thus be directed at the potentially instigating role of the private sector in the bribery of public officials, namely, private-to-public bribery.[395] This potential role of the private sector is what has been considered in the Strategy 2019–2024.

The embezzlement and misappropriation offences have been perceived as effective and comprehensive in covering as many cases as possible,[396] though the stated objective of their Act (the PPFA) is perplexing and causes fairness-related concerns.[397] There are, however, problems pertaining to the investigation of such offences: the lack of experienced prosecutors and the non-existence of prosecutorial policies (agreements) for corruption crimes. These two issues impact the effectiveness of these offences when the prosecutors are not well trained in dealing with sophisticated cases (which may lead to producing weak evidence)[398] or when the prosecutors are unable to deal flexibly with each individual case, taking into consideration the circumstances surrounding the case. Empowering the prosecutors to enter into agreements could effectively improve the embezzlement and misappropriation offences.[399] Again, an enhanced system of whistleblowing and informing would help here.[400]

In regard to the intentional harm and exploitation of office offences, the issues associated with the elements of 'harm' and 'benefits' highlight two difficulties: the difficulty in proving the officeholder's intention to cause 'harm' and the

392 See <https://www.nazaha.gov.kw/EN/Lists/News/DispForm.aspx?ID=159&Source=/en/pages/news.aspx>.
393 Official-2; Lawyer-1.
394 Boles (2014b).
395 Official-2.
396 Official-4; Official-5.
397 See section 4.3.2.2.
398 NGO-3.
399 See below section 4.4.2.2.
400 Lawyer-1.

difficulty in proving the benefits for the officeholder or others.[401] To overcome these difficulties, it is suggested that providing specialised courts with qualified judges and prosecutors could effectively help to deal with complex cases.[402] Currently, Nazaha acts as a specialised body in counter-corruption matters, with a wide range of legal powers. The designated role of Nazaha as a buffer between the reporting parties and the prosecutors enables it to perform technical functions that the courts may not be able to, such as those related to complex economic assumptions.[403] Moreover, prosecutorial agreements would avoid the difficulties regarding uncertainty associated with prosecuting those cases. Whenever a benefit is achieved for others by the act of an officeholder, the ability to arrange settlements with the defendants can secure the return of such a benefit to the state. In the existing laws, the challenge is that such benefits cannot be returned to the state unless a criminal conviction is secured, which can be uncertain given the evidential difficulties (especially if the official's intention to secure such benefits for others cannot be proved).

In terms of the conflict of interest offence, its criminal nature brings some criticism.[404] Conflicts of interest should first be subject to a preventive strategy. Instead of relying solely on the criminal law, transparency measures could perform pre-emptive functions. Officeholders most susceptible to conflicts of interest could be required to register their respective interests before the assumption of office. Having such a registry would render the officials under a constant check, both by people and by other competent public bodies. The registry would deter officeholders from engaging in conflicts of interest and/or facilitate investigations into conflicts of interest in the future. The United Kingdom has good practice in this regard. The Ministerial Code requires ministers to ensure that no conflict of interest transpires: upon appointment, they must provide a list of all relevant interests known to them that may affect their decisions in the future.[405] Three reforms to the CIA are suggested here to respond to its unconstitutionality as decided by the Kuwait Constitutional Court.[406]

First, the CIA should reconsider the social construction of Kuwaiti society, as the applicability of the CIA to the fourth-degree relative of the officeholder is problematic. Therefore, the scope of criminalisation should be limited, because of factors such as the intra-society relationships and the small population, and hence the likelihood that professional people may know each other. Second, there could be a waiver of conflict of interest in cases of relative conflict.[407] A balance between officeholders' public role and their personal interest as private citizens should be struck. Whenever an officeholder has a

401 See section 4.3.3.1.
402 Lawyer-2; Judge-2.
403 See section 4.3.3.1.
404 See section 4.3.3.2.
405 See <https://www.gov.uk/government/publications/list-of-ministers-interests>.
406 See section 4.3.3.2.
407 OECD (2003).

minuscule share in a business, or the financial interest is so remote that it is unlikely to improperly affect his/her decision, the officeholder should only have to disclose such shares/interest and should not have to leave their office/position or divest the private interest. Third, further arrangements related to managing a conflict of interest would arguably solve the issues mentioned previously. Rather than leaving office or divesting the private interest, the law may establish a recusal policy with appropriate procedures to properly manage a conflict of interest 'by having another official temporarily perform the official's duties'.[408]

Next, the criminal nature of the IEO provokes the constitutional safeguards provided for the suspect.[409] The current construction of the IEO in Kuwait law – whereby it is contingent on officials submitting financial disclosures – has some limitations. These financial disclosures are the only source of information regarding any suspicious increase in wealth and the only cause for triggering an investigation. The literature suggests additional sources for triggering investigations into suspicious illicit enrichment.[410] Of particular relevance are 'lifestyle checks' on public officials, in which enquiries are undertaken to check whether the lifestyle of an officeholder cannot reasonably be explained by his/her legal income.[411] These lifestyle checks would not replace but, rather, would complement the financial disclosures; as a result, senior, junior, and non-citizen officials would not escape liability just because they had not submitted a financial disclosure or because they were not obliged to submit one.[412]

The current misapplication of the ML offence reveals its inability to achieve its intended effect.[413] The requirement that the prosecutor must present evidence that the money is derived from a particular predicate offence is impractical. Lawyer-1 argued for reducing the difficulties provided by the burden of proof and adopting 'circumstantial evidence': whenever there is suspicion, there should be effective mechanisms to explain the money based on 'logical and reasonable justifications'. It is argued that this understanding of the ML offence is consistent with what Alldridge mentioned, that is, 'A common complaint was that there was insufficient evidence to bring prosecutions'.[414] A good example is the UK POCA 2002, which has 'gradually undermined the significance of the actual source of the funds'.[415] As stated in *R v Anwoir (Ilham)*, one of the 'two ways in which the Crown can prove the property derives from crime …' is '…b) by evidence of the circumstances in which the property is handled which

408 See OECD (2005, p. 20).
409 See section 4.3.4.
410 Muzila et al. (2012).
411 There are several safeguards to avoid abuses. See ibid., p. 43.
412 Lawyer-2 argued that bribery can be displaced to non-citizens officials. See section 4.3.1.
413 See section 4.3.5.
414 Alldridge (2008, pp. 440–441).
415 McCluskey (2009, p. 719).

is such as to give rise to the irresistible inference that it can only be derived from crime'.[416] Although there are other decisions that have reached different conclusions,[417] the general, non-specific statutory definition of 'proceeds of crime' in the Kuwaiti AML/CFT Act allows for the idea of 'irresistible inference' to be used in the courts in Kuwait. Practitioners are encouraged to adopt this understanding.

The criticism of each crime does not so much relate to the offences themselves as to the criminal law system. It can be said that what the professionals were referring to is not the difficulties affecting the effectiveness of each offence, but rather, the difficulties of the criminal law as a whole – even if they were not explicit in this regard. All of these critical points relate to the nature of the criminal law and not to the essence of the offences. One point can be inferred from the aforementioned analysis: the fact that not a single participant out of those interviewed mentioned the difficulties of the criminal law itself in countering corruption implies that they do not even conceive of instruments other than the criminal law. This inference is an indication that the philosophy underlying the current arrangements and the Kuwaiti policymakers and professional experts have a clear inclination towards, or preference for, the criminal laws to combat corruption. The criminal law is a conventional instrument and does not, at least in the case of Kuwait, provide for any innovative measures to combat corruption. The IEO is an exceptional recent development in the arsenal of counter-corruption laws. But as much as it brings in innovation, the IEO is still a measure that is criminal in nature that has been added to the existing predominant criminal responses. Also, whether or not the IEO is effective is yet to be determined. It is thought that the time has come to adopt alternative non-criminal measures to tackle the scourge of corruption; this is the subject of chapter 5.

In relation to the whistleblowing system, the discussion in section 4.3.7 generally focused on the role of individuals. As shown, the whistleblowing system in Kuwait is, to a large extent, comprehensive and bringing concrete results.[418] The Strategy 2019–2024 takes into account having an encouraging rewards scheme to secure the reporting of more wrongdoings. The Strategy aims to establish a 'comprehensive rewarding policy' and to regularly review its effectiveness regarding its potential effect on inducing individuals to come forward and report corruption incidents.[419] However, the clandestine nature of corruption keeps not only the law enforcement authorities uninformed, but also would-be whistleblowers. More attention to should be paid, then, to the role of offenders in reporting crime, since the current arrangements in this regard are arguably insufficient. Innovation is suggested in the next section.

416 [2008] EWCA Crim 1354; [2009] 1 WLR 980, 987.
417 Walters (2009).
418 See section 4.3.7.
419 Nazaha (2019, p. 98).

### 4.4.2 *Innovative measures*

The reflection on the existing criminal measures indicates that Kuwait has so far adopted adequate criminal measures to counter corruption. However, the effectiveness of such measures to deal with the problem of grand corruption in Kuwait is questionable and they lack innovation. Therefore, this section articulates innovative reforms to effectively consolidate the counter-corruption efforts and discusses how relevant to the existing criminal measures these 'innovative' reforms could be. It is argued here that the Kuwaiti criminal measures should be complemented by other instruments, powers, and approaches. This section focuses on approaches to consolidate the whistleblowing system (section 4.4.2.1) and prosecutorial agreements (section 4.4.2.2).

#### 4.4.2.1 *Bounty hunting and public mobilisation strategies*

Reflecting on what the interviews with the experts revealed, evidence-related difficulties in proving wrongdoing can be identified as a common pattern. This section is concerned with attenuating these difficulties by suggesting innovative reforms to be introduced to the existing whistleblowing system in Kuwait. The first strategy is 'bounty hunting'. This strategy is concerned with the role of perpetrators as the most informed parties and spurring them to self-report. The second strategy is 'public mobilisation'. This strategy is directed at encouraging more individuals (non-offenders) to blow the whistle.

In regard to the bounty hunting strategy, the analysis is directed more at the perpetrators. Detecting corruption is a difficult task because usually the perpetrators are the only people in the unique position of knowing about the corrupt deal. Increasing the possibility of detection is a function of whether there are incentives to induce any of the perpetrators to report to the authorities.[420] In fact, nothing is novel for the Kuwaiti law in regard to this conclusion. In pre-defined conditions, the perpetrators are already immune from punishment if they secure the punishment of the other offenders.[421] However, this immunity is permissive if the self-reporting is done after the commission of the offence.[422] Among the shortcomings, the eligibility of perpetrators for the WPP and the rewards scheme is questionable because their statutory provisions were drafted in a general sense.[423] The ACAA does not clearly articulate the intention of the legislature to apply the WPP and reward scheme to whistleblowers who are perpetrators. There is a risk that they are excluded from the rewards, especially based on the principle that no offender should benefit from his/her illegal act.

420 Rose-Ackerman (1999).

421 See section 4.3.7.

422 ACAA, s.44. However, section 160 of the CJA renders the immunity obligatory in other offences punishable for 7 years and more.

423 Nazaha (2017b, p. 7). See also <http://www.nazaha.gov.kw/en/Pages/ImportantInfo.aspx>.

The uncertainty around their entitlement to the rewards could discourage them from reporting.

The leniency programmes based on the waiver of criminal prosecution may be insufficient to encourage the perpetrators of illegal activities to self-report,[424] especially if the potential gains of the corrupt deal are too much to be waived, and the trust between the perpetrators is entrenched. Therefore, not only must the law offer immunity to spur perpetrators to self-report their misconduct, but it should also be designed to increase the risks of engaging in corruption, particularly in cooperative crime. There may be a more effective bounty hunting strategy that threatens to undermine the trust built around corrupt deals. This strategy may take advantage of the fact that corruption is vulnerable to 'opportunism'.[425] The law can position the corrupt against each other from the first moment of the criminal enterprise. For example, a mechanism called the 'conspirator dilemma' suggests that the first offender to file a lawsuit is entitled to collect the fine from the other accomplices (besides being criminally immune).[426] Each offender risks the other offender defecting and initiating a lawsuit to collect the fine from him/her as a reward. This strategy is inspired by the idea of Becker and Stigler regarding the privatisation of enforcement and the compensation of enforcers.[427]

However, the idea of private enforcement of corruption laws is not attractive to the Kuwaiti policymakers at the moment. Therefore, to introduce the 'conspiracy dilemma' to the existing whistleblowing system, some adaptations are necessary. The first offender to report to Nazaha about the other would be entitled to two advantages: criminal immunity and rewards equal to the fine that would be imposed on the other offender(s). To further encourage self-reporting earlier, the law may differentiate between whether the self-reporting is done before or after the crime is committed. If it were done beforehand, the conspirator would be rewarded the whole fine; if it were done after the crime had been committed, the offender would get a portion of the fine. In the latter case, the immunity and reward scheme must be obligatory. Interestingly, the fines in the Kuwaiti counter-corruption laws are remunerative enough to encourage an offender to report before committing the crime, waiving the illegal gains he/she would gain. With increases in the law enforcement activities, it becomes rational for the conspirator to report and get as much of the gains as possible before being detected.

The reform proposed seems to be revolutionary for the Kuwaiti legal system, because it not only involves the immunity of the offender, but also allows for one offender to take advantage of the 'carrots' – the benefits that would be gained from the criminal activity. The gist of this radical reform may be justified on

424 See sections 4.3.7 and 4.4.1.
425 Lambsdorff (2007, p. 51).
426 See Yadlin (2006, pp. 26–29).
427 See Becker and Stigler (1974).

utilitarian grounds. Since it revolves around the reciprocity inherent in cooperative corruption, there should be methods to inhibit this reciprocity: Lambsdorff argued that, 'To root out corruption, it may be necessary to risk destroying some of the confidence that goes along with it – the trust that expects corrupt favors to be reciprocated'.[428] Distrust should be created among offenders, who could be placed in a race in terms of who reports first. The point is that this suggested reform is different from the existing leniency provided for the offender. The former is generous and ensures a much larger reward, especially in the early stage of the crime, which makes defection a lucrative decision. The suggested reform is also consistent with what Dworkin and Near observed, that is, that the whistleblowing laws have undergone a shift from valuing motivation over information, to valuing information over motivation.[429]

Unlike the first strategy, the 'public mobilisation' strategy is directed at whistleblowers who are non-participants in the crime. The problematic assumption addressed here relates to 'inactive observers' who observe the wrongdoing but do not report it.[430] One cause giving rise to this problem is the ethical duality of whistleblowing: while it can be seen as an 'act of justice, serving to right a wrong', it can also be seen as 'a grave betrayal'.[431] Psychological research shows that the trade-off between fairness and loyalty values constitutes an important predictor that affects one's decision regarding whether to blow the whistle.[432] These values are arguably linked to the culture of a society. Hofstede stresses that, unlike 'individualistic' societies where the people only look after themselves and their immediate family, 'the loyalty to the group' is an essential feature of 'collectivist' societies.[433] The problem here is of a cultural nature: where the collectivist culture dominates, the loyalty value prevails and there is a tendency to overlook unethical conduct, leading, eventually, to a decrease in the possibility of whistleblowing.[434]

Studies have found that collectivist societies tend to support unethical acts as long as they lead to benefits for the in-groups.[435] Although the studies mentioned here deal with the employees within one organisation, they can be extended to broader contexts: the relationships between the whistleblowers and their in-group members. In Kuwait, where the social construction strongly comprises interpersonal relationships within cohesive in-groups (clans, tribes, and sects),[436] the loyalty value may affect one's ethical decision to report others' wrongdoing. Driven by the loyalty value, the would-be whistleblower is not

428 See Lambsdorff (2007, p. 55).
429 Dworkin and Near (1997).
430 Ibid., p. 6.
431 See Dungan, Waytz and Young (2015, p. 129).
432 See Waytz, Dungan and Young (2013).
433 Hofstede (2001, pp. 225–229).
434 Dungan, Waytz and Young (2015).
435 Sims (2009).
436 See chapter 2.3.4.1.

expected to expose the wrongdoing of a member of his/her family or tribe. In this social situation, where the loyalty value dominating the interrelations in Kuwaiti society may affect the willingness to report wrongdoing, it is important to build what may be called 'constructive dissent', where people are encouraged to express their dissent while maintaining the loyalty among in-groups.[437] Changing people's interpretation of what is beneficial for them is more plausible than changing the cultural values of a whole society.[438] Whistleblowing would be seen as an essential part of being a loyal group member by achieving the common good.[439] The role of codes of conduct within governmental bodies is of utmost importance.[440]

Whistleblowing is not just a matter of formal rules, such as laws. Other informal actors may also be involved in whistleblowing. NGOs can perform educative roles embodied in raising the awareness of people.[441] They can promote the social acceptance of whistleblowing and provide moral support for people to break any cultural barriers to whistleblowing and enable them to see it as a beneficial matter for all of society. In Kuwait, the interviewees stressed that NGOs also play a role in incentivising people to resist corruption and report misconduct.[442] Before the advent of the ACAA, in line with the TI's Advocacy and Legal Advice Centres,[443] the Kuwait Transparency Society (KTS) established the *Faz'aa* Centre for legal guidance and advocacy in February 2011. NGO-2 explained that this centre has received more than 43 reports about suspiciously corrupt practices. The success that the *Faz'aa* centre has achieved could be explained by the deliberative nature of the mechanism that the KTS has adopted in responding to the reports received.[444] NGO-2 explained this success:

> We went to the senior officials responsible for the body where the suspicious act had been committed. We succeeded in many cases. For example, we stopped a suspicious tender in the Ministry of Health in relation to nursery activities. We also succeeded on other occasions when we communicated with the Minister of Interior regarding suspicious practices during the general election.

NGO-3 also referred to the 'Report Campaign', which expressly aimed to encourage people to report bribery cases that they had confronted. Broadly speaking, the campaign aimed to consolidate the principle of accountability: 'when an officeholder is aware that people are being supported to report bribery,

437 Dungan, Waytz and Young (2015, p. 131).
438 Sims (2009).
439 Dungan, Waytz and Young (2015).
440 See chapter 5.3.2.1.
441 Myers (2014).
442 NGO-2; NGO-3.
443 See <https://www.transparency.org/reportcorruption>.
444 NGO-2.

that official will be certain that he/she can be held accountable at any time, and hence, will stop being involved in bribery'.[445] Although these examples of informal, civil society-backed initiatives are limited in terms of the financial rewards and other incentives, they are practical and help people get involved in whistleblowing informally but effectively. The official channels for whistleblowing, as Martin argues, sometimes do not work, and it is wise to first take precautionary steps.[446] The NGOs may act as experienced organisations that help whistleblowers deliver their claims in the right way. They can also help build and mobilise sympathetic supporters so that the whistleblower does not fall into the trap of 'relying solely on the truth'.[447] TI contends that especially in grand corruption cases, which are politically sensitive, reporting to the NGOs will prevent the authorities from overlooking or covering up the wrongdoing.[448]

#### 4.4.2.2 *Innovative prosecutorial policy*

Reflecting on the opinions of some of the interviewees, this section suggests an innovative prosecutorial policy to secure better delivery of justice outcomes. This policy responds to the criticism directed at the existing pre-trial prosecutorial arrangements in the Kuwaiti criminal justice system, especially those pertaining to corruption crimes. In particular, this section is concerned with improving the prosecutorial stage and introducing an alternative disposal mechanism to court proceedings. But first, a brief background on the current pre-trial provisions of prosecuting crimes is necessary to understand what Kuwait really lacks.

In Kuwait, the public prosecution has exclusive jurisdiction over the investigation and prosecution of corruption crimes.[449] The prosecutors also have discretion with respect to the disposition of the investigation.[450] The general rule on criminal prosecution is that it is mandatory, except in cases where the prosecutor can discontinue the investigation for specific reasons, such as a lack of evidence.[451] However, the CJA has some applications where the cases can be resolved at the investigation stage but under the supervision of the court. First, there can be a victim–offender reconciliation whereby they can agree upon a plan involving restitution and immunity.[452] Such reconciliation, nevertheless, is limited to specific crimes: adultery, kidnapping, insult and defamation, extortion, and predatory and property offences.[453] Second, the 'criminal order' has

445 NGO-3.
446 Martin (2009).
447 Martin (2013, pp. 15–16).
448 Transparency International (2018).
449 ACAA, s.27.
450 CJA, s.9.
451 Ibid., ss.101–104 bis.
452 Ibid., ss.240–243.
453 Ibid., ss.109 and 240.

been established by the CJA whereby the prosecutor can submit an application to the court asking it to impose sanctions on the offender in misdemeanours punishable for 1 year (and less) or a KWD 500 find (or less). The application shall be summarily decided on by the court (and it may be dismissed).[454]

Certain offences may be specified with distinct prosecutorial arrangements. First, in smuggling offences, the GCCA 10/2003 recognises an agreement between the Kuwait Customs and the offender as an alternative means to the traditional prosecutorial procedures.[455] Second, section 131 of the Capital Market Authority Act 7/2010 also allows for the Authority in stock exchange offences to offer, or accept from, the offender an agreement with specific conditions. Third, section 42 of the Electronic Transactions Act 20/2014 allows the prosecutors to accept from a non-recidivist offender an agreement to discontinue the proceedings under specific conditions. It follows that the prosecution is not mandatory in these cases and can be disposed of out of the court. Once again, there is no special legal framework governing the prosecution of corruption crimes, as analysed in section 4.3. Thus, alternative disposals by agreement could be suggested.

Corruption cases may be diverted away from the courts and resolved in other ways. Non-trial resolutions involve 'a wide array of mechanisms developed and used to resolve criminal matters without a full court proceeding … based on an agreement with an individual or a company and a prosecuting or another authority'.[456] In this context, the Deferred Prosecution Agreements (DPAs) represent a 'profound' development that provides the prosecutors with other paths to pursue for white collar crimes.[457] The prosecutors may exercise their discretion in balancing circumstances and enter into a DPA where they procure a charge against the defendant but defer the prosecution in return for the cooperation of the other party.[458] The criminal charge is dismissed once the conditions in the DPA are met: the conditions might include compliance with certain requirements, 'such as financial penalties, restitution for victims, confiscation of the profits of wrongdoing and measures to prevent future offending'.[459] The non-trial resolutions may have different outcomes across jurisdictions.[460]

DPAs have their roots in the 'pretrial diversion agreements' for individual defendants whereby the prosecution is suspended until the defendant meets the conditions of the agreement.[461] However, they have recently been developed and

454 Ibid., ss.148–149.
455 GCCA, ss.151–153.
456 OECD (2019, p. 17).
457 Spivack and Raman (2008, pp. 159–160).
458 Greenblum (2005).
459 UK Ministry of Justice (2012, p. para.5).
460 See OECD (2019).
461 Uhlmann (2013, pp. 1303–1304). For the differences between the pre-trial diversion agreements and the DPAs, see Xiao (2013).

used in the context of corporate crimes.[462] For the present purposes, DPAs will be used as an inclusive term to refer to any prosecutor–defendant settlement. Given the focus on public sector corruption, the typical clients of the DPA are assumed to be offending officeholders. The DPAs should be adapted for that purpose and employed to tackle the practical difficulties raised by the interviewees. In particular, the introduction of DPAs in Kuwaiti law would be helpful in two cases: non-serious corruption crimes and serious corruption crimes (especially those with inadequate evidence).

First, some practitioners argued that with the legal power to settle investigations, the prosecutors would be able to deal effectively and efficiently with non-serious corruption crimes.[463] The DPAs for non-serious corruption crimes may be bounded with requirements regarding eligibility on a case-by-case basis. Prosecutors may determine that the defendant is not involved in serious crime. Among the factors to be taken into consideration are that the defendant should not be a recidivist and the prosecutor should believe that the circumstances indicate that the defendant would not engage in crime in the future. It may also be required that the crime committed must not have caused substantial harms[464] and can be readily addressed through a remedial plan in which the victims (mainly, state institutions) are involved. The remedial plan may include the defendant making amends to the state or/and victims and the illegal profits being disgorged. The prosecutors may depend on the disciplinary actions taken against the defendants as an additional justification for the decision to decline the prosecution.[465]

Despite the lack of a legal framework for DPAs in Kuwait, one of the interviewees argued that the Kuwaiti legislature has addressed the need to deal with some corruption crimes flexibly, though in a somewhat primitive way.[466] In crimes against the public purse, the offender will be given 'conditional discharge' (i.e. it will be decided not to hand down a criminal conviction) whenever the trial judge believes that the crime committed is trivial and that the offender will not re-engage in other criminal activities in the future.[467] Still, the case should be dealt with in court. Judge-1 argued that introducing statutory amendments to allow prosecutors to settle investigations more quickly 'will shorten the road from the beginning'. Non-trial resolutions have been advocated, especially in regard to non-serious crimes, due to their pragmatic role in simplifying criminal justice: they empower the prosecutors to effectively respond to less serious crimes that cause no substantial harms, enable the prosecutors to avoid the preparatory work

462 King and Lord (2018).

463 Judge-1; Prosecutor-1; Prosecutor-2. The participants did not designate a specific title for these settlements and talked in general sense to refer to settlements between the prosecutor and the defendant.

464 Lawyer-1; Prosecutor-2.

465 Uhlmann (2013).

466 Judge-1.

467 PPFA, s.20. See also CLA 1960, s.81.

and save time and effort for pursuing more serious offences, and reduce the case-loads of the courts through crimes being dealt with outside of them.[468]

Second, DPAs should not be confined to less serious corruption crimes. The prosecutors should have the discretion to enter into agreements when dealing with serious corruption crimes, particularly those cases with distinct features. The practice reveals that there are cases with uncertain outcomes where there is a risk that the defendants would go unpunished. Thus, advocating the DPAs as an innovative tool in the following discussion is dictated by the reality and circumstances of corruption cases as uncovered by the practitioners.[469] As Prosecutor-1 illustrated, it is not uncommon that corruption cases, especially grand ones, are investigated after a relatively long period because, for example, 'corrupt practices by a minister might not be exposed until he/she leaves the office'. Prosecutor-1 said that this situation often causes problems. The suspect's right to defence would be undermined since the suspect would argue: 'I do not have the documents proving my innocence and it is legally prohibited to keep such documents after leaving the office'. After a long period, the case would not be effectively investigated and the illicit assets associated with that crime would be difficult to trace.[470] The result would be that the evidence gathered would be inadequate to prosecute the case, or even too weak to convince the judge that the suspect was guilty. All of these deficiencies would make the case unlikely to meet the 'beyond the reasonable doubt' standard, leading to the acquittal of the defendant.[471]

One possible solution would be to give the defendants some latitude to enter into negotiations with the prosecutor. Defendants should be allowed to demonstrate cooperation with the prosecutor, and in exchange, the prosecutor could agree to defer the prosecution. Some scholars argue that the DPAs help both the prosecutors to elicit the cooperation of the defendants and the defendants to evade the costly collateral outcomes of criminal convictions.[472] The cooperation scenario should be open to the defendant at an earlier stage of the investigation. Prosecutor-1 referred to the criticality of 'the time factor'. As an investigation progresses, the terrain of the case becomes clearer. With the help of the defence lawyer, the defendant will be aware of his/her legal status.[473] This issue has been considered by the OECD, which argues that there is no incentive without deterrence. In order for non-trial resolutions to be effective, the alleged offenders should not have a reason to believe that they can escape 'any form of judicial reckoning' because of, for example, weak enforcement efforts.[474] Therefore, defendants must be incentivised to show cooperation as soon as possible for it

468 Ashworth and Redmayne (2010).
469 Alschuler (1968).
470 Prosecutor-1.
471 Ibid.
472 Alexander and Cohen (2015).
473 Prosecutor-1.
474 OECD (2019, pp. 82–83).

seems rational, from their perspective, to evade the undesirable consequences of criminal conviction.

Some would argue that serious corruption crimes should always be prosecuted so that the perpetrators are punished.[475] However, the rationale underpinning the use of DPAs in serious crimes is different from that related to their use in trivial crimes. In trivial crimes, the DPAs aim to reserve time and efforts for more serious crimes. But in serious crimes, the DPAs may prompt the defendants to cooperate with the prosecutor to resolve serious corruption cases with less cost and effort. This argument is pragmatic especially for those cases where the prosecutors are unable to build adequate evidence. The DPAs become a more practical solution in crimes that have caused monetary damage that can be compensated.[476] Among the key findings of a recent report by the OECD, non-trial resolutions were found to be 'a prominent means for resolving economic crimes': 695 of the 890 foreign bribery cases in the OECD State parties studied were resolved using non-trial resolutions.[477] Among the factors leading to an increase in the use of non-trial resolutions were evidence-based difficulties.[478] Thus, the DPAs help the prosecutors to strike a balance in the following cases: between the need to prosecute those who are seriously guilty and the risk of acquittal (in serious crimes) and the responsibility of offenders and the collateral consequences of criminal convictions (in non-serious crimes).

The introduction of DPAs in the Kuwaiti legal system could be fraught with legal challenges and concerns.[479] First, the limited role of the judiciary in the DPAs is one of the substantial criticisms directed at the deferral mechanism.[480] The role of the judge could be confined to discretion to block the DPA negotiated, based on considerations of justice or fairness.[481] Thus, in relation to the DPA proceedings, the judge does not have the power of adjudication. DPAs then may be construed as usurping upon the authority of the courts, which may conflict with the legal tradition in Kuwait, whereby judges have full dominance on the trial stage as well as control over the prosecutorial discretion. Article 34 of the Constitution establishes that a defendant has the right to a fair trial where his/her defence is safeguarded. Sections 1–2 of the CJA require that no criminal sanctions shall be imposed unless there is a criminal trial, and that it is the courts that are statutorily mandated to try the defendants. The trial judge can void a prosecutor's decision to discontinue an investigation.[482] Also, the trial judge is not restricted to the charges and facts

475 See, for example, King and Lord (2018).
476 Xiao (2013).
477 OECD (2019, pp. 11–15).
478 Ibid., p. 21.
479 See King and Lord (2018).
480 Greenblum (2005).
481 UK Ministry of Justice (2012).
482 CJA, s.104 bis.

as initiated by a prosecutor and can always introduce alterations to them.[483] Therefore, the DPAs might be inconsistent with the constitutional arrangements in Kuwait and might truly lead judges to resist any concession to their dominance over criminal proceedings.

Second, the DPAs raise some concerns regarding fairness and legitimacy.[484] Because the prosecutor has more discretion, and the agreements are made without the involvement of the judiciary, the DPAs may reduce the 'predictability and consistency' of sentences. Although the negotiated DPAs are eventually subject to judicial review, this oversight is still limited during the stage of negotiation.[485] In the absence of clear standards and guidance on the DPAs, there is a risk of uncertainty regarding the sanction that will be imposed: each potential defendant will be subject to divergent processes and conditions during the negotiation. Thus, the DPAs may compromise legal certainty.[486] Such 'uncertainty' has been recognised in the United Kingdom as a disincentivising factor for defendants to engage and cooperate with the prosecutors.[487] However, the judicial approval, at the heart of DPAs proceedings, acts as independent scrutiny that secures certainty and public confidence: it 'is not merely a review to see that the procedure has been properly followed and the guidelines applied', but also 'a separate exercise of judgement'.[488] The limited, though significant, judicial involvement offsets against any potential 'unfair' terms during the negotiations.

Third, the DPAs could be abused to serve the interests of high-ranking political actors. There is a perception that the DPAs are an instrument that helps big businesses 'get away with' things or that they can be harnessed to 'buy their way out of trouble'.[489] This perception is relevant to the case of Kuwait where grand corruption cases are often associated with politicians and senior officials. Again, the judicial approval may serve as a safeguard in such contexts to avoid any potential abuse of the prosecutorial discretion. Although it might have a limited role regarding the terms and conditions negotiated, the court surely has a decisive role in preventing abuse of the prosecutorial authorities. The judge can retain control over a DPA, oversee and scrutinise its appropriateness, and decide whether to proceed with it.[490] This judicial oversight might protect the prosecutors from political pressure in high-ranking cases by putting the approval of the DPA in the hands of the judiciary. However, this judicial oversight is insufficient. The potential enactment of DPAs should be accompanied by guidance for the prosecutors, which clearly establishes the standards to be followed, such as the Deferred

483 Ibid., ss.132–134.
484 King and Lord (2018). See also the analysis of 'legitimacy' in chapter 3.2.1.
485 Alexander and Cohen (2015, pp. 556–557).
486 See the analysis of 'legal certainty' in chapter 3.2.1.5.
487 UK Ministry of Justice (2012, p. para.37).
488 Bisgrove and Weekes (2014, pp. 428–429).
489 Ibid., p. 435.
490 *Serious Fraud Office v Rolls-Royce Plc* [2017] Lloyd's Rep FC 249 para.7. See also UK Ministry of Justice (2012).

Prosecution Agreements Code of Practice in the United Kingdom.[491] Such a code would ensure, to a large extent, the transparency and consistency of the DPAs in relation to processes and terms.[492]

As shown above, the reality of criminal investigations in Kuwait requires that the prosecutors should be provided with more discretion in dealing with corruption offences. The introduction of DPAs is suggested as an innovative prosecutorial policy that could effectively empower the prosecutor to respond, with more flexibility and certainty, to both non-serious crimes and serious crimes. The need for DPAs is justified in Kuwait. Unlike the situation in the United Kingdom, where prosecutors have alternatives and may seek a civil recovery order,[493] the Kuwaiti prosecutors have no alternatives in the light of the existing legislation: they either prosecute or discontinue the investigation. These limited options may explain the low level of counter-corruption law enforcement, as noted by the interviewees, and one possible suggestion to increase enforcement activities could be the adoption of non-trial alternatives.[494]

## 4.5 Conclusion

The investigation of the existing criminal counter-corruption measures reveals the fact that the Kuwaiti policymakers and legislature have already responded to numerous forms of corruption misconduct. These responses have varied from core corruption crimes, such as bribery, the diversion of public funds, misconduct in public office and conflicts of interest, to other interrelated offences, including the IEO and ML offences. The existing measures also deal with other essential issues, such as the illicit gains of crime (proceeds of crime) and whistleblowing. Notably, Kuwait has always depended on the criminal law and its tools as the key response to corruption. This conclusion can be inferred from the abundance of criminal measures against corruption and from the participants interviewed, who focused on the criminal law and did not refer to other non-criminal measures. A thorough look at these measures, nevertheless, leads to the verdict that although the current criminal measures are comprehensive enough (in content and scope), criminal law alone is not adequate, or perhaps ineffective, to combat corruption. This finding is made for a number of reasons.

First, some of these measures are, in themselves, unable to counter the complexity of corruption cases because of criminal law-related requirements, such as proving the *mens rea*. Their criminal nature sometimes makes them elusive to apply, especially in complicated cases. Although some measures have been improved to capture modern forms of corruption, the substance of the criticisms can, in fact, be lodged against their criminal nature; namely, the demanding

491 Available at <https://www.cps.gov.uk/sites/default/files/documents/publications/dpa_cop. pdf>.

492 UK Ministry of Justice (2012).

493 See King and Lord (2018).

494 OECD (2019).

requirements of criminal law. To consolidate the state's efforts to combat corruption, the policymakers should always take into consideration innovative approaches that rectify the technical pitfalls of using criminal law in resolving crime: incentivising others to blow the whistle and providing the prosecutors with room for manoeuvre to elicit the cooperation of the defendants have been suggested as two possible approaches.

Second, effective counter-corruption policies should consider the broader contexts in which corruption occurs. The inherent characteristics of grand corruption cases, and the parties usually involved in them, render the resort to the criminal law a daunting task. Apart from the difficulties associated with the criminal law, it could be argued that the recourse to criminal law to resolve grand corruption cases seems to be a less amenable idea, because of the sensitivity and political character of such cases. Therefore, the policymaker should seek other more realistic paths to respond to corruption cases. Despite being necessary and essential, the criminal measures should not be the only instruments used to counter corruption. Other non-criminal measures could be brought to the fore to confront corruption, alongside the criminal law instruments, as discussed in the next chapter.

## Bibliography

Al-Assar, Y. (2015). Recent Trends in Constitutional Jurisdiction on Protection of the Right to Privacy: Comparative Study between Kuwait, Egypt and France. *Journal of Kuwait International Law School.* 3(10), pp. 35–80.

Al-Eifan, M. (2016). The Right Against Self-Incrimination in Kuwaiti Law: Analytical and Comparative Study With American Law. *Kuwait University Journal of Law.* 40(1), pp. 119–171.

Al-Haidar, F. (2018). Whistleblowing in Kuwait and UK Against Corruption and Misconduct. *International Journal of Law and Management.* 60(4), pp. 1020–1033.

Al-Kandari, F., Ghannam, G. (2006). *The Exposition of the Kuwaiti Criminal Law: The Special Part.* Kuwait: Kuwait University.

Al-Melhem, A. (1995). Kuwait: Law on the Protection of Public Funds. *Journal of Financial Crime.* 3(1), pp. 113–116.

Al-Mulaifi, O. (2018). *The Role of the Public Prosecution in the Investigation and Disposition of Public Fund Crimes.* Kuwait: Kuwait International Law School.

Al-Oumi, N. (2015). Illicit Enrichment: Comparative Analytic Study of the Decree-Law No. 24 of 2012 of the Public Authority of Anti-Corruption and the Provisions for Financial Disclosure. *Kuwait University Journal of Law.* 39(4), pp. 65–112.

Al-Oumi, N. (2018). Towards the Confiscation of Proceeds of Crime Without Criminal Conviction: An Analytic, Comparative Study on the Criminal Kuwaiti Law. *Kuwait University Journal of Law.* 42(2), pp. 89–135.

Al-Qarioti, M. (2013). Bribery Problem in Kuwaiti Administration: An Exploratory Study. In: *Proceedings of the 10th Eurasia Business and Economics Society Conference, May 23–25, 2013, Istanbul, Turkey.* Istanbul: EBES Publications, pp. 52–64.

Al-Rashidi, K. S. (2020). Proceeds of Corruption Crime: The Kuwaiti Legal Response. In: Benson, K., King, C., Walker, C. (eds). *Assets, Crimes and the State: Innovation in 21st Century Legal Responses.* Abingdon: Routledge, pp. 215–228.

Al-Zafiri, F. (2006). *Criminal Protection of Public Funds in Kuwaiti Act No. 1/1993*. Kuwait: Kuwait University.

Alexander, C., Cohen, M. (2015). The Evolution of Corporate Criminal Settlements: An Empirical Perspective on Non-Prosecution, Deferred Prosecution, and Plea Agreements. *American Criminal Law Review*. 52(3), pp. 537–593.

Alldridge, P. (2002). Smuggling, Confiscation and Forfeiture. *Modern Law Review*. 65(5), pp. 781–791.

Alldridge, P. (2008). Money Laundering and Globalization. *Journal of Law and Society*. 35(4), pp. 437–463.

Alldridge, P. (2012). The UK Bribery Act: The Caffeinated Younger Sibling of the FCPA. *Ohio State Law Journal*. 73(5), pp. 1181–1216.

Alldridge, P. (2016). *What Went Wrong With Money Laundering Law?* London: Springer.

Alldridge, P. (2018). Civil Recovery in England and Wales: An Appraisal. In: King, C., Walker, C., Gurulé, J. (eds). *The Palgrave Handbook of Criminal and Terrorism Financing Law*. London: Palgrave Macmillan, pp. 515–542.

Alschuler, A. (1968). The Prosecutor's Role in Plea Bargaining. *University of Chicago Law Review*. 36(1), pp. 50–112.

Ashworth, A. (1989). The Scope of Criminal Liability for Omissions. *Law Quarterly Review*. 105, pp. 424–459.

Ashworth, A. (2006). Four Threats to the Presumption of Innocence. *International Journal of Evidence and Proof*. 10(4), pp. 241–279.

Ashworth, A., Redmayne, M. (2010). *The Criminal Process*. Oxford: Oxford University Press.

Becker, G. S., Stigler, G. J. (1974). Law Enforcement, Malfeasance, and Compensation of Enforcers. *Journal of Legal Studies*. 3(1), pp. 1–18.

Bisgrove, M., Weekes, M. (2014). Deferred Prosecution Agreements: A Practical Consideration. *Criminal Law Review*. (6), pp. 416–438.

Boles, J. (2014a). Criminalizing the Problem of Unexplained Wealth: Illicit Enrichment Offenses and Human Rights Violations. *New York University Journal of Legislation and Public Policy*. 17(4), pp. 835–880.

Boles, J. (2014b). The Two Faces of Bribery: International Corruption Pathways Meet Conflicting Legislative Regimes. *Michigan Journal of International Law*. 35(4), pp. 673–713.

Broadbridge, S. (2001). *Proceeds of Crime Bill: Bill 31 of 2001–2002* (Research Paper 01/79). London: House of Commons Library.

Brun, J.-P., Gray, L., Scott, C., Stephenson, K. (2011). *Asset Recovery Handbook: A Guide for Practitioners*. Washington, DC: World Bank.

Dennis, I. H. (2010). *The Law of Evidence*. London: Sweet & Maxwell.

Doig, G. A. (2015). The Inter-Relationship Between Theft and POCA: Is Every Thief Also Guilty of a Money-Laundering Offence?: GH v R [2015] UKSC 24. *Journal of Criminal Law*. 79(3), pp. 165–169.

Dungan, J., Waytz, A., Young, L. (2015). The Psychology of Whistleblowing. *Current Opinion in Psychology*. 6, pp. 129–133.

Dworkin, T., Near, J. (1997). A Better Statutory Approach to Whistle-Blowing. *Business Ethics Quarterly*. 7(1), pp. 1–16.

Emmerson, B., Ashworth, A. (2001). *Human Rights and Criminal Justice*. London: Sweet & Maxwell.

European Court of Human Rights. (2019). *Guide on Article 6 of the European Convention on Human Rights – Right to a Fair Trial (Criminal Limb)*. Strasbourg: Council of Europe.

Eurostat. (2017). *Crime and Criminal Justice Statistics – Methodological Guide for Users.* Luxembourg: Eurostat.

Gallant, M. M. (2004). Alberta and Ontario: Civilizing the Money-Centered Model of Crime Control. *Asper Review of International Business and Trade Law.* 4, pp. 13–33.

Gallant, M. M. (2005). *Money Laundering and the Proceeds of Crime: Economic Crime and Civil Remedies.* Cheltenham, UK; Northampton, MA: Edward Elgar.

Gardiner, J. (2007). Defining Corruption. In: Heidenheimer, A., Johnston, M. (eds). *Political Corruption: Concepts and Contexts.* 3rd ed. New Brunswick, NJ; London: Transaction Publishers, pp. 25–40.

Gray, L., Hansen, K., Recica-Kirkbride, P., Mills, L. (2014). *Few and Far: The Hard Facts on Stolen Asset Recovery.* Washington, DC: World Bank.

Green, S. (2013). Official and Commercial Bribery: Should They Be Distinguished?. In: Horder, J., Alldridge, P. (eds). *Modern Bribery Law: Comparative Perspectives.* Cambridge: Cambridge University Press, pp. 39–66.

Greenberg, T., Samuel, L., Grant, W., Gray, L. (2009). *Stolen Asset Recovery: A Good Practices Guide for Non-Conviction Based Asset Forfeiture.* Washington, DC: World Bank.

Greenblum, B. (2005). What Happens to a Prosecution Deferred? Judicial Oversight of Corporate Deferred Prosecution Agreements. *Columbia Law Review.* 105(6), pp. 1863–1904.

Hart, H. L. A. (2012). *The Concept of Law.* Oxford: Oxford University Press.

Hatchard, J. (2014). *Combating Corruption: Legal Approaches to Supporting Good Governance and Integrity in Africa.* Northampton, MA: Edward Elgar.

Hofstede, G. (2001). *Culture's Consequences: Comparing Values, Behaviors, Institutions and Organizations Across Nations.* Thousand Oaks, CA: SAGE.

Homad, A. (1977). Bribery Crime in the Kuwaiti Legislation. *Kuwait University Journal of Law and Sharia.* 1(1), pp. 1–20.

Hosni, M. N. (2005). *Property Crimes.* Beirut: AlHalabi Legal Publications.

Hosni, M. N. (2012). *Exposition of the Criminal Law: The General Part.* Dar Alnahda Alarabiya.

Jayawickrama, N., Pope, J., Stolpe, O. (2002). Legal Provisions to Facilitate the Gathering of Evidence in Corruption Cases: Easing the Burden of Proof. In: van Dijk, J., Ruggiero, V. (eds). *Forum on Crime and Society.* Vienna: UNODC, pp. 23–31.

Jusic, A. (2017). Kuwait's Administrative Risk-Based Model for the Prevention of Money Laundering: Costs and Benefits of Compliance With the Financial Action Task Force (FATF) Standards. *Arab Law Quarterly.* 31(2), pp. 101–133.

Kalintiri, A. (2015). The Allocation of the Legal Burden of Proof in Article 101 TFEU Cases: A 'Clear' Rule With Not-So-Clear Implications. *Yearbook of European Law.* 34(1), pp. 232–256.

King, C., Lord, N. (2018). *Negotiated Justice and Corporate Crime: The Legitimacy of Civil Recovery Orders and Deferred Prosecution Agreements.* London: Palgrave Macmillan.

Kofele-Kale, N. (2006). Presumed Guilty: Balancing Competing Rights and Interests in Combating Economic Crimes. *The International Lawyer.* 40(4), pp. 909–944.

Kofele-Kale, N. (2012). *Combating Economic Crimes: Balancing Competing Rights and Interests in Prosecuting the Crime of Illicit Enrichment.* Abingdon: Routledge.

Kuwait Ministry of Justice. (2015). *Guide on International Judicial Cooperation in Criminal Matters.* Kuwait: Ministry of Justice.

Lambsdorff, J. (2007). *The Institutional Economics of Corruption and Reform: Theory, Evidence and Policy.* Cambridge: Cambridge University Press.

Martin, B. (2009). Corruption, Outrage and Whistleblowing. In: Burke, R., Cooper, C. (eds). *Research Companion to Corruption in Organizations.* Northampton, MA: Edward Elgar, pp. 206–216.

Martin, B. (2013). *Whistleblowing: A Practical Guide.* Sweden: Irene Publishing.

McCluskey, D. (2009). Money Laundering: The Disappearing Predicate. *Criminal Law Review.* (10), pp. 719–722.

MENAFATF. (2015). *Mutual Evaluation Report: 3rd Follow-Up Report for State of Kuwait: Anti-Money Laundering and Combating the Financing of Terrorism.* Manama: MENAFATF.

Miceli, M., Near, J., Dworkin, T. (2008). *Whistle-Blowing in Organizations.* London: Psychology Press.

Muzila, L., Morales, M., Mathias, M., Berger, T. (2012). *On the Take: Criminalizing Illicit Enrichment to Fight Corruption.* Washington, DC: World Bank.

Myers, A. (2014). Whistleblowing: Civil Society's Challenge. [Online]. Available from: https://whistlenetwork.files.wordpress.com/2014/01/myers-article-website-version-jan14.pdf.

Nazaha. (2017a). *First Annual Report: 2016/2017.* Nazaha.

Nazaha. (2017b). *Guidance on Whistleblowing.* Nazaha.

Nazaha. (2019). *Kuwait Integrity and Anti-Corruption Strategy 2019-2024.* Nazaha.

Nicholls, C., Daniel, T., Bacarese, A., Maton, J., Hatchard, J. (2017). *Corruption and Misuse of Public Office.* Oxford: Oxford University Press.

OECD. (2003). *Managing Conflict of Interest in the Public Service: OECD Guidelines and Overview.* Paris: OECD.

OECD. (2005). *Managing Conflict of Interest in the Public Sector: A Toolkit.* Paris: OECD.

OECD. (2019). *Resolving Foreign Bribery Cases With Non-Trial Resolutions: Settlements and Non-Trial Agreements by Parties to the Anti-Bribery Convention.* Paris: OECD.

Prakken, H., Sartor, G. (2016). A Logical Analysis of Burdens of Proof. In: Kaptein, H., Prakken, H., Verheij, B. (eds). *Legal Evidence and Proof: Statistics, Stories, Logic.* Abingdon: Routledge, pp. 223–253.

Rose-Ackerman, S. (1999). *Corruption and Government: Causes, Consequences, and Reform.* Cambridge: Cambridge University Press.

Ryder, N. (2013). To Confiscate or Not to Confiscate? A Comparative Analysis of the Confiscation of the Proceeds of Crime Legislation in the United States of America and the United Kingdom. *Journal of Business Law.* 8, pp. 767–798.

Sabrie, S., Hakala, P. (2013). *Kuwait's Political Crisis Deepens.* Brussels: European Union.

Sims, R. (2009). Collective Versus Individualist National Cultures: Comparing Taiwan and US Employee Attitudes Toward Unethical Business Practices. *Business & Society.* 48(1), pp. 39–59.

Spivack, P., Raman, S. (2008). Regulating the 'New Regulators': Current Trends in Deferred Prosecution Agreements. *American Criminal Law Review.* 45(2), pp. 159–193.

Sproat, P. (2007). An Evaluation of the UK's Anti-Money Laundering and Asset Recovery Regime. *Crime, Law and Social Change.* 47(3), pp. 169–184.

Sullivan, G. R. (2011). The Bribery Act 2010: Part 1: An Overview. *Criminal Law Review.* (2), pp. 87–100.

Transparency International. (2018). *A Best Practice Guide for Whistleblowing Legislation.* Berlin: Transparency International.

Uhlmann, D. (2013). Deferred Prosecution and Non-Prosecution Agreements and the Erosion of Corporate Criminal Liability. *Maryland Law Review.* 72(4), pp. 1295–1344.

UK Ministry of Justice. (2012). *Consultation on a New Enforcement Tool to Deal With Economic Crime Committed By Commercial Organisations: Deferred Prosecution Agreements.* London: The Stationery Office.

UNODC. (2003). *United Nations Guide on Anti-Corruption Policies.* Vienna: UN.

UNODC. (2004a). *United Nations Anti-Corruption Toolkit.* Vienna: UN.

UNODC. (2004b). *United Nations Handbook on Practical Anti-Corruption Measures for Prosecutors and Investigators.* Vienna: UN.

UNODC. (2012a). *Legislative Guide for the Implementation of the United Nations Convention Against Corruption.* Vienna: UN.

UNODC. (2012b). *Manual on Mutual Legal Assistance and Extradition.* Vienna: UN.

UNODC. (2013). *Review of Implementation of the United Nations Convention Against Corruption: Kuwait Executive Summary* (Fourth Session, 27–31 May 2013). Vienna: UN.

Volpin, C. (2014). The Ball Is in Your Court: Evidential Burden of Proof and the Proof-Proximity Principle in EU Competition Law. *Common Market Law Review.* 51(4), pp. 1159–1185.

Walters, V. (2009). Prosecuting Money Launderers: Do the Prosecution Have to Prove the Predicate Offence? *Criminal Law Review.* (8), pp. 571–575.

Waytz, A., Dungan, J., Young, L. (2013). The Whistleblower's Dilemma and the Fairness–Loyalty Tradeoff. *Journal of Experimental Social Psycholology.* 49(6), pp. 1027–1033.

Williams, G. (1963). *The Proof of Guilt: A Study of the English Criminal Trial.* London U6 - ctx_ver=Z39.88-2004&ctx_enc=info%3Aofi%2Fenc%3AUTF-8&rfr_id=info%3Asid%2Fsummon.serialssolutions.com&rft_val_fmt=info%3Aofi%2Ffmt%3Akev%3Amtx%3Abook&rft.genre=book&rft.title=The+proof+of+guilt&rft.au=Williams%2C+Glanville+Llewelyn%2C+1911&rft.series=The+Hamlyn+lectures&rft.date=1963-01-01&rft.pub=Stevens&rft.volume=7th+series&rft.externalDocID=b20285280&paramdict=en-US U7 - Book: Stevens.

Wilsher, D. (2006). Inexplicable Wealth and Illicit Enrichment of Public Officials: A Model Draft That Respects Human Rights in Corruption Cases. *Crime, Law and Social Change.* 45(1), pp. 27–53.

Xiao, M. Y. (2013). Deferred/Non Prosecution Agreements: Effective Tools to Combat Corporate Crime. *Cornell Journal of Law Public Policy.* 23(1), pp. 233–253.

Yadlin, O. (2006). The Conspirator Dilemma: Introducing the *"Trojan Horse" Enforcement Strategy. Review of Law & Economics.* 2(1), pp. 25–43.

Ziouvas, D. (2018). International Asset Recovery and the United Nations Convention Against Corruption. In: King, C., Walker, C., Gurulé, J. (eds). *The Palgrave Handbook of Criminal and Terrorism Financing Law.* London: Palgrave Macmillan, pp. 591–620.

# 5 Kuwaiti non-criminal counter-corruption measures

## 5.1 Introduction

In chapter 4, the criminal counter-corruption measures in Kuwaiti law were identified and analysed, and potential reforms were suggested. It was shown that criminal responses to corruption are necessary, but currently these are insufficient. Given those findings, Kuwaiti policymakers have also put in place non-criminal measures to counter corruption. In this regard, the legal tools provided by the civil and administrative laws have been employed. Other non-legal measures, such as regulatory responses and situational crime prevention (SCP),[1] are also considered as counter-corruption measures.

This chapter is smaller in size compared to chapter 4 given the primacy of the criminal responses to corruption in Kuwait. The significance of this chapter stems from the nature of the regulatory measures and the civil and administrative laws. These instruments have several advantages that justify their studying alongside the criminal laws. First, they may be more helpful than the criminal laws in combating corruption as they are less demanding due to the lower standard of proof. Second, these tools can properly operate under the idea of a comprehensive enforcement pyramid (section 5.3.1). With the help of the pyramid's features, the availability of alternatives to the criminal law enables the state to apply the available measures in a gradual fashion. In that sense, they are flexible in responding to the various degrees of culpability, including insignificant violations of formal duties. Third, apart from the deterrent aspect of the criminal sanctions, regulatory responses and administrative laws improve the cooperation of individuals, especially when their engagement in corruption is due to a lack of awareness. Fourth, the self-regulatory approach engages stakeholders from the private sector and secures their support and endorsement, which boosts the effectiveness of counter-corruption measures.

This chapter proceeds as follows. Section 5.2 adopts the working definition previously constructed. This working definition delineates the scope of the chapter and identifies the non-criminal counter-corruption laws and regulations. Section 5.3 explores the present framework of non-criminal counter-corruption

1 As discussed in chapter 3.3.3.

measures (regulatory, civil and administrative) and analyses their effectiveness. Section 5.4 builds on the analysis undertaken in section 5.3 to assess the adequacy of the current non-criminal counter-corruption responses and the need for innovative counter-corruption techniques to confront the problem of grand corruption. Therefore, this chapter aims to achieve two of the research objectives (the fourth and fifth objectives). In regard to the fourth objective, this chapter examines the current Kuwait non-criminal legal and regulatory measures to combat corruption. Three sub-research questions are addressed: what are the persuasive measures against corruption? what is the role of the civil and administrative laws in the counter-corruption process? and how can these two measures be assessed? In regard to the fifth methodological objective, socio-legal methodology is employed to draw upon insights from practitioners to answer part of the fourth objective.

## 5.2 Working definition for corruption in non-criminal contexts

In defining the non-criminalised forms of corruption, this chapter relies on the nature of the act: it conceives of corruption in relation to the public roles of officials.[2] The World Bank's definition – 'the abuse of public office for private gain' – is helpful here. According to Kuwaiti law, it is possible to conceptualise a broader conception of corruption that covers the non-criminal forms of corruption.[3] Corruption therefore involves violations committed by officials against the public office and their public roles. This type of corruption may be addressed by regulations and laws that set out integrity values, prohibit various acts, and specify measures that can be taken by the state. These measures include codes of conduct; civil actions, such as civil lawsuits; and disciplinary offences in the context of the civil service (see Table 5.1). This approach responds to the concerns of NGO-3, who stated that the definition of corruption should focus not only on the financial aspects of corruption, but also on the administrative forms of corruption.

## 5.3 Current non-criminal counter-corruption measures

This section explores the existing non-criminal counter-corruption measures in Kuwait. In this chapter, the measures are classified in a hierarchical way based on Ayres and Braithwaite's model of 'the enforcement pyramid'. The first section then identifies the idea of the enforcement pyramid as an innovative approach. The main thrust of the approach is to respond to corruption in a gradual fashion. The second section addresses the persuasive counter-corruption measures (codes of conduct in the civil service and self-regulation of the private sector). The third

2 Gardiner (2007).
3 See chapters 2.3.1 and 4.2.

*Table 5.1* Non-criminal counter-corruption responses

| *Act* | *Function* |
|---|---|
| Civil Law Act (Civil Act) 67/1980 | It sets out the provisions of civil responsibility |
| Administrative Disputes Act (ADA) 20/1981 | It establishes the judicial review over administrative decisions |
| Civil Service Act (CSA) 15/1979 and its Statutory Instrument (CSA-SI) | It sets out, inter alia, the disciplinary system for public officials |
| Code of Conduct of Public Officials Circular No. 11/2012 (Code 2012) | It set outs the standards of integrity and behaviours that should be followed |
| Legal Advice and Legislation Department Act (LALD Act) 12/1960 | It establishes the body that defends the interests of the public treasury in the courts |
| State Audit Bureau Act (SAB Act) 30/1964 | It sets out the financial irregularities and the Disciplinary Tribunal |

section identifies civil law measures that can potentially be used against corruption. Finally, the fourth section identifies the administrative measures.

### 5.3.1 Enforcement pyramid

The enforcement pyramid (or regulatory pyramid) is one of the most important ideas associated with the idea of 'Responsive Regulation' and is very helpful to the analysis in this chapter.[4] As can be seen in Figure 5.1, the response starts at the base of the pyramid where actions are taken to secure compliance through persuasion. After that, the enforcement is escalated to more stringent responses. If this fails to secure compliance, the enforcement will gradually be escalated upwards through civil and criminal sanctions and finally to the top of the pyramid, when the behaviour of a regulatee is not amenable. This approach deters unwanted behaviours, incentivises desired conduct, and secures compliance by educating regulatees to exhibit the behaviours expected from them. As a result, it becomes rational for regulatees to comply and cooperate in order to avoid the costs of non-compliance.[5] The relevance of the dynamism of the enforcement pyramid is that many problems can be solved through expanding the responsibilities of the regulated actors.[6,7]

Although the approach speaks to regulators of business-related activities, 'regulatory theory' in general has been applied to corruption prevention.[8] First, the enforcement pyramid has been applied to crime and other public governance activities.[9] Second, regulators and counter-corruption agencies have many commonalities. They may both use similar instruments and tools, both of them aim

4 Ayres and Braithwaite (1995, p. 35).
5 See Ivec and Braithwaite (2015).
6 Braithwaite (2011).
7 Ayres and Braithwaite (1995, p. 35).
8 Graycar and Prenzler (2013, p. 73).
9 Braithwaite (2011).

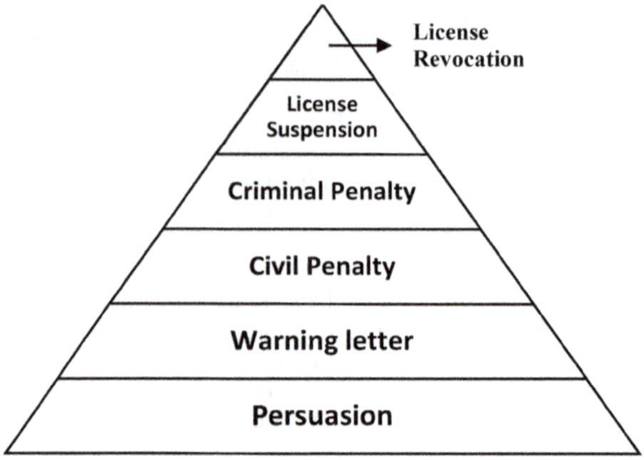


*Figure 5.1* Enforcement pyramid as suggested by Ayres and Braithwaite.

to promote behaviours that comply with specific standards, and both of them have public interest-oriented objectives 'whether that is public health and safety or public integrity'.[10] Third, while the prospective responses to corruption differ from those proposed in Figure 5.1, the idea behind the pyramid in itself is useful. Ayres and Braithwaite suggest that 'it is not the content of the enforcement pyramid on which we wish to focus during this discussion, but its form'.[11] Therefore, the logic of the enforcement pyramid can be extended beyond its context. In summary, the application of the enforcement pyramid to corruption implies that before resorting to punishing the regulated actors (here, these are public officials), their engagement in corrupt acts can be prevented by educating them.

Although Kuwait lacks a consistent strategy regarding how and when counter-corruption responses should be applied in a given context, the idea of the enforcement pyramid is helpful in understanding and assessing the various counter-corruption measures available in Kuwaiti law. It is argued here that the enforcement authorities in Kuwait, when responding to corruption, must consider different approaches before resorting to criminal law. They should use an effective mix of strategies to reduce corruption (see Figure 5.2). Minor violations should be dealt with at the bottom of pyramid, serious violations should be dealt with in the middle, and more serious violations should be dealt with at the top.

Despite its applicability in principle, the pyramid approach faces theoretical challenges in Kuwait. These challenges are predictable since Braithwaite accepts that there are some limitations of the enforcement pyramid approach (or the idea of responsive regulation) in developing countries, as it has been designed

10 Mills (2008, p. 10).
11 Ayres and Braithwaite (1995, p. 35).

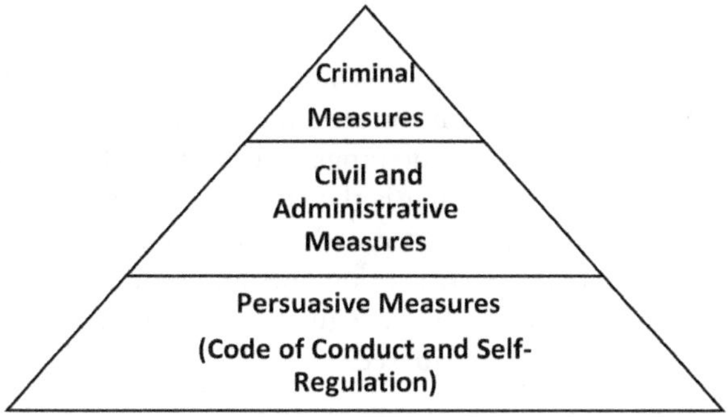


*Figure 5.2* Proposed enforcement pyramid in Kuwait.

for countries with developed economies.[12] In Kuwait, the major challenge lies at the base of the pyramid (particularly self-regulation). The dominance of the state regulator and the limited role of the regulators from the private sector have blurred the significance of self-regulation. The involvement of the private sector in corruption related regulations has been limited, and their current contributions are no more than voluntary initiatives.[13] The absence of the systematic engagement of the private sector to steer itself has some implications for the optimal utilisation of the enforcement pyramid. Thus, one of this chapter's aims is to argue for more focus on self-regulation in Kuwait.

Taken as a whole, the enforcement pyramid has many merits.[14] First, it provides an opportunity for the respectful option of persuasion and reserves the costly intervention of criminal prosecution for cases where persuasion fails.[15] Second, the enforcement pyramid is not just about the costs of enforcement; it is a 'democratic ideal' that is concerned with the legitimacy of laws and increasing the likelihood of compliance with the law.[16] This 'democratic ideal' is important for Kuwait where democracy has been adopted as a system of government.[17] Third, the enforcement pyramid approach directs the attention of Kuwaiti policymakers to the importance of non-criminal measures against corruption. In a jurisdiction like Kuwait, the dominance of criminal law in combating corruption may inadvertently overlook, or even downplay, the other means. It is based on this pyramid idea that counter-corruption responses are categorised in the following sections.

12 See Braithwaite (2006).
13 See below sections 5.3.2.2 and 5.4.
14 See Parker (2013) and the book review of Responsive Regulation by Ian Ayres and John Braithwaite at Harvard Law Review (1993).
15 Braithwaite (2011).
16 Braithwaite (2006, pp. 884–885).
17 Kuwaiti Constitution, art.6. See also chapter 3.2.1.

### 5.3.2 *Persuasive measures*

This section highlights the persuasive counter-corruption measures that are used to encourage compliance with the relevant laws and regulations. The persuasive measures could involve a wide range of responses, but the focus here is on two types of regulations. The first is the code of conduct in the civil service in Kuwait (hereinafter the civil service code), which educates and encourages officials to comply with counter-corruption laws and regulations. The second is concerned with persuasion through self-regulation and other regulations related to the codes of conduct in the private sector.

#### 5.3.2.1 *Code of conduct in the civil service*

In the civil service, ethics are a central issue when addressing the corruption problem.[18] To inculcate bureaucratic values that reduce corruption, the civil service codes can set out concrete standards defining the behaviour expected from officials and the behaviour that is forbidden, and institutionalise basic standards of performance related to, for example, fairness, integrity, and diligence.[19] The civil service codes can also contain legal obligations and values, and more critically, principles derived from those values.[20] The civil service codes are perceived to guide public life, to curb corruption, and to define how public servants should act to achieve the public interest.[21] Although there is a difference between codes of ethics (directed towards relatively constant values and principles) and codes of conduct (directed towards defining standard behaviours that are rapidly developing),[22] they are used interchangeably here due to the irrelevance of the distinction for the purposes of this section.

The role of the civil service codes has been recognised in the International Code of Conduct for Public Officials, adopted in General Assembly resolution 51/59 of 12 December 1996.[23] With the advent of the UN Convention against Corruption (UNCAC) in 2003, the civil service codes have been an essential measure of corruption prevention: state parties shall 'endeavour to apply, within their own institutional and legal systems, codes or standards of conduct for the correct, honourable and proper performance of public functions'.[24] Rothstein and Sorak argue that the civil service codes play an important role in terms of the limitation of the laws. It is impossible for the law to be formulated to take into consideration all of the circumstances that could take place in the future

18 Rothstein and Sorak (2017).
19 UNODC (2003).
20 For the differences between values and principles, see Gilman (2005).
21 Rothstein and Sorak (2017).
22 See Gilman (2005).
23 See <http://unpan1.un.org/intradoc/groups/public/documents/un/unpan010930.pdf>.
24 Article 8(2).

and what decisions should be taken in each case.[25] The civil service codes, then, act as a guidance for officeholders by establishing a set of ethics that can be relied on in unanticipated events. As the 'codes are not designed for "bad" people, but for people who want to act ethically',[26] they are consistent with the enforcement pyramid idea, regarding the ability to deal with the diverse motivations of regulatees.[27]

In Kuwait, according to the CSA 15/1979, the Civil Service Commission is the body responsible for the civil service in the public sector.[28] In 2012, the Civil Service Commission issued the Code of Conduct of Public Officials Circular No. 11/2012 (Code 2012). Yet the generality of the civil service codes may not correspond to the specificities of some jobs. In this sense, each public body may be delegated the power to issue its own code to match its roles. For example, the Kuwaiti Capital Market Authority[29] and the Kuwait Petroleum Corporation (KPC)[30] have their own codes that deal with relevant counter-corruption issues. Based on its role and mandate in setting the Kuwait Counter-Corruption Strategy 2019–2024 (Strategy 2019–2024),[31] Nazaha has collaborated with the Kuwaiti National Assembly to design a code of conduct for Members of Parliament, taking into account the constitutional concerns regarding the separation of powers.[32] Nazaha also has liaised with the judiciary to establish a code of conduct for judges, prosecutors, and court clerks.[33] However, the discussion here is limited to the Code 2012 given its applicability to all officeholders.

The Code 2012 contains numerous counter-corruption values, principle-based statements, and proscribed acts that officials should refrain from. It aims to set out the integrity standards and behaviours that should be followed, publicise the behaviours that the public should expect from officials, encourage officials to commit themselves to the ethical values of public service, and promote the professionalism of the public service and public trust in officials.[34] The Code 2012 identifies seven values: professionalism, loyalty towards the organisation, respectfulness and wisdom, equality and impartiality, confidentiality, maintenance of public property, and the rejection of gifts. Under each value, there are principle-based statements that operationalise the values in reality. For example, officials must act impartially irrespective of their political affiliation (equality and impartiality); when it is impossible to reject a gift, the official must deliver

25 Rothstein and Sorak (2017).
26 Gilman (2005, p. 7).
27 Ayres and Braithwaite (1995).
28 CSA, ss.4–5.
29 See <https://www.cma.gov.kw/documents/20622/385481/ميثاق+الشرف+لموظفي+هيئة+أسواق+المال/18cdff08-0e7f-4fc8-bb32-e95bd28090f1>.
30 See <https://www.kpc.com.kw/press/KPCPublications/CodeOfConduct/KNPC-code-of-conduct.pdf>
31 ACAA-SI, s.10(5)
32 Nazaha (2019, p. 63).
33 Ibid., p. 64.
34 See Code 2012.

the gift to his or her employer (rejection of gifts); and officials should be honest when dealing on behalf of the state (maintenance of public property). As well as the values, the Code 2012 imposes rule-based statements imposing duties on officials in terms of reporting any misconduct and the avoidance of conflicts of interest.

However, as analysed in chapter 3, combating corruption requires addressing more governance-related issues than those mentioned in the Code 2012. Therefore, in the Anti-Corruption Authority and Financial Disclosure Act (ACAA) 2/2016 and its Statutory Instrument No. 300/2016 (ACAA-SI), transparency is considered a value that Nazaha aims to promote in the economy and public administration.[35] A thorough examination of the Code 2012 reveals that no transparency-oriented standards have been mentioned. Transparency, however, has assumed a central importance with the issuance of the Strategy 2019–2024. Major reforms have been adopted in the Strategy to arguably make a shift in the way in which state institutions and resources are administered. The freedom of information (FOI) legislation and the promotion of a more transparent government have been two targets of Kuwaiti policymakers.[36] Strategy 2019–2014 therefore incorporates 'transparency' as a new value, which has been added to the existing system of values governing public office.

The Code 2012 in Kuwait can be said to be effective, at least in terms of its drafting. The inclusion of 'aspirational' values, followed by a description of desired/prohibited conduct, avoids the problem of vagueness that tends to result from general values.[37] However, the mere existence of civil service codes is insufficient. There should be an effective strategy of implementation, including 'soft' measures to make sure that officials are aware of, and encouraged to comply with, the civil service codes.[38] The problem raised here is that, after all, no code will be of value in reality if officials 'lack the technical competence to recognise an ethics problem for what it is, or if they do not know what standards their organisation expects of them'.[39] Therefore, the civil service codes arguably face two challenges in Kuwait.

The first challenge is their institutionalisation. Effective institutionalisation requires ongoing professional training and other intensive efforts. The ACAA-SI entrusts Nazaha with the responsibility to publicise the civil service codes, educate officials, and instil a culture of counter-corruption in the light of the existing codes.[40] The Strategy 2019–2024 has already taken initiatives in this regard. Nazaha and the Civil Service Commission are now setting up a specialised training institute to train junior and senior officeholders

35 ACAA-SI, s.10.
36 Nazaha (2019, p. 21).
37 See Whitton (2001, p. 4).
38 UNODC (2004, p. 146).
39 Whitton (2001, p. 3).
40 ACAA-SI, s.7.

in civil service-related matters.[41] The second is what Al-Kazemi and Zajac have described as a contradiction between the ethics that public organisations adopt in theory and what happens in reality.[42] They studied the behaviours of employees in six public organisations in Kuwait providing vital services. They found that the employees showed a high level of 'ethics sensitivity' towards unethical behaviours. Notwithstanding this conclusion, this sensitivity was not translated into ethical behaviours in reality, as a high rate of misconduct was reported within the organisations studied.[43] Although undertaken in 1999, this study brings to light an additional challenge. There is a cultural resistance to Western-based values due to the very nature of the traditional values embedded in the Kuwaiti society.[44] As a result, officials may develop indifferent attitudes towards job performance, as their personal relationships and the interests of their family and clan have superiority over the public interest.[45]

Because these challenges threaten officeholders' compliance with the laws, the Kuwaiti policymakers have realised the importance of raising awareness among officials regarding what they are required to do. One of the agenda items of the Strategy 2019–2024 is to have in place intensive training courses for officials to make them familiar with the civil service code. Having taken this seriously, the Civil Service Commission has incorporated 'the compliance with the code' as an element in the annual evaluation of officeholders. The Commission will also review the number of officials who were subject to disciplinary actions because of their non-compliance with the civil service codes (including the Code 2012) and will assess the effectiveness of the code's effects on the officials.[46]

The focus on compliance, in the first place, is linked to the problem of systemic corruption. As systems in the public institutions reinforce corruption, by engendering a criminogenic environment, officials may find themselves unable to comply. Officials therefore should be educated and empowered to make themselves familiar with the values linked to the integrity of public office. Consistent with the idea of the enforcement pyramid, before any disciplinary or criminal procedure is undertaken, the administrative capacity of officials should be enhanced so that they are given an opportunity to comply. Thus, good officials are encouraged to avoid engaging in corruption. When the state speaks 'softly' as such, this is an effective approach to securing the compliance of officials, especially when the state is empowered with 'big sticks' – legal powers to impose severe sanctions.[47] If an officeholder fails to comply, the state may escalate its response and use more legalistic measures.

41 Nazaha (2019, p. 60).
42 See Al-Kazemi and Zajac (1999).
43 Ibid., p. 360.
44 See chapter 2.3.4.
45 Al-Kazemi and Zajac (1999).
46 Nazaha (2019, p. 62).
47 Ayres and Braithwaite (1995, p. 19).

### 5.3.2.2 *Self-regulatory measures in the private sector*

Various professions from the private sector can assist in committing corruption crimes. As Jordanoska suggests, the problem here can be described as 'corruption *through* financial institutions'.[48] A lawyer could knowingly be a device for the corrupt to launder dirty money; a company may bribe public officials to abuse their position so that it wins a public tender; or a bank may turn a blind eye to dirty money. Globally, the role of businesses in this regard has been recognised by the 10th principle of the United Nations Global Compact, which states that 'Businesses should work against corruption in all its forms, including extortion and bribery'.[49] Therefore, in Kuwait, actors from the private sector can be persuaded, encouraged, and harnessed to be involved in the counter-corruption efforts alongside the state institutions. Unsurprisingly, the private sector forms the 'Second Pillar' of the Strategy 2019–2024.[50] Although the private sector can be regulated via various regulatory approaches, such as direct regulation, the focus here is on a different understanding of regulations: self-regulation.

Self-regulation decentres the task of regulating. It involves a shift in the process of regulation from the state to other actors,[51] involving, most commonly, industry-wide organisations and professions.[52] Rather than having a steering government, firms and professions from the private sector steer themselves 'in the direction that governments want them to go'.[53] Here, regulation should be seen as a continuum where pure self-regulation and government regulation are at opposite ends.[54] To avoid confusion, self-regulation in the following discussion must be understood as involving other forms of self-regulation (such as co-regulation and mandated self-regulation), 'which point toward the government regulation end involving greater and greater degrees of government oversight and ultimately, direct intervention'.[55] Self-regulation is an 'attractive alternative to direct governmental regulation', not least because businesses are more capable than the state of regulating their own activities.[56]

There are few applications of self-regulation in Kuwait whereby regulations are partially devolved to private sector professions. Some provisions of the Anti-Money Laundering and Countering Financing of Terrorism Act (AML/CFT Act) 106/2013 and its Statutory Instrument No. 37/2013 (AML/CFT-SI) are characterised as co-regulatory. Businesses are permitted to issue AML regulations that have prior legislative underpinnings.[57] Two types of businesses are

48 Jordanoska (2018, p. 165).
49 See <https://www.unglobalcompact.org/what-is-gc/mission/principles>.
50 Nazaha (2019, pp. 75–81).
51 Black (2001).
52 Gunningham and Sinclair (2017).
53 Black (2001, p. 113).
54 Gunningham and Rees (1997).
55 Ibid., p. 366.
56 Braithwaite (1982, pp. 1467–1469).
57 Black (2001).

identified: financial institutions (such as banks) and designated non-financial businesses and professions (such as estate agents and lawyers).[58] These sectors are required to set up the policies necessary for the implementation of the AML/CFT Act.[59] They are also allowed to establish due diligence measures and appropriate systems of risk evaluation to identify clients and manage the risks posed by high-risk transactions.[60] Thus, to some extent, the regulatees are able to contribute to the AML regulation.

These sectors are mainly monitored by governmental supervisory bodies, but for the legal profession (lawyers), the Kuwait Lawyers Association (KLA) is the supervisory self-regulatory body in AML matters.[61] There is one point that should be raised regarding the current regulatory approach in the AML regime. The current form of self-regulation adopted in the AML/CFT Act promotes 'intra-firm' regulation, involving the enactment of regulations inside a single company, organisation, etc.[62] Rather than 'self-regulation by a group', usually a collective professional community,[63] the current regulatees in Kuwait range from individual companies and estate agents to lawyers, who are individually required to regulate themselves.

In other areas of corruption, the current policy on self-regulation is less clear. The governmental regulators of professions have not articulated a self-regulatory policy to encourage professions to issue corruption-related regulations. In general, the Kuwaiti laws neither hinder the state from engaging professions in the counter-corruption efforts nor prevent professions from designing their respective integrity systems. The ACAA entrusted Nazaha with engaging NGOs and activating their role in combating corruption 'to widen the scope of knowledge on how corruption is fought and prevented'.[64] Therefore, the Strategy 2019–2024, in essence, is based on a 'participatory approach', whereby the private sector is brought from the periphery to the centre to play an effective role in combating corruption.[65] The Kuwaiti policymakers have realised that combating corruption effectively necessitates the involvement of all stakeholders, especially the private sector. Through self-regulation, various professions in Kuwait can have some effective input into the counter-corruption efforts, in tandem with the state. Furthermore, this regulatory approach secures a wider reach of the regulators to prevent *potential* corruption crimes, whereas other legal tools, such as prosecution, do not enable the state to take action until a crime has taken place.[66]

58 AML/CFT Act, s.1.
59 AML/CFT-SI, s.2.
60 Ibid., s.5.
61 Ibid., s.1.
62 Black (2001, p. 120).
63 Gunningham and Rees (1997, p. 364).
64 ACAA, ss.4(7) and 5(11); ACAA-SI, s.5.
65 Nazaha (2019, pp. 12–16).
66 Jordanoska (2018).

In the following part, three professional sectors are selected as examples because of their potential role in combating corruption (as facilitators or instigators of corruption): the legal profession, the commercial and industrial sector, and the banking business.

The Legal Profession Act (LPA) 42/1964 governs the legal profession. Under the LPA, the regulation of the legal profession has been partially delegated to the KLA as a self-regulatory body – a private body that finds endorsement in the law.[67] In 2018, the KLA voluntarily issued a code of professional ethics for the legal profession, expressing the common conscience of the members of the profession.[68] That code, however, is more concentrated on the intra-relations among lawyers, their role with their clients, and ethical issues related to marketing. Not a single article in the KLA code refers to any integrity or counter-corruption values or the role of lawyers in combating corruption. Furthermore, sections 35–45 of the LPA set out the disciplinary procedures that should be taken against a lawyer who violates the provisions of the LPA or his/her professional duties. Yet the LPA, and the duties of lawyers mentioned within it, do not explicitly refer to any form of corruption-related duties.

Regarding the commercial and industrial sectors, section 1 of the AML/CFT-SI states that the Ministry of Commerce is the supervisory authority for commercial entities (such as real estate agents and insurance companies) that are not supervised by the Central Bank of Kuwait (CBK). The Chamber of Commerce Act 1959 also established the Kuwait Chamber of Commerce and Industry (KCCI) as a self-financed, self-regulatory body to represent the economic and industrial interests of all businesses, as well as to be a consultant in the economic affairs in Kuwait.[69] According to its Act, all businesses can gather under the umbrella of the KCCI and contribute to issuing corruption-related regulations, such as codes of conduct in the field of pursuing business. The KCCI has taken no initiative for such regulations yet.

Regarding the banking sector, the Currency, CBK and Banking Business Act 32/1968 establishes the CBK as the statutory regulator of the financial and banking sector.[70] The statutory relationship between the CBK and the local banks (as regulatees) permits the CBK to adopt a self-regulatory approach to persuade the banks to design their own integrity policies.[71] Also, the Kuwait Banking Association (KBA) was established in 2001. The KBA is not a self-regulatory body, but a representative NGO that promotes the interests of its member banks. Representing 23 banks, the stated aim of the KBA is to strengthen the cooperation and coordination among the member banks, enable them to keep up with the development of banking systems, and improve the performance of employees. The charter of the KBA enables it to

67 Promulgated in 1963. See <http://kuwaitlawyers.com/page/1/النظام-الأساسي>.

68 See <http://kuwaitlawyers.com/page/2/ميثاق-الشرف>.

69 Sections 1 and 4.

70 Sections 13 and 15(4).

71 Currency, CBK and Banking Business Act 32/1968, ss.61, 68, and 71.

address a range of banking policies and issues, one of which is issuing codes of conduct.[72] Again, the KBA has not enacted any ethical codes or other integrity regulations yet.

In 2013, however, the Kuwait Transparency Society (KTS), in coordination with TI, studied the four biggest companies in Kuwait with regard to their counter-corruption policies. Acknowledging some limitations, such as the limited sample, the report found that those companies had achieved high scores in applying counter-corruption measures when compared with other transnational companies. Two of the biggest banks in Kuwait (NBK and KFH) have voluntarily incorporated a number of counter-corruption bylaws, including codes of conduct for their employees. Also, two of the biggest Kuwaiti companies in the commercial sector (Zain and Wataniya (Ooredoo now)) were found to have gone further and voluntarily established their own counter-corruption policies.[73]

With the potential involvement of the private sector in fighting corruption, the counter-corruption arrangements might take on complex structures that are neither public nor private. As shown above, AML regulations issued by individual firms can find endorsement in the law, and self-regulatory private bodies have been, or might potentially be, mandated to take AML measures in their field (such as in the legal profession). The blurred borders between the public and private arrangements for countering corruption may allow us to argue that corruption can be fought through an innovative approach called an 'assemblage'.[74] In the field of counter-terrorism, for example, some commentators argue that terrorist monies can be pursued through an assemblage, which 'exercises power at multiple sites and through diverse elements, that work in conjunction but may also encounter friction'.[75] Thus, the concept of an assemblage 'offers the possibility of grasping how something as heterogeneous as nation states, for instance, or regional political formations, hold together without actually ceasing to be heterogeneous'.[76] For this section, the heterogenous elements include a number of arrangements, such as laws and regulations and other non-legal measures, or even public-private interactions, which help to ensure the functionality of a strategy.[77] In the counter-corruption landscape, different actors, from international organisations, domestic political authorities and the law enforcement authorities to the professional associations and individual firms, may work in conjunction to render counter-corruption one of their objectives, although they are heterogenous in terms of their nature and formation. Thus, combating corruption is becoming neither a central nor a fully deregulated task. The state institutions should realise that, through the various mechanisms in practice, the private sector has a linkage to a broad range of corruption practices.

72 See <http://www.kba.com.kw/ar/site/page/kba-profile>.

73 See Kuwait Transparency Society (2013).

74 For further analysis of 'assemblages', see Allen (2011).

75 de Goede (2018, p. 761).

76 Allen (2011, p. 154).

77 de Goede (2018).

One strategy suggested here is self-regulation, through the delegation to the private sector of the task of establishing integrity policies. Interestingly, with the help of the advantages of the self-regulatory approach, no resistance is expected to be exerted by the private sector. The private sector is expected to effectively and positively react and cooperate to develop integrity regulations. Economically speaking, the economic losses incurred by businesses due to corrupt practices by others are persuasive enough to encourage the private sector to engage.[78] The voluntary adoption of counter-corruption regulations by some big Kuwaiti companies is an evidence of that. Thus, the more the strategy is based on persuasion, the more the private sector will feel engaged, which may justify the importance of self-regulation over the interventionist approach in some contexts.

The challenge of the fragmentation of the counter-corruption policies has just been recognised with clear responses in the Strategy 2019–2024, which has concentrated on the integrity of the private sector. The current agendas impose unprecedented requirements on actors from the private sector. Nazaha, with the cooperation of other governmental regulatory bodies, has taken three short- and long-term initiatives to develop integrity programmes in the private sector. First, private sector entities are encouraged to develop effective auditing systems with specific criteria set by the governmental regulators.[79] Second, those entities are encouraged to develop codes of conduct that are suitable in terms of the nature of the area being regulated and to have training programmes for those codes.[80] Third, companies and other entities are invited to establish appropriate governance systems where the independence of the auditors of companies is ensured.[81] Under the Strategy, it can be said that there is a governmental policy that potentially allows for the existence of what might be called true self-regulation (with its various forms). The state supervisory institutions, including the ministries and the statutory regulators, are expected to invite the private sector professions to participate in those counter-corruption activities. The role of the private sector in countering corruption in Kuwait is supposed to extend beyond the AML regime to include other areas of corruption. With the presence of government involvement in requiring self-regulation within a broad statutory framework, the involvement of the private sector is no longer 'voluntary'.[82]

### 5.3.3 *Civil law measures*

The state can resort to the Civil Law Act (Civil Act) 67/1980 to initiate civil lawsuits against individuals (who might be officials) and legal persons, whose actions cause damage to the state.[83] As private plaintiffs, public authorities can initiate

78 Hatchard (2014).
79 Nazaha (2019, p. 75).
80 Ibid., p. 76.
81 Ibid., p. 77.
82 Black (2001).
83 See Appendix 2 for extracts of the full text of the Civil Act.

civil proceedings against defendants, in the national or the foreign courts, to claim incurred damages and losses based on torts or contractual liability, or to seek the recovery of stolen assets. The civil law provides additional actions that complement the criminal and administrative measures. The civil law emphasises the interest of victims and aims at compensation and restitution.[84] Therefore, in relation to corruption, the focus of the civil law is the financial consequence of corrupt conduct. This section focuses on two issues. The first is civil lawsuits as a potential civil law measure. This remedy has been considered in the UNCAC, which aims to 'ensure that entities or persons who have suffered damage as a result of an act of corruption have the right to initiate legal proceedings against those responsible for that damage in order to obtain compensation'.[85] The second is international cooperation in these civil proceedings.

#### 5.3.3.1 *Domestic civil lawsuits*

For the purpose of this section, civil lawsuits may be triggered based on different legal grounds: tortious liability and contractual liability. In the Civil Act, torts involve any wrongful act by an individual that causes harm to others.[86] Although the Civil Act does not refer to 'corruption', it may be grounded on two types of civil liability. In terms of contractual breaches, the contractor may engage in a corrupt practice that inflicts harms and losses on the state or other entities and persons. In terms of tortious acts, officials and their accomplices may also be involved in a corrupt activity without contractual relationship. Nevertheless, to be consistent with the working definition of corruption chosen, which excludes private actors from its scope, individuals and corporations will be included based on their authorisation of, or complicity and participation in, a corrupt act.

A number of the arrangements that underpin the state's right of action are found in the Civil Act. Civil lawsuits can be based on two types of claims: proprietary and personal claims.[87] Since corrupt actors frequently engage in activities that involve stolen assets, civil lawsuits can be employed to recover the proceeds of corruption. If there are stolen assets, the legitimate owner of the assets (the plaintiff state) can initiate civil proceedings to exercise their full rights over the assets. That is the proprietary claim; it is 'a claim that one owns something and asks the court to return that item or its equivalent value'.[88] This claim is based on section 23 of the Civil Act, which establishes that public property cannot be sold or transferred, such as creating *in rem* rights in favour of a third party.[89] Without prejudice to the rights of bona fide, section 28 of the Protection of Public Funds Act (PPFA) 1/1993 renders void all acts undertaken by the

84 See Brun et al. (2014).
85 Article 35.
86 Civil Act, s.227.
87 See Brun et al. (2014).
88 Ibid., p. 49.
89 However, this rule has some exceptions. See Al-Sabah (2011, pp. 83–91).

convicted to dissipate or prevent the authorities from returning the assets. In this regard, in offences where public property is embezzled or misappropriated, the public property is subject to a proprietary claim where the defrauded public authorities can take action to claim back their property and compensation even if the criminal proceedings abate for any reason: orders to return the stolen money and/or compensate for the damages are effective against the inheritors and any third party that benefited from the offence.[90]

However, proprietary claims are not always available. A corruption act may not involve proceeds, or the proceeds of corruption may be unrecoverable or untraceable because they have been dissipated and laundered, or even transferred to a third party who does not know about their illicit origin, such as a bona fide purchaser for value. Furthermore, the state is not always entitled to the property derived from criminal activities. In those cases, personal claims are helpful in that 'the state can claim, for example, that it has suffered economic damages and demand to be paid or compensated by the person who caused the damage'.[91] The Civil Act is replete with relevant provisions providing for personal claims based on different legal bases. In terms of infringements of contractual duties, the party harmed is entitled to avoid the contract, assert a restitution claim, and claim compensation.[92] Regarding tortious liability, every natural and legal person who commits a wrongful act, resulting in damages and losses, is liable to compensate the others who incurred the damages caused.[93] In regard to unjust enrichment, each natural or legal person who was enriched without legal cause at the expense of others is liable, within the limit of the unjust enrichment, to compensate others who incurred damages.[94]

The facts of a criminal case may give rise to a civil claim.[95] Sections 111–112 of the Criminal Justice Act (CJA) 17/1960 have established a legal mechanism for victims who have suffered damages and losses from crime to initiate (as civil parties) civil proceedings as part of the criminal proceedings, either during the pre-trial stage or in the trial court, against any person or entity responsible for the harms caused by the crime. Civil claims may be adjudicated within a criminal trial; otherwise, the criminal court can defer the judgment or refer the case to the civil court if the decision on civil matters may cause a delay to the original criminal case.[96] For example, a victim can take a civil claim against an official who is being prosecuted for embezzling property belonging to that victim.[97] In analysing the interplay between criminal and civil actions, the Kuwaiti Supreme Court has decided that in criminal cases, compensation is not inevitably linked

90 PPFA, s.22.
91 Brun et al. (2014, p. 56).
92 Civil Act, s.209(1).
93 Ibid., ss.227 and 245.
94 Ibid., s.262.
95 Brun et al. (2014).
96 CJA, s.113.
97 PPFA, s.9.

to the sentence. It is possible for the court to order the defendant to compensate the plaintiff even in the case of acquittal of the former. The compensation is contingent on two conditions. The act should actually have been committed, and that act should be attributable to the defendant.[98] This path is not restricted to individuals: governmental bodies may also pursue this procedural path to initiate their respective civil lawsuits.

Kuwait depends on the general provisions regarding the compensation of victims of crime enshrined in its national legislation. These general provisions are considered to comply with Article 35 of the UNCAC, which emphasises enabling corruption victims who have suffered damages to initiate legal proceedings against the parties that caused the damages to obtain compensation.[99] In corruption cases, however, the status of the civil party in Kuwaiti law is not clear. Kuwaiti law does not define who the corruption victims are, and it does not contain special provisions allowing them to initiate civil proceedings against corrupt officials. With a lack of concepts like 'social damage', the victims of corruption may not be readily deemed as victims in Kuwait as they lack 'a direct and specific interest'.[100] A lawsuit that is only based on social harms is a public prosecution. The Supreme Court stated that, 'compensation for the injury to the national pride and the Kuwaiti people and their money generated by the crime is achieved by the punishment of those found guilty of the crime'.[101] The same court decided that compensatory claims should originate from wrongful conduct being tried and that the harms should be personal, direct and causally linked to that act.

Next, the ADA 20/1981 provides contracting governmental bodies with a right of action to bring lawsuits against other contractors in relation to administrative contracts.[102] Administrative contracts have a specific meaning in civil law jurisdictions like Kuwait. They are contracts concluded by a public body for the purpose of running a public facility, whereby that public body appears as a person of public law, in the sense that the contract will incorporate conditions that are extraordinary and unusual conditions for the ordinary civil law contracts.[103] The Administrative Court is granted jurisdiction over those contracts.[104] The ADA is different from the Civil Act, as the latter sets out the right of the government to sue as a private litigant in civil and commercial contracts. For administrative contracts, however, governmental bodies appear as a sovereign party.

In relation to how to sue within the jurisdiction of Kuwait, the LALD Act 12/1960 has established the LALD as a specialised governmental body whose

98 Case No. 721/2010, 15/1/2012 (Supreme Court – Criminal Division 1) 4.

99 Conference of the States Parties to the UN Convention against Corruption (2017).

100 Ibid., para.9.

101 Case No. 196/2000, 13/3/2001 (Supreme Court – Commercial Division).

102 ADA, s.2.

103 Al-Tammawi (1975). See also Case No. 236/2004, 4/1/2006 (Supreme Court – Commercial Division 2) 2–3.

104 ADA, s.2.

remit includes, inter alia, defending the interests of the state treasury in all suits that are brought against, or filed by, the government.[105] The LALD represents all public bodies in the courts by initiating judicial proceedings on their behalf (including civil lawsuits and administrative disputes). Furthermore, in corruption crimes, Nazaha has been mandated to coordinate and liaise with the competent bodies (such as the LALD) to initiate the lawsuits and to follow up the process of recovery of the proceeds of corruption undertaken by the governmental bodies.[106] One interviewee said that Nazaha has established the Corruption Detection and Recovery of Proceeds of Crime Unit, which has a wide range of tasks, including those related to the recovery of proceeds of crime (including following up the provisional measures taken against assets by the public prosecutors).[107]

#### 5.3.3.2 *International cooperation in civil law*

Civil litigation about corruption may have an international dimension. Grand corruption cases, due to their transnational nature, often involve assets that are located abroad.[108] Asset recovery then may require international cooperation, extending from gathering evidence and taking provisional measures to enforcing judgments and confiscating the proceeds of corruption. In civil matters, the legal bases for assistance in the international context may vary, but include multilateral conventions and bilateral mutual legal assistance (MLA) treaties.[109]

The UNCAC, Article 43, requires that 'States Parties shall consider assisting each other in investigations of and proceedings in civil and administrative matters relating to corruption'. Although some commentators argue that using the UNCAC as a basis for MLA may be restricted to criminal matters,[110] there is a strong argument that Article 43 may be used 'as a legal basis' for MLA in civil matters.[111] Article 46 of the Convention includes the general term 'judicial proceedings' when stating that 'States Parties shall afford one another the widest measure of mutual legal assistance in investigations, prosecutions and *judicial* proceedings in relation to the offences covered by this Convention'. Moreover, the Hague Convention on the Taking of Evidence Abroad in Civil or Commercial Matters was concluded in 1970 to facilitate, through a Letter of Request, the obtaining of evidence, or the performance of some other judicial act in civil and commercial matters.[112] Kuwait ratified this Convention in 2002.[113]

105 LALD Act, s.8.
106 ACAA, ss.5(6) and 5(14).
107 Official-2.
108 See chapter 4.3.6.3.
109 Brun et al. (2014).
110 Hatchard (2014).
111 Brun et al. (2014, p. 82).
112 See <https://www.hcch.net/en/instruments/conventions/full-text/?cid=82>.
113 Ratification of Convention on the Taking of Evidence Abroad in Civil or Commercial Matters Act 8/2002.

In relation to the enforcement of domestic judgments of civil lawsuits in other jurisdictions, the UNCAC, Article 55(1)(a) and Article 55(1)(b), urge the requested State Party to submit to its authorities a request from another State Party to confiscate the proceeds of crime or to give effect to a confiscation order issued by the requesting State Party. But whether the Kuwaiti judgments in civil lawsuits can be considered as 'confiscation orders' abroad is questionable. It is expected that the enforcement of these judgments abroad, under the provisions of the mentioned Articles, may face challenges related to the interpretation of their nature as civil rather than criminal; hence, Article 55(1)(a) and Article 55(1)(b) are not applicable. On some occasions, assistance has not been rendered to another state because the MLA did not cover proceedings of a civil nature; on other occasions, assistance has been rendered based on the fact 'that there can be circumstances in which a forfeiture procedure could be likened to a case of "criminal character" even in the absence of criminal proceedings'.[114] Anyway, although all of the provisions on international cooperation among states may be determined by other means (such as the domestic legislation in the requested state), it is concluded that effective international cooperation is largely contingent on the existence of MLA bilateral agreements that sanction specific modes of cooperation between Kuwait and other jurisdictions.

Faced with these potential challenges, it is preferable to resort to the option of initiating civil proceedings in the jurisdiction where the assets are located. However, determining the choice of where to file a lawsuit is subject to a number of considerations, such as the ease of enforcing judgments, personal jurisdiction, the location of the events, the location of the assets, the location of the evidence, and whether there is an existing criminal investigation.[115] When legal actions are required to be taken abroad, Article 54 of the UNCAC stipulates that State parties should enable another State Party 'to initiate civil action in its courts to establish title to or ownership of property acquired through the commission of an offence established in accordance with this Convention'. In this context, specific arrangements should be put in place. Usually, the government creates a national team consisting of professionals with extensive experience of studying the case at issue, sets up a strategy regarding the actions to be taken abroad, and cooperates with international law and accountancy firms.[116] Now, Nazaha, through the Corruption Detection and Recovery of Proceeds of Crime Unit, has a role to play in the process of recovering the proceeds of corruption both inside and outside Kuwait.[117] However, the interviewees did not raise or emphasise any point related to the international cooperation in civil matters, which may be attributable to their lack of expertise in that aspect of the counter-corruption field in Kuwait.[118]

114 See Greenberg et al. (2009, p. 96).
115 Brun et al. (2014).
116 Al-Moqatei (2009).
117 Nazaha (2017, p. 62).
118 See chapter 6.3.

The following are examples where corruption has been dealt with through civil actions abroad. Between 1989 and 1992, the investments of the Kuwaiti government in Spain through an office in London were subject to several corrupt acts, including conspiracy and the embezzlement of money; the losses amounted to $5 Billion.[119] Consequently, a national team of experts was formed to determine the legal actions to be taken and the jurisdiction for those actions. The team initiated several legal actions in 19 countries, including Kuwait, Spain, and the United Kingdom. Such actions encompassed criminal proceedings and non-conviction-based confiscation, but the main strategy was to recover the assets through private civil actions. [120] In January 2019, the Kuwaiti government filed a lawsuit against a British asset management company, Man Group Plc. The Kuwaiti government was seeking $156 million (£122.4 million) in compensation based on alleged conspiracy, including secretive deals undertaken by the company with an ex-official in a governmental body in the period 1996–2013.[121]

It can be argued that the use of civil law in corruption cases in Kuwait is limited. This limited use is unsurprising. In the context of combating corruption, the civil law remedies tend to be overlooked, though not completely neglected, despite the fact that civil actions against corruption have their own functionality.[122] Not least, given the transnational nature of grand corruption cases, the enforceability of civil law remedies in jurisdictions where proceeds of corruption are hidden becomes one critical advantage of these remedies.[123] They also serve to fill the gaps caused by not only the failure of criminal law and justice to combat corruption, but also the absence of other civil recovery regimes, such as civil forfeiture.[124]

### 5.3.4 *Administrative measures: disciplinary offences*

When exercising their functions, officeholders may commit official malfeasances, and the state can then take disciplinary action. Some Kuwaiti laws as well as the civil service codes consist of obligations, general duties, and prohibitions.[125] The discussion here, however, is concerned with violations of formal duties that amount to an abuse of public office for private gain. Such formal duties encompass maintaining public property and the way in which it can be disposed of.[126] The proscribed acts also include purchasing, selling, or renting property belonging to the governmental department where the officeholder works;[127] exploiting

119 Al-Moqatei (2009).
120 Ibid., pp. 164–165.
121 See <https://uk.reuters.com/article/uk-kuwait-litigation-man-group/kuwait-pension-fund-says-files-lawsuit-against-uks-man-group-idUKKCN1P316W>.
122 See Meyer (2009).
123 Makinwa (2009).
124 Young (2009, p. 145).
125 See Al-Farsi (2004).
126 CSA, s.24(4).
127 Ibid., s.25(1).

one's official capacity for the purposes of nepotism and favouritism;[128] and financial violations committed by an official in relation to public finance.[129] These examples are forms of non-criminalised corruption that the state is empowered to combat.

The civil service-related disciplinary offences and measures in Kuwait mainly comprise two types: administration-related disciplinary offences (hereinafter administrative violations) and public finance-related disciplinary offences (hereinafter financial irregularities). This categorisation of the disciplinary offences has been created recently.[130] To understand this categorisation, it is noteworthy to mention the legislative history of those two disciplinary offences. The SAB Act 30/1964 created the financial irregularities.[131] Later, in 1979, the CSA was enacted to be the general law that governs the civil service in Kuwait, including the establishment of the disciplinary offences. With the enactment of the CSA, the Civil Service Commission understood that the legislature intended to impliedly repeal the financial irregularities in the SAB and replace them with the disciplinary offences established by the CSA. From 1979, professionals repeatedly stated that the CSA's disciplinary measures were not intended to replace the SAB Act's financial irregularities based on the distinct nature of the latter.[132] Therefore, in 2015, the legislature intervened and settled the issue under Act No. 9/2015, which asserted that the sections of the SAB Act – that govern the financial irregularities – do not contradict the CSA and hence, are not impliedly repealed.[133] Since 2015, the financial irregularities have been re-enforced. This historical introduction underlines two features. First, it justifies why the effectiveness of financial irregularities is assessed in this book from 2015, though they were enacted in 1964. Second, it indicates the positive attitudes of Kuwaiti policymakers towards the value of accountability.

#### 5.3.4.1 *Administrative violations*

Official-1 defined administrative violations as 'those violations that are committed against the administrative regulations and do not bear serious financial harms to the public purse'. Administrative violations are subject to the CSA (and its CSA-SI) and the Code 2012. The Code 2012, however, focuses more on stating the values, principles, and obligations, representing a rich source of the duties of public office, the violation of which forms an administrative violation.[134] In terms of the disciplinary procedures, the Code 2012 refers to the

128 Ibid., s.25(4).
129 SAB Act, s.52.
130 See Case No. 1987/2018, 23/12/2018 (First Instance Court – Administrative Division 4) 7.
131 SAB Act, ss.52–53.
132 Official-6.
133 Section 36.
134 However, the distinction between administrative and financial irregularities sometimes could be blurred.

CSA and the CSA-SI, which bring in general provisions pertaining to the disciplinary measures (including formal duties and the disciplinary procedures).[135] Depending on the circumstances, either the Civil Service Commission or the governmental bodies where the violation has been committed are responsible for investigating the administrative violation.[136]

Officials who violate their formal duties or commit prohibitions prescribed in the regulations and laws will be subject to disciplinary punishments.[137] These punishments are pre-defined and can be cancelled according to specific procedures.[138] The disciplinary actions also include suspending officials due to a pending investigation or because they are on remand.[139] In any case, the retirement of officials does not prevent them from having criminal and civil responsibility.[140] The details of these provisions, however, have been left to the CSA-SI. The CSA-SI requires an investigation before punishing the officials and regulates the process of investigation, providing the officials with safeguards.[141] The sanctions that can be imposed, and the safeguards in this regard, are also regulated in the CSA-SI.[142] Nevertheless, high-ranking officials are subject to a disciplinary system that is different from that which applies to low-ranking officials.[143]

#### 5.3.4.2 *Financial irregularities*

Financial irregularities are subject to the provisions of the SAB Act. Section 52 lists eight financial irregularities mostly related to the financial and accounting rules of public finance. Each official (except the ministers) is liable to disciplinary actions if they commit one of these financial irregularities.[144] The Act also regulates how these irregularities are referred to, and investigated by, the relevant governmental departments, and the cases when the decisions regarding the administrative investigation of these irregularities can be overseen and reviewed by the SAB.[145] One of the most important measures stipulated in the SAB Act is the establishment of the Disciplinary Tribunal, which is administrative in nature and whose decisions are subject to judicial oversight.[146] The Disciplinary Tribunal has the jurisdiction to investigate financial irregularities.[147] The Act

135 Code 2012, s.3(a).
136 Official-1.
137 CSA, s.27.
138 Ibid., ss.28–29.
139 Ibid., s.30.
140 Ibid., s.31.
141 Sections 55–59, 63, 65, and 67.
142 Sections 60–62, 64, 66, 68, 69, and 70.
143 See Al-Haidar (2018).
144 SAB Act, s.53.
145 Ibid., ss.54–59.
146 Case No. 1987/2018, 23/12/2018 (First Instance Court – Administrative Division 4) 8.
147 SAB Act, s.60.

also regulates the sanctions that can be imposed on officials even if they have left office.[148]

After being re-enforced in 2015, the resurgence of financial irregularities reflects the fact that the Kuwaiti policymakers have realised the extent of the exacerbation of the corruption problem. Official-6 emphasised that the SAB has always demanded the re-activation of the provisions regarding financial irregularities on the grounds that they are valid. However, such a demand was neglected until 2015. Political attitudes towards consolidating the value of accountability, Official-6 argued, are being seen in reality: 'with the enactment of Act No. 9/2015 amending section 36 of the CSA, there has been a political will to support the counter-corruption efforts.' Later in 2019, the policymakers' inclination towards upholding the value of accountability was made evident in the Strategy 2019–2024, where public finance (and financial irregularities) is subject to further accountability-based measures.[149]

The re-enforcement of financial irregularities has made a difference. One senior official stated that 'the disciplinary measures against financial irregularities are effective' and 'with the start of holding public officials accountable for financial irregularities, the number of irregularities has decreased'.[150] The effectiveness of the financial irregularities provision was also noted by another interviewee: 'after implementing the financial irregularities system, the rate of irregularities in the governmental bodies has clearly decreased'.[151] Official-1 provided a report showing that in the year 2017–2018, the number of irregularities dropped from 293 to 245, representing a 16% drop in violations, compared with the year 2016–2017.[152] 'I believe', said Official-1, 'that this drop reflects the deterrent effect of such an accountability mechanism'. Official-1 and Official-6 stated that the reduction is a result of the enforcement of the financial irregularities, the first hearing for which was held on 15 June 2016. Official-6 stated that out of those 245 financial irregularities, 143 cases were referred to the Disciplinary Tribunal (involving 383 officeholders); he/she argued that this is deterrent enough to decrease the number of irregularities. The referrals were so serious that two cases ended with decisions to dismiss the officeholders referred. The willingness to hold officeholders to account may be evident in the number of senior officials sanctioned (see Table 5.2).

At the end of the interview, Official-1 concluded: 'I expect that the number will continue to decrease in the future, particularly with raising the awareness of the public officials.' Yet it may be impulsive to assert that the reduction is a direct result of the deterrent effect of the enforcement of the financial irregularities. Bringing the financial irregularities into action may have raised the awareness of officials and helped them to comply with the existing laws and

148 Ibid., ss.62 and 72.
149 Nazaha (2019, p. 67).
150 Official-1.
151 Official-6.
152 See State Audit Bureau (2018).

*Table 5.2* Cases referred to the Disciplinary Tribunal (2015–Nov 2018)

| *Action taken by the Tribunal* | *Number* |
|---|---|
| Convictions | 43 (of which 36 involved senior officials) |
| Acquittals | 43 |
| Cases dismissed | 27 |
| Lack of jurisdiction | 3 |
| Cases discontinued | 1 |
| *Total numbers* | |
| Total of officials referred | 383 Officials |
| Total of cases referred | 143 Cases |
| Total of decisions taken | 117 Decisions |

regulations. This view reinforces the argument made in the enforcement pyramid that officeholders should first be persuaded before resorting to more intrusive measures.

Kuwaiti law assists the public administration with a disciplinary system as one of the counter-corruption responses to official malfeasance. This system has the potential to be effective in deterring corrupt officeholders. Offending officials are liable to a wide range of sanctions, which vary from reprimand, deduction of salary, and dismissal[153] to the denial of their pension after leaving office.[154] More importantly, the system of discipline enables the competent authorities to employ the idea of the enforcement pyramid.[155] The government can respond to corruption in a gradual fashion through a hierarchy of sanctions to dissuade officials from involving themselves in corruption cases by using the disciplinary system of administrative law before resorting to the criminal law.

## 5.4 Critique of the existing non-criminal counter-corruption measures and suggested reforms

This section addresses two interrelated issues. First, it assesses, in general, the adequacy and effectiveness of the existing Kuwaiti non-criminal laws and regulations on corruption in dealing with the problem of grand corruption. The aim is to identify the points of weakness and strength in Kuwait's non-criminal responses to corruption. Second, it examines how the non-criminal counter-corruption measures can be changed to more effectively confront the problem of grand corruption. In examining these issues, this section explores innovative techniques and suggests how innovation could be incorporated into Kuwaiti laws. This task necessitates analysing how the international practice regarding corruption could be harnessed to rectify the existing deficiencies in the counter-corruption responses.

153 CSA, s.28.
154 SAB Act, s.72
155 See Ayres and Braithwaite (1995).

### 5.4.1 *Assessment of existing non-criminal counter-corruption measures*

Building on the idea of the 'enforcement pyramid', the counter-corruption responses in Kuwait can be hierarchically classified into three levels. Perhaps this classification has not been systematically adopted by the Kuwaiti policymakers, but it is possible to perceive the current counter-corruption arrangements in this light, at least from theoretical and analytical perspectives. At the bottom of the pyramid lie the persuasive measures. The civil service codes comprise a number of integrity values and principles that govern public office.[156] However, given the focus of this book on grand corruption, codes may play different roles. The nature of grand corruption complicates the perception that officials may be unaware of the governing rules of public office. Grand corruption cases tend to be committed by senior officials, who occupy high levels in public organisations. Senior officials are supposed to be fully aware of the integrity principles, because they often form the tier of policymakers that enact such principles. As a result, the civil service codes that are directed at senior officials should be different than those directed at junior officials in two respects.

First, while the former should remind high-level officials of the expected behaviours, the latter should raise the awareness of, and educate, low-level officials. Second, the civil service codes directed at senior officials may include more dedicated principles related to the integrity of decision making. Given the generality of the current codes, they may be insufficient to deal with the specificity of some state institutions, including the high-risk public bodies that are vulnerable to corruption, such as the Central Agency for Public Tenders (CAPT). The Strategy 2019–2024 sheds light on that issue and specifies a number of measures mainly directed at the tier of decision makers within the governmental bodies. The Strategy aims to promote more transparent and objective decision making at the level of governmental activities in general and the appointment of junior and senior officials in particular.

Next, self-regulation is another persuasive measure that has, arguably, not matured yet in Kuwait. The self-regulation of the private sector in the area of counter-corruption is limited to the AML regime. In other counter-corruption areas, the current contributions of the private sector are also fragmented and better described as voluntary, whereby individual firms opt to 'do the right thing unilaterally without any basis in coercion'.[157] The state-centred regulatory policy in Kuwait, based on the command and control approach, has contributed to the lack of interest among the private sector in combating corruption. Unless the government takes the initiative, it is 'too much to expect that private sector organizations will feel morally obliged to act with integrity in business

156 See section 5.3.2.1.

157 Gunningham and Sinclair (2017, p. 140). See section 5.3.2.2.

dealings.'[158] However, with the advent of the Strategy 2019–2024, the private sector has been paid much attention.[159]

Self-regulation is an appropriate device to integrate counter-corruption issues in the routines of businesses. It allows for the development of a new mode of controlling crime through the 'responsibilisation' of the private sector by devolving the responsibility for crime prevention to non-state organisations.[160] It also allows for importing potential innovations from the private sector. However, the inclination towards self-regulation is expected to be fruitful if the emphasis is placed more on industry-wide organisations. Self-regulation by industry-wide organisations would be possible through, for example, bilateral cooperation between the statutory regulators and the professional associations. The list of those who participated in drafting the Strategy 2019–2024 includes a number of professional associations, which may reveal the preference of Kuwaiti policymakers for dealing with the representatives of private entities collectively rather than individually.[161]

Nevertheless, the concept of self-regulation has some limitations. Its success depends on many factors, including the extent of adherence of the professions/businesses to the regulations they have enacted.[162] Regulation then is tied to the importance of the enforcement capacity.[163] Compliance with counter-corruption laws and regulations is not voluntary and should not be left entirely to non-state actors. Therefore, self-regulation is not said to replace the role of the state and enforcement authorities, but to complement them. Because self-regulation is based on self-policing, there is a need for credible external oversight through enforcement that reasserts the significance of compliance.[164] There is some evidence that regulatory requirements are often ignored in the absence of enforcement.[165] In the United States, the self-regulatory model was incorporated into the Foreign Corrupt Practices Act (FCPA) 1977 as a means of self-restraint to secure the compliance of corporations in regard to not getting involved in bribery. Such a self-regulatory approach, however, has failed for several reasons, including the weak presence of regulatory enforcement, especially in foreign locales.[166] In this sense, the responsive regulation captures the idea of the need for enforcement, because it ensures that punitive approaches follow when self-regulation fails.[167]

Another indicator whereby self-regulation cannot be entirely relied upon to achieve the regulatory objectives comes from the United Kingdom. The

158 Hatchard (2014, p. 236).
159 See section 5.3.2.2.
160 See Garland (1996, p. 452).
161 Nazaha (2019, p. 55).
162 See OECD (2015).
163 Haines (2011).
164 See Weismann (2009).
165 See Haines (2011).
166 See Weismann (2009).
167 Haines (2011).

Office for Professional Body Anti-Money Laundering Supervision (OPBAS) was established in 2018 'to strengthen the UK's anti-money laundering (AML) supervisory regime and ensure the professional body AML supervisors provide consistently high standards of AML supervision'.[168] In its report, OPBAS assessed the effectiveness of the professional body AML supervisors (PBSs) responsible for the accounting and legal sectors and found that the PBSs should be subject to 'ongoing assessments'. Among the findings, the PBSs assessed were found to focus more on the interests of their members than on promoting AML standards.[169] This finding goes hand-in-hand with the FATF's Mutual Evaluation Report of the United Kingdom, which identified that 'weaknesses in supervision and sanctions are a significant issue', especially at the level of the legal and accountancy sectors.[170] In sum, the adoption of a self-regulatory approach to deal with counter-corruption matters is necessary, but, at the same time, it must not be used without some interventionist policies by the state. There should always be other enforcement-oriented measures.

The upper tier in the enforcement pyramid is the civil and administrative measures against corruption. Civil proceedings enable the state to address the financial consequences of corruption, which can be effective in combating an economic crime like corruption. Civil law has its own advantages, such as the less-demanding requirements in terms of the standard of proof and the multiple options to sue based on proprietary or personal claims. However, there is still a gap that civil law may not bridge. Although civil law is helpful in the context of assets owned by the state, the options available in civil law do not always help recover the proceeds of crime, especially when the state does not have proprietary rights. The civil-based measures do not always empower the state to forfeit the criminal assets generated by the various forms of crimes. Therefore, there is a need for tools that go beyond proprietary claims. Civil forfeiture and unexplained wealth orders (UWOs) are suggested as two innovative tools.[171]

The administrative measures are useful in implementing the 'enforcement pyramid'. The disciplinary offence is a proportional option to cases where an official commits misconduct without serious consequences. The state can strike a balance between the seriousness of the official misconduct and the action to be taken. Yet in grand corruption cases that involve harmful consequences, administrative measures seem to do little. The effectiveness of these measures is also affected by the fact they are but public administration activities that are subject to judicial oversight, which may annul the decisions taken. Therefore, their effectiveness in grand corruption cases is largely linked to simultaneous criminal proceedings. Official-5 emphasised that when financial irregularities are detected, they have more of a deterrent effect when they are subject to administrative

168 See <https://www.fca.org.uk/opbas>.

169 See <https://www.fca.org.uk/publication/opbas/themes-2018-opbas-anti-money-laundering-supervisory-assessments.pdf>.

170 See FATF (2018).

171 See section 5.4.2 below.

investigation and, at the same time, referred to the public prosecution for criminal investigation. In such cases, the effectiveness of the administrative measures depends on whether they empower the governmental bodies to expeditiously intervene and suspend the suspect official from exercising his/her authorities, especially those bodies that may be the closest to the alleged crime.

### 5.4.2 *Innovative measures*

The traditional responses of criminal law that focus on imprisonment alone may not sufficiently empower the state to combat grand corruption. It was also argued that the existing criminal provisions for depriving criminals of the proceeds of crime face some challenges.[172] Therefore, this section further argues for 'civilizing the money-centered model of crime control'.[173] This encompasses adopting innovative approaches that use civil law proceedings to target property associated with crime, such as civil forfeiture and UWOs. These two tools aim to bridge the gaps, not only in the criminal provisions regarding the proceeds of crime, but also in the available civil law options in the Kuwaiti law. These tools are more workable options, especially when the use of criminal law is not well adapted to the grand corruption cases at hand, such as politically sensitive cases or cases lacking concrete evidence.[174]

#### 5.4.2.1 *Civil forfeiture*

Generally, two regimes are used in the asset forfeiture process: non-conviction-based forfeiture (civil forfeiture) and criminal forfeiture (following conviction).[175] While both regimes aim to capture the proceeds and instrumentalities of crimes, they differ in their genesis. Civil forfeiture is a 'right of action in the civil courts to recover property which is, or represents, property obtained through unlawful conduct'.[176] Criminal forfeiture requires initiating criminal proceedings and obtaining a conviction, whilst civil forfeiture does not. Criminal forfeiture then is an action against a person (*in personam*) and is part of the sentence, whilst civil forfeiture is an action against the asset itself (*in rem*). Furthermore, criminal forfeiture often requires the heightened standard of proof beyond reasonable doubt used in criminal cases, whilst civil forfeiture requires the lower standard of proof used in civil cases, that is, the balance of probabilities. Criminal forfeiture is either object-based (the prosecution should prove that the assets are proceeds of the crime committed) or value-based ('the forfeiture of the value of the offender's benefit from the crime, without proving the connection between the crime and the specific object of property'), while

172 See chapter 4.3.6.
173 See Gallant (2004, p. 14).
174 See Al-Rashidi (2020).
175 Greenberg et al. (2009).
176 See Broadbridge (2001, p. 53).

civil forfeiture is mainly object-based, requiring proof that the property is proceeds of crime.[177] However, some jurisdictions have developed value-based civil forfeiture regimes.[178] The analysis here is limited to civil forfeiture.

Civil forfeiture is provided for in Article 54(1)(c) of the UNCAC, which requires all States Parties to consider 'taking such measures as may be necessary to allow confiscation of such property without a criminal conviction in cases in which the offender cannot be prosecuted by reason of death, flight or absence or in other appropriate cases'. Recommendation 4 of the FATF's recommendations on combating money laundering and the financing of terrorism requires countries to 'consider adopting measures that allow such proceeds or instrumentalities to be confiscated without requiring criminal conviction'.[179] Despite being an 'under-theorised' means of combating crime,[180] civil forfeiture derives its significance from the policy rationales that lie behind it. The perceived failure of criminal law, caused by due process safeguards, to combat serious criminality has led to the resort to the civil techniques to target criminal assets.[181] Moreover, in the realm of organised crime, especially corruption, offenders can be leaders or high-ranking officials who tend to be far from the criminal enterprise, meaning that it may be impossible to bring them to justice.[182] Thus, civil forfeiture is able to overcome three types of difficulties. The first involves difficulties raised by the procedural safeguards of criminal law.[183] The second involves difficulties raised by the complexity of corruption crimes as white-collar crimes.[184] The third relates to the political expediency in avoiding *in personam* actions.[185] This difficulty is context-specific for Kuwait, where the use of the criminal law and imprisonment against high-profile figures may be unrealistic and politically sensitive, leaving the victimised state without alternative tools.

Despite the commitment of Kuwait to the UNCAC, its laws lack a civil forfeiture regime.[186] However, some of the statutory assets forfeiture provisions in Kuwait bring it closer to civil forfeiture, though not fully. Forfeiture/confiscation of the proceeds of crime is not impeded in cases where the defendant absconded or died after the criminal charge was instituted.[187] However, these provisions do not technically transform the existing forfeiture provisions into a fully civil forfeiture regime. First, even though securing a criminal conviction is not required to forfeit the proceeds of crime when the criminal proceedings are terminated because the offender has deceased, forfeiture is still limited in this

177 For detailed distinctions, see Greenberg et al. (2009, pp. 13–14).
178 See Kennedy (2006).
179 FATF (2012, p. 10).
180 See Hendry and King (2015, pp. 389–411).
181 Ibid.
182 Simser (2009).
183 Hendry and King (2015).
184 Ryder (2013).
185 Greenberg et al. (2009).
186 See Al-Oumi (2018).
187 See the post-conviction measures in chapter 4.3.6.2.

case because a criminal charge must have been instituted while the offender was alive. Furthermore, in determining the unlawful origin of property, Kennedy shows that, in a number of jurisdictions, it is not necessary for civil forfeiture 'to show that the conduct [the origin of proceeds of crime] was of a particular kind'.[188] Second, a criminal trial *in absentia* also requires that a criminal charge has already been instituted against an offender. Thus, such *in personam* characteristics of the existing measures further distance them from civil forfeiture: the cases mentioned are not separated from the criminal proceedings, a condition that prevails in true civil forfeiture.[189]

It is predicted that introducing a civil forfeiture regime in Kuwait would not be without challenges and concerns. However, since civil forfeiture is not part of the Kuwaiti legislation, the following discussion is based on a set of predictions rather than actual challenges. This caution is noted to justify the brevity in discussing the potential challenges, though there is much literature in this regard.

First, the effectiveness of civil forfeiture cannot be taken for granted. Although civil forfeiture represents itself as 'an alternative approach that makes use of civil processes to target criminal assets',[190] it is not necessarily more effective. On some occasions, the law enforcement authorities may fail to use civil forfeiture because of the impossibility of obtaining evidence to forfeit illicit property.[191] In the United Kingdom, for example, the Home Office proposed that the existing provisions of the Proceeds of Crime Act (POCA) 2002 that allow for civil forfeiture were not helpful in these cases.[192] In 2019, the Home Office showed that civil recovery cases represented 'a small proportion of total recovered assets in the UK'.[193] Even if the standard of proof is lower in civil forfeiture, finding sufficient evidence still impedes any potential forfeiture in the future. Therefore, investigative powers, including 'compulsory questioning powers' to collect relevant information, are necessary to secure the effectiveness of civil forfeiture.[194] The evidence-related difficulties expose the need of civil forfeiture for additional, innovative tools, such as UWOs.[195] But these difficulties do not dispel the idea that civil forfeiture would still be useful in Kuwait. As found in chapter 4, the evidential difficulties of criminal law have been identified as a pattern: for example, the prosecution of stand-alone money laundering offences (ML offences) is not possible due to difficulties in proving the unlawful origin of money.[196] The 2018 report by FATF on the law regarding

188 Kennedy (2006, p. 135).
189 Greenberg et al. (2009).
190 Hendry and King (2015, p. 399).
191 See Sproat (2018).
192 See Home Office (2016).
193 See Home Office (2019, p. 20).
194 Kennedy (2006, pp. 145–146).
195 See below section 5.4.2.2.
196 See chapter 4.3.5.

AML in the United Kingdom found that alternatives, including civil recovery, were actively sought by the United Kingdom where the prosecution of the ML offence is not possible.[197]

The second challenge relates to human rights infraction in civil forfeiture.[198] Civil forfeiture has been used 'as an uneasy and unsatisfactory substitute for the criminal process'.[199] Consequently, the introduction of civil forfeiture would be expected to be met with resistance from a number of professional experts in Kuwait. Civil forfeiture purports to be civil in character as it adopts civil proceedings. But, more precisely, although civil forfeiture employs civil legal mechanisms, it aims to achieve criminal law objectives, and those affected may be labelled criminals (despite its *in rem* nature).[200] This hybrid nature of civil forfeiture, which results from it involving civil and criminal processes, has been criticised for illegitimately circumventing the procedural safeguards provided by the criminal law for defendants.[201] As Naylor illustrates, civil forfeiture is based on a 'fiction' that it is the property and not its owner that is guilty, though it is not possible to declare that the property is proceeds of crime without 'smearing its owner'.[202] In the United Kingdom, when it was first introduced, civil forfeiture was opposed as it 'involves direct or indirect findings of guilt on the part of the property holder or persons connected to the property. These proposals undermine the presumption of innocence'.[203]

In Kuwait, the potential establishment of civil forfeiture may be covered by Article 19 of the Constitution, which allows private forfeiture following judgment. However, Article 19 uses the term of 'forfeiture' in a punitive sense when it states that 'the penalty of forfeiture should be based on judgment'. As a result, the Kuwaiti law has always dealt with forfeiture as a punitive measure. The potential for the constitutional challenge of civil forfeiture is, arguably, contingent on considering it as a criminal measure. Unlike those criteria established by the European Court of Human Rights (ECtHR),[204] there is a lack of a test or specific criteria upon which a law or mechanism can be determined criminal in character. But the fact that civil forfeiture is basically concerned with criminal wrongdoing may result in its classification as a criminal measure. Consequently, there is a strong argument to expect that civil forfeiture would evoke the Kuwaiti Constitution's safeguards that are granted to the accused in criminal cases. Additionally, private property ownership is safeguarded in Article 18 of the Constitution. Depriving individuals of their property, based on a lower

197 See FATF (2018).
198 Alldridge (2018).
199 Rees, Fisher and Thomas (2015, p. para. 6.14).
200 King (2014).
201 See Hendry and King (2017).
202 Naylor (1999, p. 41).
203 See Liberty (2001, p. 21).
204 See *Engel v Netherlands* (No. 1) App No. 5100/71, Series A No. 22 (1979–80) 1 EHRR 647.

civil standard of proof, claiming that they are derived from criminal activity, may collide with property rights that are constitutionally protected.

Criminal forfeiture has been, as Ryder describes, 'the central tenet of the international policy towards confiscating the proceeds of crime'.[205] Reflecting on the judicial attitudes of the Kuwaiti Constitutional Court,[206] the forfeiture of illicit property in the absence of a criminal conviction (and the associated set of protections) would be a radical shift in the existing criminal policies. It may also be fettered by some constitutional limitations, most notably, Article 4, which sets out the presumption of innocence and the necessary safeguards of a fair trial. Moreover, the interviews with two judicial actors showed their preoccupation with fairness concerns; they emphasised protecting suspects from the executive's arbitrary interference more than the effectiveness of the laws.[207] It is noteworthy that the problematic legitimacy of civil forfeiture is more concerned with the mechanisms used to deprive criminals of their illicit property than the end behind those mechanisms – or, as expressed by Hendry and King, the 'privileging of instrumentality over considerations of due process'.[208] Prioritisation of such a kind has already been subject to constitutional scrutiny. The Kuwaiti Constitutional Court once stated that the underpinning rationale of a law is not necessarily sufficient to 'constitutionalise' it, unless it adheres to the Constitution, especially with regard to respecting the constitutional rights of individuals.[209]

It is important then to justify the means used in civil forfeiture. Al-Oumi argues that civil forfeiture is not a radical departure from the Kuwaiti legal system. Civil forfeiture can be compared to the civil law remedy of restitution, which is based on civil liability. The state can submit a claim to order an individual to return the proceeds of crime, without the need to prove that offence.[210] The Kuwaiti legislature has already used the concept of 'restitution' rather than 'forfeiture' in offences against the public purse.[211] Since the focus of this book is grand corruption in the public sector, where state-owned assets may be a central component of proceeds of crime, civil forfeiture provisions could be imported, but adapted to the conditions and situation in Kuwait. To avoid any potential resistance, civil forfeiture could be marketed or justified, for the current phase at least, on the basis that it reinforces the ownership of the state of the proceeds of crime.

205 Ryder (2013, p. 774).
206 This may be inferred from its recent decisions wherein the Court has reiterated its emphasis on the constitutional safeguards provided for the suspects. See, for example, Case No. 1/2018, 24/10/2018 (Constitutional Court); Case No. 7/2018, 1/5/2019 (Constitutional Court).
207 Judge-1; Prosecutor-2.
208 See Hendry and King (2017, p. 746).
209 Case No. 7/2018, 1/5/2019 (Constitutional Court) 8–9.
210 See Al-Oumi (2018).
211 PPFA, s.16.

#### 5.4.2.2 *Unexplained wealth order (UWOs)*

UWOs are a relatively recent development in forfeiture and confiscation regimes that aim to strengthen the state's powers to fight crime and deprive criminals of the gains derived from criminal activities.[212] Research sponsored by the US Department of Justice studied the UWOs across a number of jurisdictions and found that full UWO laws have their own distinct features that distinguish them from other forfeiture regimes. First, the UWOs regime introduces the concept of unexplained wealth. Second, unlike *in rem* civil forfeiture, UWOs are *in personam* measures, meaning that they are directed at the asset's owner. Third, unlike *in rem* civil forfeiture, UWOs are characterised by the non-requirement of a nexus between the crime and the property. The property liable to forfeiture does not have to be proven to be proceeds or instruments of crime. What is required is that the property the person holds is unexplained wealth. Fourth, unlike traditional forfeiture, the onus of proof is on the owner of the property, who is obliged to demonstrate its legal provenance.[213]

The UWO laws can be subject to different, but subtle, arrangements across jurisdictions.[214] In the United Kingdom, UWOs have been introduced in the Criminal Finances Act (CFA) 2017, amending the POCA 2002.[215] Section 362A of the POCA, as amended by the CFA, stipulates that the High Court can grant a UWO order to a law enforcement authority in relation to any property when the court is satisfied that certain requirements are met. Among other things, this order requires the respondent to explain how he/she obtained the property at issue.[216] Failure to provide an explanation of the legitimate source of assets 'could lead to or assist a civil recovery action or criminal conviction'.[217] As such, UWOs in the United Kingdom are an investigative tool that can be used as a means to achieve the civil recovery of proceeds of crime.[218] As Keen illustrates, in the face of the evidential-based difficulties of civil forfeiture, 'UWOs address the evidential barriers that prevent law enforcement from acting when there appears to be a substantial difference between what an individual earns and what is on display, be it property, cars or expensive artwork'.[219]

Although it is too early to determine the effectiveness of UWOs in the United Kingdom (as they only came into force in January 2018), in one case two UWOs were secured.[220] The National Crime Agency, as of February 2019, had

212 Transparency International UK (2015).
213 See Booz Allen Hamilton (2011).
214 For Australia, for example, see Gray (2012).
215 For the background to the introduction of UWOs in the United Kingdom, see Keen (2017).
216 POCA, s.362A(3).
217 FATF (2018, p. para.182).
218 Sproat (2018).
219 Keen (2017, p. 7).
220 As of December 2018. See FATF (2018). For the application concerning the first UWO, see *National Crime Agency v Mrs A* [2018] EWHC 2534 (Admin).

considered 140 UWOs.[221] However, earlier research addressed the effectiveness of UWOs in the jurisdictions that apply them. Until 2011, it was found that the impact of UWOs varies across these jurisdictions: Ireland has witnessed the greatest effects of UWOs, while in Australia UWOs have been less successful.[222] Reflecting on the experiences in other countries, Keen has identified key lessons that the governments should take into account when considering legislating UWOs: 'expertise in non-conviction based asset recovery; inter-agency cooperation; resources; and political will'.[223]

Although Kuwaiti law does not provide for UWOs, many of their features might find some echoes in the ACAA. Kuwait has legislated for the IEO in the ACAA. The IEO in Kuwaiti law arguably has some key elements of the UWO regime in that it is directed at proceeds of corruption and somewhat relaxes the burden of proof. First, the AACA has criminalised illicit enrichment.[224] To that end, financial disclosures have been established to monitor the wealth of specific officials and enable Nazaha to proactively identify IEO suspects.[225] Like UWOs, financial disclosures can be considered as investigative tools. Furthermore, irrespective of the requirements of the IEO (such as prosecution), 'unexplained wealth' is reflected in Kuwaiti counter-corruption laws. In terms of the lack of a nexus between the crime and the targeted property, the IEO under the ACAA does not necessitate proving a direct nexus between the crime and the property. The mere lack of a reasonable justification for the legitimate source of the wealth can be a reason to secure the forfeiture of the assets. In terms of the third feature, reversing the burden of proof has been established in the IEO, although it is not precise to say that there has been a shift in the burden of proof. The burden of proof is first placed on the prosecutors. Then, the burden is transferred to the suspect who can refute this presumption.[226]

Despite these convergences, there are also divergences. First, the IEO applies only to certain officeholders. Second, an investigation by the IEO is only triggered by the financial disclosures submitted by those officeholders. Therefore, the criminal liability of the officials cannot be raised on the basis of the IEO unless they submit the financial disclosures required. On the contrary, UWOs represent an alternative approach to gathering information and evidence and 'allowing for action against those about whom little information is available'.[227]

In line with the commonalities identified between UWOs and the features of the IEO, the pathway to the adoption of UWOs is, to a large extent, paved in Kuwait. A number of innovative techniques, such as unexplained wealth,

221 See<https://www.riskscreen.com/kyc360/news/update-uk-looks-into-140-unexplained-wealth-orders-many-linked-to-russians-nca/>.

222 For further analysis, see Booz Allen Hamilton (2011, pp. 101–148).

223 Keen (2017, pp. 15–17).

224 See chapter 4.3.4.

225 ACAA, s.30.

226 See chapter 4.3.4.

227 Home Office (2016, p. para.20).

financial disclosures, and the reverse burden of proof, have been already incorporated into the ACAA. However, two aspects do seem to be novel to Kuwaiti law. First, UWOs are being used in the sphere of civil law, which is radical to the Kuwaiti law. Second, civil forfeiture, which does not require a criminal conviction, is required in order to effectively make use of UWOs. As illustrated previously, the potential challenges facing the introduction of civil forfeiture in Kuwait render the introduction of UWOs a high-hanging fruit. Added to that, in what follows, the discussion builds on the controversial nature of UWOs to predict a set of challenges unique to the introduction of UWOs in Kuwait, although there is scant literature on that topic.[228]

Civil liberties and human rights concerns, such as the right to privacy, are inherent in the use of UWOs.[229] Although there is a strong case to predict that UWOs portend an infringement upon individuals' right to privacy (safeguarded by Article 30 of Constitution), the Kuwaiti Constitutional Court has already argued against this claim when the financial disclosures in relation to the IEO were challenged.[230] The legitimate aim of legislation in protecting the 'national interest', as set up by the Court,[231] may represent a recourse for the justification of UWOs against privacy claims. However, the severity of privacy claims should be less severe in UWOs than in the ACAA's financial disclosures. UWOs require an explanation of the origin of identified property whenever there is a reason to suspect that its owner has been involved in crime. The judicial oversight over the issuance of UWOs may also prevent their misuse and any potential infringement upon individuals' privacy. In financial disclosures, officials are required to disclose their assets only because of their assumption of specific official positions and without any judicial involvement. Furthermore, these financial disclosures may result in penal consequences, such as imprisonment when convicted of an IEO.

Another challenge relates to the appropriateness of using evidence derived from UWOs in criminal cases. Even with the lack of civil forfeiture, UWOs are still useful in themselves. TI-UK has recognised the value of UWOs in improving the performance of suspicious transaction reports (STRs). When receiving an STR, especially with moderate evidence, law enforcement authorities may issue a UWO to collect more intelligence. In this case, a UWO is justified on the basis of the moderate evidence previously acquired in the STR.[232] Although, in that context, TI-UK argues that UWOs can be used later in the civil recovery, such value of UWOs is relevant to the misapplication of AML law in Kuwait where the standalone ML offence faces some evidential-based problems.[233] Evidence emerging from UWOs may be used to prosecute ML offences. However, UWOs

228 See Sproat (2018).
229 Transparency International UK (2015).
230 The analysis of this claim is addressed in chapter 4.3.5.
231 See Case No. 4/2017, 8/11/2017 (Constitutional Court) 7.
232 Transparency International UK (2015).
233 See chapter 4.3.5.

might not be appropriate to be used in a subsequent criminal prosecution. The Kuwaiti Constitution establishes the presumption of innocence and that 'the accused shall not be bodily or *mentally* injured'.[234] This safeguard includes the right against self-incrimination whereby the suspect is protected from being compelled to provide evidence that could be used against them.[235] One application of this principle is what section 158 of the CJA states that the suspect should not be compelled by any means to provide any statement.

The UWOs are reminiscent of the financial disclosures of the IEO, which withstood the constitutional challenge. But the constitutionality/appropriateness of the use of evidence – gathered from financial disclosures – in the prosecution of the IEO has not been raised in the Kuwaiti courts.[236] Therefore, to prevent self-incrimination, it is necessary that UWOs do not 'require a person to supply information if in doing so would disclose evidence of the commission of a separate offence, and that disclosure would expose the person to proceedings for that offence'.[237] As a result, UWOs should remain in the field of civil proceedings. With the absence of civil arrangements, such as civil forfeiture, the potential use of evidence gleaned from UWOs in criminal proceedings will be limited, if not useless.

A lack of political will has been seen as a potential inhibiting factor in regard to the implementation of UWOs.[238] Although the grand corruption cases that Kuwait witnesses from time to time may justify the recourse to more innovative techniques to respond to such types of criminality, one may question the assumption that the time to adopt UWOs has come – at least from the perspective of the policymakers. When asked about the possibility of introducing FOI legislation, one interviewee commented that Kuwait lacks the institutional capacity: 'when we met the Nazaha, they showed their unwillingness to adopt any additional measures [more than the existing ones] and that was, in part, because of their lack of capacity'.[239] Another interviewee emphasised the same point, regarding the poor institutional capacity of the counter-corruption institutions.[240] This conclusion can be applied not only to FOI legislation and UWOs, but also to any other innovative tools.

Moreover, applying UWOs to encounter grand corruption may be seen as a disproportionate measure, especially as the assets involved are often hidden outside Kuwait. This argument becomes clearer when we consider the circumstances that justified the introduction of UWO laws in other jurisdictions. For example, in the United Kingdom, 'the National Crime Agency assesses that billions of pounds of proceeds of international corruption are laundered into

234 Article 34 (emphasis added).
235 Al-Eifan (2016).
236 See Case No. 4/2017, 8/11/2017 (Constitutional Court).
237 Transparency International UK (2015, p. 29).
238 See Keen (2017); Sproat (2018).
239 NGO-2.
240 NGO-1.

or through the UK', which 'remains the largest centre for cross-border banking', and hence, 'money laundering represents a significant threat to the UK's national security'.[241] It is these circumstances that induced the United Kingdom to adopt UWOs to face these emerging threats. The comparison with the United Kingdom is not an attempt to downplay the role of UWOs in combating grand corruption in Kuwait: what this analysis wants to say is that arguably this scene should not be isolated from any attempt to justify the introduction of UWOs law in Kuwait.

## 5.5 Conclusion

This chapter demonstrates that corruption need not only be countered by criminal laws. Rather, the civil and administrative law, on the one hand, and the regulatory measures, on the other, have the potential to combat corruption alongside the criminal law. As shown, they have complementary functions, but do not substitute for the criminal law. The persuasive and educative nature of some of these responses can make them an effective and efficient tool that can prevent (or even counter) corruption by making officeholders familiar with the expected behaviours in terms of integrity, and letting professions from the private sector contribute to the counter-corruption policies in the way they see fit. These soft persuasion-based measures help the state focus more on prevention rather than enforcement. The administrative law and the disciplinary offences are also necessary instruments that enable the state to respond to less serious administrative and financial violations. More importantly, the civil law measures are argued to perform promising roles, especially when dealing with the proceeds of crime. With the advent of the Strategy 2019–2024, there have been signs of a forthcoming shift in the Kuwaiti counter-corruption framework: from the dominance of criminal laws towards non-criminal responses. However, the non-criminal measures are not being employed to their full potential in Kuwait.

There are two non-criminal areas where innovation could be introduced in Kuwait. The first is to give the private sector a bigger role in combating corruption. Through the concept of self-regulation, professions that are vulnerable to corruption could have an input in preventing corrupt practices at their source. The second is to pursue 'forfeiture' as a key policy objective; namely, to incorporate civil law-based approaches in the state's strategy in responding to proceeds of crime. The existing provisions are of a criminal nature as they are triggered in, and confined to, criminal cases either on the basis of suspicion or conviction. Reflection on the non-traditional, innovative approaches to proceeds of crime, such as those stipulated by the UNCAC, exposes a lack of civil-based measures within Kuwaiti laws.

In Kuwait, as in many other jurisdictions, civil measures are of particular importance for corruption crimes, especially when these crimes involve grand

241 Home Office (2016, pp. paras.1–3).

corruption that permeates the upper echelon of public officials that dominate the state institutions. Gathering robust evidence and subsequently securing the prosecution and conviction of those officials is difficult, due to the impunity they may enjoy. Therefore, it is concluded here that the existing forfeiture mechanisms cannot deal with a phenomenon like grand corruption. The focus of any future financial arrangements should be on the assets arising from corrupt activities rather than the corrupt actors. Taken together, these results suggest that the law enforcement authorities should be vested with more powers in relation to asset forfeiture. In particular, there should be a shift to a civil model in regard to forfeiture. The Kuwaiti policymakers must prioritise targeting the assets rather than the corrupt as this step is more realistic in grand corruption cases. Given that prosecuting high-profile offenders for corruption crimes inevitably raises issues regarding political sensitivity, targeting the assets might encounter less severe objections. The targeting of assets rather than persons, by using civil remedies, might also be more attainable when the assets are abroad (as they often are). In that eventuality, civil actions against assets might be more feasible (and rewarding) than extradition warrants against high officials.

## Bibliography

Al-Eifan, M. (2016). The Right Against Self-Incrimination in Kuwaiti Law: Analytical and Comparative Study With American Law. *Kuwait University Journal of Law*. 40(1), pp. 119–171.

Al-Farsi, A. (2004). Discipline in Civil and Military Service in Kuwait: Comparative Study. *Kuwait University Journal of Law*. 28(4), pp. 165–254.

Al-Haidar, F. (2018). Administrative Disciplinary and Grievance Procedures for Public Employees in Kuwait and UK. *International Journal of Law and Management*. 60(3), pp. 842–853.

Al-Kazemi, A., Zajac, G. (1999). Ethics Sensitivity and Awareness Within Organizations in Kuwait: An Empirical Exploration of Epoused Theory and Theory-in-Use. *Journal of Business Ethics*. 20(4), pp. 353–361.

Al-Moqatei, M. (2009). Stolen Asset Recovery: A Case from Kuwait. In: Greenberg, T., Samuel, L., Grant, W., Gray, L. (eds). *Stolen Asset Recovery: A Good Practices Guide for Non-Conviction Based Asset Forfeiture*. Washington, DC: World Bank, pp. 163–166.

Al-Oumi, N. (2018). Towards the Confiscation of Proceeds of Crime Without Criminal Conviction: An Analytic, Comparative Study on the Criminal Kuwaiti Law. *Kuwait University Journal of Law*. 42(2), pp. 89–135.

Al-Rashidi, K. S. (2020). Proceeds of Corruption Crime: The Kuwaiti Legal Response. In: Benson, K., King, C., Walker, C. (eds). *Assets, Crimes and the State: Innovation in 21st Century Legal Responses*. Abingdon: Routledge, pp. 215–228.

Al-Sabah, S. (2011). *The Legal Protection of Public Funds in Kuwaiti Law: A Comparative Study*. Master Dissertation, Gulf University, Bahrain.

Al-Tammawi, S. (1975). *Basics of Administrative Contracts: Comparative Study*. Cairo: Dar Alfekr Alarabi.

Alldridge, P. (2018). Civil Recovery in England and Wales: An Appraisal. In: King, C., Walker, C., Gurulé, J. (eds). *The Palgrave Handbook of Criminal and Terrorism Financing Law*. London: Palgrave Macmillan, pp. 515–542.

Allen, J. (2011). Powerful Assemblages? *Area.* 43(2), pp. 154–157.

Ayres, I., Braithwaite, J. (1995). *Responsive Regulation: Transcending the Deregulation Debate.* Oxford: Oxford University Press.

Black, J. (2001). Decentring Regulation: Understanding the Role of Regulation and Self-Regulation in a "Post-Regulatory" World. *Current Legal Problems.* 54(1), pp. 103–146.

Booz Allen Hamilton. (2011). *Comparative Evaluation of Unexplained Wealth Orders: Prepared to the US Department of Justice.* Washington, DC: National Institute of Justice.

Braithwaite, J. (1982). Enforced Self-Regulation: A New Strategy for Corporate Crime Control. *Michigan Law Review.* 80(7), pp. 1466–1507.

Braithwaite, J. (2006). Responsive Regulation and Developing Economies. *World Development.* 34(5), pp. 884–898.

Braithwaite, J. (2011). The Essence of Responsive Regulation. *University of British Columbia Law Review.* 44(3), pp. 475–520.

Broadbridge, S. (2001). *Proceeds of Crime Bill: Bill 31 of 2001-2002* (Research Paper 01/79). London: House of Commons Library.

Brun, J.-P., Dubois, P., van der Does de Willebois, E., Hauch, J., Jaïs, S., Mekki, Y., Sotiropoulou, A., Sylvester, K., Uttamchandani, M. (2014). *Public Wrongs, Private Actions: Civil Lawsuits to Recover Stolen Assets.* Washington, DC: World Bank.

Conference of the States Parties to the UN Convention against Corruption. (2017). *Good Practices in Identifying the Victims of Corruption and Parameters for Their Compensation* (Seventh Session, 6–10 November 2017). Vienna: UN.

de Goede, M. (2018). Counter-Terrorism Financing Assemblages After 9/11. In: King, C., Walker, C., Gurulé, J. (eds). *The Palgrave Handbook of Criminal and Terrorism Financing Law.* London: Palgrave Macmillan, pp. 755–779.

FATF. (2012). *International Standards on Combating Money Laundering and the Financing of Terrorism & Proliferation: The FATF Recommendations.* Paris: FATF.

FATF. (2018). *Anti-Money Laundering and Counter-Terrorist Financing Measures: Mutual Evaluation Report of the United Kingdom.* Paris: FATF.

Gallant, M. M. (2004). Alberta and Ontario: Civilizing the Money-Centered Model of Crime Control. *Asper Review of International Business and Trade Law.* 4, pp. 13–33.

Gardiner, J. (2007). Defining Corruption. In: Heidenheimer, A., Johnston, M. (eds). *Political Corruption: Concepts and Contexts.* 3rd ed. New Brunswick, NJ; London: Transaction Publishers, pp. 25–40.

Garland, D. (1996). The Limits of the Sovereign State: Strategies of Crime Control in Contemporary Society. *British Journal of Criminology.* 36(4), pp. 445–471.

Gilman, S. (2005). *Ethics Codes and Codes of Conduct as Tools for Promoting an Ethical and Professional Public Service: Comparative Successes and Lessons.* Washington, DC: PREM, the World Bank.

Gray, A. (2012). Forfeiture Provisions and the Criminal/Civil Divide. *New Criminal Law Review.* 15(1), pp. 32–67.

Graycar, A., Prenzler, T. (2013). *Understanding and Preventing Corruption.* London: Palgrave Macmillan.

Greenberg, T., Samuel, L., Grant, W., Gray, L. (2009). *Stolen Asset Recovery: A Good Practices Guide for Non-Conviction Based Asset Forfeiture.* Washington, DC: World Bank.

Gunningham, N., Rees, J. (1997). Industry Self-Regulation: An Institutional Perspective. *Law and Policy.* 19(4), pp. 363–414.

Gunningham, N., Sinclair, D. (2017). Smart Regulation. In: Drahos, P. (ed). *Regulatory Theory: Foundations and Applications.* Acton, Australia: ANU Press, pp. 133–148.

Haines, F. (2011). *The Paradox of Regulation: What Regulation Can Achieve and What It Cannot.* Northampton, MA: Edward Elgar.

Harvard Law Review. (1993). The Bureaucrats of Rules and Standards. *Harvard Law Review.* 106(7), pp. 1685–1690.

Hatchard, J. (2014). *Combating Corruption: Legal Approaches to Supporting Good Governance and Integrity in Africa.* Northampton, MA: Edward Elgar.

Hendry, J., King, C. (2015). How Far Is Too Far? Theorising Non-Conviction-Borthased Asset Forfeiture. *International Journal of Law in Context.* 11(4), pp. 398–411.

Hendry, J., King, C. (2017). Expediency, Legitimacy, and the Rule of Law: A Systems Perspective on Civil/Criminal Procedural Hybrids. *Criminal Law and Philosophy.* 11(4), pp. 733–757.

Home Office. (2016). *Criminal Finances Bill – Overarching Impact Assessment* (IA No: HO 0259). London: Home Office.

Home Office. (2019). *Asset Recovery Action Plan.* London: Home Office.

Ivec, M., Braithwaite, V. (2015). *Applications of Responsive Regulatory Theory in Australia and Overseas: Update* (RegNet Working Paper No. 72). Canberra: Regulatory Institutions Network (RegNet), ANU.

Jordanoska, A. (2018). The Dark Side of Finance: Policing Corruption through Regulatory Means. In: Campbell, L., Lord, N. (eds). *Corruption in Commercial Enterprise: Law, Theory and Practice.* Abingdon: Routledge, pp. 163–181.

Keen, F. (2017). *Unexplained Wealth Orders: Global Lessons for the UK Ahead of Implementation.* London: RUSI.

Kennedy, A. (2006). Designing a Civil Forfeiture System: An Issues List for Policymakers and Legislators. *Journal of Financial Crime.* 13(2), pp. 132–163.

King, C. (2014). Civil Forfeiture and Article 6 of the ECHR: Due Process Implications for England & Wales and Ireland. *Legal Studies.* 34(3), pp. 371–394.

Kuwait Transparency Society. (2013). *Transparency in Corporate Reporting – A Study of the 4 Largest Companies in Kuwait.* Kuwait: Kuwait Transparency Society.

Liberty. (2001). *Proceeds of Crime: Consultation on Draft Legislation.* London: Liberty (the National Council for Civil Liberties).

Makinwa, A. (2009). Researching Civil Remedies for International Corruption: The Choice of the Functional Comparative Method. *Erasmus Law Review.* 2(3), pp. 331–351.

Meyer, O. (2009). The Civil Law Consequences of Corruption – An Introduction. In: Meyer, O. (ed). *The Civil Law Consequences of Corruption.* Baden-Baden: NOMOS, pp. 15–20.

Mills, A. (2008). Applying the Enforcement Pyramid to Organisational Corruption Prevention. In: *Ethics and Integrity of Government Study Group, EGPA Conference, 3–5 September 2008, Rotterdam.* Rotterdam: EGPA.

Naylor, R. T. (1999). Wash-Out: A Critique of Follow-the-Money Methods in Crime Control Policy. *Crime, Law and Social Change.* 32(1), pp. 1–58.

Nazaha. (2017). *First Annual Report: 2016/2017.* Nazaha.

Nazaha. (2019). *Kuwait Integrity and Anti-Corruption Strategy 2019-2024.* Nazaha.

OECD. (2015). *Industry Self-Regulation: Role and Use in Supporting Consumer Interests.* Paris: OECD.

Parker, C. (2013). Twenty Years of Responsive Regulation: An Appreciation and Appraisal. *Regulation & Governance.* 7(1), pp. 2–13.

Rees, E., Fisher, R., Thomas, R. (2015). *Blackstone's Guide to the Proceeds of Crime Act 2002.* Oxford: Oxford University Press.

Rothstein, B., Sorak, N. (2017). *Ethical Codes for the Public Administration: A Comparative Study* (Working Paper Series 2017:12). Gothenburg, Sweden: University of Gothenburg.

Ryder, N. (2013). To Confiscate or Not to Confiscate? A Comparative Analysis of the Confiscation of the Proceeds of Crime Legislation in the United States of America and the United Kingdom. *Journal of Business Law*. 8, pp. 767–798.

Simser, J. (2009). Perspectives on Civil Forfeiture. In: Young, S. (ed). *Civil Forfeiture of Criminal Property: Legal Measures for Targeting the Proceeds of Crime*. Cheltenham, UK; Northampton, MA: Edward Elgar, pp. 13–20.

Sproat, P. (2018). Unexplained Wealth Orders: An Explanation, Assessment and Set of Predictions. *Journal of Criminal Law*. 82(3), pp. 232–244.

State Audit Bureau. (2018). *Minutes of Meeting of the Financial Irregularities Department With Annual Accounts and Audit Committee at the Kuwait National Assembly on 26 November 2018*. Kuwait: State Audit Bureau.

Transparency International UK. (2015). *Empowering the UK to Recover Corrupt Assets: Unexplained Wealth Orders and Other New Approaches to Illicit Enrichment and Asset Recovery*. London: Transparency International UK.

UNODC. (2003). *United Nations Guide on Anti-Corruption Policies*. Vienna: UN.

UNODC. (2004). *United Nations Anti-Corruption Toolkit*. Vienna: UN.

Weismann, M. F. (2009). The Foreign Corrupt Practices Act: The Failure of the Self-Regulatory Model of Corporate Governance in the Global Business Environment. *Journal of Business Ethics*. 88(4), pp. 615–661.

Whitton, H. (2001). *Implementing Effective Ethics Standards in Government and the Civil Service*. London: Transparency International.

Young, S. (2009). Why Civil Actions Against Corruption? *Journal of Financial Crime*. 16(2), pp. 144–159.

# 6 Conclusion

## 6.1 Introduction

This final chapter discusses the findings from the prior chapters and how each chapter has advanced its respective objective. Rather than restating what was done in detail, this chapter refers to the core findings regarding the corruption problem in Kuwait. The significance of the book findings is evident in a number of aspects. First, the findings determine a starting point for future researchers from which they may proceed to study corruption in Kuwait. Second, some of the book findings have direct policy implications. In particular, the findings of chapters 4 and 5, centring upon the need to innovate the current counter-corruption measures, are reform-oriented proposals which could be translated into action by policymakers. The originality of this book is further discussed in this current chapter and, in this respect, the focus on fieldwork is emphasised. Finally, issues that were not addressed in the book and which could be considered for future research are outlined.

This chapter proceeds as follows. Section 6.2 recaps the objective of each chapter and concentrates on what has been achieved. Section 6.3 emphasises the originality of this book with a particular focus on the author's experience of fieldwork and what he found useful. Section 6.4 addresses the limitations of this book and raises topics which were not covered and how these may be significant for future research. Overall, this chapter achieves the sixth objective of the book by building on chapters 2–5 in order to establish the conclusions and the findings of the book on how to counter grand corruption in Kuwait effectively.

## 6.2 Research objectives and key findings: What has been found

Although it is not a recent phenomenon, corruption has become more visible in public life in Kuwait. Citizens' concerns have become so omnipresent in the last decade that corruption has been an essential part of Kuwaiti political discourse. This reality drove the author to probe into the corruption phenomenon. The key starting questions were: what is the problem of corruption in Kuwait and what is the problem regarding Kuwaiti laws against corruption? Consequently, the general aim of this book was to address corruption in Kuwait and propose legal solutions to combat it. The author started with a general assumption that there is a problem of corruption in Kuwait. Having been influenced by his prior knowledge and experience as a lawyer (and given that this book is basically legal scholarship), the author proposed that the existing counter-corruption laws are part of that problem. Thus, the book plan was incorporated into chapter 1 where the book problem (the research assumptions), its scope, and its objectives were posited. However, because of the book methodologies adopted in chapter 1, the book assumptions were constantly subject to refinements. As a result, the contours of the problem became clearer as the book processed.

The overriding argument of this book has been that the corruption problem is primarily related to 'grand corruption'. The existing responses to grand corruption and the public discourse on combating corruption have been dominated by criminal law since corruption became more visible and discussed. There have been enough criminal law-based responses to corruption. These responses vary and have the potential to cover many forms of corruption. Some of the measures are innovative, such as the illicit enrichment offence (IEO). However, these responses are criticised from two perspectives. First, the current measures are unable to bring about their intended effects (preventing and prosecuting corruption). This is not because of the measures' inadequacies. As stated in the book introduction, 'Although there is a raft of criminal laws which are comprehensive enough (in content and scope) to cover many forms of corruption crimes, they suffer from poor enforcement'[1] and, on some occasions, they are misapplied, an example being the money laundering offence (ML offence).[2] Second, for a problem such as grand corruption, the criminal responses are insufficient in themselves: 'despite the adequacy of current criminal measures, criminal law alone is not per se adequate. Kuwait still lacks innovative measures to combat grand corruption'.[3] It was argued that an innovative approach to combat corruption should be incorporated into the current criminal law-dominated measures. This approach is mainly a non-criminal process which can be effectively harnessed as part of the state's efforts to counter corruption.[4] The foregoing key argument is a summary of what was studied in chapters 2–5 with the help of a cross-cutting methodology (chapter 1). The following discussion emphasises the key book findings of each chapter and how each objective assigned to each chapter has been achieved.

Methodology in chapter 1 addressed the book design and the multiple methodologies adopted in this book. In this regard, the chapter achieved the fifth cross-cutting methodological objective of the book to achieve a fuller understanding of the book subjects. The book is mainly a socio-legal study of grand corruption in Kuwait. First, a library-based methodology was adopted to

1 See chapters 1.1 and 3.2.2.
2 See chapter 4.3.5.
3 See chapter 1.1.
4 See chapters 4.4.2 and 4.4.2.

approach some of the research questions. In particular, two types of research were used: doctrinal legal and non-legal research. The doctrinal legal research helped to analyse the judgments and provisions of the relevant laws on corruption and other secondary legal sources. The legal analysis of these materials revealed significant findings which were not previously understood. The legal responses to corruption have been, from their inception, dominated by criminal law. Numerating and analysing the adopted criminal arrangements, it was found that the state has criminalised numerous potential forms of corruption, from traditional core offences, such as bribery and the diversion of public funds, to innovative provisions, such as financial disclosures and the IEO. The legal analysis (combined with empirical data gathered from professional experts) enabled the author to propose 'original' and 'valuable' insights related to corruption crimes, which also highlighted the insights' strengths and weaknesses. Potential legal solutions were then proposed to reflect what is needed in reality.[5]

The non-legal research was of particular importance for this book, not least because it supports the originality of the book. Such research rectified the limitations of legal research and studied the phenomenon of corruption beyond the law. Studying corruption from other social perspectives highlighted the multi-dimensional nature of corruption. The use of sources from sociocultural disciplines helped the author to investigate corruption as an embedded aspect of Kuwaiti society. Political science also crystallised corruption as a problem of the imbalance of power relations in Kuwait. An additional dimension was added to the corruption phenomenon in terms of the pursuit of the interests of corporate units and the corruption which occurs as an expected result. Analysing corruption from the perspective of the economy was also relevant. The structure of the Kuwaiti oil-dominated economy, the centralisation of economic power in the government, and the need to understand Kuwait as a rentier state, all facilitated a comprehension of the real nature of corruption in Kuwait.[6] Thus, the interdisciplinary study of corruption effectively captured the complex nature of this phenomenon in a manner that the legal approach struggles to depict fully.

Second, a qualitative methodology was also used to approach other research questions empirically. A fieldwork methodology based on semi-structured interviews was adopted as a technique. The importance of this methodology for the book is considered below.

Third, comparative legal research (confined to policy transfer) was utilised to draw lessons from, and take advantage of, other jurisdictions' experiences. This methodology directly relates to the aim of this book to propose solutions to combat corruption. The existence of leading and experienced international organisations in the field of counter-corruption, such as the United Nations (UN), World Bank, and Financial Action Task Force (FATF), renders recourse to their tools and recommendations inevitable. Furthermore, investigating how

5 See chapters 4.3 and 4.4.
6 See chapter 2.3.4.

other jurisdictions, especially the United Kingdom, are encountering corruption enabled the author to take into account the latest innovative approaches. In fact, the conservative nature of Kuwaiti policymakers was one of the reasons for considering what has been adopted elsewhere. Perhaps reluctance or conservatism on the part of stakeholders in Kuwait is responsible for the delay in adopting some counter-corruption innovative approaches, as evident in the criminalisation of IEO in 2012 despite the ratification of the UN Convention against Corruption (UNCAC) in 2006. Comparative research also enabled the author to benefit from other jurisdictions in terms of how they have addressed the potential challenges of some controversial legal instruments, such as the IEO. Thus, utilising 'policy transfer' was a valuable approach which allowed the author to take advantage of the experiences of other jurisdictions.

Chapter 2 (The Phenomenon of Corruption) essentially revolved around the literature review of corruption in order to achieve the first research objective, namely, to address the corruption phenomenon in order to understand its complexity both globally and in Kuwait. Key corruption-related issues were first visited as a preliminary step to study the problem of corruption. These issues were the definition of corruption and corruption's potential patterns, effects, and causes.[7] At first, these subjects were addressed in a general context. This step was useful and necessary in order to guide the book in terms of probing into the phenomenon of corruption in Kuwait. In light of the dearth of corruption research in Kuwait, the multiple perspectives of corruption, as highlighted in the literature, enabled the author to apply them to Kuwait. Reflecting on these issues, the parameters of the corruption phenomenon in Kuwait could be seamlessly analysed. The application of the literature of corruption to the situation in Kuwait was another original contribution of this book when approaching the subject of corruption in Kuwait.

After adopting a working definition of corruption which focuses on corruption in the public sector and investigating the potential patterns of corruption in the literature, a number of findings were concluded. The phenomenon of corruption in Kuwait is strongly linked to the public sector. The magnitude of the workforce in the public sector, the weak private sector, and the dominant role of the state in directing state institutions are factors which make corruption a problem more pertinent to the public sector than the private sector. This assumption does not mean that private sector corruption is unimportant; however, the relatively small number of transnational corporations in Kuwait, compared with other developed countries, may be one of the causes which diminish the seriousness of corporate corruption in Kuwait.

The lack of systematic data on corruption cases impeded the author from conclusively identifying any particular corruption pattern. However, the intrinsic features of Kuwait as a state helped to single out 'grand corruption' as a prevalent pattern, as confirmed by the literature. In particular, grand corruption

7 See chapter 2.2.

has lent itself as a problem which requires a deep analysis of the causes which explain its existence. The causes of grand corruption in Kuwait were analysed from a 'structural' point of view. Rather than perceiving corruption as an outcome of an 'opportunity', it was argued that it has intrinsic links with the sociocultural, political, and economic characteristics of Kuwait.[8] Driven by these three perspectives, this study of corruption in Kuwait proffered strong evidence to suggest that 'grand' corruption is the prevalent corruption pattern. This task was also facilitated by examining a number of corruption cases which indicated 'grand corruption' as the most problematic. These cases involved high-ranking officials and a large amount of money, both of which are particular characteristics of grand corruption. The identification of grand corruption as a problematic pattern in Kuwait sharpened the book problem and hence the book scope. At the beginning of the study, the research was directed to study corruption without any specification. By investigating the literature in abstract and applying it to Kuwait, the problem became clearer.

The focus on grand corruption has enlightened the analysis of other aspects of corruption and affected the direction of the analysis. When the effects of corruption were studied in general, corruption is argued to facilitate organised crime and crime in general (corruption–crime nexus).[9] However, grand corruption is expected to bring bad effects unique to the Kuwaiti context and is expressed as the 'corruption–governance nexus'. In Kuwait, there are less concerns raised by the potential link of corruption to organised crime than the effects of grand corruption on the way in which state institutions are administered. It was found that grand corruption is responsible for, for example, the distortion of expenditure on public investments, the low economic growth in Kuwait, and other managerial problems.[10]

The issues addressed in chapter 2 were helpful in identifying the parameters of the problem in Kuwait, which had implications for the other chapters. First, grand corruption implies that the problem is related to the higher tier of policymakers and officials. That the problem is associated with high-ranking officeholders means that part of the reforms should, in the first instance, be directed at them. Thus, chapter 3 partly focused on the transparency of state administration and the political and legal accountability of politicians and officeholders. Second, combating grand corruption requires distinct legal efforts which are commensurate with the difficulties raised by grand corruption. Thus, chapters 4 and 5 considered the nature of 'grand' corruption when addressing the legal and regulatory responses and when suggesting innovative approaches. The bad news is that these efforts are assumed to be constantly challenged. When the policymakers are themselves part of the problem, the changes are expected to be impeded. In this context, political dynamics and the external pressure of

8 See chapter 2.3.4.
9 See chapter 2.2.3.2.
10 See chapter 2.3.3.

international organisations (whatever the type of pressure) can play significant roles which prompt internal changes.

In order to achieve the second objective of the book, chapter 3 (Counter-Corruption: Values and Strategies) extended the analysis of the literature of corruption but from a different perspective. Two key areas related were investigated. The first was the values that should accompany and underpin efforts to combat corruption. Legitimacy and effectiveness were chosen as key values because of their relevance. Sub-values were also identified under 'legitimacy': transparency, accountability, human rights, morality of the law, and legal certainty.[11] Rather than redefining the values, the aim of applying them was to reinforce the legitimacy of the state's efforts to combat corruption. The relative democratic nature of the regime in Kuwait and the associated values of freedom, justice, and equality strongly link the values previously mentioned to the fate of any efforts against corruption. Simply put, when counter-corruption measures are perceived legitimate by subordinates, people are expected to show more compliance with laws and cooperate with state institutions. Legitimacy then reflects on the effectiveness of counter-corruption efforts.

'Effectiveness' was identified as a second key value.[12] Securing an effective legal framework and adopting evidence-based policymaking were proposed as two measures to promote the state's efforts to counter corruption. Ultimately, what enables the law enforcement authorities to combat corruption is a set of laws and powers which often need to be updated and reformed to keep up with developments in the criminality of corruption. The empirical analysis of the importance of 'effectiveness' in Kuwait opened a debate about other issues. Thus, the adequacy of current counter-corruption criminal laws, the poor enforcement of laws in Kuwait, and the lack of awareness of the role of civil law to combat corruption were identified as pertinent. The latter issue affected the reshaping of the assumptions of the book and re-shifted the analysis, in some parts, to civil law-based approaches to corruption. Addressing the prior values, and their potential links to the counter-corruption process, highlighted valuable issues which can be subject to further analysis in future research.

The second area related to corruption which was investigated concerned key relevant strategies which have been globally devised to combat corruption. These were social empowerment,[13] law enforcement,[14] and preventive strategies.[15] It was suggested that corruption should be combated using these multi-dimensional strategies: people and civil society should be empowered to help, or induce state institutions, to counter corruption, corruption cases should be prosecuted and the corrupt must be punished, and corruption should be prevented *ex ante*.

11 See chapter 3.2.1.
12 See chapter 3.2.2.
13 See chapter 3.3.1.
14 See chapter 3.3.2.
15 See chapter 3.3.3.

These strategies were addressed in abstract and reflected upon in later chapters. However, because this book mainly takes laws and regulations as key means to combat corruption, discussing the strategy of social empowerment was limited to chapter 3. Basically, two strategies of the three mentioned (law enforcement and prevention) underpinned the responses in chapter 4 and chapter 5.

Chapter 4 (Kuwaiti Criminal Counter-Corruption Measures) focused on the aim of this book to respond to corruption from a socio-legal perspective. The author analysed the criminal counter-corruption measures which have been adopted by Kuwaiti policymakers. Besides what was found in chapter 3, a number of conclusions may be inferred from chapter 4. Kuwaiti policymakers have been prolific in their counter-corruption responses, and each potential form of corruption has almost been covered, be it traditional, such as bribery, or innovative, such as the IEO. The possibility of disgorging the illicit financial gains of corruption has also increased through the introduction of the Anti-Money Laundering and Countering Financing of Terrorism Act 106/2013 (AML/CFT Act). In general, criminal law has been, and is still being, used as the key instrument. The empirically consolidated legal analysis of criminal responses revealed that they are not so much flawed as having only some typical difficulties that are inherent in the use of criminal law, such as *mens rea* problems and evidence-based difficulties. Kuwaiti policymakers have already recognised these challenges and since 2012 have introduced the IEO (and associated financial disclosures), although the fruits of this innovation have not been reaped yet.[16] A comprehensive whistleblowing system has also been incorporated into Kuwaiti laws.[17] However, extra innovation is still required.

The elusive nature of corruption crimes assumes the need to empower prosecutors with more discretion to manoeuvre. It was found that there is a lack of prosecutorial policy to deal with corruption crimes. The prosecutors are faced with rigid arrangements of criminal justice. For example, they are not able to enter into agreements to elicit the cooperation of suspects in corruption cases. Consequently, deferred prosecution agreements (DPAs) were suggested as a prosecutorial tool to settle serious corruption cases when the prosecutor decides that it is in the interest of an investigation, such as when there is a risk of acquittal because of the lack of strong evidence.[18] An innovative 'bounty hunting scheme' was suggested to break the trust inherent in corrupt deals through privileging one party of the deal who is the first to cooperate with law enforcement authorities.[19] A 'public mobilisation strategy' was also proposed to resist the cultural factors which might inhibit whistleblowing.[20] These three approaches represent part of the original contribution of this book to suggest innovative approaches to combat corruption in Kuwait.

16 See chapter 4.3.5.
17 See chapter 4.3.7.
18 See chapter 4.4.2.2.
19 See chapter 4.4.2.1.
20 See chapter 4.4.2.1.

Unlike the less controversial strategy of public mobilisation, the feasibility of the DPAs and the bounty hunting scheme need some examination, at least from the perspective of Kuwaiti policymakers. The diminished role of the judges with regard to DPAs seems to be controversial and less palatable in the context of the legal system in Kuwait where the court assumes full control of a criminal trial. However, in other areas of law, such as customs, stock exchange, and electronic transactions offences, the Kuwaiti legislator has already adopted a similar measure whereby law enforcement authorities are allowed to enter into an agreement with offenders in order to settle offences without prosecutions.[21] Although the rationales underpinning these types of settlement may differ, corruption crimes also have specificity. Agreements in corruption crimes can be inevitable in some cases. It does not matter whether the Kuwaiti policymakers import the system of DPAs as it operates in other jurisdictions. The gist of the idea is that prosecutors should always be empowered to enter into agreements with offenders in corruption crimes as long as the interests of the investigation so require.

The bounty hunting scheme, as suggested, may conflict with the idea that criminals should not benefit from their crime. However, in the context of the bribery offence in Kuwait, the briber is always encouraged to report the crime even after its commission. To that end, the briber will receive back whatever was paid as a bribe. In other forms of corruption, whistleblowing should be designed to take into account the role of offenders. Apart from outsiders (whistleblowers who are not part of the corrupt deal), the risks of mutual betrayal among the parties of a corrupt transaction must be increased to make corruption more troublesome. The idea is not to reward the corrupt; instead, individuals should be dissuaded from engaging in corruption in light of what Lambsdorff argued; namely, that 'The unreliability of corrupt counterparts induces honesty and good governance even in the absence of good intentions'.[22] Under specific requirements, Kuwaiti laws already exempt offenders who cooperate with law enforcement authorities; however, this is insufficient for lucrative corruption activities.[23] Privileging the defector, by any means, at the expense of the other criminal(s) either deters corruption *ex ante* or facilitates its detection. Nevertheless, it can be said, in general, that the need for this innovative bounty hunting scheme will be more urgent when the existing whistleblowing system fails, although it is too early to assess the scheme's effectiveness.

What is left then? The abundance of corruption laws will not achieve their deterrent role unless relevant governance issues are considered. Of particular importance here is the value of accountability. Corruption must not pay or pass unnoticed. Public officials and politicians should always be held legally accountable and none must enjoy impunity. Arguably, the focus may be more on legal than political accountability where, with regard to the former, a corrupt

21 See chapter 4.3.7.

22 Lambsdorff (2009, p. 398).

23 See chapter 4.3.7.

person faces serious consequences resulting from his/her corrupt conduct.[24] The effects of legal accountability require effective enforcement of relevant laws. On numerous occasions, the current laws have successfully secured the conviction of corrupt officials when the laws have been properly enforced. These cases have included notorious instances of grand corruption where huge sums were stolen.[25] Some cases involved assets located abroad, a situation which requires an effective framework of international cooperation to repatriate the assets to Kuwait,[26] but no technical difficulties related to criminal laws were raised in such cases. The common feature of these cases was the successful and effective employment of the accountability mechanisms. Thus, before thinking of reforming the existing laws or introducing any new tools, such attempts should be, as Naylor has suggested, subject to a qualification that the failure of existing measures is attributable to the deficiencies in the measures themselves and not because of deficiencies in the implementation and enforcement of these measures.[27] However, the use of criminal law in combating 'grand corruption cases' is sometimes challenging and may raise political sensitivity. In cases where it is not realistic to initiate criminal proceedings against high-profile actors, other non-criminal measures seem to be more workable and need to be explored.

In order to achieve the fourth objective, chapter 5 (Kuwaiti Non-Criminal Counter-Corruption Measures) complemented chapter 4 in finding appropriate responses to combat corruption. Chapter 5 identified potential non-criminal responses guided by the 'enforcement pyramid' approach.[28] This approach suggests that the state's responses to corruption should be gradual based on the seriousness of the criminal act. To this end, the current measures against corruption are categorised into four types: persuasive (civil service codes and self-regulation), civil, administrative, and criminal. Addressing the potential role of Kuwaiti non-criminal measures to combat corruption in general, and the use of an 'enforcement pyramid' to categorise these measures specifically, adds a new dimension to the counter-corruption process in Kuwait.

Civil service codes were found to play an educative role in raising the awareness of officials about the behaviour expected in public service.[29] The values and principles which govern public service should be effectively instilled in order to encourage officeholders to comply. Before punishing them, officials should be educated not to violate laws. Among other aims, the persuasive role of civil

24 See chapter 3.2.1.2.

25 See, for example, Case No. 336/2012, 21/7/2013 (Supreme Court – Criminal Division), Case No. 1200/2016, 27/03/2017 (Supreme Court – Criminal Division 2), Case No. 1499/2008, 27/6/2019 (First Instance Court – Criminal Division 10), Case No. 1246/2017, 16/12/2018 (First Instance Court – Criminal Division 2), and Case No. 1942/2015, 6/5/2018 (First Instance Court – Criminal Division).

26 See below section 6.4.

27 Naylor (1999).

28 See chapter 5.3.1.

29 See chapter 5.3.2.1.

service codes prevents officials from engaging in corrupt practices. Moreover, when officials engage in corrupt practices, the civil service codes can legitimise subsequent action taken by the state.

The private sector plays a key role in instigating corruption; however, this role can be harnessed to combat or prevent corruption. Decentring some counter-corruption regulations to the private sector through self-regulation and co-regulation is a persuasive measure to engage relevant business sectors in the fight against corruption.[30] Despite its significance, the concept of self-regulation in Kuwait is amorphous and limited to the arena of anti-money laundering (AML).[31] In other areas of corruption, counter-corruption efforts are still state-centred. The immaturity of self-regulation may be partly affected by the relatively limited size of the private sector in Kuwait, which reflects the small chance of the sector's involvement in corrupt practices. However, in areas such as public procurement, private sector companies are likely to intersect with venal officeholders, a situation which requires the former to have internal integrity systems in place which effectively prohibit any corrupt practice and promote a corruption-free business environment.

The administrative measures embodied in disciplinary offences complement the criminal measures.[32] They were found to achieve two purposes. The first is that a disciplinary offence may be proportionate to deal with trivial violations. The second is that disciplinary offences enable state institutions to take expeditious measures against the offending officials. When offenders are referred to the public prosecutor, state institutions can suspend the officials temporarily from exercising their authority. Above all, enabling state institutions to take disciplinary actions against their officials may help prevent more serious conduct from being exacerbated or even taking place. Punishing, or threatening to punish, officials at an earlier stage can effectively dissuade them from developing their criminal enterprises.

Civil lawsuits are also an alternative to criminal measures. Whenever a criminal prosecution is not possible for any reason, there are still other paths to pursue. Just because there is a lack of strong evidence which meets the criminal standard of proof (beyond reasonable doubt), we must not turn a blind eye to suspiciously dirty assets. Suspicious assets should always be targeted, and none should benefit from these assets. In any case, if the authorities are convinced that particular assets are of illicit origin (when, of course, there is evidence and not mere suspicion), the civil law provides these authorities with alternative solutions: instead of initiating criminal proceedings, *in rem* measures may be taken to disgorge those assets from their owners. In Kuwait, the existing laws provide the state with rights of action to initiate civil claims.[33] However, the current

30 See chapter 5.3.2.2.
31 See chapters 5.3.2.2 and 6.4.1.
32 See chapter 5.3.4.
33 See chapter 5.3.3.

civil arrangements are general in nature and may be used for many purposes. Although civil law provisions can be used to recover assets derived from unlawful conduct, the use of such provisions is limited. Regardless of the challenge of establishing the state's ownership of the illicit assets, it is argued that the generality of the existing provisions obfuscates their potential use in Kuwait. This generality can be responsible for the absence of civil law's role in the public discourse on combating corruption in Kuwait. As a result, ad hoc arrangements are suggested. The creation of a civil forfeiture regime that is specifically geared to use civil law techniques in the context of combating crime was analysed.[34] Not only does civil forfeiture lend itself as an alternative to criminal proceedings, but it also serves as a deterrent measure, bearing the following message to the corrupt: if you are not sent to prison, you will at least not enjoy the outcomes of your corrupt conduct.

As part of the book' commitment to provide an original contribution regarding counter-corruption in Kuwait, chapter 5 suggested a radical approach to combat corruption by shifting the focus from 'corrupt individuals' to the 'recovery of assets'; namely, from the use of criminal law means to the civil law means. However, overlooking the role of criminal law in corruption was never the gist of chapter 5. In contrast, it is proposed that, on some occasions, non-criminal means (and civil law techniques specifically) may be more realistic and workable, be it in politically sensitive cases or when there is a lack of strong evidence which meets the standard required for criminal trials. Indeed, a point which cannot be overstated is what the Asset Recovery Plan of the United Kingdom (UK) asserted that 'money is the common thread that runs through almost all offending'.[35] The potential role of civil proceedings is that they are directed at a key motivation of corruption crimes: making money. Eventually, to facilitate the gathering of evidence which makes civil forfeiture more effective, it was suggested that Kuwait should use an innovative investigative power adopted in some other jurisdictions: unexplained wealth orders (UWOs).[36]

If adopted, civil forfeiture and UWO laws may face some challenges in Kuwait, not least constitutional challenges.[37] Their introduction is feasible, though. The civil nature of civil forfeiture[38] lends itself as an amenable idea. The national interest to combat a detrimental problem such as corruption should outweigh other considerations. Whenever the use of criminal law is not possible, law enforcement authorities must not be left powerless: they should always be granted other legal instruments to pursue the corrupt, or at least their illicit assets if not the individuals. Thus, civil forfeiture can be based on considerations of efficiency and expediency. In the end, civil forfeiture is not arbitrary; it is still

34 See chapter 5.4.2.1.

35 See Home Office (2019, p. 3).

36 See chapter 5.4.2.2.

37 See chapters 5.4.2.1 and 5.4.2.2.

38 Although its nature is contested. See chapter 5.4.2.1.

an action which must go through the courts and be based on evidence. UWOs, on the other hand, would not be radical for Kuwaiti law. UWOs have a number of commonalities with the IEO and financial disclosures which are already adopted in the Anti-Corruption Authority and Financial Disclosure Act 2/2016 (ACAA).[39] In addition, restricting the use of UWOs to civil proceedings renders them less susceptible to resistance related to concerns about human rights.

## 6.3 Originality: A fieldwork study

The originality of the book has already been emphasised in chapter 1, where it was shown that this is the first legal scholarship that has encompassed the study of the phenomenon of corruption, and particularly grand corruption, from multiple perspectives.[40] Further, the originality of the book was illustrated while discussing the achievements of each chapter. However, a qualitative methodology (involving fieldwork study) is proclaimed to be one of the most important aspects which supports the originality of the book. This fieldwork enabled the author to collect original and valuable data which helped to address many of the issues in this book from an empirical perspective. In such a context, this section reflects upon the following questions: why was fieldwork relevant for this book, what did the fieldwork reveal, and how was the book's experience?

When the author chose 'corruption' as his book subject, he assumed that the related research would be fraught with challenges. At least three challenges were expected. The first is the novelty of Kuwait's experience in combating corruption. The efforts to combat the various forms of corruption started, for example, with the criminalisation of bribery in 1960 and crimes against the public purse in 1993. However, systematic efforts to combat corruption arguably started in 2012 with the enactment of the ACAA,[41] which involved the establishment of the Anti-Corruption Authority (Nazaha) and the criminalisation of IEO. Actually, ACAA was re-enacted in 2016 and actual experience should begin from that year.[42] The second challenge is the sensitivity of the topic and the lack of support which the author expected from the stakeholders in Kuwait. The third is the political nature of the topic. Corruption is a widely politicised issue which negatively affects the reliability of sources. Politicians (legislators and ministers) were more willing to speak politically about counter-corruption matters, which negatively affected the legal nature of some interview questions related to laws. Even with the scarcity of reliable sources on corruption produced by the government, academic scholars, and neutral think tanks, the author, on some occasions, was reluctant to depend upon these sources. The problem

39 See chapter 5.4.2.2.
40 See chapter 1.2.
41 ACAA 24/2012.
42 ACAA 2/2016.

became starker when the focus of the book was directed at 'grand corruption' and obscured by the frequent involvement of politicians and high-profile figures in grand corruption cases. Faced with these challenges, resorting to fieldwork to seek reliable sources, namely elite professionals, was inevitable for the achievement of this book.

First, interviewing the experts proved effective at producing original insights and enriched the analytical output of this book. The fact that the participants were chosen based on their experience in relation to counter-corruption allowed them to translate their empirical experience into comments. Their privileged positions and frequent access to corruption cases, or even their wider interest in dealing with corruption-related issues, shed light on issues which were not in the public domain. New patterns and themes were inferred from the data obtained from the interviewees. These insightful data could not have been obtained elsewhere because the experts are not encouraged to write about their views regarding the counter-corruption process, nor are they incentivised enough to conduct research (as evident in the general lack of evidence-based policymaking). Moreover, the interviews with experts helped to focus more effectively on the technicalities of complex corruption laws. When the author analysed some legal texts, many questions were unsolved. There was no possible way to answer these questions other than through a review of the opinions of experts, opinions which the documents lack. Hence, the author produced an original analysis of the issues in question.

The success of the fieldwork, in fact, was not only a result of an appropriate selection of research participants. Fortunately, the fieldwork, which lasted from October to December 2018, coincided with a campaign against corruption under the auspices of the Kuwaiti government and the National Assembly. The interest of the state in countering corruption was reified in major reforms which were being prepared by Nazaha and other state institutions. These reforms included the Kuwait Counter-Corruption Strategy 2019–2024 (Strategy 2019–2024). This governmental campaign informally encouraged the responsiveness of a number of interviewees to participate in the fieldwork.

Not only did the fieldwork succeed in achieving a large part of the planned tasks, it also yielded other valuable results. These results involved issues which pointed to critical matters which may stimulate further research in the future, although they were not part of the research objectives and have not been subject to comprehensive examination here. Among the issues observed was one pertaining to the expertise of those involved in combating corruption. Although the research sampling sought to interview participants close to the counter-corruption processes, the interviewees showed varying degrees of experience. Some participants apologised for not participating, justifying their non-participation because of a lack of knowledge. In some cases, the author was referred to other experienced participants within the same cohort. Some interviews were excluded, after being conducted, for data quality reasons. The participants involved were so inexperienced that their responses were shallow, and with some questions they were unable to respond or gave incorrect answers. The author ensured that the interviewees participated voluntarily without any coercion; indeed, they were welcoming and showed their willingness to take part.

Some participants were unsure about a number of questions. During one interviewee, Judge-1 commented, with tongue in cheek, whether I had questions about drug offences. In general, the experience of judges and prosecutors in relation to corruption crimes was confined to a limited range of such crimes, for example embezzlement and criminal damage of public property offences, which means that they did not have sufficient knowledge about other corruption crimes (such as the ML offence and the IEO). Other participants were clear from the beginning and stated that their expertise was limited to some corruption cases in which they were involved. Lawyer-2 expressed his/her desire to only answer questions related to the areas he/she dealt with. Lawyers also lacked sufficient expertise in relation to counter-corruption laws because some of them told me: 'we are more familiar with traditional crimes, such as drugs offences, than white collar crimes.'[43] The lack of experience was also noticeable regarding Nazaha. The participants from Nazaha showed some competence in answering many questions during the interviews. They could address many of the technicalities of the counter-corruption laws; however, they barely answered the questions posed. They did not meet the expectations of the author in going beyond the questions and visiting other areas of counter-corruption. For example, in a side dialogue with Official-2 about whether there is political will to introduce a civil forfeiture regime in Kuwait, he/she responded that he/she had no idea about the nature of civil forfeiture; hence, no affirmative response could be obtained.

When asked about the role of the government in upholding the role of civil society in combating corruption, NGO-1 answered: 'when we met with [a relevant governmental agency], its Director was confused as he did not have a sufficiently specialised cadre to meet the expectations of the sudden governmental campaign against corruption'. MP-2 arrived at similar conclusions about the role of this agency: 'they have not succeeded in recognising their serious and critical role'. The resort of policymakers to the United Nations Development Programme (UNDP) and the United Nations Office on Drugs and Crime (UNODC) in setting up the Strategy 2019–2024 is only one piece of evidence of their lack of expertise. Regardless of the insightful data obtained, it may be said that the fieldwork uncovered the lack of full familiarity of Kuwaiti professionals with the laws on corruption. During the fieldwork, there was a shortage of experts in the counter-corruption fields. There were many instances where the author struggled to find a specialist who could confidently speak about counter-corruption laws, policies, and regulation. The complexity of corruption laws requires more professional cadres which are aware of this complexity. Thus, ongoing training programmes for those who are involved in the counter-corruption process are indispensable, especially in the forthcoming stage in which Kuwait has many counter-corruption objectives to achieve.

43 Lawyer-2.

Another valuable observation is that the fieldwork has underlined the dissatisfaction among a number of experts with the current level of enforcement of counter-corruption laws. Paradoxically, this conclusion was inferred despite the experts' 'relative' satisfaction with the existing measures against corruption.[44] MP-2 pointed to what he/she called a 'comprehensive system of corruption laws and mechanisms.' Judge-1, at the end of the interview, emphasised that 'a raft of laws has been legislated so far to govern even the "tiny" matters'. What that interviewee wanted to say is that Kuwaiti judges have enough laws to apply to corruption cases and that the legal infrastructure of corruption laws is sufficient to correspond to the current level of criminality. However, when asked what the problem is, Judge-1 expressed his/her desire not to participate in what he/she called 'politicised questions'.

Probably one of the most convincing explanations for this paradox is to return to the issue of political will. In the corruption literature, political will is argued to be a significant factor for fighting corruption.[45] Political will includes both the initiation of the fight against corruption and the effective implementation of existing counter-corruption laws. Some commentators also link the lack of political will to the unwillingness to recover stolen assets which are located abroad.[46] Singling out isolated corruption cases, albeit sporadically, uncovers the fact that the state is able to bring corruption to justice when those who have the power want to do so. However, a sustained political motivation to target corruption is challenging in the context of 'grand corruption'. When the problem of corruption involves the policymakers themselves, it is unrealistic to expect a sustainable, genuine intent on their part to combat corruption. The environment in which grand corruption takes place, namely when corruption is systemic and an inherent part of the way state institutions operate, further complicates the problem. Thus, the impetus to counter corruption resides with those who are part of the problem. What can be concluded from this analysis is that in a small country such as Kuwait, which has many counter-corruption laws, corruption becomes, to a large extent, controllable as long as the government is willing to take action to reduce the effects of corruption.

## 6.4 Future research

This book was limited in its scope. It was restricted to investigating grand corruption, which is by its nature related to the public sector, and studying current Kuwaiti laws and regulations against corruption. Given some limitations, other significant areas were excluded from the book scope. In Kuwait, both academics and practitioners are required to conduct further intensive theoretical and empirical research to cover each potential aspect of the corruption problem,

44 See chapter 3.2.2.1.

45 See, for example, Brinkerhoff (2000).

46 See Ziouvas (2018).

and hence to capture its complexity. With this in mind, the following discussion refers to a number of topics which are suggested for future research. The importance of some of these topics was already recognised from the beginning of the book, while the importance of other subjects has been developed during the writing of the book.

The counter-corruption institutional framework in Kuwait is one of the topics proposed for further research. Future studies could focus on the role of institutions in the process against corruption. There are several relevant institutions in Kuwait. Some of these have supervisory functions in relation to public finances, such as the Supreme Audit Bureau (SAB) and the Financial Controllers Bureau (FCB). Other institutions have direct remits with regard to corruption crimes, such as the Kuwait Financial Intelligence Unit (KFIU), Nazaha, the prosecutors, and the judiciary. Some of these institutions have been studied; for example, a questionnaire-based non-legal study on the role of the SAB has been published,[47] the role of public prosecution in embezzlement and misappropriation offences has been investigated,[48] and the administrative model of the KFIU has also been analysed, focusing, inter alia, on its structural characteristics.[49] Notwithstanding these scholarly works, there is still much to do. The three studies which have been concluded so far are limited. There should be more empirical studies, adopting qualitative methodologies, to examine the aforementioned institutions. Qualitative studies are recommended here because of their advantage in enabling researchers to understand the modus operandi of such institutions. Approaching these institutions empirically contributes to an understanding of key issues: the obstacles which institutions may face, their weaknesses and strengths, and their effectiveness. For example, since the ML offence has a strong link to corruption crimes, further research is needed to analyse the role of the KFIU in preventing and combating the offence and to assess its effectiveness. Research may shed light on the operations of the KFIU, including its relationship with the public prosecutor, banks, and its counterparts in foreign jurisdictions.

Public finance has recently elicited the attention of policymakers in Kuwait as a vital sector in a state-dominated economy.[50] Future studies could illuminate new areas of public finance-focused research in Kuwait. They could ask: how can the supervisory roles of the SAB and the FCB be harnessed in the counter-corruption process? In this regard, a qualitative study would be helpful in raising numerous issues: for example, to understand the intricacy of corruption practices and how corruption takes place in the daily life of governmental bodies, how corruption practices can be detected, and how coordination and liaison between supervisory institutions and other institutions (such as the prosecutors)

47 See Al-Qarioti (2015).
48 See Al-Mulaifi (2018).
49 See Jusic (2017).
50 See Nazaha (2019).

may increase the institutions' effectiveness. Comparative innovative approaches might also help.

It would be helpful if a dedicated study were to be undertaken into the institutional role of Nazaha in preventing and combating corruption in Kuwait. The lack of studies on Nazaha is understandable, given its relative novelty. However, enough time has passed from its inception in 2012 (and its reestablishment in 2016). Nazaha now plays a key role. The outcomes of the recent investigations undertaken by Nazaha in a number of grand corruption cases (including IEO cases) should be studied to find out whether Nazaha has been successful in dealing with corruption. Moreover, this role has been emphasised with the promulgation of the Strategy 2019–2024 whereby Nazaha has been mandated with numerous duties. The implementation of the Strategy, however, is yet to be assessed. All these developments in Kuwait necessitate a focused study on how Nazaha really works.

Rose-Ackerman emphasised that 'Corruption is sometimes discussed as if it were a broad generic concept. In practice, however, it operates at the sector level'.[51] Thus, a second potential research area would involve studying corruption in risky areas. This book considered studying the corruption phenomenon in Kuwait from a holistic angle. However, it is preferable for future studies to undertake a micro-level diagnosis of the loci which are most vulnerable to corruption. The core of these studies could focus on the dynamics of corruption in vulnerable loci so that one can design a distinct institutional framework which, in combating corruption, takes into account the specificities of the sector in question. A targeted sectoral approach, which studies the causes of corruption in a specific sector and proposes counter-corruption interventions on an ad hoc basis, would be more practical with regard to locating the entry points for tackling corruption. In this context, there are a number of loci where corruption may be prevalent, such as public works, service delivery sectors, public procurement, and oil revenues management. In particular, corruption within these loci could be subject to a criminological study which addresses the corruption problem from the perspective of situational crime prevention (SCP). SCP is more able to have policy implications. Moreover, SCP, and its underpinning theories and techniques, may provide a more realistic and practical framework in which corruption can be understood, and hence tackled.

Finally, studying how to combat grand corruption has underlined the key role which international cooperation plays in the process. The transnational nature of grand corruption cases may prompt future researchers to look beyond the combating of corruption domestically and to study international cooperation in grand corruption cases between Kuwait and other jurisdictions. This area requires further research enlightenment on numerous related issues. First, studying the existing statutory provisions on international cooperation in the relevant cases. Second, fully understanding the complex process in which domestic institutions, such as Nazaha and the prosecutors, deal with cases across borders,

51 Rose-Ackerman (2010, p. 60).

with a particular focus upon the potential jurisdictions which the corrupt often target. Third, assessing the effectiveness of domestic institutions in the process of international cooperation, including eliciting the cooperation of other jurisdictions. Fourth, if needed, considering how Kuwait can improve its domestic provisions to facilitate the process of international cooperation.

This book has been based on the assumption that potential legal studies on corruption which focus only on technicalities are not enough; it is always preferable to study corruption within broader contexts. Therefore, this book has analysed the phenomenon of corruption in Kuwait in a detailed socio-legal study relating to grand corruption as reflected in law and regulation, with particular emphasis on its multiple facets (corruption forms) and how they may be combated. The book can be seen as a corrective step in the sense that it addresses the problem underpinning much of the existing studies in Kuwait, studies which have focused on corruption crimes or counter-corruption institutions. With this in mind, this study is a necessary beginning and foundation for other related studies because it has made an initial step in developing a socio-legal understanding of the problem of corruption in Kuwait. In addition, this book has considered the opinions of professional experts to suggest reforms to the existing criminal counter-corruption laws. It has also looked beyond the criminal law as a dominant means to counter corruption in Kuwait and suggested a number of non-criminal innovative approaches, which are assumed to be workable for the situation in Kuwait.

## Bibliography

Al-Mulaifi, O. (2018). *The Role of the Public Prosecution in the Investigation and Disposition of Public Fund Crimes.* Kuwait: Kuwait International Law School.

Al-Qarioti, M. (2015). Kuwaiti Audit Bureau Role in Auditing Government Agencies from Employees' Perspectives: An Exploratory Study. *Journal of Business Theory and Practice.* 3(1), pp. 61–80.

Brinkerhoff, D. (2000). Assessing Political Will for Anti-Corruption Efforts: An Analytic Framework. *Public Administration and Development.* 20(3), pp. 239–252.

Home Office. (2019). *Asset Recovery Action Plan.* London: Home Office.

Jusic, A. (2017). Kuwait's Administrative Risk-Based Model for the Prevention of Money Laundering: Costs and Benefits of Compliance With the Financial Action Task Force (FATF) Standards. *Arab Law Quarterly.* 31(2), pp. 101–133.

Lambsdorff, J. (2009). The Organization of Anti-Corruption: Getting Incentives Right. In: Rotberg, R. (ed). *Corruption, Global Security, and World Order.* Baltimore, MD: Brookings Institution Press, pp. 389–415.

Naylor, R. T. (1999). Wash-Out: A Critique of Follow-the-Money Methods in Crime Control Policy. *Crime, Law and Social Change.* 32(1), pp. 1–58.

Nazaha. (2019). *Kuwait Integrity and Anti-Corruption Strategy 2019–2024.* Nazaha.

Rose-Ackerman, S. (2010). The Institutional Economics of Corruption. In: de Graaf, G., von Maravic, P., Wagenaar, P. (eds). *The Good Cause: Theoretical Perspective on Corruption.* Opladen: Barbara Budrich, pp. 47–63.

Ziouvas, D. (2018). International Asset Recovery and the United Nations Convention Against Corruption. In: King, C., Walker, C., Gurulé, J. (eds). *The Palgrave Handbook of Criminal and Terrorism Financing Law.* London: Palgrave Macmillan, pp. 591–620.

# Appendices

## 1.1 Appendix 1: Interview guide

Section 1: Biography

| *No.* | *Question* |
|---|---|
| *1* | What is your job title? |
| *2* | Could you describe your duties or role in relation to the counter-corruption process? |
| *3* | What is your experience of corruption cases? |

Section 2: The phenomenon of corruption in Kuwait

| *No.* | *Question* |
|---|---|
| *4* | 4.1. What is the definition of corruption in Kuwaiti law?<br>4.2. Do you think that the law defines corruption in a proper way?<br>• If yes, how? Can you give any examples from your experience?<br>• If no, why? |
| *5* | Are they any features of Kuwaiti society which encourage corruption?<br>• If yes, how? Can you give any examples from your experience?<br>• If no, why? |
| *6* | Does the heavy economic dependence on oil link with the problem of corruption?<br>• If yes, how? Can you give any examples from your experience?<br>• If no, why? |

Section 3: Counter-corruption: Values and strategies

| *No.* | *Question* |
|---|---|
| *7* | 7.1. Do you know what the counter-corruption policy in Kuwait is?<br>7.2. Is it comprehensive?<br>• If yes, how?<br>• If no, why? |

| | |
|---|---|
| *8* | 8.1. In your opinion, are counter-corruption laws effective or fair?<br>• If effective, how? Can you give any examples from your experience?<br>• If fair, how?<br>8.2. What is more important (and should be prioritised)? Effectiveness or fairness?<br>• If effectiveness, why? Can you give any examples from your experience?<br>• If fairness, why? |
| *9* | 9.1. In general, are corrupt public officeholders held accountable for corruption?<br>• If yes, how? Can you give any examples from your experience?<br>• If not, why?<br>9.2. Are high officials more accountable or less accountable than low office holders?<br>• If more, how? Can you give any examples from your experience?<br>• If less, why?<br>9.3. Are politicians more/less accountable than officeholders?<br>• If more, how? Can you give any examples from your experience?<br>• If less, why? |
| *10* | 10.1. Does the civil society (including civic associations, media, and press) in Kuwait play a role in combating corruption?<br>• If yes, how? Can you give any examples from your experience?<br>• If not, why?<br>10.2. Does the government do enough to empower the civic associations (that have counter-corruption objectives, such Kuwait Transparency Society and Kuwait Association for Protecting Public Funds) to perform their role?<br>• If yes, how? Can you give any examples from your experience?<br>• If not, why? |
| *11* | Does the Parliament play a role in combating corruption?<br>• If yes, how? Can you give any examples from your experience?<br>• If not, why? |
| *12* | Do the courts play a role in combating corruption?<br>• If yes, how? Can you give any examples from your experience?<br>• If not, why? |
| *13* | Could freedom of information legislation prevent and combat corruption?<br>• If yes, how? And why does Kuwait lack such a legislation?<br>• If no, why not? |

Section 4: Counter-corruption laws

| *No.* | *Question* |
|---|---|
| *14* | 14.1. Are the bribery offences effective and fair as mechanisms against corruption in Kuwait?<br>• If yes, how? Can you give any examples from your experience?<br>• If no, why not?<br>14.2. What further steps might be taken to secure their effectiveness and fairness? |
| *15* | 15.1. Are embezzlement and misappropriation offences effective and fair as mechanisms against corruption?<br>• If yes, how? Can you give any examples from your experience?<br>• If no, why not?<br>15.2. What further steps might be taken to secure effectiveness and fairness of these offences? |

| | |
|---|---|
| *16* | 16.1. Are abuse of functions and exploitation of position offences effective and fair as mechanisms against corruption?<br>• If yes, how? Can you give any examples from your experience?<br>• If no, why not?<br>16.2. How can such offence be more effective and fairer in relation to counter-corruption? |
| *17* | 17.1. Is conflict of interest offence effective and fair as a mechanism against corruption?<br>• If yes, how? Can you give any examples from your experience?<br>• If no, why not?<br>17.2. How can such offence be more effective and fairer in prevention of corruption? |
| *18* | 18.1. Are obstruction of justice offences effective and fair as mechanisms against corruption? e.g. non-cooperation with law enforcement authorities by hiding documents related to offence against pubic purse, and influencing Nazaha:<br>• If yes, how? Can you give any examples from your experience?<br>• If no, why not?<br>18.2. How can such offences be more effective and fairer in prevention of corruption? |
| *19* | 19.1. Is the creation of illicit enrichment offence (IEO) effective and fair as a mechanism against corruption?<br>• If yes, how? Can you give any examples from your experience?<br>• If no, why not?<br>19.2. How can such offence be more effective and fairer in relation to counter-corruption? |
| *20* | 20.1. Is money laundering (ML) offence effective and fair as a mechanism against corruption?<br>• If yes, how? Can you give any examples from your experience?<br>• If no, why not?<br>20.2. How can ML offence be more effective and fairer in combating corruption? |
| *21* | 21.1. In general, are the Kuwaiti counter-corruption laws effective and fair in combating corruption?<br>• If yes, how? Can you give any examples from your experience?<br>• If no, why not?<br>21.2. Is there anything else you consider relevant in terms of existing offences or reforms which might be made? |

Section 5: Counter-corruption enforcement authorities

| *No.* | *Question* |
|---|---|
| *22* | 22.1. Are the interim and provisional measures (taken by the Public Prosecution Office) effective and fair in preventing the dissipation of criminal assets?<br>• If yes, how? Can you give any examples from your experience?<br>• If no, why not?<br>22.2. Are the investigative tools that the Public Prosecutors have effective and fair in investigating corruption cases?<br>• If yes, how? Can you give any examples from your experience?<br>• If no, why not?<br>22.3. What steps, if any, can be taken to make the Public Prosecution more effective and fairer in dealing with corruption cases? |

| | |
|---|---|
| *23* | 23.1. How does the establishment of Nazaha affect efforts against corruption? Is it positive, negative, or neither?<br>• If positive, how? Can you give any examples from your experience?<br>• If negative, why not?<br>• If no effect, why?<br>23.2. What steps, if any, can be taken to improve the effectiveness and fairness of Nazaha in dealing with corruption? |
| *24* | 24.1. Is the State Audit Bureau effective and fair in detecting and preventing irregularities/corruption in the governmental bodies?<br>• If yes, how? Can you give any examples from your experience?<br>• If no, why not?<br>24.2. What steps, if any, can be taken to improve the effectiveness and fairness of the Bureau? |
| *25* | 25.1. Is the Kuwait Financial Intelligence Unit (KFIU) effective and fair in combating corruption? Has the Unit achieved the intended effects in practice?<br>• If yes, how? Can you give any examples from your experience?<br>• If no, why not?<br>25.2. What steps, if any, can be taken to improve the effectiveness and fairness of the Unit in dealing with corruption? |
| *26* | In general, are the counter-corruption processes and institutions effective and fair in Kuwait?<br>• If yes, how? Can you give any examples from your experience?<br>• If no, why not? |

Section 6: Conclusion

| *No.* | *Question* |
|---|---|
| *27* | Is there anything else you would like to add? Or any documents you can pass to me? |

## 1.2 Appendix 2: Translation of some of the most relevant cited legislation

| *Legislation* | *Section 1* | *Anti-Corruption Authority and Financial Disclosure Act 2/2016 (ACAA)* |
|---|---|---|
| *Arabic* | الكسب غير المشروع: كل زيادة في الثروة او انتقاص في الالتزامات تطرأ – بسبب تولي الوظيفة العامة او قيام الصفة – على الخاضع لهذا القانون أو أولاده القصر او من يكون وليا أو وصيا أو قيما عليه متى كانت لا تتناسب مع موارده‌م وغير مبرره. | |
| *English* | The ACAA defines an IEO as an increase in the wealth or decrease in the obligations of an official, including his/her minor children and those under his/her guardianship, because of the assumption of public office, when that increase or decrease cannot be reasonably explained and justified in terms of their legal resources. | |
| *Legislation* | *Section 44* | *ACAA* |
| *Arabic* | يعفى من العقاب كل من بادر من الجناة بإبلاغ الهيئة او النيابة العامة او الجهات المختصة بوجود اتفاق جنائي لارتكاب احدى الجرائم المنصوص عليها في المادة ٢٢ من هذا القانون وبمن اشتركوا فيها قبل البدء في تنفيذها. ويجوز للمحكمة الاعفاء من العقوبة إذا حصل البلاغ بعد وقوع الجريمة وقبل البدء في التحقيق إذا مكن الجاني – في اثناء التحقيق – السلطات من القبض على مرتكبي الجريمة الآخرين أو ضبط الأموال موضوع الجريمة او القبض على مرتكبي جريمة أخرى مماثلة لها في النوع والخطورة. | |
| *English* | In other corruption crimes, the offender shall also be given immunity from punishment when they spontaneously report any criminal enterprise before embarking on that enterprise. Even after committing the crime, the court can exempt the offender from the punishment, if the offender, before the start of the investigation, voluntarily reports a corruption crime; and if he/she enables the investigative authority to arrest the other offenders, locate the money that is the subject of the offence, or arrest the offenders of other crimes that are similar in their seriousness. | |
| *Legislation* | *Section 1* | *Anti-Money Laundering and Countering Financing of Terrorism Act 106/2013 (AML/CFT Act)* |
| *Arabic* | أية أموال تنشأ أو تحصل - بصورة مباشرة أو غير مباشرة - من ارتكاب جريمة أصلية، وتشمل ما تدره هذه الأموال من أرباح أو فوائد أو ريع أو أي ناتج آخر، سواء بقيت على حالها أو تحويلها كلها أو بعضها إلى أموال أخرى. | |
| *English* | Proceeds of crime are defined as money that is derived or obtained, directly or indirectly, from committing a predicate crime. Proceeds of crime also refer to what this money yields, including profits, interests, rents, or any other gains – whether they remain as they are, or they are, fully or partially, converted into other forms of money. | |
| *Legislation* | *Section 1* | *AML/CFT Act* |
| *Arabic* | كل فعل يشكل جريمة بموجب القوانين في دولة الكويت، كما تشمل أي فعل يرتكب خارج دولة الكويت، إذا كان يشكل جريمة وفقًا لقوانين الدولة التي ارتكب فيها ووفقا لقوانين دولة الكويت. | |
| *English* | Predicate crime … concerns both acts constituting crimes according to the Kuwaiti laws, and acts committed abroad, constituting crimes according to the laws of the country where the act was committed and to the Kuwaiti laws. | |

*Legislation* *Section 2* *AML/CFT Act*

*Arabic*

:يعد مرتكبا لجريمة غسل الأموال كل من علم أن الأموال متحصلة من جريمة، وقام عمدا بما يلي

أ. تحويلها أو نقلها أو استبدالها، بغرض إخفاء أو تمويه المصدر غير المشروع لتلك الأموال، أو مساعدة أي شخص ضالع في
.ارتكاب الجرم الأصلي التي تحصلت منه الأموال، على الإفلات من العواقب القانونية لفعلته
ب. إخفاء أو تمويه الطبيعة الحقيقية للأموال أو مصدرها أو مكانها أو كيفية التصرف فيها أو حركتها أو ملكيتها أو الحقوق
.المتعلقة بها
.ج. اكتساب الأموال أو حيازتها أو استخدامها

*English*

A person commits the ML offence when he or she, knowing that the money is proceeds of crime, intentionally:

a converts, transfers, or substitutes the proceeds of crime, with the purpose of hiding or disguising their illicit source, or helps the offender involved in the predicate crime to avoid the legal consequences of his or her activities;
b hides or disguises the original nature, source, place, disposition, movement, and ownership of proceeds of crime, or the rights related to them; and
c acquires, possesses, or uses proceeds of crime.

*Legislation* *Section 40* *AML/CFT Act*

*Arabic*

يجب على المحكمة - في حالة الإدانة بإحدى الجرائم الأخرى المنصوص عليها في هذا القانون - أن تحكم بمصادرة الأموال
:والأدوات التالية
.أ. متحصلات الجريمة، بما في ذلك الأموال المختلطة بتلك العائدات أو الناتجة عنها أو المستبدلة بها
.ب. الدخل والمنافع الأخرى الناتجة عن عوائد الجرائم
.ج. الأموال محل الجريمة
وللمحكمة أن تحكم بما يعادل قيمة الأموال والأدوات الواردة في البنود (أ) و(ب) و(ج) والتي لا يمكن تحديد مكانها أو
.غير الموجودة لأغراض المصادرة

*English*

Section 40 of the AML/CFT Act … requires the courts to order the confiscation of the 'proceeds of crime'. In particular, the confiscation order includes the proceeds of the crime and the funds intermingled with, derived from, or exchanged for these proceeds and income and other gains from the proceeds of the crime.

However, if the forfeiture and confiscation of the proceeds of the crime is not possible because they cannot be located or are no longer available, the court shall order the offender to pay an amount of money equivalent in value to the proceeds of the crime.

*Legislation* *Section 1* *Conflict of Interests Act 13/2018 (CIA)*

Arabic

تعارض المصالح: كل حالة يكون للخاضع منفعة أو فائدة أو مصلحة مادية أو معنوية تتعارض تعارضا مطلقا أو نسبيا مع
.ما يتطلبه منصبه أو وظيفته من نزاهة واستقلال وحفظ المال العام أو تكون سببا لكسب غير مشروع لنفسه أو لغيره

المصلحة المادية: المصلحة المالية التي تتضمن كسبا او خسارة مالية فعلية او محتملة
المصلحة المعنوية: كل مصلحة غير مالية تنشأ من علاقات شخصية او عائلية او غير ذلك مما يؤثر على القرار
التعارض النسبي: كل حالة يحتمل فيها وقوع ضرر للمصلحة العامة او الوظيفة العامة
.التعارض المطلق: كل حالة يترتب عليها ضررا مباشرا ومحققا بالمصلحة العامة او الوظيفة العامة

*English*

The conflict of interest offence is defined … as any situation where the officeholder has a physical or moral interest, or can benefit from his/her official capacity, in a manner that conflicts, absolutely or relatively, with the integrity of public office, including those situations that cause illicit enrichment for an official or for others.

Physical interest … involves certain or likely financial gains or harms.

Moral interest … comprises non-financial interests, arising from personal, family, or other relationships, which affect decision making.

Relative conflict … a situation that is likely to cause harm to the public interest or the office.

Absolute conflict encompasses a situation that results in direct and certain harm to the public interest or the office.

---

*Legislation* *Section 4* *CIA*

---

*Arabic*

:يكون الخاضع في حالة تعارض مصالح تشكل جريمة فساد في احدى الحالتين الاتيتين

١. تحقق منفعة أو فائدة أو مصلحة مادية أو معنوية له أو لأي شخص من المنصوص عليهم في المادة السابقة ممن خلال قيامه أو امتناعه عن أي عمل من اعمال الوظيفة التي يشغلها منفردا او بالاشتراك مع الاخرين

٢. امتلاكه أي حصة او نسبة من عمل في أي نشاط، له تعاملات مالية مع جهة عمله

*English*

The key conflict of interest offence takes two forms.

1 The first involves any act or omission of an official's duties, individually or through participation with others, that achieves a physical or moral interest in terms of one of the categories mentioned in section 3 of the CIA.
2 The second involves an official owning any share or percentage of work in any activity that has financial transactions with his/her employer.

---

*Legislation* *Section 2* *Statutory Instrument No. 296/2018 of the Conflict of Interests Act 13/2018 (CIA-SI)*

---

*Arabic*

:يكون الخاضع في حالة تعارض نسبي وفقا لأحكام المادة 1 من القانون في أي من الحالات الآتية

أ. إذا امتلك حصة او نسبة من عمل في أي نشاط له تعاملات مالية مع جهة عمله ذات صلة بأعمال وظيفته وشارك فيما اتخذ بشأنها من اجراء دون ان يحصل على منفعة او يسبب ضررا للمصلحة العامة او الوظيفة العامة.

ب. إذا كان له أو لأولاده القصر أو زوجته أو من هم في ولايته او وصايته او من يكون قيما عليهم حصة في أي شركة او منشأة أو عمل أو نشاط يهدف إلى الربح ويتصل بأعمال وظيفته وشارك فيما اتخذ بشأنها من اجراء دون ان يحصل على منفعة او يسبب ضررا للمصلحة العامة او الوظيفة العامة.

ج. إذا قام بدور الوسيط او الوكيل او الكفيل او الاستشاري لأي شركة او منشأة خاصة يتصل نشاطها بجهة عمله دون ان يحصل على منفعة او يسبب ضررا للمصلحة العامة او الوظيفة العامة.

*English*

An official is in a 'relative' conflict in the following cases:

1 an official owning any share or percentage in any activity having financial transactions with his/her employer, if he/she participates in decisions related to those transactions and no gains are achieved and no harms are inflicted;
2 an official, or his/her minor children, spouse, or those under his/her guardianship or custody, who own a share in a company or business activities associated with that official's duties, if he/she participates in decisions related to those transactions and no gains are achieved and no harms are inflicted; and
3 an official acting as an intermediary, agent, or consultant for any private company whose activities relate to his/her employer, if no gains are achieved and no harms are inflicted.

---

*Legislation* *Section 3* *CIA-SI*

*Arabic*

يكون الخاضع في حالة تعارض مطلق - وفقا لأحكام المادة 1 من القانون في اي من الحالات الآتية:

أ-إذا كان في حالة يترتب عليها ضرر مباشر او محقق للمصلحة العامة أو الوظيفة العامة.
ب-إذا تحققت له أو لأي ممن نصت عليه المادة 3 من القانون منفعة أو فائدة أو مصلحة مادية أو معنوية من خلال قيامه او امتناعه عن اي عمل من اعمال وظيفته التي يشغلها منفردا او بالاشتراك مع آخرين.
ج-إذا تحققت له او لأي شخص طبيعي او معنوي تربطه به مصلحة مادية او معنوية خلال سنتين للحالة التي اتخذ فيها القرار او شارك فيه.
د-إذا تحققت له منفعة او فائدة مادية او معنوية من خلال قيامه بدور الوسيط او الوكيل او الكفيل او الاستشاري لأي شركة أو منشأة خاصة يتصل نشاطها بجهة عمله.

*English*

An official is in 'absolute' conflict in the following cases:

1 if the official is in a situation that certainly or directly inflicts harms;
2 if a physical or moral interest is achieved in terms of one of the categories mentioned in section 3 of the CIA by any act or omission of an official's duties, whether performed individually or through participation with others;
3 if a physical or moral interest is achieved for any natural or legal person associated with the official within two years preceding the case in which the decision is taken or participated in (related-party transaction); and
4 if physical or moral interest is achieved for an official through acting as an intermediary, agent, sponsor, or consultant for any private company whose activities relate to his/her employer.

*Legislation* *Section 78* *Criminal Law Act 16/1960 (CLA 1960)*

*Arabic*

يجوز للقاضي إذا حكم بعقوبة من اجل جناية او جنحة عمدية ان يقضي بمصادرة الاشياء المضبوطة التي استعملت او كان من شأنها ان تستعمل في ارتكاب الجريمة والاشياء التي تحصلت منها.

*English*

The courts are empowered in all 'intentional' criminal cases to forfeit any property that was used, or could be used, in committing an offence, and that extends to the assets derived from that criminal property.

*Legislation* *Section 118* *CLA 1960*

*Arabic*

كل موظف عام قبل من شخص، ادى له عملا من اعمال وظيفته او امتنع عن اداء عمل من اعمالها، مالا او منفعة بعد اداء العمل او الامتناع عنه، بصفة مكافأة على ذلك، يعاقب بالحبس مدة لا تجاوز ثلاث سنوات وبغرامة تساوي المال او المنفعة.

*English*

Second, the subsequent reward offence involves two forms … The second form refers to the case where the performance or refraining by the official did not violate his/her official duties.

*Legislation* *Section 143* *CLA 1960*

*Arabic*

كل من علم بوجود مشروع لارتكاب جريمة قتل او حريق او سرقة في وقت يستطاع فيه منع ارتكابها، وامتنع عن ابلاغ ذلك الى السلطات العامة او الى الاشخاص المهددين بها.

*English*

It is a criminal offence for anyone who was aware of a criminal project to have refrained from reporting it at a time when it could have been prevented. However, such a duty is confined to three offences: murder, arson, and theft.

*Legislation* *Section 215* *CLA 1960*

*Arabic*

لا تتوافر الاباحة المنصوص عليها في المادة السابقة الا إذا ثبت حسن نية الفاعل باعتقاده صحة الوقائع التي يسندها بقيام اعتقاده هذا على اسباب معقولة بعد التثبت والتحري، وباتجاهه الى مجرد حماية المصلحة العامة، وباقتصاره فيما صدر منه على القدر اللازم لحماية هذه المصلحة.

*English*

Public disclosures are criminally protected if they meet three requirements. First, disclosures should be based on a reasonable belief that what is being disclosed has actually occurred. Second, the intention behind the disclosure must be to protect the public interest. Third, the public disclosure must be as limited in scope and content as possible just to protect the public interest.

*Legislation* *Section 35* *Criminal Law Act 31/1970 (CLA 1970)*

*Arabic*

يعاقب بالحبس مدة لا تجاوز عشر سنوات وبغرامة تساوي ضعف قيمة ما اعطي او وعد به بحيث لا تقل عن خمسين دينارا كل موظف عام طلب او قبل لنفسه او لغيره وعدا او عطية لأداء عمل او للامتناع عن عمل من اعمال وظيفته.

ويسري حكم هذه المادة ولو كان العمل المنصوص عليه في الفقرة السابقة لا يدخل في اعمال وظيفة المرتشي ولكنه زعم ذلك او اعتقده خطأ.

كما يسري حكم المادة ولو كان المرتشي يقصد عدم اداء العمل او عدم الامتناع عنه.

*English*

Active and passive bribery offences involve situations where an official asks for, or accepts for himself/herself or for others, a promise or an undue advantage in exchange for performing or refraining from one of his/her official duties.

*Legislation* *Section 36* *CLA 1970*

*Arabic*

كل موظف عام قبل من شخص ادى له بغير حق عمل من اعمال وظيفته او امتنع بغير حق عن اداء عمل من اعمالها، هدية او عطية، بعد تمام ذلك العمل او الامتناع عنه بقصد المكافأة على ادائه او الامتناع عنه وبغير اتفاق سابق يعاقب بالحبس مدة لا تجاوز خمس سنوات وبغرامة لا تجاوز خمسمائة دينار او بإحدى هاتين العقوبتين.

*English*

Second, the subsequent reward offence involves two forms. The first includes any official, who, without prior agreement, accepts an undue advantage as a reward from someone for whom the official has already performed, or refrained from, an act in violation of one of his/her official duties.

*Legislation* *Section 43* *CLA 1970*

*Arabic*

يعد في حكم الموظف العام في تطبيق نصوص هذا الفصل:

أ- الموظفون والمستخدمون والعمال في المعالج التابعة للحكومة او الموضوعة تحت اشرافها او رقابتها.

ب- اعضاء المجالس النيابية العامة او المحلية سواء اكانوا منتخبين او معينين.

جـ- المحكمون والخبراء ووكلاء الديانة والمصفون والحراس القضائيون.

د- كل شخص مكلف بخدمة عامة.

هـ- اعضاء مجالس ادارة ومديرو وموظفو ومستخدمو المؤسسات والشركات والجمعيات والمنظمات والمنشآت إذا كانت الدولة او احدى الهيئات العامة تساهم في مالها بنصيب ما بأية صفة كانت.

*English*

The following categories of individuals are deemed officials:

1 officials, clients, and workers of both the governmental bodies and the bodies that are supervised and overseen by the government;
2 members of parliament and other local councils (elected and appointed);
3 arbitrators, members of the Experts Department, official receivers, liquidators, and debt collectors;
4 boards of directors, directors, officials, and clients of companies and enterprises in which the state has any capital contribution; and
5 every individual that is charged with a public service.

---

*Legislation* *Section 209(1)* *Civil Law Act 67/1980 (Civil Act)*

---

*Arabic*

.١- في العقود الملزمة للجانبين، إذا لم يوف أحد المتعاقدين بالتزامه عند حلول أجله، وبعد إعذاره، جاز للمتعاقد الآخر، إن لم يفضل التمسك بالعقد، أن يطلب من القاضي فسخه، مع التعويض إن كان له مقتض

*English*

In terms of infringements of contractual duties, the party harmed is entitled to avoid the contract, assert a restitution claim, and claim compensation.

---

*Legislation* *Section 227* *Civil Act*

---

*Arabic*

.كل من أحدث بفعله الخاطئ ضررا بغيره يلتزم بتعويضه، سواء أكان في إحداثه الضرر مباشرا أو متسببا

*English*

Torts involve any wrongful act by an individual that causes harm to others.

---

*Legislation* *Section 2* *Protection of Public Funds Act 1/1993 (PPFA)*

---

*Arabic*

:يقصد بالأموال العامة في تطبيق احكام هذا القانون ما يكون مملوكا أو خاضعا بقانون لإدارة احدى الجهات الآتية أيا كان موقع تلك الاموال في داخل البلاد او خارجها

.أ- الدولة

.ب- الهيئات العامة، والمؤسسات العامة

.ج- الشركات والمنشآت التي تساهم فيها الجهات المبينة بالبندين السابقين بنسبة لا تقل عن 25% من رأسمالها بصورة مباشرة او غير مباشرة عن طريق شركات او منشآت تساهم الدولة او الهيئات العامة او المؤسسات العامة او غيرها من الاشخاص المعنوية العامة في رأسمالها بنصيب ما، ويعتد في تحديد نسبة راس المال المشار اليها بمجموع الحصص التي للدولة او غيرها من كافة الهيئات ذات الشخصية المعنوية العامة او الشركات المشار اليها

*English*

Public funds comprise … property in Kuwait and abroad that is owned or administered by one of these entities (hereinafter public bodies): the state and its institutions, and companies in which the entities mentioned above, have no less than a 25 per cent stake, whether held directly or indirectly.

---

*Legislation* *Section 9* *PPFA*

---

*Arabic*

.يعاقب بالحبس المؤبد او المؤقت الذي لا تقل مدته عن خمس سنوات كل موظف عام او مستخدم او عامل اختلس اموالا او اوراقا او امتعة او غيرها مسلمة اليه بسبب وظيفته

.وتكون العقوبة الحبس المؤبد او المؤقت الذي لا تقل مدته عن سبع سنوات إذا ارتبطت الجريمة بجناية اخرى ارتباطا لا يقبل التجزئة

*English*

Embezzlement occurs when an official embezzles money, documents, or other property entrusted by virtue of his/her official capacity or position.

---

*Legislation* *Section 10* *PPFA*

---

*Arabic*

يعاقب بالحبس المؤبد او المؤقت الذي لا تقل مدته عن خمس سنوات كل موظف عام او مستخدم او عامل استولى بغير حق على شيء مما ذكر في المادة السابقة لأحدى الجهات المشار اليها في المادة الثانية او تحت يدها او سهل ذلك لغيره.

.وتكون العقوبة الحبس المؤبد او المؤقت الذي لا تقل مدته عن سبع سنوات إذا ارتبطت الجريمة بجناية اخرى ارتباطا لا يقبل التجزئة

*English*

Misappropriation takes place when an official misappropriates or facilitates others to misappropriate money, documents, or other property that is owned, or controlled, by the public bodies.

---

*Legislation* *Section 11* *PPFA*

---

*Arabic*

.كل موظف عام او مستخدم او عامل كلف بالمحافظة على مصلحة لأحدى الجهات المشار اليها في المادة الثانية في صفقة او عملية او قضية او كلف بالمفاوضة او الارتباط او الاتفاق او التعاقد مع أي جهة في داخل البلاد او خارجها في شأن من شئون تلك الجهات إذا كان من شأن ذلك ترتيب حقوق او التزامات مالية للدولة او غيرها من الجهات المذكورة فتعمد اجراءها على نحو يضر بمصلحة هذه الجهات ليحصل على ربح او منفعة لنفسه او لغيره

*English* The intentional harm offence involves any act by an official in violation of his/her duties whereby he/she wilfully inflicts harm on a public body to achieve benefits for himself/herself or for others. This offence occurs when that official is charged with maintaining the interest of that public body in a transaction, process or case, or is assigned to negotiate or contract with any party in relation to the affairs of that body.

---

*Legislation* *Section 12* *PPFA*

---

*Arabic* كل موظف عام او مستخدم او عامل له شأن في ادارة المقاولات او التوريدات او الاشغال المتعلقة بإحدى الجهات المشار اليها في المادة الثانية او يكون له شأن في الاشراف عليها، حصل او حاول ان يحصل لنفسه بالذات او بالواسطة او لغيره باي كيفية غير مشروعة على ربح او منفعة من عمل من الاعمال المذكورة.

*English* The exploitation of office offence refers to an official, who, directly or indirectly, illegally obtains, or conspires to obtain, benefit for himself/herself or for others from contracting, procurement or works related to a public body. The official should have the duty to manage or supervise those works.

---

*Legislation* *Section 20* *PPFA*

---

*Arabic* لا يجوز تطبيق المادة 81 من قانون الجزاء بأي حال على جريمة من الجرائم المذكورة في هذا القانون الا إذا بادر الجاني برد الاموال موضوع الجريمة كاملة قبل اقفال باب المرافعة في الحالات التي يجب فيها الرد. ومع ذلك يجوز للمحكمة في الجرائم المنصوص عليها في هذا القانون وفقاً لما تراه من ظروف الجريمة وملابساتها إذا كان موضوعها او الضرر الناجم عنها يسيرا ان تقضي فيها بدلا من العقوبات المقررة لها بعقوبة الحبس مدة لا تزيد على ثلاث سنوات وبغرامة لا تزيد على ثلاثة الاف دينار او بإحدى هاتين العقوبتين.

*English* In crimes against the public purse, the offender will be given 'conditional discharge' (i.e. it will be decided not to hand down a criminal conviction) whenever the trial judge believes that the crime committed is trivial and that the offender will not re-engage in other criminal activities in the future.

---

*Legislation* *Section 28* *PPFA*

---

*Arabic* تعتبر باطلة التصرفات التي اجراها المحكوم عليه في الاموال المتعلقة بالجرائم المنصوص عليها في هذا القانون او من آلت إليهم هذه الاموال إذا كانت هذه التصرفات بقصد تهريب هذه الاموال او تفويت حق الجهة المضرورة في استيفاء ما عسى ان يحكم به عليه. ولا يسري البطلان المنصوص عليه في الفقرة السابقة على التصرفات التي تمت بعوض والى الاشخاص حسني النية.

*English* Without prejudice to the rights of bona fide, section 28 of the Protection of Public Funds Act (PPFA) 1/1993 renders void all acts undertaken by the convicted to dissipate or prevent the authorities from returning the assets.

---

# Index

Note: Page numbers in *italics* indicate figures, **bold** indicate tables and with "n" indicate endnotes in the text

www.ingramcontent.com/pod-product-compliance
Lightning Source LLC
LaVergne TN
LVHW011116300926
849160LV00008B/399

*9780367721794*